The Politics
of Policies

Economic and Social Progress
in Latin America

2006 REPORT

Ernesto Stein
Mariano Tommasi
Koldo Echebarría
Eduardo Lora
Mark Payne
Coordinators

INTER-AMERICAN DEVELOPMENT BANK

**DAVID ROCKEFELLER CENTER FOR LATIN AMERICAN STUDIES
HARVARD UNIVERSITY**

The Politics of Policies

©2005 Inter-American Development Bank
1300 New York Avenue, NW
Washington, DC 20577

Co-published by
David Rockefeller Center
for Latin American Studies
Harvard University
1730 Cambridge Street
Cambridge, MA 02138

To order this book, contact
IDB Bookstore
Tel: 202-623-1753
Fax: 202-623-1709
E-mail: idb-books@iadb.org
www.iadb.org/pub

ISBN: 1-59782-010-5
ISSN: 0095-2850

Cover photos: Getty Images

A good government implies two things:
first, fidelity to the object of government,
which is the happiness of the people; secondly,
a knowledge of the means by which
the object can best be obtained.

James Madison,
The Federalist Papers, No. 62

Preface

The 1990s were a period of intense reform in Latin America and the Caribbean. Frustration in the wake of the so-called "lost decade" of the 1980s, and the promise offered by the apparently simple recipe of the Washington Consensus, convinced political leaders to enact fiscal and monetary measures to control inflation and to adopt a series of reforms to open up their economies to trade, liberalize their financial systems and privatize State enterprises in order to accelerate economic growth.

With the modest success in terms of economic growth, and reduction of poverty and inequality, enthusiasm for reform has diminished in recent years. In its place are doubts about the efficiency of these reforms and debate over what the future course of economic and social policy should be in order to achieve the elusive goal of sustainable growth with equity to which all Latin American societies aspire.

This report aims to contribute to this debate, but not from the economic perspective from which entities such as the Inter-American Development Bank (IDB) have traditionally analyzed development policy. Instead, the report looks at the problem from a political and institutional angle—one that has been much less studied but is essential for understanding the possibilities for success of economic and social policies.

The focus of this report is not the content of policies, or their effects on major economic and social variables, but rather the process by which these policies are discussed, approved, and implemented. In presidential democracies like those in the majority of the Latin American countries, the process of adopting and implementing public policy occurs in political systems in which a variety of actors participate, ranging from the president to voters in small rural communities and including congressmen, judges, public opinion leaders and businessmen.

The complex interaction among these actors is influenced by the institutions and political practices of each country. This interaction is the subject of this report, which uses an approach that combines comparative analyses for Latin American presidential systems as a whole with a variety of country and sector case studies. Institutions and political practices help explain why reforms endure in some countries, why some countries can easily change policies that are not working well or why some can adjust better when circumstances demand it.

Institutions and political practices are not the only factors influencing the quality of economic and social policy. History, the beliefs and attitudes of citizens, and leadership are at least as decisive. This report recognizes these factors even though it does not do justice to these idiosyncratic, albeit equally important, aspects of the development of each country.

As Managers of the Research Department and the Sustainable Development Department of the IDB, which were responsible for its production, it is our pleasure to introduce to the public discussion this report, which, though it does not necessarily reflect the opinions of the Bank or its management, does reflect the environment of intellectual openness, analysis and debate that has characterized this institution. For fostering this environment and for his interest in this report, we would like to thank Enrique V. Iglesias, former president of the IDB. We are confident that governments, politicians and students of development will find in these pages reasons to persevere in their efforts to build more prosperous, just, equitable and democratic societies.

Guillermo Calvo
Chief Economist and Manager
of the Research Department

Carlos M. Jarque
Manager of the Sustainable
Development Department

Contents

Preface   v

Acknowledgments.   ix

PART I. Overview and Methodology.   1

Chapter 1
Overview   3

Chapter 2
Understanding the Politics of Policies: A Methodological Approach   11

PART II. Actors and Arenas in the Policymaking Process   23

Chapter 3
Political Parties, Legislatures, and Presidents   27

Chapter 4
Cabinets, the Bureaucracy, Subnational Governments, and the Judiciary.   61

Chapter 5
Actors from Civil Society   91

PART III. The Policymaking Process and Policy Outcomes   125

Chapter 6
Political Institutions, the Workings
  of the Policymaking System, and Policy Outcomes   129

Chapter 7
Country Experiences in Policymaking   157

PART IV. The Policymaking Process in Action 181

Chapter 8
The Art of Tax Policies 185

Chapter 9
Politicization of Public Services 203

Chapter 10
Two Kinds of Education Politics 221

Chapter 11
Decentralization, Budget Processes, and Feedback Effects 243

PART V. Conclusion 253

Chapter 12
A New Lens for the Future 255

Data Appendix 261

References 277

List of Acronyms 289

Acknowledgments

Economic and Social Progress in Latin America is the flagship publication of the Inter-American Development Bank. This issue was a joint production of the Research Department and the Sustainable Development Department coordinated by Luis Estanislao (Koldo) Echebarría, Eduardo Lora, and Mark Payne, as well as Ernesto Stein and Mariano Tommasi, who were overall leaders for the project. Nancy Morrison edited the report, with input from Rita Funaro, who served on the editorial committee. Carlos Andrés Gómez-Peña, who was project assistant, completed the coordinating team.

The principal authors by chapter were:

Chapter 1: Eduardo Lora, Ernesto Stein, and Mariano Tommasi, with contributions from Koldo Echebarría.

Chapter 2: Ernesto Stein and Mariano Tommasi, with contributions from Koldo Echebarría.

Chapter 3: Mark Payne, drawing on work by Mark Jones (political parties), Sebastián Saiegh (legislatures), and Mark Payne (presidents), with contributions by Ernesto Stein.

Chapter 4: Mark Payne and Koldo Echebarría, drawing on work by Cecilia Martínez-Gallardo (cabinets), Laura Zuvanic and Mercedes Iacoviello (bureaucracy), Francisco Monaldi (subnational governments), and Mariana Sousa (judiciary), with contributions by Carlos Scartascini and Gabriel Filc.

Chapter 5: Mark Payne and Koldo Echebarría, drawing on work by Ben Ross Schneider (business), Sallie Hughes (media), María Victoria Murillo (unions), María Mercedes Mateo and Koldo Echebarría (social movements), and Javier Santiso and Laurence Whitehead (knowledge actors).

Chapter 6: Ernesto Stein and Mariano Tommasi.

Chapter 7: Ernesto Stein and Mariano Tommasi.

Chapter 8: Eduardo Lora, Mauricio Cárdenas, and Valerie Mercer-Blackman.

Chapter 9: Mario Bergara and Andrés Pereyra.

Chapter 10: Juan Carlos Navarro.

Chapter 11: Gabriel Filc, Carlos Scartascini, and Ernesto Stein.

Chapter 12: Koldo Echebarría.

Data Appendix: Laura Clavijo.

In addition, Lee J. Alston, Cristóbal Aninat, Raquel Ayala, Mauricio Cárdenas, Juan Carlos Cortázar, Erick Coyoy Echeverría, Robert Daughters, Carlos González Tablada, Roberto Junguito, Fabrice Lehoucq, John Londregan, Gustavo Márquez, Daniel Maceira, Andrés Mejía Acosta, Marcus André Melo, Bernardo Mueller, Patricio Navia, Mónica Pachón, Carlos Pereira, Juan Cruz Perusia, Gustavo Porras Castejón, Rosa Tock Quiñónez, Joaquín Vial, and Raquel Zelaya Rosales provided useful background material. Overall research assistance was provided by Carlos Andrés Gómez-Peña, Laura Clavijo, Carolina Mandalaoui, and María Miyar Busto. Additional research assistance was provided by

Valentina Calderón, Eric Cárdenas, Ian Cox, Arturo Harker, Elton Mancilla, Luis Daniel Martínez, Mariela Semidey, Aimee Verdisco, and Juan Vázquez-Zamora.

Many other individuals participated in the preparation of the report, including Manuel Agosin, Pablo Alonso, Euric Bobb, Fernando Carrillo-Flórez, Eduardo Fernández-Arias, Edmundo Jarquín, Phil Keefer, Jaime Millán, Gina Montiel, Esteban Piedrahita, and Pablo Spiller. The authors also thank many other Bank staff who participated in internal discussion workshops, and who provided comments on background papers, as well as the 166 policy experts in 20 countries who responded to the State Capabilities Survey.

The IDB's Office of External Relations was responsible for the editorial production of the report, under the coordination of Dan Martin and Rafael Cruz. Álvaro Correa, Stella Covre, Roberto Donadi, Gabriel Dobson, Larry Hanlon, Paula Irisity, and John Dunn Smith were translators. Editorial revision was done by Cathy Conkling-Shaker, Gerardo Giannoni, Michael Harrup, Nancy Morrison, Claudia Pasquetti, John Dunn Smith and Elisabeth Schmitt. Leilany Garron and Dolores Subiza created the cover and graphic design and typeset the volume.

Part I

Overview
and Methodology

*Democracy has its own way of developing
public policies. Decisions grow out of a
negotiated equilibrium of interests; they conform
to transparent rules; and they are made in
the public arena....Policies do not reflect the
supposed omniscience of illuminated technocrats;
instead, they represent the harmonization
of legitimate interests, in a concert of wills,
including that of the government itself.*

Fernando Henrique Cardoso,
speech presented to ECLAC in August 2003

Chapter 1

Overview

The significant problems we face today cannot be solved at the same level of thinking we were at when we created them.

—Albert Einstein

Beyond Technocratic Policies

The history of economic and social development in Latin America is dominated by the search for new paradigms: simplified ways of understanding how the economy and society function that offer governments a variety of policy alternatives. Latin America has ridden the waves of successive paradigms from the State-run, inward-looking development of the postwar era to the macroeconomic discipline and trade liberalization of the Washington Consensus in the 1990s. As with other paradigms, the region's enthusiasm for the Washington Consensus has waned, and it is now in search of a new paradigm that offers better economic results, more stability, and greater equity.

This report questions the logic behind this search. The Fountain of Youth and the City of Gold were fantasies, and so are magic formulas for accelerating growth and eradicating poverty. Certain simple ideas can help to mobilize society, but they are rarely sufficient for understanding the processes of fundamental change. Sadly, there are no shortcuts to the Promised Land of sustainable development and prosperity for all.

Previous editions of this report have analyzed various aspects of economic, social, and institutional reform and have discussed the pros and cons of diverse policy options. What is clear is that, whatever the policy area, there is no single formula applicable to all circumstances; policies' effectiveness depends on the manner in which they are discussed, approved, and implemented. Therefore, instead of focusing on the substance and orientation of particular policies, this report concentrates on the critical processes that shape these policies, carry them forward from idea to implementation, and sustain them over time. It takes as its starting point the premise that the processes of discussing, negotiating, approving, and implementing policies may be at least as important as the specific content of the policies themselves.

A strictly technocratic approach toward policymaking short-circuits these steps of discussion, negotiation, approval, and implementation, which have at their core the messy world of politics. This report views the political process and the policymaking process as inseparable. To ignore the link between them when pursuing policy change may lead to failed reforms and dashed expectations.

This study, like the background research and accompanying analysis it draws upon, takes a detailed look at the institutional arrangements and political systems at work in Latin America, as they shape the roles and incentives of a variety of actors (some of them professional politicians, others members of civil society) that participate in the policy-making process. It then goes on to explore the way in which this process contributes to shaping policy outcomes and takes a long look at the political economy of specific countries and sectors: the dynamic between politics and economics that is so central to a nation's development.

This body of work additionally advances a framework of the policymaking process that helps in understanding the complex variables and interactions that come into play as policies are discussed, approved, and executed. Taken together, the framework, research, case studies, and analysis can help demonstrate that, while some worthwhile changes can take place, not every reform is politically or institutionally feasible.

The hope is that this study will be of use to those who participate in policymaking processes and want to understand the limitations and the potential of public policies and attempts at reform. However, this report does not offer recipes or magic potions. On the contrary, it serves as a warning to those who believe that a policy's chances for success can be judged abstractly on its theoretical or technical attributes without considering the institutional, political, and cultural context in which it is applied.

This report does not cover countries with parliamentary systems. The core institutional setup of these countries is different from that of the countries in Latin America with presidential systems. Not only do the former have parliamentary political regimes, but they have also inherited, from their institutional tradition, party systems, professional bureaucracies, and justice systems that differ from those in the rest of Latin America. The study of institutions, policymaking processes, and policy outcomes in these countries constitutes a very important next step in the research agenda. This next step has already begun, with a study of policymaking in Jamaica, which is reflected in Box 3.1 in Chapter 3.

A Varied Landscape

For the last 15 years, Latin America has experimented with a wide range of policies and reforms. Nonetheless, the success of those reforms and more generally, the quality of public policy, have varied considerably.

- While some countries can maintain the basic thrust of their policies for long periods of time, thus creating a predictable and stable environment, other countries experience frequent changes in policies, often with every change in administration.

- While some countries can adapt their policies rapidly to changes in external circumstances or innovate when policies are failing, other countries react slowly or with great difficulty, retaining inappropriate policies for long periods of time.
- While some countries can effectively implement and enforce the policies enacted by congress or the executive, others take a great deal of time to do so or are ineffective.
- While some countries adopt policies that focus on the public interest, in others, policies are filled with special treatment, loopholes, and exemptions.

Why this variation? What determines the ability to design, approve, and implement effective public policies? To answer this question, this study brings to bear an eclectic and interdisciplinary approach, described in Chapter 2, drawing on both economics and political science. It also draws on a wealth of background research produced by a network of researchers across Latin America, which provides insights into the workings of the policymaking process and its impact on policy outcomes. This background material includes:

- Detailed studies of the workings of political institutions and policymaking processes in 13 countries.
- Studies that focus on the role of different actors (legislators, political parties, presidents, business, the media, and others) as they participate in the policymaking process in a variety of arenas.
- Comparative studies focusing on the link between policymaking processes and policy outcomes in a number of specific sectors, such as education, health, social protection, decentralization, budget processes, and tax policy, as well as the privatization and regulation of public utilities.

The research agenda and this study build on other work, notably the effort that culminated in the publication by the Inter-American Development Bank (IDB) in 2002 of the book *Democracies in Development: Politics and Reform in Latin America*.[1] That document was primarily concerned with the effect of alternative arrangements of democratic institutions on a broad definition of democratic governability. It focused on a number of distinct institutional dimensions of democratic systems (such as legislative electoral systems), one at a time.

This report is part of a further effort, focusing more explicitly on the process of policymaking and on the characteristics of the public policies that result from different policymaking environments. Rather than taking institutional traits one at a time, it looks into the interactive effects of multiple institutional rules on political practices, as well as the effect of these practices on policymaking.

Since the approach is systemic, this report does not evaluate the performance of individuals responsible for making or implementing policy. However, this does not imply that the report ignores the important role that the leadership and competence of public

---

[1] Payne and others (2002).

actors play in policy outcomes. Instead, the systemic approach simply attempts to understand the constraints and incentives that condition the actions of presidents, legislators, judges, public servants, and other actors that participate in the policymaking process.

Given an emphasis on complex interactions, part of the research agenda behind this report takes a country-centered, historically grounded approach. A first output of that effort is reflected in the Political Institutions, Policymaking Processes, and Policy Outcomes project, conducted under the auspices of the Latin American Research Network of the IDB.[2]

This report takes an additional step in advancing that agenda. It looks deeper into *cross-country comparisons* of the roles and characteristics of the main actors and arenas of the policy process. It develops *new indicators* of policy characteristics and of some properties of political systems. And it develops *comparative cases* in a number of policy areas.

This report should be taken as one stage of a work in progress. It raises more questions than it answers. Unlike previous editions of *Economic and Social Progress in Latin America*, which presented the culmination of years of research, this report is still writing an agenda. Research, analysis, and synthesis will continue. The main messages of the work to date are summarized in the rest of this chapter.

---

[2] The results of the project, which benefited from the input of practitioners and academics from several disciplines, are available for examination at http://www.iadb.org/res/index.cfm?fuseaction=LaResNetwork.StudyView&st_id=82.

Main Messages

Ten main messages can be extracted from this year's report.

1. Processes matter!

The process by which policies are discussed, approved, and implemented (the policy-making process) has an important impact on the quality of public policies, including the capacity of countries to provide a stable policy environment, to adapt policies when needed, to implement and enforce policies effectively, and to ensure that policies are adopted in pursuit of the public interest.

2. Beware of universal policy recipes that are supposed to work independently of the time and place in which they are adopted.

Recent experience of countries in Latin America with the reforms of the Washington Consensus shows that reforms with similar orientation and content can have very diverse results. One of the pitfalls of advocating the adoption of universal policy recipes—and one of the driving motivations for this report—is that policies are not adopted and implemented in a vacuum. Rather, they must proceed within the context of a country's political institutions. These political institutions, as well as the policymaking processes they in turn help shape, can have a profound impact on the success or failure of any policy.

3. Certain key features of public policies may be as important in achieving development goals as their content or orientation.

The impact of public policies depends not only on their specific content or particular orientation, but also on some generic features of the policies. An "ideal" policy that lacks credibility and is poorly implemented and enforced may be more distortionary than a "suboptimal" policy that is stable and well implemented. This study examines six such key features: *stability, adaptability, coherence and coordination, the quality of implementation and enforcement, public-regardedness* (public orientation), and *efficiency*. These key features have a great deal of bearing on whether policies can actually enhance welfare, can be sustained over time, and can contribute to overall development.

4. The effects of political institutions on policymaking processes can be understood only in a systemic manner.

Policymaking processes are very complex, as a result of the multiplicity of actors with diverse powers, time horizons, and incentives that participate in them; the variety of arenas in which they play the game; and the diversity of rules of engagement that can have an impact on the way the game is played. A focus on a few institutional characteristics (such as whether the country has a presidential or parliamentary system, or whether the electoral rules are of the plurality or proportional representation variety) will only produce a very fragmented and unsatisfactory understanding of these processes. In order to understand them more fully, the institutional setup needs to be addressed by a systemic or "general equilibrium" approach.

5. Political and institutional reform proposals based on broad generalizations are not a sound reform strategy.

A corollary of the previous point is that the merits of potential changes in political and institutional rules must be considered carefully, with an understanding of how these rules fit within the broader institutional configuration. Broad generalizations about the merits of different political regimes, electoral systems, or constitutional adjudication of powers among branches are not very useful. Partial equilibrium views that stress the importance of a single institutional dimension may lead to misguided institutional and policy reforms. Understanding the overall workings of the political process and of the policymaking process in each specific country, with its specific historical trajectory, is a crucial prerequisite for developing appropriate policy reform proposals and institutional reform proposals.

6. Policy or institutional reforms that have important feedback effects on the policymaking process should be treated with special care, and with an understanding of the potential ramifications.

Policy reforms often have feedback effects on the policymaking game. In some sectors, these feedback effects are likely to alter the specific sector's policy game by creating new actors or changing the rules of engagement among them. But some reforms (particularly in sectors such as decentralization, budget processes, or civil service reforms) can have a much broader impact and alter the dynamics of the country's policymaking process. Policy or institutional reforms that have important feedback effects on the policymaking process should be considered with special care, and with an understanding of the potential ramifications.

7. The ability of political actors to cooperate over time is a key determinant of the quality of public policies.

Multiple actors (such as politicians, administrators, and interest groups) operate at different points in time over the policymaking process. Better policies are likely to emerge if these participants can cooperate with one another to uphold agreements and sustain them over time. In systems that encourage cooperation, consensus on policy orientation and structural reform programs is more likely to emerge, and successive administrations are more likely to build upon the achievements of their predecessors.

8. Effective political processes and better public policies are facilitated by political parties that are institutionalized and programmatic, legislatures that have sound policymaking capabilities, judiciaries that are independent, and bureaucracies that are strong.

- *Well-institutionalized political parties (especially parties that have national and programmatic orientations).* Institutionalized, programmatic parties tend to be consistent long-term policy players. A political system with a relatively small number of institutionalized parties (or coalitions) is more likely to generate inter-temporal cooperation, and to lead to the emergence of consensual sustained policy stances on crucial issues (*Políticas de Estado*).
- *A legislature with strong policymaking capabilities.* Policies tend to be better when legislatures develop policymaking capacities and constructively engage in national policymaking, rather than when they simply adopt a subservient role, rubber-stamping the wishes of the executive.
- *An independent judiciary.* A well-functioning and independent judiciary can be a facilitator, fostering bargains among political actors by providing enforcement that binds them to their commitments, and by ensuring that none of the players oversteps its boundaries.
- *A well-developed civil service.* A strong and technically competent civil service can contribute to the quality of public policies by making policies more stable, by enhancing the overall quality of implementation, and by preventing special interests (which often choose to wield their influence during the policy implementation stage) from capturing the benefits of public policies.

9. Most of these "institutional blessings" are not granted overnight. Building them, and keeping them in place, depends on the political incentives of key political actors.

The incentives of professional politicians such as presidents, legislators, and party leaders (as well as their interaction with the rest of society) are crucial for the workings of institutions. Improving the capabilities of congress requires that legislators have incentives to develop such capabilities. Independent judiciaries are built only over time, but they can be destroyed overnight. Adopting the best civil service law in the world will not work if patronage involving positions in the bureaucracy remains an important currency used by politicians to reward their partisan base.

10. Leadership, if functional, can be a vital force for institution-building.

Individual leaders can play a vital role as catalysts in the development of institutions. Functional leadership can encourage deliberative processes that allow policies and institutions to adapt to the needs and demands of society. Leadership, however, can also be dysfunctional. Rather than contributing to institution-building, dysfunctional leaders can have the opposite effect. Their accumulation of power allows them to get things done, but at the expense of weakening institutions.

Chapter 2

Understanding the Politics of Policies: A Methodological Approach

The policymaking process can be understood as a succession of bargains among political actors, interacting in formal and informal arenas.

In a technocratic approach toward policymaking, policies are objects of choice by benevolent policymakers. Anyone interested in fostering better social outcomes would simply need to identify policies that would induce those better outcomes and communicate those policies to policymakers. Chapter 1 warned against the dangers of such an approach—which, among other shortcomings, takes policies as exogenous: that is, as originating from outside the system. This study examines the processes by which countries discuss, decide on, and implement public policies over time. Accordingly, this study treats policies (as well as some characteristics of policies) as largely endogenous. Policies are viewed as the outcome of the policymaking process. This study focuses on the characteristics and determinants of policymaking processes, with particular emphasis on the workings of political institutions.

Focusing the study on institutions and processes does not imply denying the influence of other, more structural variables on the configurations of polities, policymaking, and policies. Social and economic structures give rise to different configurations of actors in different countries at different times; these societal and economic actors exercise influence not only on the making of policy but also on the making of institutions. The country studies that serve as background to this report pay attention to the important role of such structures in each case.[1] The history of policymaking in Venezuela cannot be understood without reference to the political economy of an oil economy; policymaking in Argentina cannot be understood without reference to the complex relations between

---

[1] These country studies were conducted as part of the IDB Latin American Research Network project on Political Institutions, Policymaking Processes, and Policy Outcomes (www.iadb.org/res/index.cfm?fusea ction=LaResNetwork.StudyView&st_id=82).

the national government and the provinces—which in turn are affected not only by the formal institutions of that federal republic, but also by underlying economic and social structures throughout the country; and so on.

These important underlying forces cannot be ignored by anyone attempting to understand (let alone influence) the workings of these polities. Yet, since it is impossible to do everything at once, this report focuses mainly on the aspects of these complex polities that are more directly related to the formal and informal political and policymaking institutions.[2] This is a particularly timely focus, given that the democratization processes of most Latin American countries over the last few decades have increased the importance of political institutions, and given that such institutions are the focus of much debate (and in some cases, reform) in many countries in the region.

The workings of institutions and their influence on development outcomes have become a central concern in international policy circles, as well as in academic ones. For a long time, institutional capacity was perceived mostly as an "unexplained residual."[3] Development was conceived of as mainly a function of capital accumulation, with the implicit assumption that institutional capacity would follow resources. Institutions were viewed as the formal organizations in charge of implementing policies and projects. As pointed out by Arturo Israel, "Institutional development was everybody's problem, but nobody's problem."[4]

That rather dismissive view of institutions was discredited by the failure of policies and investments for lack of institutional capacity, leading to a rather pessimistic mood about the possibility of overcoming institutional weaknesses. This turn was among the reasons leading to a paradigm shift toward markets and away from State-led distortions.

The difficulties experienced by countries of the former Soviet bloc in their transition to market economies, and the relative success of the Asian "tigers," turned the spotlight again toward the role of institutions in development. This renewed interest was influenced by the conceptual and analytical advances of the so-called *new institutionalism*. The new institutionalism is a broad heading covering diverse schools of thought scattered throughout multiple disciplines (including economics, sociology, history, and law) that emphasizes the central role of institutions in explaining political, economic, and social behavior. Within the field of economics, economic historian Douglass North has led the way in generating new ideas on the relationship between institutions and development.[5] These "new institutional" studies have highlighted the fact that (economic and political) institutions are themselves a product of human choice at some point. Some of the most dynamic current lines of inquiry trace the origins of institutions back to colonial times.[6]

---

[2] Chapter 5 provides some insights on the role of some key informal societal actors in the policymaking process.

[3] Hirschman (1967).

[4] Israel (1987).

[5] See, for example, North (1990). Shirley (2005) provides an excellent survey of this literature.

[6] See, for example, Acemoglu, Johnson, and Robinson (2001, 2002).

This report takes an intermediate view with respect to the issue of endogeneity or exogeneity of institutions. The authors of this report recognize that institutions are endogenous to past arrangements and occurrences, and to some extent to more recent configurations of political power, socioeconomic structures, and other deep determinants. This study focuses on the *impact* of particular configurations of political institutions on policymaking processes, and hence on policies. Political institutions are being debated and even reformed in many countries in the region, and these debates are not just blunt exercises of power. Instead, they are informed by a discussion of the possible effects of reform on political practices and outcomes. Hence, this study tries to take a middle way, attempting to increase awareness of the importance of political practices and institutions in the policymaking process—without falling into a totally deterministic mode in which everything that happens is determined by forces absolutely beyond the control of individual or collective actors. Leadership can sometimes be an extraordinary force in the political process, but its possibilities and implications are closely intertwined with the institutional setting (see Box 2.1).

The report aims to provide guidance and orientation to politicians, policymakers, organizations, and social actors interested in participating in the debate about improving policies and institutions to foster development goals. Increased awareness of policymaking processes and their institutional foundations might help in the promotion, design, and implementation of policy reforms that are more likely to achieve desired development objectives, given the particular political institutions and practices of each country. It might also illuminate discussions about reforming political institutions.

In studying these issues, the report draws from an extensive literature in political science about the effects of alternative arrangements of institutions on many important political and policy outcomes.[7] These alternatives include whether the political regime is presidential or parliamentary; whether the State is centralized or decentralized; whether the electoral system is majoritarian or proportional; whether parties are weak or strong, numerous or few; whether business organizations, trade unions, or the media are active participants in the policy processes; whether the bureaucracy is meritocratic or clientelistic; and so on.[8] Since each country has a specific configuration of all these and several other important characteristics, this report emphasizes the interactions of all these variables. As several examples in the following chapters show, these interactions are nonadditive, in the sense that the effect of one particular institutional rule or characteristic depends on the whole array of institutional rules and characteristics.

---

[7] These discussions have also been addressed by some important work on political economy by economists. For instance, Persson and Tabellini (2000, 2003) study the impact of different forms of government and electoral rules on a number of fiscal policy outcomes.

[8] Part II provides references to that literature and summarizes some findings that are relevant for the purposes of this study. Given that most of the background work for this study has focused on the presidential democracies of Latin America, the distinction between parliamentarism and presidentialism is not emphasized in this report.

Box 2.1   The Role of Leadership in Political Processes

Functional leadership renews institutions. Dysfunctional leadership "deinstitutionalizes" them, as the personal accumulation of power weakens institutions.

The role of leadership—the ability to effectively influence the achievement of certain goals—plays a critical role in political processes, often at critical times. The central role of leadership has encouraged a tendency to view politics more as a matter of personal interaction than as the interplay of institutional incentives. This report urges a careful look at the interplay of institutions, players, rules of the game, and incentives. Nonetheless, it is important to bear in mind the implications of individual leaders' behavior.

Leadership is the ability of individuals to exert influence that goes beyond the scope of their formal authority. Leadership entails a combination of purpose, commitment, and ability to relate on a personal level that produces outcomes beyond what would be expected in the normal functioning of institutions. Leadership is demonstrated through distinct types of behavior, many of them symbolic. Leadership, thus understood, may be functional or dysfunctional, according to its effects on the structure of institutions and the quality of policies.

Functional leadership facilitates cooperation and inter-temporal bargains that improve the quality of public policy. The value of leadership is best appreciated in moments of change, when imbalances arise that alter the effect of rules on actors' incentives and generate opportunities for institutional reform. Functional leaders, if they are to exercise influence and power to contain tensions in times of crisis, need to direct change toward renewing institutional frameworks. The region offers many examples of such a positive trend during the transition to democracy. The recent changes of government in countries such as Brazil, Mexico, and Uruguay, which are considered turning points in the political processes of these countries, represent an exercise of leadership, on the part of outgoing as well as incoming governments, that institutionalizes new rules of the game.

In a democracy, functional leadership can rarely be attributed to a single person. Democracy is associated with multiple leaders who serve as catalysts of deliberative process that permit policies and institutions to be adapted to the demands of an open society. One of the challenges facing these leaders is the articulation of political and technical rationales to produce policies of high quality. The region has a rich experience with such leadership, both at the national and subnational level, where cities such as Bogotá and Montevideo have enjoyed innovative and constructive leadership.

Box 2.1	Continued

Dysfunctional leadership is different in nature. A single person can dominate. While at first its perverse effects may be hidden by the charisma of an individual leader and his effective exercise of power, those perversities eventually come to light. The fundamental characteristic of dysfunctional leadership is that it "de-institutionalizes," as the personal accumulation of power weakens institutions. There is a significant risk that the accumulation of unchecked power might lead to arbitrary rule and corruption.

In times of crisis, dysfunctional leaders can hold an irresistible attraction for the public. Leaders can present themselves as having the answer to all problems, while promising to spare society as a whole and individual citizens from confronting their own problems and taking responsibility for them. This interaction between a leader's charisma and followers' escape from reality has historically been the route to a dangerous brand of politics.

The Methodological Approach[9]

While this study takes a rather eclectic approach, drawing insights from different disciplines, it has a guiding framework, which is described briefly below. The framework is presented graphically in Figure 2.1. In keeping with the nature of the methodology, and for ease of explanation, it is best to start from the dependent variable (some key features of public policies) and work back to its political and institutional determinants.

The framework views public policies as the outcomes of complex exchanges among political actors over time.

Characteristics of Public Policies: The Dependent Variable

Policies are complex undertakings. Bringing any particular "policy reform" to fruition is a process that involves multiple actors through many stages of the policy process. It requires specific responses from economic and social agents, and therefore necessitates several forms of cooperation and positive beliefs about the durability and other properties of the policy. That is, policies require a great deal more than a magical moment of special politics to introduce "the right policy" in order to produce effective results.

A universal set of "right" policies does not exist. Policies are contingent responses to underlying states of the world. What might work at one point in time in a given coun-

---

[9] An expanded description of this framework is provided in Spiller, Stein, and Tommasi (2003), the design paper for the IDB's Political Institutions, Policymaking Processes, and Policy Outcomes project.

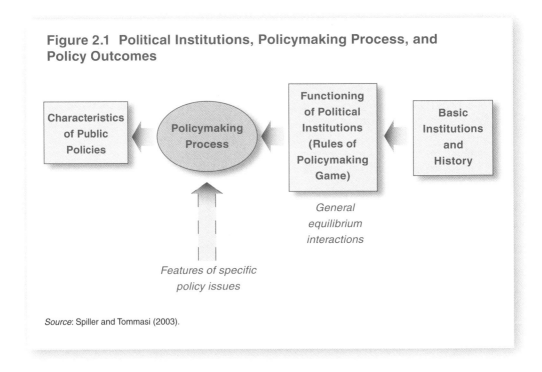

Figure 2.1 Political Institutions, Policymaking Process, and Policy Outcomes

Characteristics of Public Policies ← Policymaking Process ← Functioning of Political Institutions (Rules of Policymaking Game) ← Basic Institutions and History

General equilibrium interactions

Features of specific policy issues

Source: Spiller and Tommasi (2003).

try might not work in a different place or in the same place at another time. In some cases, some particular characteristics of policies or the details of their implementation might matter as much as the broad type of policy. For instance, Dani Rodrik analyzed six countries that implemented a set of policies that shared the same generic title—"export subsidization"—but had widely different degrees of success.[10] Rodrik relates their success to such features as the consistency with which the policy was implemented, which office was in charge, how the policy was bundled (or not) with other policy objectives, and how predictable the future of the policy was.

One important characteristic of policies that has been widely recognized in recent work on macroeconomics, trade policy, regulation, and other areas of economics is policy credibility.[11] The effects of policies on the final economic and social outcomes of interest depends on the actions and reactions of economic and social agents, who take into account their expectations about the future of the policies in question before deciding on their responses. As Rodrik explains, in reference to trade reform, "it is not trade liberalization per se, but *credible* trade liberalization that is the source of efficiency benefits. The predictability of the incentives created by a trade regime, or lack thereof, is generally of much greater importance than the *structure* of these incentives. In other

---

[10] Rodrik (1995).

[11] See, for example, Barro and Gordon (1983); Calvo (1996, Section V); Drazen (2000, Section II); Levy and Spiller (1994); and Rodrik (1989).

words, a distorted, but *stable* set of incentives does much less damage to economic performance than an uncertain and unstable set of incentives generated by a process of trade reform lacking credibility."[12]

It is for these reasons that the policy outcome to be explained in this report is not the content or type of policies (whether some particular taxes are high or low), but certain characteristics or key features of public policies that affect their quality. For operational purposes, this study has defined and attempted to measure several such characteristics, listed below, but future work should identify and attempt to measure others.

The features of public policies examined in this report include:

- *Stability*—the extent to which policies are stable over time
- *Adaptability*—the extent to which policies can be adjusted when they fail or when circumstances change
- *Coherence and coordination*—the degree to which policies are consistent with related policies, and result from well-coordinated actions among the actors who participate in their design and implementation
- *Quality of implementation and enforcement*
- *Public-regardedness*—the degree to which policies pursue the public interest
- *Efficiency*—the extent to which policies reflect an allocation of scarce resources that ensures high returns.

Chapter 6 of this report discusses these characteristics in more detail; presents measures of them for most countries in Latin America, along with an overall index of the quality of public policies (based on these characteristics); establishes some links between the quality of public policies and various measures of welfare and economic development; and relates these policy properties to variables characterizing the workings of political institutions.

The Policymaking Process

The process of discussing, approving, and implementing public policy is collectively referred to as the **policymaking process** (PMP). In democratic systems such as those in Latin America, these processes play out on a political stage featuring a variety of political **actors** (or **players**, in the parlance of game theory). Players in this **game** include official State actors and professional politicians (presidents, party leaders, legislators, judges, governors, bureaucrats), as well as business groups, unions, the media, and other members of civil society. These actors interact in different **arenas**, which may be formal (such as the legislature or the cabinet), or informal ("the street"), and may be more or less transparent.

The PMP can be understood as a process of bargains and exchanges (or transactions) among political actors. Some of these exchanges are consummated instantly (spot transactions). In many other cases, current actions or resources (such as votes) are exchanged

---

[12] Rodrik (1989, p. 2). For models formalizing the effects of policies of uncertain duration in several economic contexts, see Calvo (1996, Section V) and Calvo and Drazen (1998).

for promises of future actions or resources (they are **inter-temporal transactions**). The type of transaction that political actors are able to engage in will depend on the possibilities provided by the institutional environment. Issues of credibility and the capacity to enforce political and policy agreements are crucial for political actors to be able to engage in inter-temporal transactions.

The behavior of political actors in these exchanges, and the nature of the exchanges themselves (for example, support for the government on a crucial policy issue in exchange for a job in the public bureaucracy; or support for reform in a particular policy area in exchange for concessions in a different policy area), depend on the actors' **preferences**, on their **incentives**, and on the **constraints** they face. They also depend on the expectations these actors have regarding the behavior of other players. These interactive patterns of behavior constitute what in the parlance of game theory are called **equilibria**. Thus the characteristics of public policies depend on the equilibrium behavior of policy actors in the policymaking game.

The behavior of political actors in the policymaking process, which are shaped by the roles they play, the incentives that motivate them, and the constraints they face, will depend, in turn, on the workings of political institutions (such as congress, the party system, and the judiciary) and also on more basic institutional rules (such as electoral rules and constitutional rules) that determine the roles of each of the players, as well as the rules of engagement among them.

Policymaking processes, like policies, are very complex. Multiple actors with diverse powers, time horizons, and incentives interact in various arenas. There are diverse rules of engagement which can have an impact on the way the game is played. For these reasons, it is not possible to fully understand these processes by focusing on a few institutional characteristics (such as whether the country is presidential or parliamentary, or whether the electoral rules are of the plurality of proportional representation variety). The institutional setup must be understood in a systemic way (or, in economic jargon, in **general equilibrium**).

Such a systemic view can be accomplished only by means of detailed country studies, which take into account a variety of key institutions and their interaction, as well as historical and cultural legacies (such as fundamental cleavages, shared values, and whether a country has a history of stable democracy or has suffered frequent constitutional interruptions). This is the reason why the 13 country studies from the IDB Latin American Research Network project Political Institutions, Policymaking Processes, and Policy Outcomes play such an important role as background material for this report. Chapter 7 of the report offers a glimpse of the workings of the PMP in a few of these countries, and provides a sense of the complexity involved.

To characterize the workings of the PMP in specific settings, the following questions were asked in regard to each of the countries studied:

- Who are the key actors that participate in the PMP?
- What powers and roles do they have?
- What are their preferences, incentives, and capabilities?

- What are their time horizons?[13]
- In which arenas do they interact, and what are the characteristics of those arenas?
- What is the nature of the exchanges/transactions they undertake?

The information gathered from the country studies was complemented with a series of studies focusing on the comparative role that some key actors play in the PMP across Latin America. Political actors and arenas covered by these studies include political parties and the party system, legislatures, presidents, cabinets, bureaucracies, judiciaries, regional actors, business interests, the media, workers' unions, social movements, and sources of technical expertise ("knowledge actors"). In each case, the studies focused on the key roles (both formal and informal) played by these actors in the PMP, their preferences, incentives, and institutional capabilities, and the way in which they interact with other actors in different arenas. This research is reflected to a large extent in Part II of this report.

Policymaking Processes and Policy Outcomes: The Role of Cooperation

One insight of this report is that important features of public policies depend crucially on the ability of political actors to reach and enforce inter-temporal agreements: that is, to cooperate. In political environments that facilitate such agreements, public policies will tend to be of higher quality, less sensitive to political shocks, and more adaptable to changing economic and social conditions. In contrast, in settings that hinder cooperation, policies will be either too unstable (subject to political swings) or too inflexible (unable to adapt to socioeconomic shocks); they will tend to be poorly coordinated; and investments in State capabilities will tend to be lower.[14]

Under what conditions is cooperation more likely? Drawing on intuitions from game theory, it can be argued that cooperative outcomes are more likely if:

- There are good "aggregation technologies" so that the number of actors with direct impact on the policymaking game is relatively small.
- There are well-institutionalized arenas for political exchange.
- Key actors have long time horizons.
- There are credible enforcement technologies, such as an independent judiciary, or a strong bureaucracy to which certain public policies can be delegated.

---

[13] Time horizons are very important determinants of political behavior. Actors with long horizons are much more likely to enter into the inter-temporal agreements necessary to sustain effective policies. By contrast, actors with short horizons will tend to maximize short-term political and policy benefits, to the detriment of long-term institutional buildup, and of the credibility and quality of policies. This emphasis on time horizons draws inspiration from an important literature on institutional economics and its application to politics. See, for instance, Dixit (1996) and references therein.

[14] This link between cooperation and features of public policies such as stability, adaptability, and coordination has been modeled by Spiller and Tommasi (2003).

Box 2.2	A Complementary Analytical Approach: Veto Players, Decisiveness, and Resoluteness

Another approach, complementary to the one used in this study, also emphasizes interactions among characteristics of polities: the **veto player approach**. This approach, first proposed by George Tsebelis, zeroes in on what it takes to replace the status quo.[1]

In order to introduce any new policy, a number of actors must agree to the proposed change. Some of these actors are individuals, like the president; others are collective, like a house of congress. These actors are called **veto players** in the political science literature. Every political system has a configuration of veto players. The number of veto players may vary; players may have differing ideologies; it may be harder or easier for them to cooperate (the internal levels of cohesion may vary); and so on. These various configurations limit the set of outcomes that could possibly replace the status quo. Only some changes will be acceptable to the particular group of veto players. If few policies are acceptable as replacements for the status quo, policy will be hard to change: that is, policy will be very stable.

Gary Cox and Mathew McCubbins have taken the notion of veto players and applied it to study some characteristics of policies.[2] They suggest that one of the most important trade-offs in policymaking is that between the ability to change policy ("decisiveness") and the ability to commit to a given policy, once it is enacted ("resoluteness"). These concepts are similar to some of the policy characteristics emphasized in this report: in particular, adaptability and stability.

Different configurations of institutions (electoral rules, number of chambers, legislative procedures, and so on) give rise to different configurations of veto players. Countries with more veto players will tend to have more resoluteness and less decisiveness. That is, it will be harder for them to change policy, but once they do, they will commit to the change.

The effective number of vetoes increases when a polity has many institutional veto points ("separation of power"), and political actors with diverse interests control those veto points ("separation of purpose"). Matthew Shugart and Stephan Haggard suggest links between key institutional variables (powers of the president, legislative institutions, federalism, electoral rules) and different degrees of separation of power and separation of purpose.[3] Some of these suggested links are utilized in the rest of the report.

---

[1] Tsebelis (2002).
[2] Cox and McCubbins (2001).
[3] Shugart and Haggard (2001).

These conditions are associated with some characteristics of key players and arenas such as congress, the party system, the judiciary, and the bureaucracy. These intuitions about the determinants of cooperation help guide the analysis of some of the main policy actors and arenas in Part II. Box 2.2 presents a complementary approach, based on the notion of "veto players," which is also useful in the analysis of Part II.

Part III starts (in Chapter 6) by discussing and measuring the characteristics of policies that constitute the dependent variable. The rest of Chapter 6 and Chapter 7 attempt to identify aspects of the workings of the PMP that affect those characteristics of policies. According to the framework discussed above, effective public policies require political actors with relatively long horizons, as well as institutionalized arenas for the discussion, negotiation, and enforcement of political and policy agreements. Chapter 6 constructs some empirical counterparts of such characteristics, looking into the incentives of executives, the policymaking capabilities of congress, the independence of judiciaries, and the development of civil service systems, and relates them to the characteristics of policies using statistical techniques. Chapter 7 discusses several specific country cases, illustrating in greater detail some of the interactions among the multiple factors at play.

The PMP in Action in Specific Sectors

Much of this report looks into the general characteristics of policymaking in different countries, with the implicit assumption that such general characteristics will tend to permeate policymaking in all areas of public policy. Yet it is a well-known maxim in political analysis that "each policy has its own politics." That is because the set of actors and institutions that are relevant in each case, as well as the nature of the transactions required for policy implementation, may differ across sectors. For example, pension reform requires very long time horizons, as well as trade-offs between generations. Trade policy expands the arena beyond purely domestic considerations to introduce international actors and international rules and enforcement. Education brings to the table a very powerful specific actor: the teachers' union.

The chapters in Part IV look into the making of policy in a number of different sectors, with different degrees of proximity to the general PMP of each country. (Tax policy tends to involve all the main actors of the general PMP, while education policy brings in a more idiosyncratic set of actors.)[15] They provide cross-country comparisons of policymaking in these sectors, and show how policy outcomes in each of them can be linked to the characteristics of their PMP. The last chapter in Part IV (Chapter 11) is somewhat different in nature. Rather than looking at the impact of the PMP on policy outcomes, it focuses on feedback effects from policy reform to the PMP. These chapters constitute an important step toward one of the main purposes of this report: to provide some guidance and orientation toward understanding the policymaking processes surrounding specific reform initiatives in particular areas in particular countries at particular points in time.

---

[15] The policy examples are chosen to illustrate some of the general messages of the report; the coverage is far from exhaustive.

Part II

Actors and Arenas in the Policymaking Process

Democracy is never a thing done.
Democracy is always something
that a nation must be doing.

Archibald MacLeish, American
poet and public official
(1892–1982)

The policymaking process is a dynamic game among actors that interact in what can be called **arenas**. Some **actors** are formal, such as political parties, presidents, cabinets, legislatures, courts, and the bureaucracy. Their policymaking roles are formally assigned in the constitution. Other actors are informal, such as social movements, business, and the media. They do not have any formal role, but have emerged on many occasions as powerful players.

The extent and exact nature of the role that actors play—and their interactions—are shaped by a variety of underlying factors (formal and informal rules, interests, preferences, and capabilities), as well as by the expected behavior of other actors and the nature of the arenas where they meet. Some arenas are more formal (such as a legislative committee); others are less formal ("the street," where social movements and others mobilize). Some are more transparent (courtrooms); others are less transparent (closed-door negotiations). Actors' actual roles often deviate from the roles that one would expect based on formal rules and formally ascribed roles. Thus their real roles in the policymaking process must be analyzed carefully. Part II does precisely that.

- *Chapter 3* focuses on political parties, the legislature, and the president: actors that are central to the formal political system and to the policymaking process.
- *Chapter 4* examines the roles of other actors with formally ascribed roles in the policymaking process: cabinets, the bureaucracy, subnational actors such as governors, and the judiciary.
- *Chapter 5* examines business, unions, the media, social movements, and sources of policy expertise (so-called "knowledge actors"). Actors such as these can be considered "informal" in the sense that they are generally not regulated by the constitution or other organic laws or assigned specific roles in the process of making public policies.

Part II looks at the actors one by one in order to consider in depth the characteristics of the actors that affect the characteristics of public policies. The interactions among actors, as they participate in policymaking processes in a variety of countries and policy sectors, are examined in the rest of the report.

Chapter 3

Political Parties, Legislatures, and Presidents

Political parties are the worst form of organized political participation, except for all the others.

—Osvaldo Hurtado, Former President of Ecuador
(paraphrasing Winston Churchill)

This chapter is the first of three that examine the role of a range of actors in the policymaking process. It focuses on a group of actors that are central to policymaking in democratic systems: political parties, the legislature, and the president. These form the inner core of actors, with important roles in democratic representation, in framing the policy agenda, and in formulating, adopting, and implementing policies. Clearly, their roles in these stages of the process are not exclusive. They share these roles with other actors with a formal presence in the constitution, such as the cabinet, the judiciary, and the bureaucracy, as well as with a wide range of actors with more informal roles, such as business groups, unions, the media, social movements, and international organizations.

The operation of the democratic system and the characteristics of policy outcomes are importantly influenced by the interactions among factors related to the nature of the political party system, the structure and functioning of the legislature, and the constraints and incentives facing presidents. Chapter 3 begins by highlighting the importance of examining the interactions among these key actors and the rules of the game.

Different institutional configurations may help or hinder a president in passing his agenda.

Key Actors and Their Interactions

A useful point of departure relates to the interaction between two actors, the president and the legislature, that play a leading role in the game of policymaking as it is played in one of the most important arenas, congress. The discussion begins by looking at the ability of the president to pass his policy agenda through congress. It is natural to begin by centering the analysis on the role of presidents for a number of reasons. First, presidents have in fact acted as agenda-setters during most of the recent reforms undertaken in Latin America. Second, the rules of legislative engagement in most Latin American countries formally endow presidents with prerogatives that help them lead the policy-making process. Third, because they are elected by nationwide constituencies, presidents tend to have more "encompassing" interests in national public goods than legislators. (Presidents may also, however, have incentives that may cause them to stray from the public interest, a matter returned to below.)

The inability of presidents to pass their agendas has been at the heart of a raging debate on the merits of presidential democracies versus parliamentary systems, which fuse the selection and governing responsibilities of the executive and legislative branches. Scholars have expressed concern about the capacity of presidents to govern under divided government: that is, when their party does not control the legislature.[1] The problem is much more than an academic concern. Latin America has experienced several interruptions of democratic governance that have resulted, at least in part, from the inability of presidents and legislatures to agree on policies.

The debate in political science regarding the problems of presidential democracies under conditions of divided government has been cast mainly in terms of its impact on political outcomes: in particular, on the stability of the democratic regime itself. Although this is a very important concern, this report takes a different focus: the impact on the quality of public policies. In particular, the ability of the president to pass his agenda is a very important determinant of one of the key features of public policies emphasized in this report: policy adaptability.

What determines the ability of the president to pass his agenda? In presidential democracies, one key ingredient is the share of seats controlled by the governing party. If the president's party controls a majority of legislative seats in congress, then it will be easier for him to pass his agenda, assuming he can retain the support of his own legislators. As a result, public policies are likely to be adaptable, given that the transaction costs associated with policy change are likely to be relatively low. The size of the president's contingent, in turn, depends on the nature of the party system and electoral rules, among other things.

What if the president's party does not control the legislature? In that case, presidents have alternative ways of advancing their agendas. They can form a coalition based on the stable support of other parties, for instance. Or they can use different bargaining chips to persuade legislators to support particular legislative measures on an ad hoc basis. These rewards include appointments to political offices, policy concessions or changes that benefit legislators' constituencies or parties' bases of support, local investment projects, budgetary transfers, and/or public employment and governmental contracts. These options are not mutually exclusive, as even in the case of stable coalitions, presidents need to use different inducements such as cabinet positions or policy concessions to form coalitions, or to keep them together.

---

[1] Linz (1990), Di Palma (1990), and Linz and Stepan (1978).

Coalitions also vary in their degree of formality, cohesion, and durability. Some are very strong and long-lasting, as in Chile, where coalitions function in important respects as parties and have provided the government with a reliable majority in the lower house (see Chapter 7 for a detailed discussion of policymaking in Chile). Some coalitions, such as those in Ecuador, are much more informal, ad hoc, and short-lived. They are often based on exchanges of various types of immediate and targeted rewards for short-term legislative support. As a consequence, in Ecuador coalitions have not provided presidents with a stable base of legislative support and thus have undermined policy adaptability and stability. Between these two extremes lie coalitions, such as those in Brazil and Uruguay, that may be formalized through participation of multiple parties in the cabinet and/or through agreements on core policies. On occasion, these coalitions do not last the entire presidential term or do not provide as firm a guarantee of support.

The stability of coalitions varies across countries and across administrations, and it depends at least in part on the extent to which there is a match between what the president is able to offer legislators and what legislators want. What a president can offer depends on factors such as his appointment powers, his agenda-setting powers, and his budgetary powers. What legislators want (whether policy concessions, local investment projects, or transfers for their constituents) depends on factors shaping their incentives, including electoral rules. For example, where there is a strong electoral connection between legislators and voters (that is, where voters have a great degree of influence on who gets elected), legislators may want local investment projects for their communities. Such is the case in Brazil, where the distribution of such projects has been an important inducement used by presidents to gather political support.[2]

The potential of such exchanges to sustain coalition support also depends on the existence of commitment mechanisms that ensure that the president and parties (or individual legislators) honor their promises. In Paraguay, for example, the absence of commitment mechanisms has led to a different kind of reward: public employment. Not surprisingly, the quality of the bureaucracy in Paraguay is greatly undermined by the use of public employment as a patronage resource.[3]

One thing that should be clear from this discussion is that different institutional configurations may help or hinder a president in passing his agenda. Passing the president's agenda is possible within a two-party system with majority rule; under a system of strong and stable coalitions, as in Chile; or even under very fragmented party systems, if and when there is a good match between what legislators or legislative parties need and what the president can commit to deliver.

However, when the political system fails to provide the president and his administration with the ability to pass the president's agenda, the consequences may be very serious, even leading to interruptions of democratic governance (see Chapter 6).[4] And such a failure may also lead to a lack of adaptability of policies, implying an inability to

---

[2] See Alston and others (2005a) and Chapter 7 of this report.

[3] See Molinas and Pérez-Liñán (2005).

[4] Chasquetti (2004) provides strong empirical evidence of these consequences, analyzing a sample of 51 Latin American governments between 1980 and 2000. Of the ten governments that failed to achieve a near-majority in the legislature, either by themselves or within a coalition, in six either the executive or the members of the legislature did not complete their constitutionally mandated terms.

move away from failed policies, to adjust in response to shocks, and/or to pass welfare-enhancing reforms, even if these have been clearly identified.

While the inability of presidents to pass their agendas can have harmful political and policy consequences, an institutional setting that allows the president to pass his agenda is not a sufficient condition for good public policies. The discussion that follows highlights two problems that may arise, even when the president has the tools to get what he wants. To tie the discussion to this study's general framework, the discussion links each of these problems to one of the features of public policies introduced in Chapter 2.

Public-regardedness. Are public policies better if the president gets what he wants? Not necessarily. Because presidents are elected by national constituencies, they tend to have more encompassing interests in national public goods than legislators, who tend to favor their local constituencies. However, presidents do not always act like the idealized social planners described in economics textbooks, who seek to maximize social welfare. While they care about the public interest, presidents, like any politician, also have personal and political ambitions.

What determines the president's incentives? Among other factors, the nature of the party system may play an important role. For example, if the workings of political parties are dominated by clientelistic politics, presidents and other politicians will care more about generating the resources needed to maintain the clientelistic system that is the basis of their political support, and less about whether policies are "good" or "bad" from the standpoint of the longer-term public interest. If the president is thought of as a social planner, anything that stands in the way of passing his agenda will reduce the quality of policy outcomes. Once one departs from the naive social planner view, then checks on one's ability to pass one's agenda will be seen to involve trade-offs. These checks can reduce the extent to which the president caters to narrow interests, but they may lead to less decisiveness and less adaptability.

Like the president, members of congress can also seek to derive private or narrow benefits from their public role in the policymaking process. Various types of institutional checks and balances, including those between the executive and legislative branches, can limit the scope for all players involved to cater to narrow interests.[5] Additional actors that can enforce more public-regarding policy choices and policy implementation include an independent and impartial judiciary and a professional and politically neutral civil service. The role of these actors is considered in Chapter 4.

Policy stability. The ability of the president to pass his agenda may also lead to policy instability under some circumstances. Consider a hypothetical country with a two-party system. Each of the parties has stable support of close to half of the electorate. As a result, they alternate in power. Both parties are programmatic, so they compete primarily on the basis of distinctions in their policy ideas and proposals, which tend to be stable over

---

[5] For the classic argument in favor of checks and balances, see *The Federalist Papers*. Authors James Madison, Alexander Hamilton, and John Jay called special interests "factions" and argued that pitting one faction against another, in a system of checks and balances and limited government, would be the best way to promote the public good.

time. Electoral rules tend to produce majority governments and disciplined parties, so policies are adaptable. Some analysts would consider this to be a favorable scenario for presidential democracies. Yet even this rosy scenario of stable parties with stable preferences does not guarantee a very important feature of public policies: policy stability.

If, for example, one of the parties is on the Right and the other on the Left in ideological terms, policies could shift from one extreme to the other every time there is a change in administration.[6] Trade openness and privatization could be followed by increased protection and nationalization of assets; primary education could shift from a focus on public provision to private; and so on. The inefficiencies associated with policy volatility are obvious. While those on the Right and the Left may disagree on their preferred policy options, they would probably agree that cycling between extremes represents the worst possible scenario. The question is how to make sure that the parties "compromise," engaging in inter-temporal agreements to adopt an intermediate policy that is acceptable to both, rather than adopting their preferred one-sided option every time they gain access to power.

Now that it has been established how important it is to examine the interactions among actors and their underlying characteristics to understand the policymaking process, the rest of the chapter will focus in greater detail on each of these central political actors. The purpose is to highlight the potential roles that the actors play in the policymaking process and what characteristics of the actors may affect the extent and nature of their role, as well as to describe some of the characteristics of these actors across the Latin American region.

Political Parties[7]

Political parties are key players in the policymaking process, as they are in the workings of a democratic system more generally. An indispensable element of democracy is the holding of regular electoral contests to allocate control of governmental positions and legislative seats. Parties recruit candidates for such offices, mobilize electoral support, and define their policy aspirations, should they win a place in the government. Apart from their direct roles in elections, parties play other key roles in forming governments, organizing the work of the legislature, and articulating and aggregating citizen interests and preferences.[8]

Party systems influence the workability of executive-legislative relations, the possibilities for coordination in congress, and the incentives of elected officials to cater to narrower or broader sets of social interests.

More related to the topic of this report, the policymaking process in a country is strongly influenced by the structure and organization of political parties, both directly

---

[6] Unstable parties and unstable preferences could potentially make policy volatility even worse, resulting in policy shifts even within an administration.

[7] This section draws extensively on Jones (2005).

[8] Mainwaring and Scully (1995); Sartori (1976); Lipset and Rokkan (1967).

and indirectly. For instance, in some countries, parties—even when they are out of power—are important actors in defining and articulating broad policy programs and can engage effectively in public policy debates, on occasion with the help of affiliated think tanks (see Chapter 5). Characteristics of the party system also affect the policymaking process somewhat more indirectly: influencing, for example, the workability of executive-legislative relations; the possibilities for coordination in congress; and/or the incentives of elected officials to cater to narrower or broader sets of societal interests.

Not only do the characteristics of the party system interact with one another, they also interact with other institutions and actors, such as the presidency, the legislature, and the judiciary. Thus the expected effects of party system (and other institutional) characteristics highlighted in this part of the report may not be observed in all countries, given that the particular impact of each institutional feature depends upon its interaction with other institutional characteristics of the country.

In the discussion that follows, several party system characteristics and their expected impact on the policymaking process are considered: their degree of institutionalization, degree of fragmentation, and degree of nationalization.

Party System Institutionalization

A first important characteristic of party systems is their *level of institutionalization*. Party systems can be considered institutionalized when:

- Patterns of inter-party competition are relatively stable.
- Parties have reasonably strong links with organized societal interests, and citizens tend to be attached to particular parties.
- Parties and elections are perceived as decisive in determining who governs.
- Party organizations are well developed and influential in shaping the policy directions and leadership of the party.[9]

Institutionalized party systems are more likely to promote greater policy consistency over time and a greater potential for inter-temporal agreements. This is because, from one election to the next, the partisan identity and relative political importance of the main players in the policymaking game in the executive and the congress are less likely to change dramatically. Moreover, because parties play a strong role in political recruitment, and political elites strive to promote and protect the value of the party label (which implies maintaining relatively consistent policy positions over time), institutionalized parties are less likely to change their basic policy stances very often. In addition, it is more likely that elected presidents will enjoy some degree of partisan support in the legislature and/or will be better able to build somewhat stable party-based coalitions.

Institutionalized party systems tend to be programmatic. That is, they compete and derive support on the basis of differences in their policy orientations and achievements.

---

[9] See Mainwaring and Scully (1995).

But institutionalized parties—parties with relatively durable bases of political support—can also be clientelistic. In such cases, they compete for and obtain support based on the distribution of selective benefits to voters (such as public sector jobs, governmental contracts, cash, or meals) and are judged by voters primarily on their ability to deliver these benefits.

Parties that are institutionalized and programmatic are likely to improve democratic accountability by enhancing citizens' ability to select parties and candidates that best match their policy preferences. Incentives should also be stronger for investments in public goods, such as education and well-functioning public utilities, and for policy reforms aimed at advancing broader public interests.

By contrast, policymaking in clientelistic systems is likely to be constrained by the need to maintain the parties' clientelistic system of support. Targeted government spending on public works is likely to be favored over investments in more wide-reaching public goods. Implementing policy reforms that can undermine the pillars of the clientelistic system may necessitate making large side payments to clients that have been favored by the party in the past.

To gauge the extent and dimensions of party system institutionalization, this study used an aggregate index of party system institutionalization developed by Mark Jones.[10]

- *The stability of inter-party competition* is measured on the basis of measures of the volatility in party shares of votes and legislative seats between recent elections.
- *The extensiveness of parties' roots in society* and *the legitimacy of parties and elections* are measured on the basis of responses to questions in the Latinobarometer public opinion survey and a survey of legislators.[11]
- *The strength of party organizations* is gauged based on a measure of the age of significant parties and responses to a question from the survey of legislators, asking them to rate the permanence and strength of their party's organization.[12]

To analyze the extent to which party systems are programmatic, this study used another index constructed by Mark Jones. This index attempts to capture the extent to which parties develop distinct approaches to policy and the extent to which citizens are aware of these differences. But it does so indirectly, by examining legislator and citizen perceptions of differences between parties in Left-Right ideological terms, rather than directly observing whether parties' policy programs and positions adhere consistently to distinct ideological perspectives.[13]

---

[10] See Jones (2005). The index is based on the four dimensions set forth in Mainwaring and Scully (1995).

[11] *Proyecto de Elites Latinoamericanas* (PELA), 1994–2005.

[12] For details on the construction of the component indices and aggregate index, see Data Appendix and Jones (2005).

[13] For details on the construction of the index, see Data Appendix and Jones (2005).

Figure 3.1 plots the countries according to their scores on the two aggregate indices. According to these measures, parties are relatively institutionalized and programmatic in Uruguay, Nicaragua, El Salvador, and Chile.[14] They are weakly institutionalized and least programmatic in Guatemala, Ecuador, and Peru.

Figure 3.2 shows the marked contrast between Argentina and Chile in the degree to which parties are programmatic, as measured by one component of this index: legislator perceptions of differences between parties on the Left-Right ideological scale.

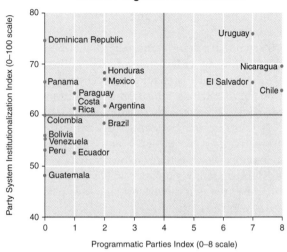

FIGURE 3.1 **Comparing Party Systems in Latin America: Degree of Institutionalization versus Programmatic Character**

Source: Jones (2005).

Party System Fragmentation, Presidential Contingents, and Party Discipline

Several other party system characteristics interacting with one another also have an important influence on the interaction between the executive and legislative branches. These are the level of *legislative fragmentation*; the size of the presidential legislative contingent; and the extent of party discipline (that is, the degree to which members of the president's party in the legislature are responsive to the instructions of the party leadership and/or president).

Party system fragmentation and the size of presidential legislative contingents, in turn, are influenced by characteristics of the electoral system. *Proportional electoral systems*, in which multiple members of congress are elected per electoral district, encourage more fragmented party systems than *plurality systems*, in which only one legislator is elected per district. Among proportional systems, greater party system fragmentation is more likely in systems with larger districts (that is, more legislators elected per district) and those with more equitable formulas for translating the vote shares of parties into shares of legislative seats.

---

[14] Nicaragua's scores on the two indices may be misleading. The two-party system that makes Nicaragua appear institutionalized is in part the result of legislation advanced by the leaders of the two main parties to restrict the ability of other parties to become legally registered and effectively compete. In addition, while the parties differ in ideological orientation, their actual conduct appears to be more clientelistic than programmatic.

FIGURE 3.2   **Ideological Self-Placement of Legislators**

a. **Argentina**

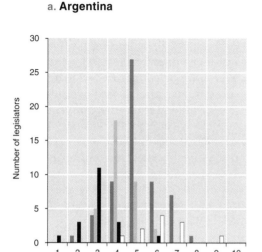

b. **Chile**

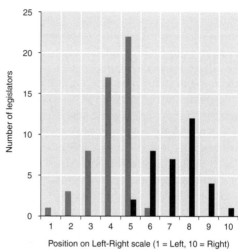

Source: PELA (2005).

Other aspects of the electoral system are also relevant. Always holding legislative elections at the same time as presidential elections favors a greater concentration of votes and legislative seats in the president's party than when such elections are held separately, or when legislative elections are held in the middle of the presidential term. The system used for electing the president can also have indirect effects on party system fragmentation. *Majority run-off systems*[15] tend to discourage the formation of inter-party alliances and favor the proliferation of parties, while plurality systems tend to encourage a concentration of votes in fewer parties.

The share of seats controlled by the governing party, the degree of party system fragmentation, and the cohesiveness of the governing parties have an important impact on the ability of the executive to pass its agenda. They also affect the nature of the bargaining game and the types and loci of trades that the executive engages in to gain legislative support. For instance, if the president controls a majority of seats in the legislature and can enforce discipline within this contingent, he is more likely to choose to govern through statutes (laws passed in the legislature) and to use partisan levers of influence to maintain support. But if the president's legislative contingent is relatively small and the

---

[15] In these systems, for a candidate to win in the first round, he must obtain a majority of the total votes cast (50 percent plus one). If no candidate wins a majority, the two candidates who received the most votes in the first round face one another in a second (run-off) round.

party system is fragmented, the executive must attempt to assemble some type of legislative coalition. These arrangements can range from being a fairly stable coalition among parties to a shifting coalition of parties and even individual legislators. In this case, the president will likely need a broader array of inducements, including offering cabinet or other governmental positions, making policy concessions, or promising favored treatment in allocating public resources and contracts. If the president expects gaining legislative support to be problematic (because stable coalitions cannot be formed), or too costly (in terms of the president's policy agenda or in terms of public resources), then he may choose to govern unilaterally through his constitutional legislative powers (decree or agenda-setting powers) or "paraconstitutional" powers (such as discretionary powers to shift funds within the budget or use unilateral rulemaking authority extensively).[16]

Consistent governmental majorities and disciplined parties can promote policy adaptability. While such a scenario may promote governmental "decisiveness,"[17] it may, in the absence of effective checks on executive authority, result in deficiencies in the public-regardedness of policy outcomes. In addition, policy volatility can result, if power tends to alternate among disciplined and relatively polarized parties.

On the other hand, party system fragmentation, especially if very high and combined with polarization, can complicate executive-legislative relations, making it difficult to obtain stable support for the executive agenda. This can lead to gridlock or prompt presidents to pursue unilateral strategies, which can endanger the durability of democratic institutions.

The level of fragmentation in the legislature directly influences the size of the presidential legislative contingent. It also affects the number of partners with which the president must form some type of legislative coalition or structure piecemeal alliances specific to individual pieces of legislation to implement his policy agenda. The level of legislative fragmentation in the lower house (or national assembly) is measured in Table 3.1, using an index of the effective number of parties based on the two most recent legislative elections in each country.[18] Brazil, Ecuador, and Bolivia are in the fragmented extreme, with a multitude of political parties winning legislative seats. By contrast, politics in Chile, Honduras, and Nicaragua tends to be dominated by two political parties.[19]

Table 3.1 also shows the average percentage of seats held by the president's party in the lower house (or national assembly) in the two most recent legislative elections, as well as an index of the proportionality of the design of the electoral system. In several countries, including Chile, Nicaragua, Paraguay (lower house), and Honduras, the president's party has typically enjoyed a majority of the legislative seats. In others, including Argentina and Uruguay, the president's contingent, while not reaching a majority, has

---

[16] Cox and Morgenstern (2002).

[17] Cox and McCubbins (2001).

[18] This index aims to measure the number of parties in a way that captures the party system's effects on the real functioning of the political system. For instance, if three parties each obtain close to an equal share of the legislative seats available, then the index value is about 3. But if two of the parties receive 45 percent of the seats and the third receives 10 percent, then the index value is 2.4. The index value is lower since this system would be expected to have more in common with a two-party system in terms of how it functions. See Data Appendix and Jones (2005) for details on the construction of this index.

[19] In Chile, the stable electoral alliances in place since 1989 are considered parties.

Table 3.1 Party System Fragmentation and the Presidential Legislative Contingent (average from two most recent legislative elections)

Country	Effective number of legislative parties	Presidential party's contingent in lower house or national assembly (percent)	Proportionality of design of election system
Brazil	7.81	19	4.90
Ecuador	6.71	25	3.23
Bolivia	5.21	27	4.44
Colombia	5.00	20	3.14
Venezuela	4.75	34	3.32
Peru	4.24	41	3.12
El Salvador	3.50	34	3.16
Guatemala	3.46	43	3.11
Argentina	3.18	48	3.21
Costa Rica	3.12	40	3.62
Panama	3.09	39	1.97
Mexico	2.79	37	2.50
Uruguay	2.73	43	5.00
Paraguay	2.73	51	3.06
Dominican Republic	2.52	41	3.77
Nicaragua	2.39	54	3.15
Honduras	2.30	50	3.47
Chile	2.02	55	2.00

Note: The index of the effective number of legislative parties is computed by taking the inverse of the sum of the squares of all parties' seat shares (Laakso and Taagepera 1979). The index of the proportionality of the design of the election system ranges from 1 to 5, where 1 = majority system (average district magnitude [ADM] = 1); 2 = low proportionality (ADM = 2–4); 3 = moderate proportionality (ADM = 4–10); high proportionality (ADM = 10–20); and 5 = very high proportionality (20–national district).

Sources: Jones (2005) and authors' calculations.

been reasonably high (above 40 percent). In several countries, however, the size of the president's legislative contingent has been very low, including Brazil, Colombia, Ecuador, and Bolivia.

From Table 3.1 it is clear that there is some correlation between party system fragmentation and the proportionality of the electoral system, but that correlation is imperfect. This is likely due to the fact that the structure of party systems is also affected by longer-term historical factors, as well as the salience of socioeconomic, ethnic, and geographic cleavages.

There is considerable debate in the scholarly literature regarding the consequences for governance in general and policymaking in particular of presidential legislative contingents that are below majority status.[20] While some observers consider small presidential contingents (especially those that are around 33 percent and below) to be problematic for democratic governance, others do not. However, there is more agreement that, in instances where the president's party lacks a majority of the seats in the legislature (or does not at least approach a majority, with at least 45 percent of the seats), the president must form some type of legislative coalition in order to be able to govern effectively. Where coalitions are not formed and sustained, governance problems are likely to emerge.[21]

The increasing fragmentation of party systems and the decreasing probability of single-party majorities (reflected in Table 3.1 above) has meant that the viability of governments increasingly depends upon the formation of some form of coalition government. Whether a stable majority government can be formed, on the basis of either a single party or a coalition of parties, is likely to be a key factor in shaping whether inter-temporal agreements among political actors are possible and whether policies are adaptable and stable over time and implemented effectively.

From 1990 to 2004, in a sample of 18 Latin American countries, only 20 percent of presidential-congressional periods[22] were characterized by single-party majorities—or 36 percent, if cases in which the governing party has a near-majority are also included.[23] During the period, single-party majorities (or near-majorities) were common in such countries as Argentina, Costa Rica, Honduras, and Mexico. Stable, or at least relatively stable, coalition governments were common in Brazil, Chile, and Uruguay, among others. By contrast, minority governments were especially common in Ecuador and Guatemala (Table 3.2).

But it is an oversimplification to focus only on the share of seats controlled by the governing party or coalition, since the degree to which parties act as a cohesive block in the legislature varies considerably across countries and even across parties within the same party system. The ability of presidents (and the central party leadership) to enforce discipline within their party's ranks in the legislature has an important effect on their success in advancing their legislative agendas.

The level of responsiveness of legislators to national party leaders is affected by incentives provided by the electoral system and the process of nominating candidates, as well as by other forms of reward and punishment that might be utilized by party leaders or the president. This study uses a Party Centralization Index to capture how responsive legislators are to national party leaders (Figure 3.3).[24] The index centers mostly on the sources of leverage that party leaders have that stem from the electoral system. But there

---

[20] See Foweraker (1998) and Cheibub, Przeworski, and Saiegh (2004), for example.

[21] See Chasquetti (2004). The formation of stable coalitions may be complicated when fragmented party systems are combined with high levels of ideological polarization. But it is hard to determine the exact threshold at which this is likely to become a problem. As stated above, some degree of programmatic difference among parties is likely to be beneficial for effective democratic governance.

[22] Presidential-congressional periods change when the president changes (because of elections, resignation, impeachment, or coup) and when a new congress is elected in the middle of a presidential term. There were 95 presidential-congressional periods between 1990 and 2004 in the 18 Latin American countries.

[23] A near-majority is defined as a case in which the president has more than 45 percent of the seats in both houses of congress (or the national assembly).

[24] The index was constructed by Mark Jones. For more details, see Jones (2005).

Table 3.2 Types of Governments in Latin America, 1990–2004

	Majority or near-majority	Minority
Single-party	Argentina (1990–)	Costa Rica (2002–)
	Colombia (1990–98)	Dominican Rep. (1990–96; 1998–2000; 2004–)
	Costa Rica (1990–2002)	El Salvador (1990–)
	Dominican Rep. (2000–2004)	Paraguay (1990–94; 1997–)
	Guatemala (1996–2004)	Peru (1990–92; 2001–)
	Honduras (1990–)	Venezuela (1993–99)
	Mexico (1990–2000)	
	Peru (1993–2000)	
	Venezuela (1989–93; 2000–)	
Coalition	Bolivia (1989–97)	Bolivia (1997–)
	Brazil (1993–)	Brazil (1990–92)
	Chile (1990–)	Colombia (1998–2002)
	Colombia (2002–)	Ecuador (1990–)
	Dominican Rep. (1996–98)	Guatemala (1990–96; 2004–)
	El Salvador (1994–97)	Mexico (2000–)
	Panama (1989–99)	Panama (1999–)
	Uruguay (1990–)	

Note: Governments are counted as majority coalition governments if the coalition is sustained for more than half of the presidential term. Otherwise, such governments are categorized as minority coalitions.

Sources: Martínez-Gallardo (2005b) and calculations based on data from Payne and others (2002).

are other incentives, such as leaders' control over the appointment of legislators to committees and control over the legislative agenda.

The first component of the index focuses on the extent to which national party leaders or individual candidates are responsible for determining who is able to run for office and their position on the electoral list. When national party leaders largely determine whether legislators can run for reelection and their position on the party list, then legislators have greater incentive to conform to the party line in the legislature.

A second dimension of the index focuses on core features of the electoral system, including the territorial dimension of electoral districts (national, regional, single-member, or some mixture thereof) and whether voters may choose among individual candidates instead of only among pre-selected party lists. Centralization is greater where legislators are elected in a single national district or large districts with closed party lists.

Four other factors affecting the degree of party centralization are included in the index: whether presidential and legislative elections are held concurrently; the degree of autonomy of subnational authorities (in particular, governors); the extent to which parties are internally democratic; and the extent to which presidential candidates have

FIGURE 3.3 **Party Centralization Index (2005)**

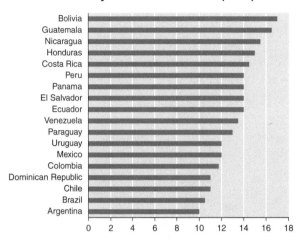

Note: The index is a simple sum of six individual components. The theoretical range of the index is from 6 to 18.

Source: Jones (2005).

been selected through primaries. Parties will be more centralized, and national party leaders more powerful, when elections are concurrent; when governors are not competing with national party leaders for the control of legislators; and when the power of the national leaders to nominate candidates is not diluted by primaries or other forms of intra-party democracy.

Values for the Party Centralization Index for various Latin American countries are shown in Figure 3.3. Presidents would be expected to have the most influence on legislators from their own parties in Bolivia, Guatemala, Nicaragua, Honduras, and Costa Rica. The president should not expect especially disciplined legislators in Chile, Brazil, and Argentina, and one would expect coalitions in those countries to be formed primarily through negotiation with regional/factional leaders of political parties or with individual legislators.

Party and Party System Nationalization

A final characteristic of party systems that can affect the functioning of democracy and policy outcomes is their *degree of nationalization*. A nationalized party system implies that parties are generally national in scope and that they tend to speak and act with a common national orientation, rather than being divided according to regional or subnational issues and focused upon them. In highly nationalized party systems, national issues are likely to be central to legislators' careers. Executives might have a greater ability to forge legislative coalitions centered on national issues, given the need to negotiate with only a few key national party leaders. Under conditions of weak party nationalization, the central party leadership may be less able to speak for the entire party and to deliver its legislative support.

Differences in nationalization are also likely to have public policy consequences. Where a party's base of support is relatively constant across geographic units, it will be more likely to treat all units equally with respect to decisions in relation to such matters as transfers to subnational units, administrative reform, public investments, and subsidies. By contrast, where its support varies widely across geographic units, it will be more likely to base its decisions in part on the degree of electoral support it receives in specific geographic units. Under a nationalized party system, public policy is likely to be more oriented toward working for the national common good.

A partial approach to assessing the nationalization of party systems is to examine the distribution of the popular vote for parties across territorial jurisdictions of the country.[25] Figure 3.4 shows the scores on an index of party system nationalization for Latin American countries constructed on the basis of votes in the lower house elections held closest to 2002. On the basis of this measure, parties would appear to be most nationalized in Honduras, Chile, Uruguay, and Nicaragua and least nationalized in Peru, Argentina, Venezuela, and Brazil.

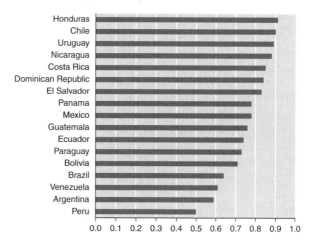

FIGURE 3.4 **Party System Nationalization Index (based on data from elections closest to 2002)**
(*0–1 scale*)

Source: Jones (2005).

Legislatures[26]

Legislatures are critical institutions in the effective functioning of a democratic system and in the policymaking process. Legislatures are expected to represent the needs and wishes of citizens in policymaking; identify problems and formulate and approve laws to address them; and oversee the implementation of policies by monitoring, reviewing, and investigating government activities to ensure that they are transparent, efficient, and consistent with existing laws and regulations.

The extent and nature of the role played by legislatures in the policymaking process vary greatly from country to country. At the more proactive and constructive end of the spectrum, legislatures such as the U.S. Congress are able to develop their own legislative proposals and thus participate along with the executive in directing the policy agenda. Given their policy capabilities, such legislatures are also

Legislatures in the region do not exist solely to rubber-stamp executive decisions.

---

[25] This measure would not correctly assess the nationalization of the party system if regional chapters of parties differ in their programmatic orientation or their bases of support.

[26] This section draws extensively on Saiegh (2005).

likely to be active and effective in overseeing policy implementation.[27] At the other end, legislatures may be fairly marginal players, serving as a rubber stamp on the executive's legislative proposals and having little capacity or willingness to scrutinize the conduct of government.[28] Between these two extremes, there is a wide area in the middle where legislatures can exhibit different degrees of activity either in simply blocking much of what the executive proposes or in reformulating and/or amending executive initiatives. Among such legislatures, there can also be considerable variation in the intensity and effectiveness with which they perform the oversight role.

How the legislature plays its policymaking roles can have an important effect on the nature of policy outcomes. If the legislature is a marginal actor, this will give the executive free rein to enact policy changes that it perceives to be necessary. But the lack of legislative deliberation as policies are formulated and the weakness of oversight may mean that the policies adopted are poorly conceived in technical terms, poorly adjusted to the real needs or demands of organized interests and citizens, lacking consensus and therefore politically unsustainable, and/or inefficiently or unfairly implemented. On the other hand, legislatures that are involved more heavily in policymaking in a constructive sense can contribute to the adoption of policies that are more sustainable because they are based on a broader social and political consensus and are more carefully scrutinized in technical terms. In addition, in a constructive legislature the effective oversight of policy implementation should increase the likelihood that policies fulfill their intended objectives rather than being carried out for the benefit of particular individuals, groups, or sectors.

Legislatures with limited capacity to play a constructive role in policymaking may nonetheless be important players in the sense of obstructing or vetoing much of what the executive proposes. Such legislatures have many of the potential negative traits of more marginal legislatures in regard to policymaking, and they may also prevent the executive from advancing a positive agenda of policy reform. Given their limited capacity, such legislatures are also unlikely to play an effective role in overseeing the implementation of policies.

Against the backdrop of the region's history of dictatorial rule and *presidencialismo*, scholars had tended to consider legislatures in Latin American countries to be largely irrelevant throughout much of the 20th century and not worthy of study in and of themselves. Some prominent experiences in the past two decades, such as the closing of the legislature by President Fujimori in Peru and the frequent use of decree powers by President Menem in Argentina, continued to reinforce the commonly held view that Latin American legislatures often abdicate (or are forced to abdicate) their constitutional prerogatives to the executive. But recent studies suggest that, while legislatures in the region in general may not be heavily involved in formulating and advocating policy change, they are nonetheless relevant to policy outcomes. Legislatures in some countries are active in policymaking in the sense of mainly being blunt veto players, blocking

---

[27] Morgenstern (2002).

[28] A marginal legislature may go hand-in-hand with a dominant president/chief executive or a situation in which policy is made through discussion between the executive and legislators from the governing party, without the legislature as a whole being brought in to play a significant role.

legislation proposed by the executive. Others, however, are involved in negotiating policy issues behind the scenes with the executive or in amending or reformulating executive legislative initiatives.

That legislatures in the region do not exist solely to rubber-stamp executive decisions is evident from data on the success rates of executive legislative initiatives. As is evident in Table 3.3, the rate of approval of executive initiatives varies from a low of 41 percent in Costa Rica from 1986 to 1998 to a high of 96 percent in Mexico from 1982 to 1999.[29]

But such raw measures are of limited value in assessing a legislature's full influence on policymaking. Aside from pro-

Table 3.3 Success of Executives in Gaining Approval of Their Legislative Initiatives

Country	Legislative success rate (percent)
Mexico (1982–99)	96
Paraguay (1990–99)	83
Honduras (1990–96)	79
Brazil (1986–98)	72
Chile (1990–2000)	69
Venezuela (1959–88)	68
Peru (2001–2004)	65
Argentina (1983–2000)	64
Uruguay (1985–2000)	57
Colombia (1995–99)	51
Peru (1996–99)	50
Ecuador (1979–96)	42
Costa Rica (1986–98)	41

Source: Saiegh (2005).

posing or killing legislation, legislatures can approve bills with extensive amendments. They can also exert influence, outside the formal legislative arena, through bilateral negotiations between legislative leaders and executive officials, as to which bills get introduced and the form that such legislation takes. In addition, the executive, not wanting to face the humiliation of a legislative defeat, can anticipate the legislature's reaction in the way that it designs policy proposals.[30] Thus the task of appraising the legislature's policymaking role in any given country is a very difficult task that requires detailed study of individual cases.

The nature of the role that legislatures play is likely to influence the way that citizens view them. At the same time, the level of citizen trust in congress affects the likelihood that investments can be made in building its capacity. In addition, in cases in which congress has little credibility, it is likely to be less effective in representing societal interests, and the executive will have a greater incentive to seek to bypass or minimize the legislature in the policymaking process.

As seen in Table 3.4, neither the general public nor international business executives have a high degree of confidence in the congress in most countries of the region. On average over the past decade, according to the Latinobarometer, the general public has the most favorable view of congress in Uruguay, Chile, Honduras, and Costa Rica and the

---

[29] Saiegh (2005).

[30] Morgenstern (2002).

Table 3.4 Confidence in Congress

Country	Confidence in congress, average, 1996–2004 (percent)	Confidence in congress, 2004 (percent)	Effectiveness of lawmaking bodies, 2004–2005 (1 = very ineffective; 7 = very effective)
Chile	36.0	29.7	3.7
Brazil	24.9	34.8	3.1
Uruguay	38.2	30.0	2.7
Colombia	20.3	24.4	2.7
Honduras	30.8	31.1	2.6
Costa Rica	29.9	35.3	2.2
Paraguay	25.0	19.5	2.2
El Salvador	27.7	21.8	2.1
Dominican Republic	n.a.	43.6	2.0
Mexico	27.4	23.1	2.0
Panama	22.5	24.8	1.8
Guatemala	19.9	19.2	1.8
Bolivia	19.9	15.5	1.8
Peru	22.1	14.5	1.7
Ecuador	13.3	8.3	1.7
Argentina	20.5	20.7	1.6
Nicaragua	23.1	16.1	1.6
Venezuela	27.8	30.6	1.4

n.a.: not applicable. As the Dominican Republic was included only in the 2004 survey, no average is shown.

Note: The first and second columns are the average percentage of respondents from 1996 to 2004 and the percentage of respondents in 2004, respectively, in the Latinobarometer survey who stated that they had "a lot" or "some" confidence in the congress. The third column is the mean score given by business executives in the 2004–2005 World Economic Forum survey to the question "How effective is your national parliament/congress as a lawmaking and oversight institution?"

Sources: Latinobarometer (1996–2004) and World Economic Forum (2005).

least favorable view in Ecuador, Bolivia, and Guatemala. By contrast, the average ratings given by business executives, as reported by the World Economic Forum, are highest in Chile and Brazil and lowest in Venezuela, Nicaragua, and Argentina. The most important differences in the views of the general public and business executives are for Venezuela and the Dominican Republic, where in each case the general public has a comparatively more favorable view than business executives.

Factors Affecting the Legislature's Role in Policymaking

The role of the legislature in the policymaking process is shaped by a variety of factors, including the extent of its constitutional powers relative to the executive branch; the balance of partisan forces in the executive and legislative branches; the structure, organization, procedures, and technical capacities of the legislature; and the goals of its members, derived from electoral-based and party-based incentives.

Macro-Structure of the Legislature

A first characteristic that may affect the role played by the legislature in policymaking is its unicameral or bicameral structure. Nine countries in the region—Argentina, Brazil, Bolivia, Chile, Colombia, the Dominican Republic, Mexico, Paraguay, and Uruguay— have bicameral legislatures. Depending upon such factors as how the members of the two houses are elected and the balance of legislative powers between the two chambers, a bicameral legislature can provide a separate veto point in the policymaking process and also affect the extent to which territorial interests are represented. For instance, a senate elected from a single national district concurrently with the president and on a single ballot (as in Uruguay) is less likely to act as an additional veto point and does not dramatically change how territorial interests are represented. But when senators are elected separately from the president on the basis of provincial districts (as in Argentina), and representation is not tied to population, then there is a greater possibility that the upper house can become a separate veto point and accentuate the extent to which regional interests are represented in policymaking. Given the complexity that consideration of the senate adds, and the relative lack of comparative information, the analysis that follows focuses mainly on the lower house, or national assembly in the case of unicameral congresses.

Constitutional Powers

Although all the Spanish- and Portuguese-speaking Latin American countries considered in this report have adopted a basic presidential form of government similar to that of the United States, considerable differences exist with respect to the relative powers the constitution assigns to the executive and legislative branches. Several Caribbean countries and Suriname and Guyana, on the other hand, use either parliamentary or semi-presidential systems, which entail differences in the nature of the relationship between the executive and legislative branches and the expected role that legislatures play in the policy process. Box 3.1 underlines some of these differences through a discussion of the case of Jamaica.

Two fundamental characteristics of presidential systems distinguish them from parliamentary systems: the head of state is elected separately from the congress, and the terms of the president and congress are fixed. In relation to these core features, the only notable deviation among this set of countries is Bolivia, where congress has the responsibility of choosing among the leading two vote-winners in the presidential race if no candidate obtains an absolute majority in the first round.

| Box 3.1 | Policymaking in a Parliamentary System: The Case of Jamaica* |

Jamaica's parliamentary system is based on the British Westminster model and shares many of its fundamental characteristics. The electorate votes for representatives to the 60-member House of Representatives. An upper house (the Senate) also exists, which performs a role somewhat similar to that traditionally performed by the British House of Lords. The legislator that commands majority support in the lower house—invariably the leader of the majority party—is invited by the Governor-General to be prime minister and, in turn, appoints the cabinet ministers. The government is responsible to the House of Representatives, which can end the government's term of office if a majority supports a motion of no confidence. Elections must be called within a five-year period from the previous election, but the timing is at the discretion of the prime minister, with the approval of the Governor-General, who, like the Queen in Britain, acts as a mostly ceremonial head of state.

The first-past-the-post electoral system, and the resulting recurrence of single-party majorities in the House of Representatives, favor the concentration of decision making authority in the executive, as in the British system. Aside from appointing the cabinet ministers, the prime minister, in effect, "appoints" the majority of senators (formally this is done by the Governor-General), as well as officials to fill the top positions in the bureaucracy and other special agencies of government. The system's parliamentary structure, broad prime ministerial appointment powers, and the important role of parties in helping members of parliament secure reelection have encouraged strong party discipline and a limited role for the legislature in policymaking.

The dynamics of inter-party competition, especially since 1990, have favored political stability. Since 1962 power has alternated between two parties—the People's National Party (PNP) and the Jamaica Labour Party (JLP)—but each instance of change has been followed by at least two successive terms of office (four successive terms, for the current governing party). As a consequence, cabinet ministers and other officials tend to stay in their positions much longer than their counterparts in Latin American countries. By the 1990s, the moderation of the traditionally more Leftist PNP had led to an increasing convergence in the policy orientations of the two parties.

One would expect that these characteristics of the Jamaican policymaking process would favor the ability of the government to adopt needed policy changes (policy adaptability) and, at the same time, the stability of broad development policies and consistent policy implementation. In addition, the existence of a merit-based and relatively professional bureaucracy, as well as a fairly independent judiciary, would be expected to favor the enforcement of long-term policy agreements and contribute to the stability and long-term quality of public policies.

In some instances, governmental decisiveness has been clearly evident, such as the response to the banking crisis in 1997 and decisions regarding entry into the Caribbean Community (CARICOM). But the government has been less adept in crafting

| **Box 3.1** | **Continued** |

timely and adequate policy reforms in relation to some other problems, such as the large fiscal deficit and public debt and the escalating crime rate. For example, in relation to the fiscal deficit, governments have been able to increase tax rates and improve revenue collection but have been less successful in abolishing tax exemptions and reducing business tax evasion. Reforms to reduce public sector salaries have only recently been implemented. The reasons for the slowness to adapt in such areas are complex, but stem in part from the inability of the government to impose losses on some powerful organized groups whose support—or at least, acquiescence—is required to implement reforms. Underlying this inability to adopt public-regarding reforms are some limitations on the intensity and fairness of electoral competition and representation, related to gerrymandering and the clientelistic practices of the political parties.

---

* Based on Mejía Acosta (2005).

Once one looks beyond these two defining characteristics, there are important differences among countries. The relative powers that constitutions assign to presidents and legislatures are a key factor in shaping the policymaking role of the congress.

Though presidents have the power to appoint and remove cabinet ministers in all Latin American countries,[31] in some cases, such as Colombia, Peru, Uruguay, and Venezuela, legislatures also have the power to remove them through censure procedures. Given the difficulty of obtaining the majorities required for censure and the president's full discretion in naming a successor, this power has not been used to a significant extent in most countries. However, the power of censure may still act as a constraint on the president's discretion in controlling the composition of his cabinet.

Aside from appointment powers, constitutions grant presidents other tools with which to insert themselves into policymaking. Generally speaking, the stronger and more diverse these powers, the more constrained the legislature is likely to be in undertaking an active and effective role in policymaking and developing its capabilities.

The presidential powers that contribute to the president's ability to unilaterally change the status quo can be referred to as *proactive powers*.[32] These powers include decree powers, agenda-setting powers, and budgetary powers. *Reactive powers*, by contrast, allow the president to preserve the status quo against efforts by the legislature to change it. These powers include package veto and partial veto powers, and exclusive powers to initiate legislation in given policy areas.

---

[31] A partial exception is Uruguay, where (as in the United States) the president must seek legislative approval for cabinet appointments.

[32] Mainwaring and Shugart (1997).

In several countries the constitution grants presidents the power to enact new legislation by decree, even without the legislature first delegating this authority. This authority is applicable across most policy areas in Argentina, Brazil, and Colombia, but limited to economic matters in Ecuador and fiscal matters in Peru. Although in most cases congress has the authority to rescind the decree, this power nonetheless helps the president control the legislative agenda and obtain outcomes that would otherwise not be possible. For instance, in Brazil, the president can legislate through provisional decrees (*Medidas Provisórias*), which need to be ratified by the congress within 60 days to remain in effect. If a provisional decree is not acted on within the first 45 days, it is automatically sent to the top of the legislative agenda. If the congress does not approve the provisional decree in this first 60-day period, the president can reissue the provisional decree, but only once.

Constitutions also grant many presidents in the region important agenda-setting powers. For instance, presidents in Brazil, Colombia, and Uruguay can declare a legislative proposal "urgent," thereby requiring congress to act within a set timeframe. In Uruguay, a bill becomes law if the congress does not act within the allowed timeframe. Another form of agenda-setting power, found in Brazil and Chile, is the president's ability to convene a special legislative session in which only those initiatives set forth by the executive can be debated.

In many countries, the legislature's role with respect to budgetary policymaking is curtailed by restrictions on the legislature's authority and by special presidential prerogatives. For instance, in Chile the executive sets the spending limits in the budget and has the sole responsibility for estimating revenues. The legislature cannot increase expenditures for any budget item or introduce amendments that increase total spending; it can only reduce expenditures or reject them. Moreover, if congress fails to approve a budget law within 60 days, the executive's original proposal becomes law.

The constitutions of many of the region's countries also provide presidents with mechanisms to prevent attempts by the legislature to change the status quo policies without the president's assent. The package veto, in which presidents can refrain from signing an entire bill approved by the legislature into law, is common in many presidential systems, including the United States. But many Latin American presidents are also given the power to reject individual items of bills approved by the legislature.

Another form of reactive power is when the president is given the exclusive authority to initiate legislation in some policy areas. For example, in Colombia, this restriction on the legislature applies to the structure of ministries, salaries of public employees, foreign exchange, external trade and tariffs, and the national debt, among other areas. Presidential legislative monopolies (that is, areas of exclusive initiative) are also fairly extensive in Brazil and Chile.

Finally, the power of presidents to put to a vote of the citizens general matters of policy or particular laws (plebiscite powers) can be valuable, even when not used, to put pressure on legislators to support the president. The magnitude of this power depends on the breadth of its applicability across policy areas and whether this power is also shared by congress.

As Table 3.5 shows, the overall legislative powers of presidents are greatest in Chile, Brazil, Ecuador, and Colombia. Proactive powers are also sizeable in Peru. Legislative pow-

Table 3.5 Legislative Powers of Presidents in Latin America

Country	Proactive powers			Reactive powers				Plebiscite powers	Overall legislative powers[b]
	Decree powers[a]	Budget powers	Proactive powers subtotal[b]	Package veto	Partial veto	Exclusive initiative	Reactive powers subtotal[b]		
Chile	0.33	0.73	0.50	0.85	0.85	0.67	0.77	1.00	0.66
Brazil	1.00	0.91	0.96	0.15	0.15	0.67	0.38	0.00	0.62
Ecuador	0.33	0.73	0.50	1.00	0.69	0.33	0.62	1.00	0.59
Colombia	0.67	0.64	0.66	0.31	0.31	0.67	0.46	1.00	0.59
Peru	0.67	0.73	0.70	0.15	0.15	0.33	0.23	1.00	0.50
Argentina	0.33	0.45	0.38	0.85	0.85	0.00	0.48	0.50	0.44
Panama	0.17	0.55	0.33	0.77	0.77	0.33	0.58	0.00	0.43
Uruguay	0.17	0.64	0.37	0.54	0.54	0.33	0.45	0.00	0.38
El Salvador	0.00	0.82	0.35	0.77	0.00	0.00	0.22	1.00	0.33
Venezuela	0.33	0.64	0.46	0.08	0.08	0.00	0.04	1.00	0.30
Guatemala	0.33	0.18	0.27	0.77	0.00	0.00	0.22	1.00	0.29
Dominican Republic	0.00	0.64	0.27	0.92	0.15	0.00	0.31	0.00	0.27
Honduras	0.33	0.36	0.34	0.77	0.00	0.00	0.22	0.00	0.26
Mexico	0.17	0.36	0.25	0.92	0.00	0.00	0.26	0.00	0.24
Bolivia	0.00	0.27	0.12	0.85	0.00	0.33	0.38	0.00	0.23
Costa Rica	0.00	0.64	0.27	0.77	0.00	0.00	0.22	0.00	0.23
Paraguay	0.00	0.64	0.27	0.23	0.23	0.00	0.13	0.00	0.19
Nicaragua	0.00	0.73	0.31	0.15	0.15	0.00	0.09	0.00	0.19

[a] Included in this measure are both the power of presidents to unilaterally make law (decree powers) and the power to shape the legislative agenda (agenda-setting powers), such as by declaring legislation "urgent," implying a reduced timeframe for congress to take action.

[b] Weighted averages.

Note: Legislative power variables are normalized on a scale of 0 to 1 based on the range of possible scores for each variable.

Source: UNDP (2005).

ers of presidents are weakest in Nicaragua, Paraguay, Costa Rica, and Bolivia.[33] While significant legislative powers give the president important levers for bargaining and shaping the legislative agenda, they usually do not substitute for the need for adequate partisan support. Decrees can be overturned, "urgent" legislative initiatives can be defeated, and vetoes can be overridden. Thus factors related to the party and electoral system are also key in shaping the legislature's role and the nature of executive-legislative relations.

[33] UNDP (2005).

Party Dynamics and Electoral Incentives

As discussed, the likelihood that the president will be able to pass his agenda is affected by the typical size of the president's legislative contingent, the degree of legislative fragmentation, and the extent of party centralization (or discipline). These factors are also likely to affect the role that the legislature plays in policymaking.

When presidents can count on the support of a disciplined majority party or coalition, the role of the legislature can be limited. For example, despite having relatively weak constitutional powers, Mexican presidents before 1997 dominated policymaking, since they could count on solid majorities for the governing *Partido Revolucionario Institucional* (PRI) in both houses of congress. Now that the currently governing *Partido Acción Nacional* (PAN) lacks a majority, the legislature has become a much more active player in policymaking and the success rate for executive initiatives has dropped considerably.

While a highly fragmented party system is likely to result in a more active legislature, it may tend to limit the legislature's role to being mainly a veto player or a site of bargaining over particularistic expenditures—rather than an arena for proactive policymaking or effective oversight of the executive. Having a large number of parties, especially when they are internally factionalized, is likely to limit the possibilities for coordination over policy both within the legislature and between the executive and the legislative branches.

Differences in the extent to which parties are centralized and disciplined also entail trade-offs with respect to the legislature's policymaking role. On the one hand, party centralization may help presidents secure support in the legislature and facilitate interparty negotiations in the formation of governing coalitions, thus contributing to adaptability. Centralized parties that are also programmatic in orientation may encourage legislators to adopt a policy focus oriented toward national public goods, rather than a focus on the delivery of more targeted and narrow benefits.

On the other hand, high levels of party centralization are likely to limit legislators' incentives and possibilities of responding directly to their constituents, as well as their incentives to participate independently in the policymaking process and in oversight responsibilities. Subservience to party leaders, especially when parties tend to be clientelistic, can contribute to a weak policy role for the legislature and weak incentives for legislators to invest in developing the capacities of congress. But while decentralized parties may encourage greater policy independence among legislators and more accountability of individual legislators to voters if parties are less cohesive, this can limit the ability of voters to hold representatives accountable on the basis of national policy positions and accomplishments and encourage an orientation among legislators toward satisfying narrow geographic interests.[34]

Election rules and the degree of centralization of candidate nomination processes can also affect legislators' career ambitions and incentives, as well as their experience. Given the very high rates of reelection (around 90 percent) and fairly decentralized party structures of the U.S. Congress, analysts assume that legislators' main motivating goals are to obtain reelection and to advance their careers in the legislature. By contrast, in Latin America, where the rate of reelection tends to be much lower, legislators typically

---

[34] Carey and Shugart (1995).

have an incentive to work toward advancing a career outside the legislature (such as in national, state, or local government) and are also less experienced. Their career objectives are often furthered by satisfying party leaders rather than centering their attention on satisfying constituents' interests and demands.

As shown in Figure 3.5, the rates of immediate reelection to the congress vary greatly across countries. In Chile and Uruguay, around 60 percent of legislators are immediately reelected; in Peru and Argentina, less than 20 percent return for a second consecutive term. In

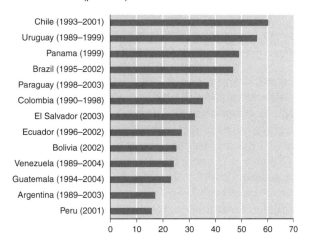

FIGURE 3.5 **Rates of Immediate Reelection to the Lower House of the National Assembly**
(*percent*)

Sources: Saiegh (2005) and authors' compilation.

Costa Rica and Mexico (not shown in the figure), immediate reelection is not permitted, and only about 13 percent and 11 percent of legislators, respectively, are eventually reelected.

The complex interactions among various electoral rules and party system characteristics, rather than any particular factor, are what shapes the legislature's policymaking role, as illustrated by the following examples.

In Argentina, local party leaders control the construction of the local party list. Thus legislators' ability to pursue a legislative career independently is significantly restricted. Instead, they typically seek to continue their political career in other elective or appointive offices. As a consequence, Argentine legislators have a strong incentive to maintain a good relationship with their local party leaders. These leaders have a complex political objective: they want to maximize their party's performance in their province, but at the same time they want to safeguard their position within the provincial party structure. The threat of challenge by popular legislators provides local party leaders with a strong incentive to reduce the national and provincial visibility of their local subordinates by rotating them among the various jobs the provincial party can offer. The electoral risks associated with nominating lesser-known candidates are mitigated by Argentina's electoral rules, especially the use of party-supplied ballots and closed-list proportional representation. Voters tend to vote for the party list, not for the individuals on the list. A president's ability to influence legislators of his own party thus depends in part on whether the provincial party leader supports the administration.[35]

---

[35] Jones (2005). See also Jones and others (2002).

In Colombia, the party system is characterized by high intra-party competition. In the last 15 years, small parties and movements have proliferated. At the national level, 45 movements/electoral lists obtained at least one seat in the lower house in the 2002 election, and more than 900 participated in the elections. The existence of high intra-party competition has weakened political leadership, ultimately fragmenting party organizations. Parties no longer have a means to control the career paths of local political leaders and candidates (see Chapter 7).

In Chile, the binominal electoral system, with two members elected per district, creates strong incentives for the formation of two electoral coalitions. Parties or electoral alliances can win the two available seats only if the winning list receives at least twice the total vote of the list that obtains the second-most votes. Given electoral incentives, legislators concerned with keeping their seats in congress know that dropping out of one of the main coalitions entails significant electoral risks. The imposition of this voting system in a country characterized by around five effective political parties has resulted in majority control of the Chamber of Deputies by the governing *Concertación* coalition since the return to democracy in 1989. Thus electoral system–based incentives have contributed to strong legislative support for bills initiated by the executive.

Organization of the Legislature

The legislature's policymaking role is also affected by its organizational characteristics, which in turn are influenced by environmental factors, such as constitutional stipulations, party system dynamics, and electoral incentives.

Given the unwieldy size and lack of specialization of the full congress, if legislatures are to play an active role in shaping the content of policy and overseeing the executive, they must do so through capable committees. Most legislatures in Latin America have permanent committees with specific policy jurisdictions. Legislation is routinely referred to them before being taken up by the larger chamber. The roles of committees vary across countries depending upon procedural rules, the resources and degree of specialization of the committees and their legislative members, and broader political factors, such as the strength and organization of political parties.

The number of committees varies greatly and does not necessarily correspond to the size of the legislature. If there are a large number of committees relative to the size of the chamber, legislators may be required to serve on several committees simultaneously, which may limit their ability to concentrate their efforts and develop specialized knowledge. In addition, the efficiency of the legislature can be impaired if legislation is commonly sent to multiple committees because of overlap among committees' policy jurisdictions.

Legislative rules also shape the size of committees, how members and committee leaders are selected, and the number of committees on which each legislator can serve. If committees are too large, this can limit their ability to function effectively. If committee memberships and leadership rotate frequently, this is likely to limit the degree of expertise that members develop and thus their policymaking effectiveness. To the extent that party leaders can exercise control over committee assignments and appointments to leadership positions, this can give them leverage in maintaining party discipline. In Brazil and Colombia, such prerogatives of party leaders to manage the committees, organize the legislative agenda, and direct public resources help impose some party discipline, despite electoral rules that allow or encourage legislator independence.[36]

In most Latin American countries, committee and leadership assignments are made on a partisan basis. The composition of the committees is expected to reflect the partisan composition of the legislature as a whole. Instead of allocating important committee assignments and leadership positions on the basis of seniority, as has been the practice in the U.S. Congress until recently, in most Latin American legislatures party leaders or party caucuses allocate these slots on the basis of other criteria, such as party loyalty.

The existence of an ample and competent staff to assist legislators with the tasks of administration, research and analysis, and document preparation is vital to enable committees to evaluate bills initiated by the executive and supervise policy implementation effectively. While the scope of committee staffing varies widely from one country to another, in most countries it is deficient relative to the roles assigned to the committees. For example, in El Salvador, each committee has only one technical assistant and one secretary, but they are expected to perform all three types of functions.

In a few countries, professional staff are available to assist legislative committees (and parties) with research and analysis. For example, in Brazil, a research office that has about 35 professionals assists the budget committee of the lower house. Chile has a (relatively small) legislative budget research office; several professional staff persons also advise the budget committee. In Colombia, a relatively large number of professional staff members assist the budget committee.

Grouping Legislatures According to Type

Despite the recent proliferation of research on executive-legislative relations in Latin America, comparative knowledge of how legislative institutions operate is still quite limited. Thus a detailed and empirically precise classification of Latin American legislatures in terms of their policymaking role is not possible at this time.

This section presents a tentative categorization of Latin American legislatures, based on available information, which is still far from complete. Legislatures can be grouped according to the nature of their policymaking role and the intensity with which they carry out that role.[37] In part, the nature of the role is shaped by their capabilities, including the experience and qualifications of legislators, the strength and degree of specialization of committees, and the availability of professional support staff and research units. But as has been discussed, the role is also affected by electoral and party-based incentives and the balance of constitutional and partisan powers between the executive and legislative branches. In the categorization employed here, a major focus is on legislative capabilities, but a more qualitative assessment of the actual role performed by legislatures is also made.

---

[36] Alston and others (2005a); Cárdenas, Junguito, and Pachón (2005).

[37] The typology, with some differences in the definition and labeling of the categories, is taken from Morgenstern (2002).

- *Relatively limited legislatures* generally approve the initiatives of the executive with only minor changes and are not very active or effective in overseeing the executive.
- *Reactive obstructionist legislatures* are potentially more active in policymaking, but their role is primarily one of a blunt veto player, generally either blocking or approving executive initiatives. This type of legislature only rarely engages deeply in refining the technical or distributional character of the policies proposed by the executive or in actively supervising the implementation of policies.
- *Reactive constructive legislatures* may perform the roles that characterize reactive obstructionist legislatures, but they can significantly shape the content of policies by amending executive initiatives. They can also fulfill the oversight function somewhat effectively.
- *Proactive legislatures*, in addition to performing the roles of the reactive obstructionist and reactive constructive legislatures, can on occasion also take the initiative in shaping the policy agenda and developing policy proposals. No legislature in the region has persistently exhibited such proactive characteristics.

Legislatures that have more experienced legislators, well-developed committee systems, and ample support staff will tend to be more constructive and/or proactive. Legislatures with weaker capabilities will tend either to play a limited policymaking role or to be active, but only in a fairly obstructionist way rather than a constructive one.

Table 3.6 compares Latin American legislatures according to several indicators that attempt to measure some of the dimensions of legislative capabilities. Five are quantitative, objective measures. The first two assess the confidence of citizens and businesspeople in the performance of congress. The third and fourth indicators—average years of legislator experience and percentage of legislators with university education—attempt to gauge the qualifications and experience of legislators. The average number of committee memberships per legislator attempts to measure the degree of specialization of legislative committees, and thus their effectiveness. The next three measures—strength of committees, whether the legislature is a good place to build a career, and technical expertise—were constructed by Sebastián Saiegh, drawing from a variety of secondary sources, but especially from the legislator survey of the University of Salamanca.[38] The final column places the legislatures into categories of "high," "medium," and "low" on the basis of the aggregate index that results from combining all these indicators.[39] The inclusion of the subjective variables does not substantially change the overall index or the corresponding country groupings.[40] However, it is important to point out that the Congress Capabilities Index should be seen only as a preliminary and imperfect effort to capture this important aspect of countries' policymaking capabilities.

---

[38] Saiegh (2005), drawing on PELA (2005).

[39] Countries were placed in the different groupings using cluster analysis, a statistical technique employed to sort cases into groups, or clusters, so that the degree of association is strong between members of the same cluster and weak between members of different clusters.

[40] The correlation between the Congress Capabilities Index and an objective index that excludes the subjective variables is 0.91.

Table 3.6 Summary of Measures of Legislatures' Capabilities

Country	Confidence in congress, average[a]	Effectiveness of lawmaking of bodies[b]	Average experience of legislators (years)	Percentage of legislators with university education[c]	Average number of committee memberships per legislator	Strength of committees	Place to build career	Technical expertise	Congress Capabilities Index
Argentina	20.5	1.6	2.9	69.6	4.50	Medium	Low	Low	Low
Bolivia	19.9	1.8	3.3	78.4	1.66	Medium	Medium	Medium	Medium
Brazil	24.9	3.1	5.5	54.0	0.92	Medium	High	High	High
Chile	36.0	3.7	8.0	79.4	1.95	High	High	High	High
Colombia	20.3	2.7	4.0	91.6	0.86	High	High	Medium	High
Costa Rica	29.9	2.2	2.6	80.4	2.09	High	Medium	Low	Medium
Dominican Republic	n.a.	2.0	3.1	49.6	3.54	Low	High	Low	Low
Ecuador	13.3	1.7	3.5	83.1	1.26	High	Medium	Low	Medium
El Salvador	27.7	2.1	3.9	64.0	2.44	Medium	High	Low	Medium
Guatemala	19.9	1.8	3.2	68.4	3.24	Low	Medium	Low	Low
Honduras	30.8	2.6	3.0	73.1	2.34	Low	Low	Low	Low
Mexico	27.4	2.0	1.9	89.5	2.43	High	Medium	Medium	Medium
Nicaragua	23.1	1.6	3.5	85.6	1.96	Low	Medium	Medium	Medium
Panama	22.5	1.8	5.8	81.3	1.86	Medium	High	Low	Medium
Paraguay	25.0	2.2	5.5	75.4	3.15	Low	High	Low	Medium
Peru	22.1	1.7	5.2	92.9	2.44	Low	Low	Low	Low
Uruguay	38.2	2.7	8.8	68.4	0.98	High	High	Low	High
Venezuela	27.8	1.4	4.9	74.6	0.97	Medium	Medium	Low	Medium

[a] Latinobarometer (1996–2004).
[b] World Economic Forum (2004–2005).
[c] PELA (2002).

n.a.: not applicable. As the Dominican Republic was included only in the 2004 survey, no average is shown.

Sources: Latinobarometer (1996–2004); World Economic Forum (2005); PELA (various years); and Saiegh (2005).

Table 3.7 Legislature Capabilities and Legislature Types

Congress type	Congress Capabilities Index		
	Low	Medium	High
Reactive limited	Argentina (1989–present) Peru (1993–2000)	Panama (1989–present) Paraguay (1989–93) Venezuela (1999–present)	
Reactive obstructionist	Argentina (1983–89) Guatemala (1985–present) Peru (2001–present)	Bolivia (1982–present) Ecuador (1979–present) Nicaragua (1990–present) Venezuela (1989–98)	
Reactive constructive		Costa Rica (1978–present) Mexico (1997–present) Paraguay (1993–present)	Brazil (1985–present) Chile (1990–present) Colombia (1991–present) Uruguay (1985–present)

Sources: Saiegh (2005) and authors' compilation.

Table 3.7 then compares the assessments of legislature capabilities that arise from the previous analysis with a qualitative assessment of the actual roles played by legislatures in the region. Legislatures with greater capabilities tend to play a more constructive role in the policymaking process. But the partisan balance of power has an important role in determining whether a legislature with relatively limited capabilities is fairly inactive or active but obstructionist.

How would the characteristics of legislatures be expected to affect the key features of public policies? Relatively marginal legislatures would typically not interfere with policy adaptability. But such legislatures would be likely to generate greater policy volatility, except in cases of long-term dominance by a single party or low levels of ideological polarization. Moreover, fewer constraints against private-regarding policy outcomes would be likely, given the deficiencies in the representation of citizens in the policy process and in oversight of the executive.

Obstructionist legislatures would be likely to lessen policy adaptability, given the greater difficulty of gaining approval for executive-initiated reforms. At the same time, if a fragmented congress impedes inter-temporal bargaining to a great extent, policies might not be designed so as to be durable over time.

Reactive constructive legislatures should contribute to greater public-regardedness, given their greater capacities with respect to representation and oversight. They also might limit volatility by facilitating inter-temporal agreements and providing a check on ill-conceived policy changes.

Presidents

In Latin America, presidents play a preeminent role in setting the policy agenda and formulating policy proposals. How does the president's central role affect policy outcomes? What is the actual experience of presidents in terms of their ability to pass their agendas and maintain their influence and prestige, and in terms of their orientation toward serving the public interest? Answers to these questions must focus on the factors constraining, enabling, and motivating the president's choices and actions. Moreover, since the office of the president has special weight in Latin America, certain personal qualities of leadership also play a role (see discussion below and Box 2.1).

Constraints

Among the factors constraining the president's strategic options and policy choices are his constitutional and partisan powers.

- *Constitutional legislative powers*, such as decree and budgetary powers, provide presidents with bargaining leverage, influence over the legislative agenda, and a means—potentially—to bypass a recalcitrant legislature.
- *Non-legislative powers*, such as the power to appoint cabinet officials, are important for shaping the policy effectiveness of the administration, as well as for building political support across parties and strengthening party discipline.
- *Partisan powers* relate to the share of seats controlled by the president's party in congress and the cohesiveness of the governing party/parties.

Traditional measures of presidential powers only imperfectly capture the actual experience of presidents in terms of their ability to pass their agendas and maintain their influence and prestige.

In general, presidents with greater partisan and constitutional powers have more room to maneuver in developing and implementing their policy agendas. Presidents with weak partisan powers may be able to compensate for this limitation by using their constitutional powers to broaden their political support and/or increase their negotiating leverage in relation to congress. Figure 3.6 shows the relationship between the overall constitutional powers of presidents and their partisan powers, as measured by the average share of seats their party controlled in the legislature as a result of the last two elections.

In some countries, such as Chile and Argentina, presidents are fairly powerful in constitutional terms, and their parties typically control a significant share of the seats in congress. In others, such as Bolivia, presidents are relatively weak in terms of both their legislative and their partisan powers. Brazil, Colombia, and Ecuador stand out as cases in which presidents are powerful in constitutional terms but their parties' weight in the congress is small. The reverse has typically been the case in Honduras and Paraguay.

Such traditional measures of presidential powers only imperfectly capture the actual experience of presidents. For example, despite the fact that Brazilian and Ecuadorian

FIGURE 3.6 Constitutional Powers versus Partisan Powers of Presidents

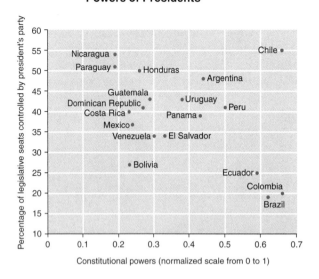

Sources: Based on data from UNDP (2005) and Jones (2005).

presidents are each strong in constitutional terms but weak in partisan terms, their experience over the past decade has been remarkably different. While in Brazil, presidents (since 1994) have tended to retain their popular standing and reasonable levels of legislative support throughout their terms of office, in Ecuador the last three elected presidents struggled to pass legislation and were unable to complete their terms of office.

Examples such as these imply that presidents face additional constraints besides those considered in Figure 3.6. Given the interaction among these various constraining factors, traditional measures of presidential power are not enough to explain such differences in outcomes and behavior. Differences in presidential incentives may be playing a role in explaining differences in outcomes as well.

Incentives

Because presidents are elected by a majority or plurality of the national vote, their electoral-based incentives are more "encompassing" than the electoral-based incentives of individual legislators, who are typically elected from smaller regional constituencies, and thus may not focus to the same extent on the provision of national public goods. Thus presidents may be more national in outlook and more encompassing in the constituent base they serve. But it is evident from the corruption scandals that have sometimes affected Latin American presidents, during or after their terms, that the ambitions of presidents are not always limited to serving the public good—and even if this remains their intention, they do not always succeed in doing so.

Beyond the goal of serving the public interest, presidents, like most politicians, are driven by personal and political goals. On the one hand, most presidents are concerned with increasing and/or maintaining their public esteem, political influence, and power, in part to increase their effectiveness as leaders, but also to increase the chance that their visions and programs will triumph over those of others. On the other hand, presidents are also driven by somewhat narrower personal and political ambitions, such as retaining their leadership over a political party, seeking reelection as president (if this is permitted by the constitution, or if the constitution is not too difficult to change), rewarding friends and allies who helped them get to the presidency and are helping to keep them there, or bolstering the popular following and power of their party for the long term.

In some institutional environments, these personal and political ambitions do not seriously interfere with the goal of serving the general public interest. A president's desire to build his stature within a party, to strengthen the party's base of support, or to be reelected, for instance, may be best served in some contexts mainly by maintaining or expanding the diffuse support of citizens or party supporters for his presidency. In other institutional contexts, these narrower ambitions, or the necessities of the exercise of power, may result in greater deviations from the public interest.

The extent to which parties are clientelistic, for instance, is an important constraint on public orientation. In clientistic party systems, the president may focus on generating and redirecting the public resources needed to maintain the party's clientelistic network of support, rather than on adopting policies in the general public interest. Similarly, if parties are relatively decentralized, as for example in Argentina, then the president may be forced to negotiate with regional party leaders and distribute resources to districts where the support of such power brokers is vital to passing legislation and maintaining authority within the party.

Other types of pressures to deviate from the general public interest are likely to be generated in contexts where the party system tends to be clientelistic and highly fragmented, as in Bolivia and Ecuador. Given the large number of parties that typically need to be involved in coalition-building and the divergent and typically geographically concentrated interests the parties represent, the costs of maintaining political coalitions and societal support in terms of policy concessions to special interests, and the distribution of patronage and particularistic expenditures, can result in considerable deviations from optimal policies.

The implications of such acute constraints on presidential incentives are clear in the case of Ecuador. When asked by a reporter whether he expected to complete his term of office after the premature ouster of the two previously elected presidents, President Gustavo Noboa (2000–2002) said, "I'm like the members of Alcoholics Anonymous. I take things one day a time."[41] Clearly, if presidents in Ecuador experience such difficulty in assembling support in congress to approve their policy initiatives and must concern themselves merely with day-to-day survival, their time horizons will tend to be quite short and not conducive to reaching inter-temporal bargains with other actors for the sake of improving policy outcomes.

Numerous other institutional configurations could create presidential incentives favoring deviation from the pursuit of the public interest. While excessive political fragmentation has its own costs, an electorally dominant governing party, strong presidential powers, weakly institutionalized parties, a weak congress, and/or a politically captured supreme court can encourage presidents to put their own power or material ambitions ahead of serving the public good. In the absence of sufficient checks and bal-

---

[41] Andrés Oppenheimer, "Region May Need European-Style Prime Ministers," *Miami Herald*, April 24, 2005.

ances, presidents elected at one moment with a majority or plurality of the popular vote may use this temporary authority and control of the State to further remove potential challenges to their power and distort the electoral process in their favor.

Overcoming Constraints

To some extent, presidents can overcome constraints and shape the outcomes of their administration through strategic choices, such as how to portray and order their policy priorities, whether to take issues to the public, whether to use their legislative powers or negotiate with potential opponents in the legislature, and how to use their powers to appoint cabinet ministers and other governmental officials.

Moreover, presidential power, beyond its formal functions, seems to be surrounded by what has been called institutional charisma. This is a type of influence derived from the way in which the office is perceived by others, which on occasion gives it a much greater range of action, especially in times of crisis. Institutional charisma acquires much more value in combination with interpersonal skills that can significantly increase the real power of the presidency. It is not possible to measure objectively the extent to which these traits increase presidential authority, but experience shows that their contribution to the policymaking process and the implementation of policy can be decisive.

Chapter 4

Cabinets, the Bureaucracy, Subnational Governments, and the Judiciary

Justice and power must be brought together, so that whatever is just may be powerful, and whatever is powerful may be just.

—Blaise Pascal, French mathematician, physicist, philosopher (1623–1662)

This chapter focuses on four more actors that have formally ascribed roles in the policymaking process (PMP): the cabinet, the bureaucracy, subnational governments, and the judiciary. As with the actors examined in Chapter 3, the extent and nature of the roles performed by these actors vary considerably across countries, in part because of differences in the formal and informal rules associated with the actor, and in part because of interactions with characteristics of the broader policymaking process. Given the focus of this report, the discussion of subnational governments is restricted to an analysis of their potential role in influencing national policy decisions or their implementation.

Characteristics related to the stability, coordination, and formation of cabinets are likely to have important effects on the key features of public policies.

Cabinets[1]

The policymaking role of cabinets is somewhat more ambiguous in presidential systems than in parliamentary systems. Executive power in "pure" presidential systems is concentrated in one person: the president. Thus cabinet ministers tend to have a narrower role as aides to the president. By contrast, in parliamentary systems, cabinet ministers typically also serve as members of parliament and, along with the head of government,

---

[1] This section draws on Martínez-Gallardo (2005b).

are collectively responsible to it. In part because of the cabinet's ambiguous status, the cabinet as a collective body in most presidential systems in Latin America does not appear to have an important influence on policy. But given the informal way cabinets generally function and the private nature of meetings in Latin American countries, little is known about how decisions are actually made, including who participates and how often the cabinet meets collectively.

Nevertheless, it is clear that cabinet ministers, at least as individuals, play key roles in every stage of policymaking. Cabinet ministers and those directly under them in the bureaucracy provide the knowledge and expertise necessary to formulate policy. The legislature and political parties rarely have comparable resources at their disposal that allow them to participate as centrally in the formulation of public policy. Cabinet ministers also advocate and defend specific policy proposals and decisions and guide bills through the legislature. Cabinet ministers are involved in interpreting and putting into practice enacted legislation through the executive's rulemaking authority. They direct large bureaucratic agencies and are in charge of evaluating and supervising the details of policy implementation. Cabinets additionally serve as a tool for building governmental and legislative coalitions. Presidents whose parties lack a majority in the legislature can help secure the support of members of other parties through cabinet appointments.

Features of Cabinets and Policymaking

Characteristics related to the stability, coordination, and formation of cabinets are likely to have important effects on the key features of public policies.

Stability of Cabinets

To promote long-term policies and to allow ministers to see programs and policy implementation through to completion, a certain degree of stability for officials in cabinet posts is likely to be necessary. Frequent turnover of cabinet ministries is likely to promote a more short-term orientation to policy and more frequent changes in policy direction. Longer tenures also facilitate and improve the efficiency of delegating responsibilities and tasks to bureaucrats, which is essential for effective policy implementation. Frequent changes in the cabinet can leave leadership vacuums that may contribute to bureaucratic inertia and even corruption. In addition, longer tenure allows ministers to accumulate valuable expertise specific to the policy area in which they work and to develop political and managerial skills that are likely to improve the quality of their performance in their different policymaking functions.

Cabinet stability is generally low in Latin America. Between 1990 and 2000, almost a quarter (22 percent) of all ministers in a sample of 12 Latin American countries remained in the same portfolio for less than six months. Three-quarters (75 percent) of all ministers had tenures of less than two years (while presidential terms vary between four and six years). Figure 4.1 compares countries in terms of the average number of different individuals who served in a given ministry from 1988 to 2000. The countries with the greatest cabinet instability are Ecuador, Brazil, Venezuela, and Colombia. Cabinets are most stable in Uruguay, Costa Rica, and Chile.

Capacity for Coordination

The ability of governmental ministries to coordinate among themselves and to cooperate with other institutions, including the bureaucracy, is likely to have a large effect both on the policymaking process itself and on the characteristics of policy outcomes. One factor affecting the capacity for coordination has to do with the partisan make-up of the cabinet. The more parties that participate in the cabinet and the greater the divergence of ideologies and interests among them,[2] the more likely it will be that difficulties in coordination will arise, and the greater

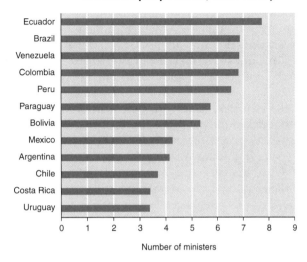

FIGURE 4.1 **Cabinet Instability (number of ministers per portfolio, 1988–2000)**

Number of ministers

Source: Martínez-Gallardo (2005b).

those difficulties are likely to be. Single-party majority governments tend to be able to minimize the costs of reaching agreements and making decisions, while coalition governments may find it more difficult to coordinate policy.

The contrast between the *Partido Revolucionario Institucional* (PRI) governments in Mexico and coalition governments in Argentina is illustrative. During the period of PRI hegemony in Mexico, cabinet coordination was aided by the centralization of power in the president, who was the de facto leader of the party, and by the high degree of ideological cohesiveness in the cabinet. By contrast, during the De la Rúa administration in Argentina, although most ministries were headed by politicians from the president's party, the Radical Party, politicians from a rival party, *Frepaso*, were given the labor and social affairs ministries. Power was further divided within ministries through the appointment of vice-ministers from a party different from the minister's. This presented problems of coordination, since vice-ministers sometimes answered to their party leader instead of to the minister and *Frepaso* ministers in some cases answered to their party leaders rather than to the president.[3]

Coordination with the bureaucracy is likely to be enhanced by relative cabinet stability, as well as by the appointment of senior (nonpolitical) civil servants to cabinet and undersecretary positions.

---

[2] The divergence may not be only ideological, but also in regard to interests in broader terms. For instance, cabinet members may be from different parties that are concentrated in particular regions of the country or that represent very different sets of societal interests.

[3] Martínez-Gallardo (2005a).

The most common institutional instrument used for fostering cabinet coordination across Latin America is thematic cabinets or interministerial committees. In Mexico, for instance, the Zedillo administration had a Security Cabinet, an Economic Cabinet, and an Agrarian Affairs Cabinet. During the Fox administration, the thematic cabinets have been Growth with Quality, Order, and Respect; and Human and Social Development. In Argentina, several attempts have been made since 1993 to establish a special cabinet for social policy. In both Mexico and Argentina, evidence suggests that these thematic cabinets have had limited effectiveness in promoting improved coordination among the ministries.[4] The frequency of meetings has depended upon the president and the priorities of the political agenda; at some points in an administration's term the special cabinets have hardly met at all.

An important feature of Latin American cabinets has been the central role of the finance ministry and, more widely, of a limited number of technical ministries. The finance ministry has dominated the budget process and been able to prioritize its goals on the presidential agenda. Thus it has been in a privileged position in respect to other ministries and, in some cases, in relation to regional governors. This dominant role has been supported in some instances by constitutional provisions, by the relative weakness of the legislature in the budget process, and by the more competitive recruitment and greater stability of personnel in the finance ministry and its superior institutional capacity. The predominance of one ministry in the cabinet may improve coordination in respect to some policy goals, while weakening it in relation to others.

Another potential source of poor coordination relates to the structure of the cabinet. An excessively large number of cabinet ministries or policymaking units with jurisdiction over policy in a particular area could be expected to limit the capacity to develop policy that is consistent over time and implemented coherently. However, the sheer number of ministries might not accurately reflect the potential for an overlap of jurisdictions or the tendency for frequent changes to be made to their areas of competence.

A case in point is Argentina. Although the number of ministries is fixed by law, ministerial reorganization has typically involved a redistribution of jurisdictions at the level of secretaries and undersecretaries.[5] Presidents have worked around these legal restrictions by creating secretaries with ministerial rank. During President Menem's term, for example, the ministries of agriculture and infrastructure were placed under the ministry of the economy as a way for the latter to enhance control over spending. President Duhalde, on the other hand, created a ministry of production as a signal of the importance of industry. The existence of multiple agencies with overlapping jurisdictions and the existence of a parallel bureaucracy composed mainly of temporary officials typically has made coordination difficult—among ministers, and among ministers and the bureaucrats in their agencies—and has made it harder to attain coherent policy.[6]

---

[4] Martínez-Gallardo (2005b).

[5] Oszlak (2003).

[6] Martínez-Gallardo (2005b).

Cabinet Formation

How presidents use their power to appoint and dismiss members of the cabinet can have important effects on their ability to obtain sufficient legislative support to enact policies and on the stability and the effectiveness of government policymaking.

Cabinet appointments can be effective in securing political support, since they provide a means for political parties as a whole and politicians as individuals to influence policy to a degree that is not possible through positions in the legislature. Cabinet positions potentially give parties and politicians control over important patronage and budgetary resources that can be used for political ends. However, incentives for sustaining inter-party coalitions and for coalition legislators to adhere to the government's position are likely to be weaker in presidential systems than in parliamentary systems. This is the case since the head of government and legislators are elected separately and their terms of office are fixed; thus their survival in office does not depend upon maintaining majority support for the government.

In choosing who will serve in their cabinets, presidents must balance the objectives of maintaining political support with those of ensuring that the individuals appointed have sufficient policy expertise, will follow policies reasonably consistent with the president's thinking, and will be able to work sufficiently well together. The latter two concerns are especially relevant when individuals from different parties are appointed for the purpose of building coalition governments. The case of Bolivia, discussed in Box 4.1, illustrates how cabinet appointments have been used to sustain governmental coalitions.

The capabilities of cabinet officials as experts in their field, as managers, and as advocates of the government's policies are likely to have an important effect on the characteristics of policy outcomes. To the extent that cabinet members are selected purely either on the basis of their personal loyalty to the president or because of their political party connections, this may detract from their ability to design sound policies and manage their bureaucratic agencies effectively. But, since policymaking is not a purely technical matter, and political and managerial skills contribute to a minister's effectiveness, broad criteria of competence, rather than narrow training in the policy field, may be most suitable.

The bureaucracy fulfills varied and contradictory roles in the PMP, depending on whether it serves mainly as a neutral and professional actor or functions mainly as a private resource of political parties or of civil servants.

The Bureaucracy[7]

The bureaucracy is one of the institutional anchors for the effective functioning of the democratic system and the enforcement of the rule of law. The bureaucracy is more than a stock of human resources, an organizational apparatus, or an employment system.

---

[7] This section draws on Zuvanic and Iacoviello (2005).

Box 4.1	Using Cabinet Appointments to Consolidate Coalitions: The Case of Bolivia

The process of government formation in Bolivia is unique in the region. If no presidential candidate wins a majority of the vote, congress elects the president from the top two candidates (the top three candidates until the electoral reform in 1995), as in a parliamentary system. This system of indirect presidential election, in the context of a fragmented party system, has encouraged the formation of coalitions and constant negotiations between parties (and sometimes between factions within parties). All these arrangements induce the major parties to seek compromises with potential coalition partners. These negotiations usually include decisions regarding who is to serve in the cabinet. Positions in the cabinet have been traditionally used as a token of exchange for maintaining coalitions.

As the share of legislative seats of the party of the winning presidential candidate has decreased, the number of ministries offered to other parties has increased. For example, in his first term, President Sánchez de Lozada offered only two ministries to other parties after he won a majority in the upper chamber and nearly a majority in the lower chamber. In his second term, when his party won less than half the seats in the upper chamber and less than one-third of the seats in the lower chamber, he offered seven ministries to other parties.

Because the number of ministries is not fixed in the constitution, presidents have also altered the number of ministries to accommodate other parties in the cabinet—while maintaining the majority of the positions. Since the transition to democracy, there has been a negative correlation between the share of the legislative seats controlled by the president's party and the total number of ministries. During the Paz Zamora presidency, the governing party obtained less than a third of the seats in both chambers, and the number of ministries fluctuated between 16 and 17. Sánchez de Lozada reduced the number of ministries from 16 to 11 in his first term. In the Bánzer/Quiroga administration that followed, in which the government coalition was formed by four parties (three, later on in the presidency), the number of ministries gradually increased to 16. In the second Sánchez de Lozada administration, also supported by a coalition of four parties, the number of ministries grew even more, to 19.

Presidents, Legislative Support, and Ministers in Bolivia since 1989

President	Period	Party	Party share of lower house	Coalition Number of parties	Coalition Share of lower house	Coalition Share of upper house	Total number of ministries[a]	Number of ministries[b] Other party	Number of ministries[b] Indep.	Number of ministries[b] Total
J. Paz Zamora	1989–1993	MIR	25.4	29.6	54.6	59.3	16.3	—	—	—
G. S. de Lozada	1993–1997	MNR	40.0	63.0	60.8	66.7	11.6	2.0	1.5	3.5
H. Bánzer Suárez	1997–2001	ADN	25.4	40.7	66.0	74.8	15.0	6.4	0.6	7.0
J. Quiroga	2001–2002	ADN	25.4	40.7	60.8	70.4	16.0	4.0	3.0	7.0
G. S. de Lozada	2002–2003	MNR	28.0	40.7	56.1	63.0	19.0	7.0	1.0	8.0

[a] Average during the period.
[b] Average offered to other parties or independents during the period.
— not available.

Note: Fractional numbers indicate change during the period. The number of ministries and their affiliations are approximate given the usual changes that took place within specific years. They serve only illustrative purposes.

Source: Authors' compilation.

Rather, it is an articulated set of operating rules and guidelines regulating the executive branch that aims to give continuity, coherence, and relevance to public policies, while ensuring a neutral, objective, and non-arbitrary exercise of public authority. The bureaucracy is a key actor for encouraging inter-temporal agreements, especially through its role in putting such agreements into practice. A neutral and professional bureaucracy limits the scope for the adoption of opportunistic policies and enhances the trust of actors that commitments made as a part of policy agreements will be fulfilled.

Latin America has traditionally been viewed as a region with large but weak States, with little capacity to respond to the needs of citizens. Historically, much of this weakness has been associated with the lack of a stable professional bureaucracy. The bureaucracy has been perceived as an employment system or a resource in the hands of politicians and corporate interests—and thus far removed from the Weberian ideal type characterized by regularized and impersonal procedures and employment decisions based on technical qualifications and achievements.

The weakness of the bureaucracy has contributed to the weakness of the executive branch in Latin American countries, particularly in its relations with other political actors and with special interests. Bureaucratic weakness has been one cause of the ineffectiveness of development policies in the region, for which the State historically has been an important actor. This contrasts sharply with the development experience of the Asian "tigers." A strong and autonomous State, supported by a highly professional and meritocratic bureaucracy, has been considered a key factor in the success of the Asian tigers. The Southeast Asian countries rank considerably higher in cross-national indicators of the quality of the bureaucracy, even relative to the more advanced countries of Latin America.

Despite its role as an institutional foundation of the rule of law, the bureaucracy holds a subordinate position to the government in the constitutional system. The bureaucracy is not legally an autonomous and responsible agent of the political system, but rather a part of the executive branch and responsible to the government.

The transition from authoritarian to democratic regimes has been linked to a certain tendency to further subordinate the bureaucracy to political control. In many cases, this has led to a reversion to clientelistic practices. This situation may arise from the need to use public employment as a resource to reward the members of the winning party with jobs (the spoils system) and from the need to reduce the technical autonomy that bureaucratic officials frequently obtain in certain sectors, which limits the scope for political action by the government. Historically, democracy has been slow to overcome this dilemma.

The bureaucracy plays varied and contradictory roles in the policymaking process, depending on how closely it approaches the ideal of being a neutral and professional actor that guarantees the stability, adaptability, and public interest of policies or mainly functions as a private resource: either of political parties, which use it to obtain votes, or of civil servants, who defend their own interests while being protected by job security. The degree to which the bureaucracy fills one or the other role affects some of the characteristics of public policies.

Characterizing Latin American Bureaucracies

An analysis of the bureaucracy requires an analysis of
public employment, its main
element. Public employment
has both a quantitative and
a qualitative dimension. The
qualitative dimension is the
more relevant for understanding the capacity and effectiveness of the bureaucracy. Thus
this study does not devote
much attention to analyzing
quantitative measures of the
bureaucracy, although the evidence presented below indicates that the size and quality
of the bureaucracy are not
closely correlated.

FIGURE 4.2 **Bureaucratic Merit Index**
(*0–100 scale*)

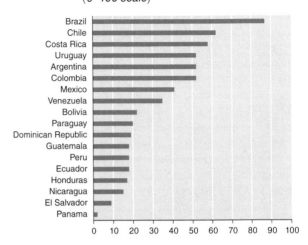

Source: Based on information from comparative studies of civil service systems in 18 Latin American countries carried out as a part of the IDB's Network on Public Policy Management and Transparency.

A qualitative approach ex-
amines the extent to which bureaucracies are endowed with the institutional attributes
required to perform the regulatory roles assigned to them in a representative democracy.
In carrying out this analysis, this study uses the data, indices, and conclusions of an institutional diagnostic study of the civil service conducted in 18 countries of the region.[8]

The degree of autonomy of the bureaucracy can be measured using the merit index
(Figure 4.2), which evaluates the degree to which effective guarantees of professionalism in the civil service are in place and the degree to which civil servants are effectively
protected from arbitrariness, politicization, and rent-seeking.[9]

Three groups of countries may be distinguished. The top performers, Brazil, Chile,
and Costa Rica, have indices between 55 and 90 (out of 100), reflecting a widespread
acceptance of the principles of merit in decisions regarding the hiring, promotion, and
dismissal of public officials. A middle group of countries, with indices between 30 and
55, includes Argentina, Colombia, Mexico, Uruguay, and Venezuela. Practices based on

---

[8] Comparative studies of the civil service systems in 18 Latin American countries carried out as a part of
the IDB's Regional Policy Dialogue on Public Policy Management and Transparency.

[9] The Bureaucratic Merit Index (Figure 4.2) and the Bureaucratic Functional Capacity Index (Figure 4.3)
have been developed within the framework of the work of the Bank's Regional Policy Dialogue on Public
Policy Management and Transparency. An analytical framework was elaborated with detailed criteria
for the assessment of these variables, and a team of consultants applied it to the countries. The national
reports and the resulting indices were reviewed for consistency with the analytical framework and sent
to the representatives of the countries for their observations and comments. For further information,
see Data Appendix.

FIGURE 4.3 **Bureaucratic Functional Capacity Index**
(*0–100 scale*)

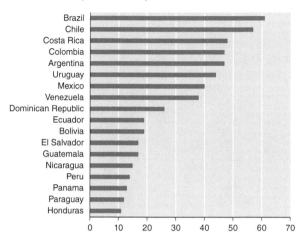

Source: Based on information from comparative studies of civil service systems in 18 Latin American countries carried out as a part of the IDB's Network on Public Policy Management and Transparency.

merit coexist with traditions of political patronage. A third group of countries, comprised of Bolivia, Paraguay, Dominican Republic, Peru, Ecuador, and all of the Central American countries except Costa Rica, have indices below 30, reflecting a strong politicization of decisions on hiring, promotion, and dismissal.

To be able to perform substantive roles in designing and implementing public policies, the bureaucracy also requires adequate technical capacities and incentives for effective performance. The functional capacity index (Figure 4.3) is a good approximation of these characteristics. It rates the characteristics of salary compensation systems and systems for evaluating the performance of public officials.[10]

Brazil and Chile stand out, with indices near 60 out of 100. Their scores reflect rational systems of salary management, with relative internal equity and processes to improve salary competitiveness, as well as evaluation processes that begin to relate individual performance to group and institutional performance. The next group of countries, with indices ranging between 35 and 50, includes Costa Rica, Colombia, Argentina, Uruguay, Mexico, and Venezuela. These countries have gone through the process of rationalizing the salary system, although internal inequity continues and problems of salary competitiveness persist at managerial levels. The group with the worst results has indices between 10 and 25 and is made up of the Dominican Republic, Ecuador, Bolivia, El Salvador, Guatemala, Nicaragua, Peru, Panama, Paraguay, and Honduras. These countries are characterized by diversity of payment criteria, lack of information on compensation, high levels of inequity, and an absence of performance evaluation.

Considering both indices together, the countries analyzed can be grouped into three levels of bureaucratic development. The first group has bureaucracies with only a minimum level of development, in which the civil service system cannot guarantee the attraction and retention of competent personnel, and lacks the management mechanisms necessary to promote efficient performance on the part of civil servants. This group includes countries with low scores on both indices: Panama, El Salvador, Nicaragua, Hondu-

---

[10] See Data Appendix.

FIGURE 4.4 **Bureaucratic Size versus Quality**

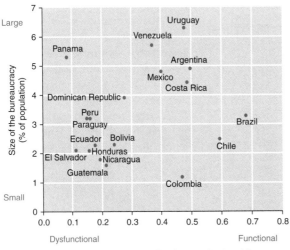

Note: Size of the bureaucracy represents the size of public employment as a percentage of the population. The Index of Civil Service Development is a combination of merit, efficiency, and capacity indices.
Sources: Carlson and Payne (2003); Longo (2005).

ras, Peru, Guatemala, Ecuador, the Dominican Republic, Paraguay, and Bolivia. The second group has civil service systems that are fairly well structured but that have not been consolidated in terms of merit guarantees and management tools that would allow for an effective utilization of capabilities. This group consists of Venezuela, Mexico, Colombia, Uruguay, Argentina, and Costa Rica. The countries in the third group, Brazil and Chile, excel on both indices and are more institutionalized relative to other countries, despite having different profiles in terms of their civil service systems.

Figure 4.4 relates the bureaucracy's size to its quality. To measure quality, the indices of merit and functional capacity are combined with an index of efficiency into an aggregate civil service index.[11] The size measure is the percentage of the total population employed in the public sector. The result highlights the fact that quantity and quality are barely correlated (0.26), since among the countries whose bureaucracies are dysfunctional, some are large and some are small.

Bureaucratic Configurations and Prevailing Roles

The bureaucracies in the Latin American countries are not homogeneous actors. In reality, they are a set of complex and interdependent organizations that vary in terms of their autonomy and capacity. This heterogeneity may provide some keys to understanding the internal dynamics of the State apparatus and the degree to which different parts of the bureaucracy may fulfill different and even contradictory roles in the same country.

Starting with this assumption, Figure 4.5 presents a basic categorization of the different types of bureaucracies found in the countries of the region. The placement of the bureaucratic types (and country examples), though based on qualitative case studies of civil service systems in the region, is not precise, and is performed for illustrative pur-

---

[11] See Data Appendix.

FIGURE 4.5   **Types of Bureaucracies**

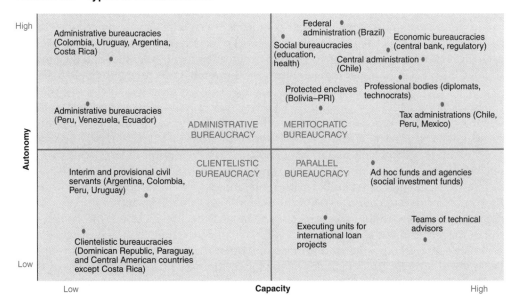

Source: Authors' compilation based on information from comparative studies of civil service systems in 18 Latin American countries carried out as a part of the IDB's Network on Public Policy Management and Transparency.

poses only. The prevalence of these types of bureaucracies varies across countries, and the types also coexist within countries. Each is shaped within historic contexts and by predominant political practices. In addition, each type of bureaucracy tends to perform certain roles in the policymaking process, although exceptions may exist that exceed the scope of this analysis.

Administrative bureaucracy. This classic form of bureaucracy is characterized by low capacity and a relatively high degree of autonomy. It includes the apparatus that exercises administrative functions in the various ministries and sectors of the State. These areas are normally covered by formal standards of merit, which are not applied in practice. In effect, they represent frustrated or partial attempts to develop a traditional Weberian bureaucracy (that is, one that is rational, hierarchical, and merit based). Civil servants are hired on the basis more of political than meritocratic criteria, but they have some job security. The degree of their technical competence and orientation toward good performance is low. These are the areas most affected by budget cuts (in some countries, such as Peru or Uruguay, funding to these bodies has been frozen). The bureaucracies of Peru, Venezuela, and Ecuador (on the lower end in this category in terms of autonomy and capacity) and of Argentina, Colombia, Costa Rica, and Uruguay (at the higher end) fall into this category, with varying degrees of autonomy and capacity.

This type of bureaucracy has a limited ability to play an active role in the different stages of policymaking. This lack of ability prevents it from effectively exerting influence at the decision making stage. Decisions are usually made in the policy section of the ministries. It may perform some role in policy implementation, although with a tendency toward formalism and control through conformity with bureaucratic procedures, rather than through the effective management of services. Its potential as a resource for political exchange is limited because of the relative lack of regular turnover of staff and the progressive decline of its importance due to reductions in overall levels of public employment.

Clientelistic bureaucracy. This form of bureaucracy is characterized by low autonomy and low capacity. It is made up of public officials who temporarily enter government because of loyalty or party affiliation. Ministerial rotations or changes of government are likely to affect the stock of human resources and may even result in large-scale turnover of civil servants. For a subset of these bureaucracies, control over access and permanence lies not with the party system but with trade unions. The most notable cases occur in the Central American countries (with the exception of Costa Rica) and in the Dominican Republic, Paraguay, and Bolivia (except in some meritocratic enclaves). In Mexico, control of the government apparatus has traditionally been divided between the governing party for managerial positions (until recently, when the Career Law was approved), and the trade unions for the remainder of the jobs. Other countries exhibit some of these characteristics as well. Examples include temporary appointments or contracted employees in Argentina, Colombia, Peru, and Uruguay, under the protection of transitional or special regimes of employment that grant the government greater flexibility in appointing and dismissing public officials.

The roles performed by clientistic bureaucracies are related to their nature primarily as a political resource of the governing party to exchange jobs for votes or political support. This type of bureaucracy is an extension of the political party. It has some veto power over the professional or meritocratic segments of the bureaucracy, with which it may come into conflict. Its role in designing and implementing policies is virtually irrelevant, except in relation to the operational level of the most simple and routine tasks.

Parallel bureaucracy ("technical teams" or "project teams"). This form of bureaucracy is characterized by low autonomy and high capacity. It is comprised of managers hired under flexible contractual agreements, a practice that has spread to a majority of Latin American countries since the early 1990s. The employment system is usually governed by laws relating to service contracts or other legal arrangements. Those hired are not part of the permanent structure of the civil service, although in several countries the contracts of these officials are routinely renewed. These groups of officials do not, strictly speaking, owe allegiance to any political party, and they possess expert knowledge in certain areas of policy. In the majority of cases they have been hired to cover certain technical needs. In some cases they have developed political as well as technical skills ("technopols"). Parallel institutions, or what have come to be called "parallel ministries," are usually configured either outside or within the regular agencies. These structures encounter varying degrees of resistance from other internal bureaucratic actors and achieve varying degrees of success.

In some cases, teams of technical advisors perform a key role in designing policy alternatives, working closely with the chief executive. In other cases, they are more centered on ensuring the execution of policies or projects or the effective delivery of certain public services. This category includes the diverse organizations that manage projects with international financing or social funds. They are characterized by different degrees of autonomy and capacity. However, parallel bureaucracies do not contribute to the strengthening of the inter-temporal capacities of the public sector, since they remain isolated and concentrated in very limited roles in the policymaking process and do not become institutionalized in the broader public sector.

Meritocratic bureaucracy. This form of bureaucracy is characterized by high autonomy and high capacity, in various combinations. It is composed of permanent civil servants recruited on the basis of merit and incorporated into professional careers, with varying incentives favoring professional job performance. It is made up of administrative bureaucracies in which merit and capacity have been preserved, as in the case of Chile or Brazil (government careers and posts), specialized agencies connected to the fiscal or economic bureaucracy (such as central banks, regulatory agencies, or tax administrations, including the *Superintendencia Nacional de Administración Tributaria* [SUNAT] and the Internal Revenue Service in Chile and Peru), and professional corps that have established their own personnel regulations based on merit and capacity (the diplomatic service in various countries, including Brazil and Mexico, government administrators in Argentina, and some expert professionals in other countries, such as economists, lawyers, and engineers). Social sector bureaucracies (personnel from the education and health sectors) can be placed midway between the administrative and meritocratic bureaucracies, depending on the countries and sectors involved.

These bureaucracies express opinions and act. Most have a specific purview: thematic areas of public policy that require a degree of training or specialized knowledge, which gives them a voice in and influence over the area in which they are acting. This makes them a major actor in maintaining the stability and public interest orientation of policies. This type of bureaucracy constitutes an actor with a specific culture, sometimes insulated, and with a strong *esprit de corps*, which can result in corporative biases. This characteristic can make such bureaucracies prone to participate more in the design than in the implementation of policies and to demand decision making autonomy that in many cases brings them into conflict with other governmental agencies. They may make alliances with other agencies and even with external societal interests. While this may give them a capacity to intermediate among these different interests, it also makes them susceptible to capture by such interests.

In recent years, numerous countries have sought to expand and strengthen their meritocratic bureaucracies. The reform experiences have varied greatly, and in some cases significant advances have not resulted. Although many countries have adopted new civil service laws, these laws have not always been implemented effectively because of a mix of political factors (related to the value that public employment continues to have as a currency of political exchange), and of fiscal factors (related to the inflationary risk associated with public employment reform). The countries that have succeeded in putting the reform on a steady trajectory have done so in situations in which the strengthening of State capacity is made a priority and when the reforms are undertaken in a manner consistent with broader fiscal policy.

Subnational Authorities[12]

Most Latin American countries have undergone a process of political and fiscal decentralization over the last several years. Mayors are now elected in most countries in the region, rather than being appointed by the national government. The four federal countries—Argentina, Brazil, Mexico, and Venezuela—along with Colombia, Paraguay, and Peru, also elect regional (provincial) authorities. A number of important government functions and fiscal resources have additionally been decentralized to lower levels of government. This process has induced important democratizing dynamics in many of the countries, as well as important changes in the provision of local public goods.

Governors and mayors are also players in the national policymaking game, whether through their role in policy implementation or through their political role in parties and the party system.

Subnational officials, elected or not, have always had an important role in the implementation of certain public policies. The trends of political and fiscal decentralization have only increased their importance. Whether through their role in policy implementation or through their political role in parties and the party system, subnational officials are also players in the national policymaking game. In keeping with the focus of this report, this section briefly analyzes the role of subnational political authorities in national policymaking, concentrating on the role of governors.

Subnational actors can affect the national PMP through different channels. At the implementation stage, they can exert influence by obstructing, delaying, or reshaping national policies. They can also use some of their "local" policies as strategic weapons in negotiations with national authorities. For instance, subnational governments can take actions that may compromise national macroeconomic stability. This provides them with bargaining power with respect to the national government. In some countries, subnational officials are important political players within parties and have an important say in the nomination of candidates to the national legislature. National legislators in those countries thus view provincial governors as their political patrons. In those cases, subnational actors can have an effect on the drafting or vetoing of the national legislative agenda.

The exact role that subnational actors have in the national PMP depends on their incentives, and on the formal and informal rules of their engagement in the national PMP. Governors typically have incentives to obtain resources for their provinces or regions, as well as to try to build their bases of political power. Alongside the beneficial effects of giving more voice to local interests that might otherwise "get lost" in the national policymaking arena, this role of governors can generate a coordination or "commons" problem, given their excessive focus on local and regional issues rather than on broader public goods. In some Latin American countries, such as Argentina, the province is one of the key arenas for the accumulation of party power and influence, and provincial party elites, particularly governors, are crucial players both in provincial politics and in the articulation of national political coalitions.

---

[12] This section draws on Monaldi (2005).

Rules That Affect the Role of Subnational Authorities in National Policymaking

The willingness and ability of subnational political actors to influence national policy-making depends on a configuration of rules determining their incentives and capabilities. Some of the most salient such rules include the following:

Method of selecting subnational authorities. Governors play a more important role when they are popularly elected, rather than appointed.

Federal constitutional structure. In general, governors have played a more significant role in the national policymaking process in the four federal countries, compared to the other countries in the region. The influence of governors has arisen more gradually and recently in Mexico and Venezuela than in Argentina and Brazil because competitive elections have been institutionalized more recently as the means for selecting subnational authorities.

Territorial bicameralism. Some countries, especially federal ones, have territorial chambers (senates) that are based on the representation of subnational political units, such as provinces, rather than on population. These territorial chambers tend to increase the power of subnational political actors.

Overrepresentation of underpopulated provinces in the legislature (malapportionment). Malapportionment strengthens the political power of the majority of the provinces in the national legislature relative to the few, more populated provinces, including the capital. As a consequence, overrepresented states typically receive disproportionately higher resources per capita, controlling for other factors. By strengthening the presence of smaller provinces in the legislature and by giving them a disproportionate share of resources, malapportionment tends to increase the power of regional authorities in national policymaking.

Electoral and party system. Characteristics of the system used for selecting representatives to the national legislature are important because they shape legislators' incentives. Among the relevant factors are the nature of the mechanisms used by parties for nominating candidates, particularly the role that regional authorities play in the nomination process; the extent of influence of regional executives on the political careers of national legislators, including their likelihood of obtaining positions in regional government; whether provinces/states are used as the electoral districts; and whether presidential elections coincide with national legislative elections and with regional elections. When regional authorities influence the nomination, election chances, and future political career possibilities of legislators, this enhances their influence on legislators from their provinces—and thus on national policymaking. Likewise, when legislative elections are held simultaneously with elections for governors but not necessarily the presidency, when legislative electoral districts coincide with the provinces/states, and when other aspects of the electoral system favor denationalized and decentralized party structures, the influence of subnational officials in policymaking will be encouraged.

Federal fiscal arrangements. The incentives of subnational political actors are strongly affected by their dependence on national funding decisions to finance their spending responsibilities. Many details of federal fiscal arrangements are important in determining the overall "federal fiscal game." These details include the distribution of taxing authorities and spending responsibilities of provinces; the way in which transfers to cover "vertical fiscal imbalances"—imbalances between the amount provinces spend and the amount they collect in revenues—are decided and implemented; and the borrowing authority of provincial governments.[13]

Table 4.1 focuses on five Latin American countries where subnational actors are important, and summarizes some of the main factors affecting the role of subnational actors in the national PMP. In each of these cases, governors and mayors are now elected by popular vote.

These institutional factors interact, so that a given feature can have different effects depending on the full institutional context. For instance, the role of regional leaders in the senate might be increased by malapportionment and by the fact that senatorial candidates are nominated at the subnational level by regional leaders. Factors addressed in other parts of this report, such as the budgetary powers of the president, also affect the equilibrium behavior of key players. The actual effects of any of these features are conditional on the dynamics of each particular country case. To illustrate how these institutional factors combine to affect the role of governors, the cases of Argentina, Brazil, and Mexico are discussed below. In Argentina, governors play a very important role. In Brazil, the role has been significant but has declined over the past decade. In Mexico, governors are still secondary players, but their role is growing because of political and fiscal decentralization.

The Role of Governors in Argentina, Brazil, and Mexico

Argentina

In Argentina, subnational political actors, particularly provincial governors, are quite important in national politics and in national policymaking. The particular way in which governors enter the game, together with other institutional features of the country, helps to explain why Argentina has a relatively noncooperative policymaking process oriented to the short term. This lack of cooperation and focus on the short term has repercussions for some of the characteristics of public policies identified in Chapter 6.

Argentina has a long federal tradition. As in the United States, the power of the State is defined in the constitution as being derived from the provinces, not the central government. The political importance of Argentina's provinces has been somewhat obscured during periods of strong national leadership (like that of Perón) or during the many military dictatorships from 1930 to 1983. Since the latest transition to democracy, however, subnational political actors have reemerged as crucial players in the national political arena.

---

[13] Several of these features were themselves policy choices at some previous point, but can be considered fixed in the short run for the discussion of other policy areas. Tommasi (2002) analyzes these dynamic interactions for the case of Argentina.

Table 4.1 Factors Affecting the Role of Subnational Actors in Policymaking

	Argentina	Brazil	Colombia	Mexico	Venezuela
Federal structure	Yes	Yes	No	Yes	Yes
Extent of fiscal resources available to governors	High	High	High	Moderate	Moderate
Territorial chamber	Yes	Yes	No	Yes	No
Malapportionment	High	High	Moderate	Low	Low
Are legislative elections concurrent with elections for governors or presidents?	Partial with governors and presidents	Yes; in 1986 and 1990, with governors; after 1994, with presidents and governors	Neither	Neither	Yes until 1999; only very infrequently with one or the other thereafter
Do legislative districts coincide with regions or provinces?	Yes	Yes	Only lower chamber	Only senate	Yes
Do governors play a major role in nomination/ election chances of legislators?	Yes	Moderate	Moderate	Moderate	Moderate
Can governors reward legislators with positions?	Yes	Yes	No[a]	Yes	Yes
Are governorships launching platforms for successful presidential campaigns?	Yes	Yes	Yes	Yes, since 1990s	Yes, since 1990s

[a] Mayors of major cities in Colombia tend to have more resources with which to reward legislators than governors do.

Source: Authors' compilation.

Governors, who have been elected for most of Argentina's democratic history, play a central role in Argentina's national policymaking process. Provincial governments have authority over significant policy areas, and their authority has increased over the last two decades, as Argentina's expenditure decentralization is the highest in Latin America. However, tax collection is fairly centralized, creating a large vertical fiscal imbalance, which makes provincial governments heavily dependent on national funding. The situation is further complicated by Argentina's bicameral congress, with a territorially based senate. Argentina has the highest level of malapportionment in the upper chamber in the Latin American region, and the third highest in the lower chamber. This confers a disproportionate degree of influence on the governors of small provinces.

The organization of party politics is heavily centered on the provincial arena. Political careers, especially successful ones, are often built from provincial bases of power. The overrepresentation of small provinces in both chambers of the legislature, the methods used for nominating candidates, the characteristics of federal fiscal arrangements, and the clientelistic nature of local political loyalties all contribute to making the province a crucial arena of political exchange. The importance of governors is reflected in the fact that three out of the five presidents since the return to democracy have been governors (Menem, Duhalde, and Kirchner).[14]

The electoral system is based on closed lists with the provinces as electoral districts. This allows provincial party leaders in general and governors in particular to play a very influential role in the nomination process for legislative elections. As mentioned in Chapter 3, Argentina has a fairly denationalized party system, and the main parties in the country can be described as confederations of subnational bases of power. Subnational party leaders are crucial players in the nomination of candidates for the national congress, and national legislators tend to view these local leaders as their bosses. This and other factors of the Argentine institutional system help to explain why the national congress has a relatively weak role with respect to the adoption of national public policies. Scholars have characterized Argentine legislators as professional politicians but amateur legislators, since they tend not to get reelected and have relatively weak incentives to invest in the policymaking capabilities of congress.[15] Instead, they tend to focus on the short term, which has an adverse effect on the quality of public policies.

Several of the crucial political and policy decisions of the last decade have been negotiated in meetings of the president or some key minister with provincial governors. The arenas for these political and policy exchanges, in turn, are not very well institutionalized. This, together with a judiciary that plays a limited enforcement role and a relatively weak bureaucracy, tends to create a policymaking process that concentrates on the distribution of short-term benefits, to the detriment of longer-term, broader concerns.

These tendencies are exemplified by the frequent exchanges of provincial support of national policies for fiscal benefits to the provinces. This contributes to creating a political system that tends to operate more on the basis of clientelistic exchanges than of policy debates and consensus-building. As a consequence, policies tend to be volatile

---

[14] Rodríguez Saá, who served for one week following the resignation of De la Rúa, also had been a governor.

[15] Spiller and Tommasi (2003); Jones and others (2002).

and obtain credibility only if they are "hard-wired." Policies also have a tendency not to be well coordinated or enforced, and often tend to favor specific constituencies instead of more public-regarding objectives.

Brazil

In Brazil, several factors inherited at the time of the return to democracy in the mid-1980s at first contributed to giving state governors a significant role in national policy-making. Yet recent trends have tended to water down the significance of this role. These trends have followed from the institutionalization of democracy, as well as from some institutional reforms adopted in response to the severe fiscal crisis the country experienced in the early 1990s.

During the transition to democracy, governors were directly elected seven years before the first direct election of the president. This conferred legitimacy on the governors and empowered them to play a crucial role in the elite's bargaining game. This particular distribution of power and legitimacy resulted in a constitution that reflected the relatively strong position of the governors.

The Brazilian Constitution vests a number of policy domains as well as revenue authority in the states, which at the same time enjoy administrative autonomy. In this context, if the policy preferences of governors and the executive diverge, governors have some power to advance their preferences. Because governors are not primarily concerned with fiscal stability at the national level, and they have a preference for higher federal public spending and geographically concentrated investments, fiscal policy usually has been a matter of conflict.

The influence of governors has always been indirect, stemming from their role during the democratic transition and the substantial tax authority that the constitution grants them. Brazil's version of the value-added tax—the ICMS—is collected by the states and represents the single most important tax in the country, accounting for one-third of tax revenues.

Given the influence that they could have on the political careers of legislators at the state level, governors had the capacity to influence the behavior of federal deputies and senators in congress. The relative dependence of legislators on support from governors was reinforced by the fact that until 1994 legislative elections coincided with elections for governors and state legislators, but not for the presidency. This meant that congressional candidates coordinated their campaigns around gubernatorial candidates and the electoral and other resources they could provide, not presidential candidates or national parties, which did not fund legislative candidacies. The economic autonomy enjoyed by governors allowed them to provide valuable support to candidates.

However, the influence of governors faded as political actors at different levels began sharing in the legitimacy conferred by direct popular election, and with the shift to simultaneous presidential and congressional elections. The inflation crisis, and the Real Plan implemented to solve it, allowed the federal government to impose certain conditions on the states. This undercut the power of governors, who were forced to privatize banks and public enterprises. The governors also lost vital resources with which to influence national and subnational politics.

In sum, throughout most of the last decade, the national executive has been able to implement its agenda by recentralizing the political game. This has included passing legislation that adversely affected state governors, such as the Social Emergency Fund (FSE). This constitutional reform, passed in 1993, allowed the Franco administration to use revenues to reduce the central government deficit that had previously been earmarked in the 1988 Constitution for specific expenditures that ultimately benefited the states. As the financial sovereignty of subnational governments has weakened, regional authorities have also lost much of their influence on the nomination process for national legislators.

Mexico

Two of the most relevant features of Mexico's PMP during the 20th century have been the hegemonic position attained by the PRI in the party system and the federal nature of its regime. Governorships have always been important in a federal country with a political system that could not resolve its political and power struggles within the electoral system. In fact, state governorships were the most valuable positions delivered by the president to party leaders; they were even preferred to senate seats. Notwithstanding their importance in the PRI hierarchy, governors were not autonomous agents in the PMP.

The importance of these positions motivated legislators to compete for the PRI nomination for governor alongside prominent federal politicians and mayors of large municipalities. Governors had control over a considerable system of patronage, as they stood at the center of the promotion structure at the state and municipal levels.[16] Governorships became even more important as the institutional features changed.

As in many other countries, because the decentralization process developed gradually, the degree of political, fiscal, and functional decentralization was not homogenous. Fiscal decentralization was the factor that started the drive toward broader decentralization, and the federal government's decision to initiate the decentralization of fiscal relations was probably based on the desire to stave off the PRI's political decline.[17] As the PRI lost its ability to guarantee economic growth, the federal government was forced to relinquish some control over tax expenditures and policymaking to local governments, which, in turn, were better able to cultivate support with new resources.[18] Control of resources is directly related to the role governors play on the national stage.

The decentralization of fiscal relations fundamentally changed the once centralized and opaque PMP because it opened the door to the insertion of local interests into national politics. Indeed, decentralization has increased the importance of local leaders in national politics more generally. This process was strengthened when, for the first time, the PRI lost a governorship in 1989 and regional elections started to become competitive. Since then, governors have increasingly played a relevant role in national policymaking. The position of governor is now a key stepping-stone to the presidency, in contrast

---

[16] Lehoucq and others (2005).

[17] Rodríguez (1997).

[18] Lehoucq and others (2005).

with the PRI-dominated era, when national executive positions were key. Furthermore, the patronage network that governors control has allowed them some influence over legislators. This influence has been small but growing, particularly with respect to the nomination of legislative candidates and to some extent with respect to determining the future career of legislators, who are barred from reelection.

These decentralizing processes generated a fundamental realignment of the interests represented in the national congress, which then had broader implications. First, states have gained political leverage over the federal government. Additional taxes have been placed within the national tax revenue sharing system (SNCF)[19] and the percentage of total tax revenues allocated to state governments has increased. Total transfers to states increased by nearly 20 percent, on average, in the early 1990s.[20] Second, within Mexico, opposition-controlled states and poorer states appear to have gained additional leverage over the federal government during negotiations on the distribution of federal revenue transfers. Thus the political and fiscal components of the decentralization process have mutually reinforced one another.

The Judiciary[21]

Another actor that can potentially play an important role in policymaking is the judiciary. Historically, in much of the region the judicial branch has been characterized by dependence on the executive and a lack of activism in interpreting the law, in challenging the legality of executive actions, or in reviewing the constitutionality of laws. Along with the broader process of democratization, the judicial reforms adopted over the last two decades have changed the structure and the operation of the judicial system in the region. The potential for the courts' involvement in the policymaking process (reflected in the levels of judicial independence) has increased significantly. As a result, in some countries the judiciary is assuming a more active and independent role in the adoption, implementation, and enforcement of public policy.

The judiciary is taking on a greater importance in both public policy and politics in Latin America.

With the establishment of institutional structures that are conducive to higher levels of judicial independence, courts have become less subservient and the judiciary has repositioned itself in relation to other branches of government. The number of judicial rulings against the executive's preferences has generally increased in many Latin American countries. Overall, court decisions are assuming greater importance in both public policy and politics.[22]

---

[19] The National System of Tax Coordination replaced the national sales tax with a federal value-added tax (VAT). To join the SNCF, states relinquished authority over additional state-level taxes in exchange for guaranteed shares of the VAT.

[20] Rodríguez (1997).

[21] This section draws extensively on Sousa (2005).

[22] Tate (1992); Shapiro and Stone Sweet (2002).

The Potential Policymaking Roles of the Judiciary

Judiciaries can assume a number of different roles in the policymaking process. These potential roles can be divided into four categories: veto player, policy player, impartial referee, and societal representative. The role of judiciaries in Latin America varies in terms of which of these roles is performed and the degree of activism and independence with which they are carried out.

Veto player. In this role, the judiciary vetoes legislation on constitutional grounds, but also partly on the basis of its own preferences. If the judiciary is independent and performs the veto player role, it may be more difficult to change policy arbitrarily, and the legislature and the executive may have to take into account the preferences of the judiciary. The veto role is more extensive and has a more profound impact when the courts' decisions apply to the law in general rather than to just a specific case. Given the trend toward "hard-wiring" many aspects of public policy into constitutions, the role for the judiciary in this regard has expanded.

Policy player. When the courts review laws to determine legislative intent or when they give new interpretations to legislation on the basis of their views of the legal system as a whole, they are imposing their own policy preferences on policy outcomes. Institutional features favoring this kind of role include those in which the courts can make rulings in the absence of a concrete case, before the law is even adopted, and when the courts' rulings on the constitutionality of laws are applicable in general, rather than to just a specific case.

Impartial referee. Courts can be called upon to ensure that public policies are effectively applied by acting as an external enforcer of agreements undertaken by others (including those encoded in the constitution) and a mediator between contracting parties. This role is being played when the court makes sure the executive does not exceed its powers, for example, by legislating by decree on matters to which this power is not supposed to apply; when it stops the government from enforcing taxes it is not supposed to levy; or when it protects the autonomy of an independent central bank in monetary policy. An effective performance of the impartial referee role can facilitate the forging of political agreements needed to adopt policy reforms and contribute to the fair and efficient implementation of those reforms.[23]

Societal representative. It is often difficult for certain sectors of the population (such as the poor and rural farmers) to influence the formation of policies. Because judiciaries can help enforce constitutional stipulations for equal protection under the law and for the defense of civil and social rights, they can provide a voice for marginalized groups and an alternative channel for societal representation.

---

[23] An example of this role occurs when, in the middle of a privatization reform, the government reneges on agreements previously made and decides to nationalize a segment of the economy. If the courts strike down the nationalization decision, the judiciary has engaged in its referee role.

The scope of judicial activism in ten Latin American countries in relation to these four potential roles is portrayed in Table 4.2.[24] The impartial referee role is performed especially actively in Brazil and Chile. In these countries, the courts also actively perform the veto player and policy player roles. Particularly as a result of the 1991 constitutional reform, the newly created Constitutional Court in Colombia has played an increasingly active role in blocking and/or interpreting legislation (veto and policy player roles). Conversely, in Argentina, Ecuador, Paraguay, Peru, and Venezuela, the judiciary has tended to be more dependent on the executive. This has limited its ability to play a significant role as an impartial referee or as a policy player.

An active and independent judiciary is likely to affect the policymaking process and the key features of public policies in several ways. First, as an impartial referee, the judiciary can help ensure the effectiveness of the implementation and enforcement of policies. Second, as an external enforcer of agreements, it can help facilitate inter-temporal political transactions, such as commitments by the executive to regulate privatized firms effectively or enact pension reforms that reduce benefits now in exchange for the greater security of benefits in the future. This can encourage greater stability of policies, since some agreements (or policy equilibria) in the public interest will be possible that would not be otherwise. Third, in performing the societal representation role, the courts can contribute to making policies more public-regarding.

Fourth, the judiciary can contribute to adaptability. For example, when policies have been delegated to an autonomous agency (like the central bank), and the judiciary upholds the terms of that delegation, the agency can then manage some area of policy as it sees fit, without the need for safeguards that would prevent opportunism at the cost of rigidity.

Fifth, when judiciaries are active as veto players, policies are likely to be more stable, since policy changes must be consistent with the preferences of another institutional actor, with the constitution and existing laws, and with the preferences of other actors that may act through the judiciary to challenge policy changes. However, in performing this role, the judiciary might make policies less adaptable, depending upon how its preferences match with those of the executive and the legislature. As policy players, the courts could potentially make policies more volatile.

Factors Affecting the Judiciary's Policy Independence and Activism

The level of independence of the judiciary in a given country is related to both the potential for individual judges to act according to their own policy objectives and the potential for courts—collectively—to be involved in the policymaking process.

Judicial independence can be defined as the judiciary's ability "to make decisions according to the law and not based on external or internal political factors."[25] It has four inter-related dimensions: substantive independence, or the power to make judicial decisions and exercise official duties subject to no other authority but the law; personal

---

[24] Table 4.2 is based on the ten country studies originally included in the PMP project carried out using this report's methodology, as well as other qualitative case studies.

[25] Dakolias (1996, pp. 7–8).

Table 4.2 Roles Played by Judiciaries in Latin America

Country	What roles has the judiciary undertaken the most?	In what issue areas has the judiciary been the most active?
Argentina	Veto player. Limited judicial review powers and judicial independence is tempered by strategic behavior of judges.	Human rights and economic affairs.
Brazil	Some evidence of veto player, policy player, and impartial referee. To a lesser extent, societal representative (via *Ministério Público*).	Tax, pension, and land reform issues.
Chile	Impartial referee, veto player (especially in human rights issues) and policy player.	
Colombia	Veto player and policy player; societal representative because of the *Acción Pública de Inconstitucionalidad*.	Fiscal.
Ecuador	Veto player.	Fiscal and exchange rate policy.
Mexico	Veto player and policy player.	Electoral disputes and issues regarding the redefinition of federalism. Also taxation.
Paraguay	Until 1993, the judiciary was dependent on the executive. Since 1993, it has been somewhat autonomous but not very capable. It is to some extent a veto player.	Policies of regulatory or redistributive intent.
Peru	The judiciary has not played effective roles in defining the national policy agenda, promoting inter-temporal cooperation, and providing checks and balances on executive power.	
Uruguay	The Supreme Court has limited ability to rule on the constitutionality of laws. However, the Supreme Court can be an effective veto player when a bill has been approved by congress and an individual citizen has been affected by it. There is also some evidence of a policy player role.	Social and financial policies.
Venezuela	Recently there have been constitutional reforms increasing the number of supreme court justices.	

Source: Sousa (2005).

independence, or stability of tenure and freedom from intimidation or threats; collective independence, or judicial participation in the central administration of courts; and internal independence, or independence from judicial superiors and colleagues.[26]

Among the characteristics of the judiciary that affect judicial independence, several stand out: the extent of budgetary autonomy; the level of transparency and the extent of the use of meritocratic criteria in the process for nominating and appointing judges; the stability of the tenure of judges; and the reach of judicial review powers. Effective judicial independence also depends upon the behavior of other actors, such as whether the president or political parties regularly interfere with the courts. This, in turn, depends upon these actors' incentives.

Judicial Budget Autonomy

In the context of public budget scarcity, the reliability and autonomy of the judicial branch's budget is essential to judicial independence. Although in many countries, the judicial branch itself prepares the annual budget (Costa Rica, Guatemala, and Uruguay, for example), in most cases the budget's execution still depends on the approval of either the legislature or the executive, thus hindering the branch's ability to administer its own resources. In some countries—mostly in Central America—the minimum budget dedicated to the judicial branch is stipulated by law. However, that does not necessarily mean that this amount is allocated in practice.

The share of the public sector's budget dedicated to the justice sector varies significantly across countries, from over 3 percent in Costa Rica to less than 1 percent in Ecuador and Peru.[27] Although the size of the budget alone does not ensure efficiency, it is an important indicator of the amount of funds available to the judiciary to carry out its operations.

Appointment System

Beyond financial resources, the judiciary needs to have qualified judges with appropriate incentives to ensure efficiency and the rule of law. The ways in which judges are chosen affects the extent to which judges are motivated to apply the law independently and impartially and to perform their role efficiently.

A wide variety of systems are used to select supreme court judges. In Argentina, Brazil, and Mexico, candidates are nominated and appointed by the president with the approval of the legislature (or one of its chambers).[28] In other countries, such as Bolivia, El Salvador, Guatemala, and Honduras, the candidates are nominated by a judicial council or nominating board and then appointed by the legislature (or one of its chambers). In another group of countries, including the Dominican Republic and Peru, supreme court judges are appointed by a judicial council. Other things being equal, nonpartisan and

---

[26] Shetreet (1985).

[27] See Sousa (2005).

[28] This system is similar to the one used in the United States.

multi-member councils would be expected to be more effective in promoting judicial independence than processes in which the executive and legislature play a substantial role in nominating and appointing judges.

The degree of transparency with which the nomination and appointment process takes place is also important for favoring or hindering judicial independence. Some countries, such as Chile and Guatemala, have put in place recruitment procedures that encourage competition, transparency, and the participation of renowned magistrates and academics in the selection of new judges.

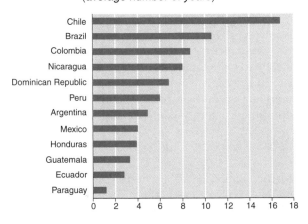

FIGURE 4.6 **Tenure of Supreme Court Judges, 1960–1995**
(*average number of years*)

Source: Henisz (2000).

Nonetheless, the simple creation of laws, judicial councils, and training programs may not correspond to the reality of the appointment system in the judicial sector. Many of the new requirements for choosing judges may be completely bypassed or implemented poorly.

Terms and Tenure

The reasoning behind establishing longer (or lifelong) terms for judges is to provide greater job security so that judges' concerns about holding their position or being promoted do not influence their decisions. Thus, moving away from short terms that coincide with presidential and congressional elections is likely to favor judicial independence.

Some countries, including Argentina, Brazil, Chile, Ecuador, and El Salvador, have adopted lifetime tenure for judges (in some cases limited by a mandatory retirement age). For other countries, such as Bolivia, Colombia, and Costa Rica, only lower-court judges have lifetime tenure, while supreme court judges have fixed terms. In Paraguay, supreme court judges have life terms, while first- and second-tier judges can remain in their jobs for only five years. Finally, in some countries, such as Guatemala and Peru, judges have fixed terms, which must be periodically renewed.

It is important to highlight the gap between the letter of the law and reality. Despite the existence of lifetime tenure for judges in Ecuador, for instance, President Lucio Gutiérrez removed 27 of 31 supreme court judges in December 2004. Thus longer *de jure* tenure for supreme court judges has not necessarily translated into the lengthening of tenures in many countries. Figure 4.6 shows the average tenure of supreme court judges in selected Latin American countries from 1960 to 1995.

Box 4.2	An Expanding Judicial Role in Mexico*

Mexico's experience in the past decade shows how a combination of changes in the parameters of inter-party competition and judicial system reforms can contribute to the emergence of a judiciary that assumes a more proactive role in policymaking.

From the late 1920s until 1994, the Supreme Court did not have the means or the incentives to assert its independence. Both the constitutional rules regulating the process for nominating Supreme Court judges and the dominance of the political system by the PRI led to that equilibrium. During this time, the Court's powers of judicial review were limited mainly to *amparo* suits, which generally were restricted to cases pertaining to the regulation of individual rights, and the results applied only to the parties to the case.

As electoral support for the governing PRI began to erode, reforms were adopted in 1994 that increased the threshold for appointment of justices in the senate from a simple majority to a qualified majority of two-thirds; created another form of judicial review (the "action of unconstitutionality"), which allows the Supreme Court to declare laws or administrative actions unconstitutional; and extended the types of "constitutional controversies" that the Court could decide upon.

Judicial system reforms, along with the decline in the PRI's hold on elected offices, led to a sharp increase in Supreme Court rulings against the governing party. While the Court ruled against the PRI only 15 percent of the time between 1995 and 1997 (in cases in which the PRI was a defendant in constitutional controversies), it did so 66 percent of the time between 1997 and 2000, when the PRI lost its majority in the Chamber of Deputies for the first time, and 69 percent of the time after 2000, when the PRI lost the presidency.

These patterns suggest that the Supreme Court has emerged as an important veto player. If divided government persists and control of the presidency shifts between parties, the Court could develop capacities as an impartial enforcer of inter-temporal agreements among actors in the PMP.

---

* Lehoucq and others (2005).

Judicial Review Powers

Judicial review is the power of a court (generally the supreme court, or in some cases, the constitutional court) to declare laws and other administrative acts unconstitutional. This power can vary according to whether it can be applied only to a specific case or to a hypothetical case (concrete or abstract), whether it can be applied before or only after a law is enacted (*a priori* or *a posteriori*), and whether only the supreme court can

Table 4.3 Independence of the Judiciary

Country	Judicial independence[a] (1–7 scale)	De facto judicial independence[b] (0–1 scale)
Argentina	1.80	0.33
Bolivia	1.70	0.56
Brazil	3.90	0.49
Chile	4.60	0.58
Colombia	3.10	0.53
Costa Rica	3.80	0.92
Dominican Republic	3.60	—
Ecuador	1.90	0.39
El Salvador	2.90	—
Guatemala	2.20	0.53
Honduras	1.90	—
Mexico	3.30	0.71
Nicaragua	1.60	0.32
Panama	2.20	0.39
Paraguay	1.40	0.49
Peru	1.90	0.16
Uruguay	4.80	0.45
Venezuela	1.20	0.40

— not available.

[a] World Economic Forum. This variable is the average response of surveyed business executives in each country to the statement "The judiciary in your country is independent from political influences of members of government, citizens or firms" (1 = no, heavily influenced; 7 = yes, entirely independent).

[b] Feld and Voigt (2003). The de facto judicial independence index of Feld and Voigt is based on objective criteria such as actual tenure of supreme court justices, deviations from de jure tenure, removal of justices before the end of their terms, increases in number of justices on the court, and changes to the budget of the supreme court and to real income of justices, among other things (see Data Appendix).

Sources: World Economic Forum (2004); Feld and Voigt (2003).

engage in judicial review or lower courts can do so as well (centralized or decentralized authority).[29]

Despite the continuing shortcomings in constitutional adjudication provisions, there is a consensus that they have been strengthened considerably in the past two decades. (Box 4.2 presents the case of Mexico, where the supreme court has emerged as an important veto player.) The control of the constitutionality of laws is especially relevant

---

[29] Navia and Ríos-Figueroa (2005).

in democratic contexts in which the constitution is detailed and there is a jurisdictional overlap of government responsibilities (as in the case of federal democracies). In these circumstances, conflicts and questions regarding constitutional issues arise frequently.

Despite recent reforms, there is still considerable variation in the region in respect to the scope of judicial review powers, in terms of the breadth of mechanisms for bringing issues to the attention of the courts, the extent of the applicability of judicial decisions based on individual or institutional complaints, and whether individual complaints can provide a basis for rulings on the general constitutionality of laws.[30]

The structural characteristics described above suggest that the impact of Latin American judiciaries on the policymaking process and public policy is uneven across the region. This variation in the potential for courts' involvement in politics is corroborated by available indicators of de facto judicial independence. Table 4.3 presents two such indicators. The first one, published by the World Economic Forum in 2004, is a subjective indicator based on survey responses of business executives. According to this index, Uruguay, Chile and Brazil appear at the top of the ranking. The second one, developed by Feld and Voigt,[31] is based on objective criteria, such as the actual tenure of supreme court (or constitutional court) justices and its deviation from de jure tenure, whether justices were removed before the end of their term or the number of justices was increased, and whether the budget of the supreme court or the income of the justices was reduced in real terms, among others. According to this index, Costa Rica, Mexico and Chile appear at the top of the list.[32]

---

[30] Brewer-Carías (1997).

[31] Feld and Voigt (2003).

[32] While the Feld and Voigt indicator has the advantage of being objective, it has some disadvantages of its own. First, the information gathered by these authors remains incomplete, and several countries were coded on the basis of a small subset of the criteria included in the index, as a result of problems with data availability. Second, in situations in which a country's courts respond to the wishes of the executive, and in turn the justices are not removed and their budget and income are not reduced, the country's judiciary would be rated as independent according to this index. Given these shortcomings, and the fact that the Feld and Voigt measure is available for a smaller set of countries than this study's sample, the index of judicial independence used in the rest of the report is the one published by the World Economic Forum.

Chapter 5

Actors from Civil Society

Politics is too serious a matter to be
left to the politicians.

—Charles de Gaulle, President of France (1890–1970)

The actors discussed in Chapters 3 and 4 have formally defined roles and functions in the national policymaking process (PMP). Rules have been established that govern how they function, who participates, how individuals within them are selected, what specific policy functions they are to perform, and how they are to relate to one another. However, these "formal" actors do not always behave according to their formal roles and functions. They may not fulfill the roles expected of them, or they may perform additional (informal) roles not specified in the constitution, or they may perform policymaking roles through mechanisms that are not specified in the rules.

Moreover, there are other—informal—actors (and arenas) that may play significant roles in national policymaking in some countries, although they are not formally assigned such roles in the constitution or are not associated with the formal political system. This chapter briefly analyzes the role of five such actors: business; the media; labor unions; social movements; and sources of policy expertise, or "knowledge actors."

Given the nature of these actors, their role in the policymaking process is less analyzed and understood than that of the more formal actors described in Chapters 3 and 4. Thus the goal of this chapter is to set the stage for a more in-depth and systematic study of the role of such actors. The selection here is admittedly partial. Limitations of space prevent the analysis of other actors that potentially can play quite significant roles in policymaking. These include civil society organizations in general, the church, multinational corporations, international organizations, foreign governments, and the armed forces.

Business[1]

Business is usually a key participant in policymaking. Of all the social groups with strong interests, businesses have the most resources to spend. They also have a variety of means to influence the policymaking process in their favor, including, in democratic settings, business associations, lobbying, campaign contributions, personal and policy networks, and corruption.

The challenge from a policy perspective is not to eliminate the influence of business, but rather to channel it so that it contributes to achieving good policy outcomes.

Different forms of business influence affect the characteristics of public policies in different ways. Behind-the-scenes networking or payoffs to corrupt politicians, for instance, may yield private advantages to particular businesses at the expense of the public welfare. Conversely, business associations that are relatively encompassing (those that represent a diverse array of economic sectors and business interests) may support broad-based reform measures vital to increasing economic growth and competitiveness.

Some types of opportunities for influence (such as contributing to the campaigns of party candidates for the legislature) are relatively fixed by features of the political system (such as the structure of the electoral and party system). Other opportunities can be created or closed by political leaders, such as appointing businesspeople to positions in the government, or giving business associations a role in policymaking and thus encouraging their development. By opening or closing opportunities for different forms of business influence, the State and society can affect the quality of public policies.

The discussion that follows examines the types of influence business can exert and offers some general observations about *when* businesses tend to participate in the policymaking process, for *which* types of policies, *how* intensely, and *what* the impact is on the quality of policies. The section concludes with a discussion of ways to make business participation more public-regarding, transparent, and inclusive.

A Typology of Business Participation

Business participation in the policymaking process varies considerably by country, by type of policy and policy area, and over time. Thus it is difficult to capture the patterns of business participation in a simple framework. However, some generalizations are useful.

Business participation can be organized and collective, or dispersed and individual, as in personal networks. It can be open and formal, as in business associations, where activities are typically known to many and are often covered by the press. Or it can be closed and informal, as in corruption.

In general, the more wide-ranging the interests of business, the more open the form of participation, and the more transparent the activities, the more public-regarding the influence of business will be (public-regarding in the minimum sense of not favoring

---

[1] This section draws extensively on Schneider (2005).

particular interests and promoting greater allocative efficiency), and the more public-regarding will be the policies that result.

In choosing to participate in the policymaking process, businesses must contend with the free rider problem. Some businesses will be tempted to free ride on the efforts of others: that is, to reap some of the benefits without incurring any of the costs. If businesses cannot reap the full benefits of their policy-related activities, they will undertake them with less intensity—or choose not to participate at all. Thus, unless firms can organize collectively to influence policy, they may choose to engage in activities in which free rider problems are less severe, such as personal networking or lobbying to win a contract or resolve a dispute. By their very nature, these activities tend to generate benefits that are very specific to the firms that engage in them, and thus are private-regarding.

Businesses are more likely to organize collectively and act effectively together if certain conditions hold:

- They share similar interests.
- They are fewer in number, thus making it easier for them to capture the benefits of acting together (and thus controlling the free rider problem).
- The State is providing some clear benefit to them, such as regular access to top policymakers or control over public funds.
- The State is imposing a clear cost, such as higher taxes.

Forms of Participation

Businesses can choose to participate in the policymaking process in a variety of ways. The form of participation has an impact on the quality of the policy.

Individual firms. Businesses can act on their own. As noted, the more wide-ranging their business interests, the less narrow their policy orientation is likely to be. Larger, diversified conglomerates that span several sectors may have more encompassing interests than smaller, more specialized firms. Combined with their huge size and small number, they are more likely to engage in collective action and coordination, and to push for policies that have broader benefits (that are more public-regarding), particularly policies that are designed to improve the functioning of the economy as a whole.

Sectors. Firms in a given economic sector (industrial or agriculture, for example) that share interests and may have a homogeneous nature are more likely to engage in collective action, especially in response to policies that distribute costs or benefits disproportionately to their sector.

Associations. These can be voluntary or state-chartered, economy-wide, industry-wide, or geared to a particular product or commodity. They may represent primarily large or small firms.

Personal or policy networks. Individual businesspeople can participate directly in the policymaking process through appointment to government positions or through close connections with top policymakers. These personalized networks may arise out of social, school, or family ties, or career movement between the public and private sectors. Businesspeople are common in government in Argentina, Brazil, Peru, and especially Colombia.

Capital mobility. Through their ability to move capital, businesses can have a direct, uncoordinated, impersonal effect on policies as policymakers try to anticipate policies that are likely to keep and attract capital. Capital mobility is not a deliberate form of business participation in policymaking. However, it serves as a constraint and tends to narrow the range of policy options that policymakers consider.

A Portfolio of Options

Businesses "invest" in politics through a range of political activities. In principle, rational businesspeople will balance their "portfolio" of political investments to take advantage of evolving opportunities: that is, they will shift political investments to activities that generate the greatest return. Precisely where they concentrate their investments will depend, in large part, on their perceptions of the opportunities for influence offered by the political system.

Businesspeople will often use a number of these channels at the same time, but certain ones tend to prevail, given the nature of the issue and the political setting of the country. These options are discussed below.

Business associations. Associations offer members direct contacts with policymakers, and members may serve on consultative or policy councils. The most important way business associations influence politics may be through the media, as the association presents the views of its members and tries to inform the public and influence public opinion.

Lobbying. Lobbying is becoming increasingly important in some countries in the region. It is generally done by individual firms, rather than by associations. This tends to make business's influence more fragmented, particularistic, and ineffectual on general issues. Lobbying is more important during the implementation and enforcement stages.

Elections and campaign contributions. Most countries in the region have reformed their campaign finance laws to reduce dependence on business contributions. Yet millions of dollars, legal and illegal, flow from business to politicians during elections. Firms often contribute to more than one presidential candidate as a form of insurance to keep their channels of access open, rather than as a way to influence policy in one direction or another.

Personal and policy networks. Personal networks operate as informal, personal relations that connect businesspeople to government elites. Business influence through networks tends to be opaque and sometimes secretive. Narrow and exclusive networks can foster private-regarding policies. To the extent that businesses perceive they have access through networks, they may be less likely to invest in encompassing associations.

Table 5.1 Portfolios of Business Politics (intensity of use)

Country	Associations	Lobbying	Elections and campaign contributions	Networks	Corruption
			Type of participation		
Argentina	Low	Medium	Medium	Medium	High
Brazil	Low	Medium	Medium	Medium	Medium
Chile	High	Low	Low	Low	Low
Colombia	High	Low	Medium	High	Medium
Mexico (1990s)	High	Low	Low	Low	Medium
Mexico (2000–present)	Medium	Medium	Medium	Medium	Medium

Source: Schneider (2005).

Outright corruption. Businesses sometimes try to buy influence directly through outright corruption. Obviously, this is a highly secretive and opaque form of influence. Corruption tends to be connected to very specific policies and is usually linked more to policy implementation (when funds, contracts, and other opportunities are distributed to particular firms) and enforcement (when penalties are assessed and administered).

As noted, businesspeople would be expected to rebalance their portfolios of political investments to take maximum advantage of the opportunities offered by the political system. For example, in countries like Argentina and Brazil, where policymakers pay less attention to associations, businesses tend not to invest much time or money in them. Where governments have drawn on associations for business input, businesspeople have strong incentives to invest in associations and build up their institutional capacity for the long term. This has been evident in Chile and Mexico (particularly as a result of business involvement in trade negotiations), as well as in Colombia.

Business investment in politics also varies by the amount the government can actually accomplish. Thus in Mexico, the business association luncheons and dinners that were so valuable to business in the heyday of market reform under the Salinas administration (1988–94) have meant much less under the current administration (2000–present), in which the government has found it more difficult to pass new policy initiatives through congress.[2]

The prevalence of the various forms of business participation in the policymaking process in the five countries studied by Schneider is summarized in Table 5.1.[3]

---

[2] Schneider (2005).

[3] Schneider (2004, 2005).

Table 5.2 Intensity of Business Involvement, by Distribution of Costs

Short- or long-term nature of costs	Certainty of costs	
	Certain	Uncertain
Immediate	• Changes in tax rates • Pension reform	• Privatization • Deregulation • Pension privatization
Longer term	• Future scheduled changes in taxes or pension benefits	• Trade liberalization • Reregulation

Note: Shaded portion indicates more intense business involvement.

Source: Schneider (2005).

Types of Policies and the Type and Intensity of Business Involvement

The type and intensity of business involvement in the policymaking process is affected by the type of policy. In gauging their involvement, businesses consider whether the costs and benefits of policies are certain or uncertain, and whether they are immediate or longer term. Some policies, such as changes in some tax rates and pension benefits, have immediate and certain costs. Other policies, especially many recent market-oriented reforms, have more uncertain costs. In the case of privatization, for example, it is well-known that new owners normally lay off workers—but how many workers, and when, is uncertain. Social policy (education and health care) and administrative reform require large, long-term investments in institutional reform and have uncertain consequences.

Generally, businesses, like other groups, are most likely to mobilize when costs are immediate and certain (Table 5.2). When reforms are longer term and costs and benefits are uncertain and diffuse, businesses are less likely to engage in a sustained way, either for or against the proposed change.

The scope of policy also matters to business: whether broad, such as across-the-board changes in tax rates or education policy, or narrow, such as privatizing a certain type of enterprise (Table 5.3). Most businesses have a hard time acting collectively with regard to policies that are broad. Thus businesses are not likely to invest in broad policies, except through encompassing associations. This can be a boon for policymakers if they fear business opposition, as in the case of trade liberalization, collective business opposition to which has not materialized.

Businesses are more likely to undertake intense business investments when faced with narrower policies that directly affect their interests in the shorter term. The challenge in the case of issues like these is to prevent policy capture by the most intensely interested groups.

Table 5.3 Intensity of Business Involvement, by Scope of Benefits and Speed of Implementation

Speed of implementation	Scope of benefits	
	Narrow	Broad
Rapid	• Privatization • Deregulation • Elimination of specific tax loopholes and exemptions	• Uniform changes in taxes, pensions, or tariffs • Fiscal decentralization
Lengthy	• Sectoral regulation (public utilities such as energy and telecom)	• Administrative reform • Education policy • Trade agreements

Note: Shaded portion indicates more intense business involvement.

Source: Schneider (2005).

Opening the System

In countries in which the State is relatively weak, such as Guatemala (see Box 5.1), business interests often dominate the policymaking process. While it is important to foster strong States that can check the power of business elites, it is unrealistic to try to keep business out of policymaking. Closing some formal channels of participation would probably lead to channeling of that influence into other, less transparent forms. Thus the challenge from a policy perspective is not to eliminate the influence of business, but rather to channel it so that it contributes to achieving good policy outcomes.

Several conditions can contribute to better policy:

Greater transparency. Businesses are encouraged to take more public-regarding positions when the policymaking process is more transparent. Transparency is encouraged by media coverage, formal business representation through such means as associations or policy councils, disclosure of political donations, and the general openness of the policymaking process.

Longer-term commitments among policymakers and businesses. Two types of business participation favor longer commitments. The first is business representation on policy councils. If business representatives and policymakers interact repeatedly in these arenas, they have incentives to develop good reputations and to honor agreements reached in the policy council. Conversely, if they know they will not meet and negotiate again, they have greater incentives to renege, and any inter-temporal commitments they make will be less credible.

Box 5.1 The Power of Business: The Case of Guatemala

The business sector plays a role in policymaking throughout Latin America, but nowhere more than in Guatemala. Its influence reflects not only the strength of the private sector, but also the relative weakness of the other institutions in the country. Guatemala's business organizations have proved to be powerful enough to alter the course of important economic policies, such as taxation (see Chapter 8).

The ability of Guatemalan business to influence the policymaking process rests on the fact that it is the best-organized sector in the country, and has been since colonial times, when power resided in the hands of large farmers and traders. The effectiveness of the Guatemalan business sector contrasts with the limitations of other organized sectors of society and of the State itself. Unions, peasant and indigenous movements, public servants, academics, and much of the rest of civil society have had limited influence throughout much of Guatemala's modern history.

The country's political parties are largely lacking in programmatic platforms and clear ideological or strategic alignments. Thus Guatemala ranked 13th of 17 countries in strength of voter affiliations with political parties (in the 2003 Latinobarometer survey) and 13th of 18 countries in perceived legitimacy of political parties (in the 2004 survey, which included the Dominican Republic). Guatemala has the lowest ranking in the overall index of party institutionalization (see Chapter 3).

Guatemala's bureaucracy and civil service have limited capabilities and are susceptible to pressure from special interests, paving the way for business groups to influence policymaking at the implementation stage (see Chapter 4).

Clearly, the business sector is the dominant player in the Guatemalan public policy arena not just because of its own strengths, but also because of the limited influence of other players.

Similarly, longstanding policy networks facilitate the exchange of information and help members develop trust. Repeated and positive interactions generate expectations that when problems or shocks arise, they will be worked out in a reasonable fashion. However, if these networks are not inclusive and transparent, they may lead to favoritism for network members, at the expense of nonmembers.

Finally, when States include business associations in policy decision making and implementation, this can encourage investments by businesspersons in building their institutional capacity, thereby promoting a more long-term and collective capacity for intermediation, which can counterbalance a tendency toward narrowly self-interested backroom deals and other private arrangements.

If the State and society can close some opportunities for narrow business involvement (such as restricting lobbying at the implementation stage and curtailing corruption) and open opportunities for encompassing action (such as encouraging publicly minded associations), the quality of policies is likely to improve.

Media[4]

Researchers usually view the media as a passive link between elite messages and mass opinion. This view fails to capture a much more complex interaction among the media, public opinion, and policymaking.

Indeed, while researchers understate the role of media, Latin American politicians and policymakers perceive a huge media influence on policymaking. This influence includes the ability of news coverage to set the policymaking agenda, accelerate the pace of decision making, change incentives for policy support, and increase the costs of narrow or self-interested behavior.

In addition to perceiving the influence of the media, politicians and policymakers take concrete steps to attempt to influence news, journalists, media outlets, and political communication. These include:

Strategic communication. This approach aims to develop and communicate a message that promotes a political goal, whether getting elected, which is most typical in Latin America, or promoting a public policy, which is less common. Strategic communication specialists use polls, focus groups, and reaction groups of opinion leaders to shape messages that target specific audiences, typically the mass media. These techniques are used not only to gather better information to guide politicians in their policy decisions, but also to find "the right language to sell already-made decisions to the public."[5] Most countries in the region have created full-time offices dedicated to conducting polls, focus groups, and other strategic marketing techniques to shape public opinion and test political messages for the media.[6]

News management. These techniques aim to enhance the uniformity, saliency, and credibility of messages about government, policy, and politicians carried by the news media. The ultimate aim of news management is not only to insert messages in news coverage, but also to influence the interpretive frames that journalists use when covering a news issue or event. The frame—for instance, whether street protest is represented as a legitimate pressure tactic or an inconvenience to motorists—shapes the sources used and questions asked by journalists in developing their news stories and also their perceptions of what information is most relevant.[7] Setting and influencing news frames is crucial for policymakers. Reformers in Brazil, for instance, were able to frame administrative reform as a way to empower State action by generating greater efficiency rather than as part of a neoliberal plot to slash unionized government jobs, as some who opposed the reform

---

[4] This section draws extensively on Hughes (2005).

[5] Bennett (2003, p. 141).

[6] Hughes (2005).

[7] Altheide (1996); Bennett (2003).

might have characterized it.[8] Politicians and officials use such techniques as staging events (or pseudo-events) that will satisfy journalists' commercial need for interesting pictures, timing statements and actions to meet news deadlines, staying "on message" to emphasize well-chosen campaign themes, and "spinning" the news to shape journalists' reports to partisan advantage.[9]

Cooptation and control. This includes cronyism and propagandist use of State media. It also includes such steps as protecting broadcasters from competition, while distributing broadcast frequencies to friends, family, or political allies, manipulating the awarding of government advertising contracts, creating media outlets that personally attack journalists, or buying off other media owners outright.

In addition, threats and violence against the press occur in several countries, including Colombia, Guatemala, and Mexico.[10] The sources of violence are diverse, at times including guerrillas, paramilitary groups, drug dealers, corrupt police, and corrupt politicians, sometimes working together. Weak government efforts to prosecute the masterminds of threats against journalists complicate the situation and do little to deter future harassment. In many countries, the press faces legal restrictions, such as libel and slander laws, which are holdovers from previous authoritarian eras and the result of politicians' desire to limit press criticism and/or investigation of potential wrongdoing. These barriers often lead journalists to practice self-censorship.

Against this backdrop, how can media's role in the policymaking process be delineated? The discussion that follows traces the influence of the news media at each stage of the policymaking process.

Media and the Policymaking Process

Policy formation (agenda-setting). In this stage, issues in need of policy attention are identified and prioritized. Media can bring to light issues that policymakers had not considered or did not view as urgent. This agenda-setting function can sometimes be powerful. In effect, politicians scan media as a form of "surrogate public agenda," especially when opinion polls are lacking.[11]

Coverage of policy-related issues or events is characterized by intense scrutiny, followed by periods of scant interest. Media attention can be diverted or channeled by a variety of factors, such as pseudo-events of news management carried out by politicians and other opinion-makers, calculated leaks, and the personal and professional interests of media owners and journalists. Scandals or "irruptive" policy issues, such as street demonstrations, are covered prominently, while technical, incremental, or chronic problems such as poverty are generally ignored, unless they can be personalized or

---

[8] Bresser-Pereira (2003).

[9] Swanson (2004).

[10] See Freedom House (2004).

[11] Pritchard (1992).

dramatized. The result of this tendency toward sensationalism and lack of profession-alism in investigating and reporting stories is to miscue policymakers, diverting their attention from more pressing problems—or focusing their attention on problems that do not warrant it.

Policy formulation. At this stage, choices are narrowed and decisions are made about the specifics of policy. Media have two main effects on policy at this juncture. First, since media tend to portray events or issues in terms of crises, media coverage prompts policymakers to act quickly and visibly and to adopt symbolic measures, rather than to develop long-term solutions. This pressure is especially strong when coverage is nega-tive, as is most policy-relevant news coverage. For instance, as inflation in Argentina spiraled upward or protests erupted, news accounts demanded that policymakers "do something"—but did not specify what should be done.

Second, media influence the formation of policies through the frames they use to structure news stories. Journalists use interpretive frames to organize news stories, even simple ones. Such frames, by focusing on some aspects as "newsworthy" and not others, confer legitimacy on certain actors, policy proposals, and views of the world. They can also effectively block certain options from entering the public consciousness.

Policymakers may make their own attempts to frame or reframe an issue. In Uru-guay, for instance, policymakers tried to frame administrative reform in ways that reso-nated with a national political culture that values the role of the State in the economy. They consequently adopted a low-key strategy in order to avoid extended debate. They also spread the reform throughout a large budget bill and decentralized its implementa-tion, in a successful attempt to avoid press scrutiny.

Policy adoption. The role of the news media during this phase depends on the vol-ume of media attention. When coverage is scant, reform can stall for lack of urgency. However, out of the public eye, policymakers have more room for bargaining—or pro-moting special interests or even rent-seeking. On the other hand, greater coverage can encourage public debate and deliberation. Monitoring by the press can raise the costs for policymakers of acting in their own interest or the interests of a favored group at the expense of public welfare. In general, the media are less interested in covering the adoption phase unless some aspect fulfills the narrative needs of news stories for drama and personalization.

The news media can influence the policy adoption process directly by acting as interest groups themselves, advocating or opposing certain policies. This is especially the case when the policies directly affect the media's business or professional interests, such as telecommunications reform or issues related to the journalism profession. In Mexico, for instance, lobbying by associations of media owners and large commercial networks has derailed attempts to open the radio and television concession process to greater competition. Conversely, major newspaper outlets in Mexico joined forces with academic specialists to write and lobby for their own version of a law granting greater access to government information.

Policy implementation. News coverage is usually sporadic at this stage. When it occurs, it tends to be focused on high-impact policies that can be fragmented into particular incidents or a few connected stories, personalized through the portrayal of villains, victims, or heroes, and dramatized in terms of conflict or moral transgression.

At times the media take on the role of watchdog. Notably, coverage of public corruption grew dramatically in Latin America after the return to democratic rule. This type of media monitoring raises the costs of transgressions and helps establish chains of accountability. Press denunciations may embolden the legislature and the courts, but even when they do not, they may inflict enough damage on a corrupt official's career to temper enthusiasm for extortion and influence-peddling.

Media-fueled scandals have been the origin of numerous presidential crises in the past decade across the region (see the discussion on social movements in this chapter). Many of these incidents unfolded against the backdrop of pressures related to economic crises and the implementation of unpopular structural adjustment policies. The eruption of governmental corruption into media scandals was a new factor in the policymaking process. Scandals brought those suffering the most as a result of economic difficulties and structural adjustment policies to the streets and emboldened opponents to try to bring down presidents and with them, their policies. In some cases, the media played a role in legitimizing and even rallying protesters.

Implications for the PMP

What implications do these media influences have for the creation of sustainable, coherent, and publicly focused policy in Latin America? Four propositions are explored below.

Sustaining or impeding cooperation. Policymakers anticipate media effects when deciding whether to maintain or withdraw their support for unpopular policies ("defect"). Negative coverage focusing on the costs of the policy, the increase in conflict, or the possibility of corruption increases the incentives for policymakers to defect from cooperative pacts because it can increase the short-term costs of cooperation. Alternatively, positive coverage focusing on policy benefits, beneficiaries, or proponents increases incentives for long-term cooperation. How policies are framed in the press in terms of costs is especially important. Whether corruption is linked directly or indirectly to unpopular policies also matters.

Making negotiations more or less inclusive. Coverage can influence the number of actors included in negotiations, the issues that must be addressed, and the balance of power among actors. Actors can gain legitimacy if the media cover them. For instance, quoting social movement leaders alongside cabinet ministers and bankers confers legitimacy on their causes, and may even extend their power beyond their bases. Even negative coverage of social movements may increase their standing among some groups, while hurting them with others. The absence of these issues and actors from press coverage weakens their position in policy negotiations because it diminishes their power to mobilize support outside their bases.

Increasing or decreasing the observability of players' moves. News coverage can expose secret actors or moves during policy negotiations and implementation, including who benefits and what their motives are. This can increase the visibility of players' moves and decrease the payoffs for secrecy. Such monitoring by the press requires assertive journalism and a diversity of media outlets, because media owners' particular interests can bias coverage. Exposure of secret moves can result from investigative journalism or from information leaked strategically by opponents during the bargaining process.

Improving or undermining policy design and enforcement. Media monitoring can promote appropriate policy enforcement design, including the designation of neutral bureaucracies to implement and enforce policy. On the other hand, irruptive demands for rapid, high-profile responses to events framed as crises can lead to merely symbolic action or poorly designed policy. In general, the press in Latin America does not pursue a type of journalism that holds policymakers accountable for their promises and monitors their performance over time. Such accountability journalism could potentially have an important positive impact on policy.

The Political Economy of the Media and Media Performance

Media performance in the policymaking process varies according to the environmental and institutional conditions in which news organizations, media owners, and journalists operate.

As the region has moved toward electoral democracies and selectively liberal economies, formerly authoritarian media systems and news organizations have developed different orientations. One is civic in outlook and oriented mostly toward serving citizens. The other views journalism as a means of serving any number of powerful actors or forces, including the market, certain State actors, or the allies of media owners.

To some degree, these orientations vary according to the type of media. In general, commercial television and radio are more prone to a market-driven version of journalism, while large daily newspapers, some niche-oriented cable news programs, and community media are more likely to follow a civic orientation.[12] The news produced on many State-run television stations on occasion resembles propaganda.

Latin Americans most use and trust information from commercial television. When asked recently which source they most trust to deliver objective news, nearly half (49 percent) chose television and only 8 percent chose newspapers.[13] Commercial television, however, is a medium more susceptible to sensationalism and distortion in the advancement of the owners' interests. This tendency is less worrisome where citizens have access to many kinds of information and where advertising dollars and media ownership are not concentrated. However, systematic access to information from cable television, the Internet, and professional newspapers is out of reach for the large majority of citizens in most countries. Commercial television and radio are by far the most accessible sources of political information and are often controlled by a handful of media groups.

---

[12] See Hughes (2005).

[13] Latinobarometer (2004).

The Future of Latin American Media

The current state of the Latin American environment for objective civic-minded news production is not the ideal. In some countries, government advertising and control of broadcasting concessions are used effectively to influence media coverage. Other factors limiting media balance in various countries include the concentration of private sector advertising and the small number of economically viable media outlets. Impunity from criminal prosecution for attacks on journalists remains high in some countries, and journalists self-censor in the face of physical threats or criminal prosecution for libel and slander.

Despite recent improvements in some countries, such as Mexico, Nicaragua and Peru, journalists in several Latin American countries work in the netherworld of a partially free media environment. According to data from Freedom House, media operate in the most problematic environments in Colombia, Guatemala and Venezuela. In contrast, Chile, Costa Rica and Uruguay have the best environments in the region for the free operation of the press.

The environment for autonomous, assertive, and diverse news production is not always favorable in Latin America, but journalism that can encourage public-focused policymaking survives where editors and reporters still have the professional autonomy and environmental space to practice it.

Labor Unions[14]

Latin American labor unions have traditionally been key participants in the policymaking process, but their influence has declined over the last two decades. As one of the few well-organized groups that could provide electoral constituencies for emerging elites following World War II, labor unions were crucial actors in the establishment of Latin American countries' postwar party systems. Their bargaining power was enhanced by import substitution industrialization policies, which protected their employers from competition and furthered the growth of employment in the manufacturing sector. The subsequent decline in the relative number of unionized voters and the effect of economic liberalization on their bargaining power has curbed the political influence of labor unions. However, labor unions still influence the policymaking process, depending on the nature of their alliances with political parties and other social actors and on their capacity for collective action in the public sector.

Labor Organization and Political Alliances

Labor unions organize to defend the interests of their members through collective action (collective bargaining, strikes), political strategies (lobbying, general strikes), and

---

[14] This section draws extensively on Murillo (2005b).

social services (cooperatives, health insurance, pensions). All of these strategies involve delegation from union members to labor leaders. These leaders organize workers' behavior in exchange for concessions to improve their lot, as well as payoffs for their representation. The payoffs to leaders can include material or policy benefits of different types. Because, historically, most governments in the region have tried to prevent workers from organizing, political strategies to obtain the right to organize and strike developed early on. In Latin America, these strategies often involved forging alliances with labor-based parties. These parties were not class-based, but included labor unions as important constituencies. The alliance with labor-based political parties in the post-Depression period provided labor unions with material benefits for workers while facilitating labor organization.

Labor influence in the policymaking process has remained dependent on political alliances and unions' bargaining power, mainly in the public sector.

The links established at that time between labor unions and political parties, such as the Argentine Peronist Party (PJ), the Brazilian Labor Party (PTB), the Mexican Institutional Revolutionary Party (PRI), the Peruvian Popular Revolutionary Alliance (APRA), and the Venezuelan Democratic Action Party (AD), structured the future loyalties of the party system and the policy preferences of the labor-based parties.[15] They also generated labor legislation with different incentives for labor organization and benefits for workers. When political parties had greater need for labor constituencies and unions were stronger, labor legislation tended to be more favorable to workers and provided incentives for labor organization—thus generating stronger ties to labor-based parties.

Moreover, the labor laws enacted usually regulated the selection of union leaders and facilitated the control of labor unions by leaders affiliated with labor-based parties.[16] Policy choices during the postwar period further increased labor influence and bargaining power. Specifically, economic strategies of import substitution industrialization and State-led development limited trade competition, perpetuated higher labor costs and transferred them to consumers, and established publicly owned management that was more interested in political considerations (including increasing the public sector labor force) than in efficiency. Labor-based political parties favored those policies, along with promoting higher levels of unionization and greater benefits for workers, so as to maintain labor support. In some of the smaller countries of the region, where on occasion labor movements had been repressed, and import substitution industrialization was less developed, labor movements were weak and often radicalized toward Left-wing political parties.

Countries that had labor-mobilizing party systems and had chosen economic strategies that favored labor experienced higher adjustment costs and deeper economic down-

---

[15] In contrast, business has usually lacked the partisan links of labor unions—even if businesspeople have partisan affiliations as individuals. Thus business associations exercise policy influence based more on their economic power and personal links, as described earlier in the chapter and by Schneider (2005).

[16] Collier and Collier (1991).

turns in the aftermath of the debt crisis that erupted in the early 1980s. This encouraged labor-based parties to change their policy preferences toward economic liberalization and State reform.[17] Yet even after labor-based parties pragmatically shifted their policy orientation from populism to more free-market-oriented policies in response to economic duress, labor unions usually continued to support their political party allies—in return for compensation of various types, including labor reforms that protected employment and regulated benefits. The labor-based identity of these parties increased their credibility in promoting the need for free-market-oriented policies. Meanwhile, labor union trust, built up through past cooperation, facilitated inter-temporal agreements between the government and the labor movement. In general, labor participated in the policymaking process by lobbying the executive directly, although sometimes labor acted through the legislature as well.[18]

Labor Organization, Preferences, and Bargaining Power

The policy preferences of labor unions are shaped by the organizational characteristics of the labor movement, as well as the patterns of competition for leadership (that is, the number of political groups competing for workers' support). The level—company, industry, or national—at which collective bargaining takes place shapes the extent to which labor tends to push for policies beneficial to all workers. Only industry-wide or economy-wide union confederations (peak organizations) with authority to negotiate at the national level can avoid the free riding of other unions, which may seek to obtain a better deal exclusively for themselves in relation to their company or industry. The presence or absence of peak central organizations influences the capacity of labor to coordinate its behavior in any inter-temporal exchange with either business or the government. The degree of unionization reflects how representative labor unions are and how well they can assess the effect of policies on their members. Finally, patterns of leadership competition affect the incentives of labor leaders, who, in entering into inter-temporal agreements on policy, also want to make sure that they will not lose their role as agents of workers. As shown in Table 5.4, unions vary across Latin American countries in regard to these features.

The structure of the labor movement is often a legacy of labor legislation, which regulates levels of collective bargaining, patterns of leadership competition, and incentives to organize peak confederations. In turn, these organizational features shape policy preferences based on the scope of their effects and the authority of confederations over their members, as well as the union leaders' incentives for entering into inter-temporal agreements.

For instance, labor preferences for encompassing policies whose benefits accrue to all workers, such as macroeconomic stability, are more likely if a centralized confederation can impose the cost of wage restraint on all workers, and thus prevent wage drift within the most competitive sectors. In Mexico, for example, although the Mexican Workers'

---

[17] Roberts (2002).

[18] See Etchemendy and Palermo (1998).

Table 5.4 Union Structure

Country	Unions as a percentage of the economically active population	Dominant level of unionization	Number of peak confederations	Leadership competition[a]
Argentina	36.1	Industry	Single	No[b]
Brazil	29.0	Local	Multiple	Yes
Chile	10.2	Firm	Single	Yes
Colombia	9.3	Firm/craft	Multiple	Yes
Mexico	13.5	Industry/local	Dominant	No
Peru	13.5	Firm	Multiple	Yes
Uruguay	20.9	Industry	Single	No
Venezuela	19.3	Local/industry	Dominant	Yes

[a] The competition takes place among labor leaders associated with different political parties.
[b] There has been some increasing competition since 1996, with the official recognition of a second central confederation of workers.

Sources: McGuire (1997) and authors' calculations.

Confederation (CTM) is not the only peak organization, it is the most important. It has strong authority with respect to leadership selection and collective bargaining over its member organizations, which are individual unions across all sectors. As a result, during the 1980s, it was easier to negotiate price caps in Mexico than in Argentina, where the General Confederation of Labor (CGT) has no authority over members and industrial collective bargaining facilitated free riding at the expense of other industries.

Partisan links between the governing PRI and the CTM in Mexico were also instrumental in allowing inter-temporal agreements surrounding wage caps (labor unions had to restrain the growth of wages to achieve lower inflation in the future). By contrast, in Brazil, efforts to reach wage agreements failed during the 1980s, in part because the different confederations could not coordinate the behavior of their members, but also because the main confederation was affiliated with an opposition party, which increased its incentives to defect from any agreement that might have been reached.

Partisan links do not necessarily guarantee inter-temporal agreements if labor unions face competition for leadership. In Venezuela, although the dominant confederation was allied with the governing *Acción Democrática* during the 1990s, leadership competition among Left-wing parties within the Venezuelan Workers' Confederation (CTV) led *Acción Democrática* labor leaders to oppose President Carlos Andrés Pérez's stabilization policies in 1989–91, for fear of appearing to be selling out to an ally in power. Thus in defining labor's policy preferences, it is important to analyze not only labor's links with political parties, but also its ability to deliver on promises and its incentives to enter into inter-temporal agreements.

Policy Reform and Labor Influence

As noted, the policy influence of Latin American labor unions has declined as the policy preferences of labor-based parties have shifted and the number of unionized voters has declined. Economic liberalization has reduced employment in the highly unionized protected sectors while increasing exposure to international trade. This has undermined labor's bargaining power. The reduction of State payrolls, and especially privatization, have eroded employment in the highly unionized public sector, while making firm managers more concerned about the impact of labor costs on profitability and competitiveness.[19] Finally, a large informal sector (as well as unemployment) has further reduced the pool of unionized workers. This has eroded the importance of formal workers as electoral constituencies and reduced their political influence.[20]

In a context of declining membership and power, labor unions have invested their dwindling resources in fighting certain kinds of reforms: those characterized by both a broad scope and intense costs for their members. Table 5.5 presents a classification of policy reforms in terms of their scope and intensity. The *scope of policies* depends on what proportion of union members are subjected to the costs of the reform. While labor law reform affects all union members, for instance, privatization of the telecommunication company generates costs only for telephone workers who may lose their jobs or be exposed to more competition. The *intensity of policy costs* depends on how large the relative stake of union members is or how deep the effects of each policy change are. If the effect is concentrated on members, the intensity of the policy cost is high. This would be the case if members faced the risk of job loss—either because of a broad policy, such as labor reform, or a narrow policy, such as telecom privatization. By contrast, if the effect is diffused, members bear a more limited cost, and thus the intensity is low. This could be true with respect to a narrow policy, such as sectoral regulation of public utilities, or a broad policy that affects all sectors of the economy, such as tax reform.

In a context of declining political influence, labor unions are more likely to invest their resources in resisting the adoption of policies of broad scope that have intense effects on their members (the shaded portion of Table 5.5). Labor unions are more likely, for example, to invest their resources in resisting labor law reform, which is a policy of broad scope (affecting all union members) and high intensity (affecting workers' job security, compensation, and so on).

The success of labor unions in influencing the policymaking process is also dependent on how costly it is for governments to make concessions in each policy area, which groups benefit from each reform, and how important those groups are to the government. Consider the case of labor law reform. The cost of not reforming labor legisla-

---

[19] Public sector employment as a share of urban employment declined by one-third in Argentina, Honduras, Panama, and Peru and by one-fifth in Costa Rica and Ecuador from the late 1980s to the late 1990s (ILO 1999).

[20] The level of open unemployment reached double digits in Argentina, Colombia, Panama, Uruguay, and Venezuela by 1998. The informal sector accounted for as much as 59 percent of urban employment in Ecuador in 1998 (ILO 1999).

Table 5.5 Reforms Classified According to Their Effects on Labor Unions

		Scope	
Effects		Broad	Narrow
Intensity of costs	**High**	Labor law	Privatization Social sector reform
	Low	Tax reform	Deregulation of a particular sector

Note: Shaded portion indicates more intense effect on labor unions.

Source: Murillo (2005b).

tion mainly falls on employers (and perhaps unemployed workers, who lack political representation). By contrast, the cost of not privatizing may be spread to all taxpayers, through the fiscal deficit, and to most consumers, if it involves service delivery. Governments are thus more likely to yield to labor demands with respect to labor reform than with respect to privatization. This makes investments of labor's political efforts more worthwhile in relation to labor law reform.[21] Thus labor movements are more likely to unite in resisting labor policy reform than privatization—even though both entail costs that are concentrated among some labor constituencies.

In fact, labor reforms have lagged behind other market reforms in the region, and those that have occurred have been modest. Further evidence of this effect is provided by a comparison of reforms to individual labor laws and collective labor legislation from 1985 to 2000, when market reforms were sweeping the region. Individual labor laws regulate work conditions, such as the work schedule, compensation, and termination, whereas collective labor legislation deals with the rights pertaining to labor organizations, such as unionization, collective bargaining, and the right to strike. In the 1985–2000 period, 10 of 16 individual labor reforms in Latin America tended to reduce the scope of regulations (deregulatory), whereas 13 of 18 modifications to collective labor law were regulatory in orientation.[22] Thus, while individual labor laws tended to be relaxed (thereby hurting union members), collective labor laws were reformed so as to enhance the rights of labor to organize. This difference in the orientation of labor reform reflects the fact that while collective labor law affects only unionized workers, individual labor legislation covers all workers in the formal sector: that is, it also covers potential members. Thus the labor movement's greater capacity for collective action with respect to collective labor law allows it to be more successful in achieving a favorable reform outcome.

The success of labor in achieving pro-labor reforms highlights the mechanisms through which it can exert an influence on the policymaking process. Labor-based gov-

---

[21] Murillo and Schrank (2005).

[22] Murillo (2005a); Murillo and Schrank (2005).

erning parties that are implementing market-oriented economic reforms have advanced regulatory-oriented labor reforms (favored by labor) in return for labor support on economic policy reforms. Exchanges of this type played a role in the regulatory reforms to collective labor laws, as well as in the exceptions to the deregulatory trend in individual labor law. These exchanges occurred mostly in countries with strong labor movements, which had developed mainly during the period of import substitution industrialization.[23]

Meanwhile, labor has allied itself not only with traditional partners—labor-based parties—but with new partners: transnational actors such as consumers in the United States and other countries that are concerned about fair labor practices and can demand trade sanctions against countries that limit labor rights.

Labor movement alliances with transnational labor advocates explain the success of regulatory-oriented reform of collective labor laws in countries where labor movements have been weak and have had no strong domestic allies, a combination that tends to occur in countries in which import substitution industrialization never became established.[24]

Labor influence on policies of high-intensity effects with more limited scope, such as privatization or social service reform, is based on long-term labor political alliances or short-term coalitions with groups of domestic consumers. Because labor-based parties have more credibility in promoting the need for such policies, labor unions can accept these policies in return for concessions to compensate union members and their leaders. For instance, in Argentina, Peronist labor unions accepted President Menem's privatizations in return for an allocation of shares of the privatized companies to workers and labor union acquisitions of privatized assets. In Mexico, the teachers' union took advantage of its relationship with the government to push for the creation of a comprehensive set of salary and career benefits for teachers in return for accepting the decentralization of education. Also in Mexico, telecom workers obtained subsidized participation in the sale of the State telecommunications company, Telmex, in return for their support of privatization.[25] By contrast, when Uruguayan governments, which lacked links with the labor movement, tried to privatize the State telecommunications company, labor unions allied with consumers and the main opposition party to prevent the implementation of the reform—which was overturned by congress in the face of certain citizen rejection in a referendum (see Chapter 9 on privatization and regulation of public services). In El Salvador, consumers were not included in the coalition against privatization, and labor resistance was not effective.

In addition to partisan links, labor can also exercise policy influence based on its ability to protest or disrupt labor relations. This power is strongest in relation to public services, which are not exposed to international economic competition and in which employers are subject to the public pressures of consumers as voters. As a result, since

---

[23] Murillo (2005a).

[24] Murillo and Schrank (2005).

[25] Murillo (1999).

the 1990s, public sector workers have increased their bargaining power relative to private sector workers and public sector unions have become more militant. Moreover, through their lack of cooperation (or even outright resistance), public sector workers can prevent public service reforms from being implemented effectively, even if they cannot prevent those reforms from being adopted. An example of this is the case of the failed attempt to privatize the Costa Rican Electricity Institute (ICE). Although the bill authorizing the privatization of the ICE passed congress (by an overwhelming majority) in early 2000, massive opposition to the privatization from a broad coalition of social groups mobilized by the unions led the government to withdraw the legislation shortly afterward, before it could be implemented. A new legislative commission, with substantial representation from those who would be affected by the ICE privatization, was instead formed to study the issue further.

In many cases, public sector protests are defensive strategies to protest arrears in the payment of wages or declining wages, rather than efforts to influence the policymaking process. Thus it is important to differentiate defensive strategies, which are more likely to involve militancy, from influence in the PMP, which often does not require more than the threat of protest actions. But unions have not always adopted an adversarial stance towards reform. The modernization of public employment in Chile has been a joint effort of the government and ANEF (*Agrupación Nacional de Empleados Fiscales*), which signed an agreement on new working conditions that was later enacted into law.

The Future Influence of Unions

Labor influence in the PMP has remained dependent on political alliances and unions' bargaining power, mainly in the public sector. Labor political alliances have moved beyond the corporatist ones of the postwar era as new labor-based parties emerged in Brazil (the Workers' Party), Mexico (the Party of the Democratic Revolution, PRD), Uruguay (the Broad Front), and Venezuela (*Causa R*), among others. Yet only in one country did the labor movement achieve its preferred policies: Venezuela, where the pro-Chávez National Workers' Union (UNT) established strong links to the government. In the other cases, labor-based parties have not delivered the preferred policies of labor unions because of fiscal constraints and the political weight of other constituencies. In a context of dwindling resources, labor unions are concentrating their policy influence on labor legislation and other policies of broad scope but with concentrated costs for their members. In doing so, they are continuing to use alliances with political parties, and forging new coalitions with domestic and transnational consumers. Unions have proved less able to engage the growing number of informal workers or the unemployed.

In the public sector, where strikes can disrupt not only the reform process but also the daily operation of crucial services for the population, labor strikes still seem effective—although they are often limited by pressures for fiscal restraint. Because public sector managers are political appointees and these sectors are not exposed to trade competition, it is likely that such areas will remain open to policy influence by labor unions. As reflected in a 2002 survey for the United Nations Development Programme, Latin American leaders concur with these conclusions. In general, they perceive labor unions as a potentially powerful actor, but with more of a veto than a proactive power, and with influence centered on labor issues. At the same time, they recognize the increasing influence of public sector unions relative to private sector unions.[26]

In sum, labor unions exercise less influence in the PMP than in the past, but they still influence it, especially if labor-based parties are in government, if they are organizing public sector workers, and if they are able to forge broader alliances with consumers or transnational allies, such as consumers in the United States.

Social Movements

The past decade has witnessed a dramatic increase in the power of social movements in Latin America, significant not only in terms of their number but also in terms of its political impact. Democracy has made possible a broad exercise of rights and freedoms of expression, assembly, and demonstration. Drawing on these rights and freedoms, social protest has turned into a powerful political instrument, which in some cases has reached a sufficient scale and intensity to lead to the forced resignations or removal of presidents (see Table 5.6).

Social movements have become complex and influential political actors.

Traditional perspectives viewed social movements as emerging from behaviors that deviate from the norm, essentially a result of processes of social atomization, alienation, and frustration. However, a different perspective has gained ground that suggests that these movements are composed of individuals who are rational, socially active, and well integrated into the community, but who seek to assert their interests through channels other than those offered by established institutions. Given the generally peaceful and self-managed nature of these movements and the support they receive from the media, which help to publicize, legitimate, and amplify them, social movements have become complex and influential political actors. Social demonstrations may on occasion become an instrument for effective action by political actors who are well established within the traditional political system.

Explaining the Rise of Street Power

What factors explain the spread of this phenomenon and its powerful impact on the political processes of the region? Three different crises of the political system can be linked to the rise of street power. These crises can be described as the "weakness of the State," the "weakness of representative democracy," and the "weakness of the nation."

Weakness of the State. The first crisis is linked to the weakening of the State, both with respect to maintaining the income of the sectors that traditionally have supported it (organized labor, agricultural landowners, and the urban middle class), and with respect to providing adequate services for the most disadvantaged sectors of the population, which

---

[26] UNDP (2005).

Table 5.6 Civil Demonstrations That Played a Significant Role in the Deposing of a President

Country	President	Date of deposition	Crisis factors
Argentina	De la Rúa	December 21, 2001	• Widespread dissatisfaction with socioeconomic performance and with the political class • Collapse of the economy • Cases of corruption
Bolivia	Sánchez de Lozada	October 17, 2003	• Widespread discontent due to socioeconomic situation • Demands of indigenous peoples • Exportation of natural gas
Bolivia	Mesa	June 6, 2005	• Lack of sufficient social support and political backing • Demands for nationalization of natural resources and a greater State role in the economy; better representation of indigenous communities; and regional autonomy
Brazil	Collor de Mello	December 29, 1992	• Economic crisis, including hyperinflation • Human rights violations • Corruption, personal scandals
Ecuador	Bucaram	February 6, 1997	• Corruption, patronage, nepotism • Institutional disorder • Attempt to privatize major State enterprises • Elimination of public services subsidies
Ecuador	Mahuad	January 21, 2000	• Economic crisis • Loss of confidence in the banking system (freezing of savings) • Dollarization of economy
Ecuador	Gutiérrez	April 20, 2005	• Partisan struggle for control over Supreme Court and unconstitutional dismissal of judges • Struggle for governability in the context of a highly fragmented and regionalized party and political system • Deep disenchantment with congress and political system • Loss of support of armed forces

(continued on next page)

Table 5.6 Civil Demonstrations That Played a Significant Role in the Deposing of a President (continued)

Country	President	Date of deposition	Crisis factors
Guatemala	Serrano Elías	June 1, 1993	• The *Serranazo* (attempted "self-coup" by Serrano) • Suspension of the constitution • Dissolution of congress, Supreme Court, and Constitutional Court
Paraguay	Cubas	March 23, 1999	• Amnesty of General Oviedo • Congress, the attorney general's office, and the Supreme Court declare pardon unconstitutional • Assassination of Vice President Argaña
Peru	Fujimori	November 19, 2000	• Authoritarian practices/concentration of power • Electoral fraud • Large-scale political corruption
Venezuela	Pérez Rodríguez	May 20, 1993	• The *Caracazo* uprising: popular revolts violently repressed • Broad disenchantment with traditional political parties and the political system • Economic crisis and austerity measures • Social programs abandoned • Two attempted coups d'état: February 3, 1992, and November 27, 1992 • Allegations of corruption

Source: Authors' compilation.

have obtained new political power as a result of democratization. On the one hand, fiscal austerity measures and the end of the old monopolies are breaking up the old corporatist and patronage State, eliminating privileges, and terminating old social alliances. On the other hand, the expectations generated by democracy have been frustrated by the need to deal with unfavorable economic circumstances. A weak State unable to fulfill the expectations for improvement generated by democracy is one of the sources of discontent and social mobilization.

In Argentina the resignation of President Fernando De la Rúa was related to this first type of crisis. It resulted from a series of corruption scandals, a protracted economic recession followed by economic collapse, and deep disenchantment with politicians, reflected in the rallying cry of protesters, *"¡Que se vayan todos!"* ("Let's get rid of them all!"). The Argentine crisis gave rise to a broad spectrum of social movements, from *los piqueteros* ("picketers")—a social protest movement formed by disadvantaged but heterogeneous sectors susceptible to political manipulation—to powerful multipurpose social organizations created to make up for the inability of public institutions to respond to social needs. It must be pointed out that these movements have failed to institutionalize an approach to representation that could replace the traditional institutions of democracy, such as political parties.

Weakness of democracy. The practice of democracy in the region has generally failed to produce significant progress in satisfying unmet social needs and in creating governments that are transparent, free from corruption, and free from capture by special interests. Moreover, the greater exposure of democratic governments to the scrutiny of public opinion has tended to exaggerate their transgressions in comparison with those of authoritarian regimes, which protected themselves from criticism using repressive means. Underlying weaknesses in democratic processes have failed to prevent authoritarian practices, patronage, populism, corruption, and the capture of public institutions and policies by special interests. This failure of democratic processes has also had repercussions with respect to the fulfillment of key State missions, such as the delivery of efficient services and the promotion of development. Public policies are perceived as having failed to incorporate and respond to the needs and demands of all the citizens, resulting in vast sectors of the population being excluded from the benefits of growth. Traditional political parties and parties in general have become a principal casualty in this loss of confidence in democratic processes, further deepening the crisis of representative institutions.

The protests that erupted in relation to the electoral fraud and corruption committed by the government of President Alberto Fujimori in Peru can be associated with this type of crisis. The demonstrations that culminated in the deposing of Presidents Fernando Collor de Mello in Brazil, Raúl Cubas in Paraguay, and Jorge Antonio Serrano in Guatemala are also largely attributable to factors related to the deficiencies of democratic processes. The fall of President Carlos Andrés Pérez and the subsequent collapse of the traditional party system in Venezuela can be attributed to a mix of the factors at play in the two crisis dimensions: street reaction to the prolonged failure of the State to deliver improvements in living standards (and the costly adjustment measures adopted by the government), and the perception of widespread corruption in the political class.

Weakness of the nation. A third crisis is the absence of a shared sense of nationhood. To generate a feeling of national identity, the State needs to be capable of producing a vision for a shared future from which a community of citizens with obligations and rights can be created. The systemic failures related to the other two types of crises compound the difficulties of dealing with this third type of crisis. When it is perceived that benefits are concentrated in a minority while sacrifices are always being asked of the same groups—which are precisely the major groups that are absent from decision making processes—it is very difficult to facilitate the emergence of a sense of belonging to the same political community. In this context it is typical for movements to appear that create parallel identities that have distinct visions of the nation. This type of crisis is the hardest to resolve, since it entails fundamental conflicts about the practical definition of rights and responsibilities of different groups of citizens, as well as how to structure the State in territorial terms to best incorporate the divergent interests of these groups.

Bolivia and Ecuador share elements of this third type of crisis. The ongoing deficiencies in governmental performance with respect to the promotion of equitable development and to the representativeness of their democratic processes are compounded by conflicts over nationhood, reflected in the mobilization of indigenous communities for greater voice in the system and in demands for greater autonomy from different regions of the country. In Bolivia and Ecuador, these crises have resulted in the resignation of several presidents, and the political landscape remains unstable.

Social movements are rooted in *structural* factors and *circumstantial* factors. Circumstantial factors, such as an increase in tariffs on fuel or a proposal to privatize a State enterprise, can launch a wave of social protest. Behind these circumstantial factors are usually hidden structural factors, such as long-term economic stagnation, widespread poverty, a lack of employment opportunities, or political corruption. These structural factors explain the deeper discontent of citizens. Thus the new social movements at times are quiescent, but have the potential to become active when they are triggered by particular events. These events become catalysts with which social leaders can mobilize the population to take to the streets.

Types of Social Movements

Social movements can be classified along two dimensions, as depicted in Figure 5.1. The first dimension, shown on the horizontal axis, represents the relative generality or specificity of the issue underlying the social movement, and thus the breadth of the population mobilized. Along this dimension, the demands of specific sectors or regional or ethnic identities are classified toward the "specific" end of the continuum. The second dimension, shown on the vertical axis, represents the degree to which the social movement seeks to change public policy constructively in a given direction ("proactive") or merely to veto government proposals or express dissatisfaction with public officials ("reactive").

Some cases are difficult to categorize according to these dimensions and are placed between the two extremes. For example, while it may be said that the *Arequipazo* uprising in Peru against President Alejandro Toledo in June 2002 (discussed further in Chapter 9) emerged in relation to a particular cause, in one region (Arequipa), and from a very specific issue—the privatization of the *Egasa* and *Egesur* electric companies—it immediately resonated at the national level.

Similarly, the social reaction to the governmental attempt to privatize the energy and telecommunications markets in Costa Rica falls into this category of a movement that arose from a fairly specific cause but ended up having broader objectives and impact. The effort to privatize the Costa Rican Electricity Institute (ICE) generated demonstrations for three weeks in March and April 2000, during the presidency of Miguel Ángel Rodríguez, which led to an important decline in his popularity. The first opponents were the ICE's own employees and environmental groups. But the enactment by congress of the bill privatizing ICE triggered massive protests that received broad social support.

FIGURE 5.1   **Classification of Social Movements**

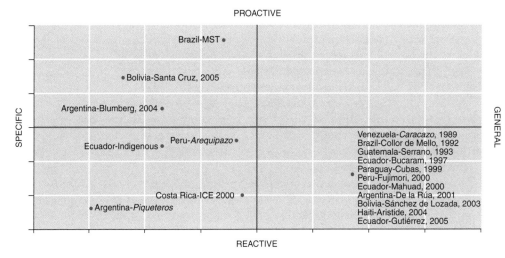

PROACTIVE

SPECIFIC — GENERAL

Brazil-MST ●

● Bolivia-Santa Cruz, 2005

Argentina-Blumberg, 2004 ●

Ecuador-Indigenous ●   Peru-*Arequipazo* ●

Venezuela-*Caracazo*, 1989
Brazil-Collor de Mello, 1992
Guatemala-Serrano, 1993
Ecuador-Bucaram, 1997
Paraguay-Cubas, 1999
● Peru-Fujimori, 2000
Ecuador-Mahuad, 2000
Argentina-De la Rúa, 2001
Bolivia-Sánchez de Lozada, 2003
Haiti-Aristide, 2004
Ecuador-Gutiérrez, 2005

Costa Rica-ICE 2000 ●

● Argentina-*Piqueteros*

REACTIVE

Source: Authors' compilation.

An example of a specific movement, but one with a more positive focus, is the Landless Peasant Movement (MST) in Brazil. This movement defines its purpose as fighting for land and for agrarian reform in Brazil. More than just a protest movement, the MST has built an entire organizational network through which it offers housing; medical and learning centers; cooperatives for credit, production, distribution, and consumption; and opportunities for improving productivity—all of which confers upon it a legitimacy that goes beyond what is normally expected for an opposition movement.

One of the most striking features of Figure 5.1 is the absence of cases with both "proactive" and "generalist" characteristics (the upper right-hand quadrant of the figure). There have been few demonstrations in the region that have mobilized a broad cross-section of the population that have also been capable of articulating constructive proposals. All the movements that resulted in the deposing of a president share the characteristics of being massive (general) civil demonstrations, while being essentially negative—in the sense that they clearly articulated opposition to something or someone, but did not advocate a constructive alternative.

The Role of Social Movements in Policymaking and Their Effects on Democratic Governance

Social movements in each of the quadrants in Figure 5.1 can have a different effect on the policymaking process. Social movements organized around specific demands tend to play a role as agenda-setters, if they are constructive, or merely as veto players, if they are not. The agenda-setting role is illustrated by the Blumberg case in Argentina. In April 2004, President Néstor Kirchner faced numerous demonstrations by citizens clamoring for greater security and a strengthening of anti-crime laws. The movement, started by Juan Carlos Blumberg, whose child had been kidnapped and later murdered, protested against rising insecurity and crime, mainly in the province of Buenos Aires. The protests induced the government to incorporate the fight against crime into the political agenda and led to the adoption in record time of several reforms to the criminal code.

By contrast, unstructured and spontaneous mass movements tend to become a general destabilizing factor in the policymaking process, with consequences for policies that are not always foreseeable. Most of the time, they bring about policy instability, as new governments attempt to distance themselves from the policies that brought down the previous governments. In countries in which such movements occur repeatedly, they contribute to imparting a short-term focus to other political actors, and may discourage investments in policy capabilities.

The increasing prominence and impact of social movements raises an important question: are they good or bad for democratic governance? The answer is not straightforward. On the positive side, it can be argued that a participatory and organized civil society (of which organized social movements are an example) can be an important component of an efficiently operating representative government. These movements have resulted in the incorporation into the political system of new actors that previously had played only a marginal role, thus enhancing the inclusiveness of the democratic system.

On the negative side, these movements are often subject to manipulation by established political actors or emerging leaders, as well as by special interests. Many of the cases analyzed above had an element of manipulation, in the sense that the movements have at some point been co-opted by other actors in pursuit of their own objectives (such as mounting powerful opposition to the government and eroding its authority). In addition, social mobilization clearly becomes a problem if the resort to mass protest becomes a structural device rather than a circumstantial mechanism for engaging in politics, and if traditional democratic institutions become incapable of supporting legitimate and effective governance. In this case, the effect is more likely to be chronic political instability than enhanced citizen participation.

The adoption of direct democracy instruments, such as referenda, popular initiatives, and recall petitions, can potentially facilitate social participation, while avoiding the instability that can result from persistent demonstrations and social unrest. Such mechanisms can help clarify the positions held by citizens and deflate protests by building legitimacy for a given course of action. The referendum on natural gas held in Bolivia during the presidency of Carlos Mesa was an attempt to contain popular pressure and to seek an effective decision making channel. Likewise, participatory budgets try to bring decisions on the use of certain resources closer to the beneficiaries. Some have argued that giving citizens a direct hand in the process of drafting public policies through consultative processes can strengthen democratic governance by legitimizing the decisions made. This logic underlies the referenda held in Uruguay to consult public opinion on decisions regarding the privatization of public enterprises.

Nevertheless, mechanisms of direct democracy can weaken representative democracy, in which political parties and public authorities, as social representatives, must articulate and aggregate societal interests. A referendum on a single issue can lead to the veto of critical elements of the general program of an elected and legitimate government, thus compromising its room for maneuver. This is what happened with the privatization referenda in Uruguay. Moreover, it is debatable whether in highly complex cases and in acute crises, these mechanisms are sufficient to contain protests and social unrest, as illustrated by the referendum in Bolivia, which failed to stop the protests that had prompted it.

Knowledge Actors[27]

The quality and thus the effectiveness of public policies depend in part on the extent to which technical policy expertise is included in the policymaking process. Various technical experts, or knowledge actors, can improve the quality of public policy debates, introduce policy alternatives, help set the policy agenda, and monitor and strengthen implementation by improving the knowledge base upon which other actors may serve. These knowledge actors serve as intermediaries or brokers between knowledge and policy.

Integrating technical rationality with policy rationality can help policymaking proceed in a more open and balanced way.

In most democratic countries, most of the mediation between knowledge and policymaking takes place in public bureaucracies, which are the main site of specialized knowledge because of their permanent professional structures.

In most Latin American countries, however, the bureaucracy is limited in its development as a stable professional structure. This has led to a historical weakness in the institutionalization of knowledge. In recent years, this weakness has been redressed in part by the strengthening of some of the fiscal bureaucracies (central banks, regulatory and audit agencies, and ministries of economy). At the same time, in some countries the relevance and functions of central planning and analysis units, such as advisory offices, ministries, or planning departments, which played an important role in the past, have been downgraded.

Meanwhile, other actors have emerged, partly because of the increasing specialization of knowledge and partly because of the difficulties of adapting the bureaucracy to the dynamic nature of events in the region. The discussion that follows briefly examines other knowledge actors that play an important role in the public policymaking process.

Emerging Knowledge Actors

Legislative advisory offices. Some countries have developed technical capacity in the legislature. As discussed in Chapter 3, a congress with good technical capacities in the policymaking process is an important factor in shaping the key features of public policies.

---

[27] This section draws extensively on Santiso and Whitehead (2005).

In Brazil, advisory offices in the upper and lower houses of congress have about 500 professional staff members altogether. These offices have been recognized as a key factor in ensuring that the political agreements and transactions that take place in congressional negotiations are not achieved at the cost of the technical quality of the laws. Moreover, there is evidence that with the support provided by these offices, the political debate has become more rigorous, the dialogue between the executive and legislative branches has become more sophisticated and demanding, and media coverage of the debates has focused more on the technical aspects of the laws.[28]

Institutes linked to political parties. Political parties are responsible for formulating policy programs consistent with the principles that they uphold and the interests of their electoral constituency. As parties build up their technical capacities, they can gain a better basis for a more solid and consistent programmatic platform.

Despite the democratization process in the region and the progressive increase in the accountability of public officials, few parties have built up these capacities extensively. This has impeded the emergence of a party system with the capacity to offer voters something more than particularistic incentives or unrealistic promises of improvement in policy outcomes.

The exception is Chile, where the opposition parties and the government have political think tanks to support their policymaking processes. The role of these think tanks was tested in the corruption crisis of 2003, because the specialists who devised the reforms came mostly from the party institutes.

International organizations. Various international nonfinancial and financial organizations operate in Latin America and the Caribbean and provide technical assistance. They serve as important knowledge mediators, transferring the experience that they have gained in other countries to the region. The nonfinancial organizations, such as the United Nations agencies—particularly the United Nations Development Programme (UNDP) and the Economic Commission for Latin America and the Caribbean (ECLAC)—provide technical assistance and capacity for policy analysis, diagnosis, and dialogue from a national or regional perspective. The financial organizations—the International Monetary Fund (IMF), the World Bank, the Inter-American Development Bank (IDB), and the Andean Development Corporation (CAF), among others—contribute to the stabilization and development of the countries by financing projects and programs. Such financing is increasingly accompanied by technical assistance, not only in the phase of preparing operations but also in the diagnosis of needs and the identification of policy alternatives.

This makes the financial organizations, especially in the countries that depend most on their financing, important actors in the policymaking process. First, they support macroeconomic stability, providing incentives for coherent policies with basic requirements of economic rationality. Second, through their work in the preparation of strategies and projects, they transfer the experience that they have amassed in public policymaking to the countries of the region.

---

[28] Alston and others (2005a).

Analysis and research centers (think tanks). Research centers involved in policymaking, also known as think tanks, play a very important role in some countries in the region. There are many such organizations, although they differ considerably from country to country. Argentina, Brazil, Chile, and Colombia have many think tanks, while in other countries they are less developed. FIEL and *Fundación Mediterránea* (Argentina), TENDEN-CIAS (Brazil), CIEPLAN (Chile), FEDESARROLLO (Colombia), FUSADES (El Salvador), CIEN and ASIES (Guatemala), and CERES and CINVE (Uruguay) are among the most significant examples in the area of economic policymaking. In some cases, such as *Grupo APOYO* in Peru, these institutes are more of a consulting firm than a think tank, although this distinction is not always clear. In other cases, such as INCAE in Costa Rica, they are more akin to universities, but with a greater orientation toward public policymaking.

Such think tanks are characterized by important financial and technical capacities, although they may not be as advanced as their counterparts in countries such as the United States and Germany, where donors (such as foundations) contribute generously to their financing, permitting greater independence from the government and more autonomy in their work agenda. In Latin America the relative lack of financial independence means that think tanks are sometimes obliged to act as paid consultants, in many cases for the government. This tends to orient them more to justifying official policies than to providing a rigorous technical analysis of problems and alternatives.

Nongovernmental organizations with research units. Some NGOs have developed their own research capacities in connection with issues with which they are concerned. They produce research studies to promote awareness of issues or propose reforms consistent with their ideas. An example is the network of organizations in the region affiliated with Transparency International. Some have carried out specific studies to analyze cases of corruption. Others, such as Transparency Colombia, have prepared indices for evaluating the transparency of governmental agencies. Still others, like Citizen Power in Argentina, have concentrated their efforts on legal reforms to promote governmental transparency.

The strength of these actors depends on their capacity to influence the policymaking process with their ideas and proposals. A very important factor is the follow-up and support they stimulate in public opinion through the media. Because of their activist nature, they are important in influencing the policy agenda, especially when a window of opportunity creates a favorable climate for their ideas (such as in the case of legislative initiatives against corruption), or when they can use their capacity for mobilization to block a decision or initiative that contradicts their ideas.

Research units of companies and corporations. Large companies and corporations contribute to the production and diffusion of knowledge through their research units and centers. In the sphere of economic knowledge, the teams of analysts of the large banks are particularly important. The major Spain-based banks have the largest teams focusing on Latin America, with about 100 analysts each.

With these services, the financial entities provide information, analysis, and very often, advice. Through their presence in the media, their interactions with government officials, and their analyses, they are constantly influencing the policy agenda, based on their business interests. Prominent executives, directors, and economists from these entities also serve in the public sector, formally or informally, and bring their experience and knowledge with them.

The extent to which the different types of knowledge actors are present and active in seven countries of the region is shown in Table 5.7. The presence of these actors varies considerably across countries. In particular, there is a serious imbalance between the presence of actors that operate within political institutions, such as political party institutes and legislative advisory units, and those that operate outside public institutions, such as think tanks and NGOs. Only in Brazil and Chile is there something approaching a balance.

The Role of Knowledge in a Representative Democracy

The institutionalization of knowledge in the policymaking process in a democracy is not easy. There is an implicit tension between two different types of approaches to policy-making. To simplify, these can be called technical rationality and political rationality. Technical rationality emphasizes the use of scientific methods of analysis to choose policies that are optimal from the standpoint of some aspect(s) of the outcomes they are expected to produce. Political rationality emphasizes the ideological content of policies and the effect that given policy choices will have on political support for the government and governing party.

A political system focuses on one or the other to its detriment. When decisions are made solely according to political considerations, there is a risk that public policies will not best address the needs of citizens. The cost can be the sacrifice of the long term for the short term, exaggerated dependence on public opinion, and disproportionate attention to the sectors of the population that have the most power or are best represented in the political process.

On the other hand, strict reliance on technical rationality presents its own problems. In quite a few countries in the 1990s, for instance, key policymaking responsibilities, particularly for economic policy, were transferred during a period of adjustment and structural reform to a core group of technocrats. This delegation of decision making to technocrats has led to some difficulties. The low degree of legitimacy of policies adopted in this fashion has compromised their sustainability and limited the possibility of expanding the reform process to new areas, in some cases. The aftermaths of the presidencies of Carlos Menem in Argentina and of Alberto Fujimori in Peru underscore the potential costs of this approach. Similarly, the discrediting of privatization in the eyes of the public, despite the empirical evidence of its positive results, is another example of costs associated with failing to build a political consensus in support of reforms.

What is needed in an effective and democratic policymaking process is not an exclusive emphasis on one type of knowledge or the other, but a combination of both. Such a combination can provide different and necessary perspectives, and promote different combinations of incentives and preferences.

However, linking these two types of logic in the policymaking process in a democratic system is not simple. Achieving this link requires a high degree of institutional maturity. Until recently in Latin America, the executive tended to delegate its decision making capacity to independent technocrats, either under autocratic regimes, which

Table 5.7 Presence of Knowledge Actors in a Sample of Countries

Actors	Argentina	Brazil	Chile	Colombia	Mexico	Peru	Venezuela
Political analysis evaluation units	Absent	Stable	Stable	Some	Weak	Absent	Absent
Legislative support offices	Absent	Stable	Some	Absent	Absent	Absent	Absent
Institutions of political parties	Weak	Weak	Stable	Absent	Absent	Absent	Absent
Think tanks	Some	Some	Some	Some	Some	Weak	Weak
NGOs	Stable	Stable	Stable	Some	Some	Some	Some

Note: Absent: Absent or almost non-existent
Weak: Small number and low or poor technical capacity
Some: Some well-established capacity
Stable: Well-established and stable capacity

Source: Santiso and Whitehead (2005).

removed most decisions from the realm of public discussion, or under highly presidentialist regimes, which shielded the technocrats from the political game, offering them isolation and protection. This approach not only risks marginalizing other technical perspectives, but it also fails to legitimize policies among the broader public—which in a democratic system makes them difficult to sustain.

In recent years, some countries have continued to keep the spheres of technical and political knowledge separate. At the same time, a new pattern has emerged, in which actors with policy expertise ("knowledge actors") are integrating themselves into the political process.

Thus the decision making process is becoming more inclusive. The role of knowledge is also being expanded and extended, as it is being democratized: taken out of the corridors of the bureaucracy or the meeting rooms of international experts and exposed to public opinion.

An illustration of the constructive linkage between technical and political approaches to policymaking can be found in Brazil in the progressive change in relations between the executive and legislative branches, based on the development of transparency in the decision making process, and of the technical capacities of congress through the strengthening of the Legislative Advisory Office. This new dynamic is exemplified by the process of preparing the Fiscal Responsibility Law. The improvement in the technical quality of the work of the legislature, combined with the increased decision making responsibility of the executive, achieved the political adjustments needed for passage of the law, and contributed technical solutions that improved its effectiveness. This process has also encouraged the media to provide more technically informed coverage of the process of policy formulation and adoption. This is an example of how the enrichment of the decision making process through the participation of the executive, the legislature, and the broader public does not have to occur at the cost of the technical rationality of the solutions.

Another example is Chile's response to the cases of corruption that became public in early 2003. Within a few months of a political pact among all of the political parties with congressional representation, a package of political and institutional reforms was adopted that ended the crisis engendered by the corruption revelations and led to major changes in political and administrative institutions. One of these reforms was the creation of the High-Level Public Management System (*Alta Dirección Pública*) with responsibility for a merit-based selection process for 735 management positions that had previously been filled on an entirely discretionary basis. The process is supervised by a council whose members are elected by a majority of four-sevenths of the senate. The interesting aspect of this reform is that it was possible, first, because of a combination of timing and political consensus, and second, because of the availability of accumulated knowledge in institutes and think tanks linked to political parties and universities, which had worked on various proposals with many elements in common. Against the backdrop of this volume of knowledge, the reform could be negotiated, adopted, and implemented rapidly and effectively.

As these examples show, a policymaking environment needs to be created in which technical rationality is politicized, and political rationality is made more technical, thus weakening the barriers that traditionally separate them. The result can be policymaking that proceeds in a more open and balanced way. This can increase the likelihood that "magic solutions" and universal policy recipes will be rejected. Perhaps as a result of these changes, the trend in the region is toward more experimental and gradualist approaches in which various heterodox combinations of policies and institutions can prove to be effective.

In sum, institutionalizing rationality does not mean imposing a single solution, but keeping policies within a basic range of objectivity and reason. To do this, it is essential to develop knowledge actors and to put in place institutionalized channels that allow technical expertise to be incorporated into policymaking processes, backed by a clear mandate and in a clear and transparent way.

Part III

The Policymaking Process and Policy Outcomes

It is not the strongest of the species that survive nor the most intelligent, but the most responsive to change.

Charles Darwin

Part II examined the role of a variety of actors—formal and informal, professional politicians and members of civil society—as they interact in different arenas in the policymaking processes of Latin American countries. The chapters in Part II discussed these actors' incentives and capabilities, as well as the rules of the game (the institutions) that help shape their behavior.

Part III takes a step toward relating several key institutional features to policymaking processes, and to the characteristics of resulting policies. Chapter 6 takes a cross-country approach. It builds empirical measures of the characteristics of public policies and relates those characteristics to several of the institutional features suggested by the framework of Chapter 2 and studied in Part II. Chapter 7 presents highlights from detailed country cases, focusing on some of the interactions among the various institutional features in specific historical contexts.

Chapter 6

Political Institutions, the Workings of the Policymaking System, and Policy Outcomes

This chapter presents a first effort at linking political institutions to the quality of public policies, such as stability, adaptability, and the quality of implementation.

This chapter offers a first look at the links between political institutions and policy outcomes. Rather than focusing on the content or orientation of policies, it emphasizes a number of characteristics of public policies—including their stability, their adaptability, and the extent to which they pursue the public interest—along with their institutional determinants.

The material in this chapter should be considered exploratory. It is a first effort at relating the policy features emphasized in the framework established in Chapter 2 to some measures of institutional characteristics. The small number of countries for which the detailed data on policies and institutions utilized are available prevents the statistical analysis from going beyond basic correlations at this point.

The cross-country approach adopted in this chapter is complemented by more detailed country cases and comparative sector studies in the chapters that follow. Together, the cross-sectional analysis, the country cases, and the sector studies offer important insights on the links between political institutions, policymaking processes (PMPs), and policy outcomes.

Yet this report does not pretend to offer the last word on these important issues. Rather, the goal is to set an agenda in motion to improve our collective understanding of policymaking processes, their institutional determinants, and their impact on policy outcomes. The hope is that other researchers will take up the challenge and contribute to the understanding of these issues by refining the methodology, by extending the sample of detailed country studies, and by focusing on other sectors in order to provide additional insights into the complex world of policymaking.

Key Features of Public Policies

Normally, the political economy literature concerns itself with the *content* of public policies: will exports be subsidized or taxed, which sectors get more or less protection, who benefits from and who pays for income redistribution, and so on. Instead, this study focuses on some *key features* of public policies:

- *Stability*—the extent to which policies are stable over time
- *Adaptability*—the extent to which policies can be adjusted when they fail or when circumstances change
- *Coherence and coordination*—the degree to which policies are consistent with related policies and result from well-coordinated actions among the actors who participate in their design and implementation
- *Quality of implementation and enforcement*
- *Public-regardedness*—the degree to which policies pursue the public interest
- *Efficiency*—the extent to which policies reflect an allocation of scarce resources that ensures high returns.

There are a number of reasons why this study focuses on these key features. First, from the standpoint of development, these features are as important as the content of policies themselves as ingredients for economic development.

Second, in many cases the link between the content of policies and the nature of the PMP is rather tenuous. Consider the case in which two parties with very different preferences alternate in power, in a political system that produces majorities for the president in congress and few incentives for cooperation among parties. In such a scenario, the content of policies may shift back and forth (from low protection to high protection, from open capital accounts to capital controls, from capture of regulatory agencies to expropriation of privatized assets). In contrast, one important characteristic of public policies will tend, ironically, to persist: policy instability.

Third, from the analytic standpoint, these variables can be used across varied policy domains, thus generating more "data" and allowing for a more precise mapping between policymaking processes and policy outcomes.

The discussion that follows describes each of these key features of public policies. They constitute the dependent variables in the framework of this report: that is, the features of public policies that this study is trying to explain. In addition to discussing their relevance, this study attempts to measure these features across countries, relying on indices developed from two main sources of data. The first is the Executive Opinion Survey of the World Economic Forum's *Global Competitiveness Report* (GCR), which covers more than 100 countries and has been published annually since 1996.[1] The second is an

---

[1] One shortcoming of the GCR data is that they are subjective and tend to be affected by the macroeconomic cycle. When countries are doing poorly, business executives tend to rate them poorly across all variables. This is dealt with to some extent by averaging the indices over all available years. Still, it may negatively affect countries, such as Argentina, which have suffered from poor economic performance for most of the period for which GCR data are available.

opinion survey conducted for this report, inspired mostly by the work on State capabilities by Kent Weaver and Bert Rockman.[2] This survey, the State Capabilities (SC) Survey, questioned more than 150 experts in 18 Latin American countries, including public policy analysts, economists, political scientists, and former policymakers (including a few former presidents), regarding the capabilities of the State in a number of dimensions identified as crucial by Weaver and Rockman (see Box 6.1).

Key features of policies, such as their stability or the quality of their implementation, are as important as the specific content of those policies as ingredients for economic development.

While each of the data sources has important shortcomings and none is free from measurement error, in combination they provide a good sense of the characteristics of public policies in different countries in the region. Before discussing each of the relevant features of public policies and their measurement in more detail, however, a couple of caveats are in order. First, respondents to the State Capabilities Survey were explicitly asked to base their answers not on the performance of public policies under the current administration, but rather on performance in the last couple of decades, or since the country's return to democratic rule.[3] Thus the position of the different countries according to the indices does not necessarily reflect the quality of public policies under the current administrations.

Second, the objective in measuring these features of public policies is not to single out countries as doing things "right" or "wrong," but rather to use the information as an important ingredient in establishing links with the institutional variables introduced in Chapters 3 through 5. In line with this objective, rather than presenting the countries' actual scores on indices, this report groups countries on each dimension in three different categories ("low," "medium," or "high," depending on the value of the index).[4]

Stability

Some countries seem capable of sustaining most policies over time. In other countries, policies are frequently reversed, often at each minor change of political winds (whether a change in administration or even a change in some key cabinet member or senior bureaucrat). Having stable policies does not mean that policies cannot change at all, but rather that changes tend to respond to changing economic conditions or to failure of previous policies, rather than to political changes. In countries with stable policies, changes tend

---

[2] Weaver and Rockman (1993).

[3] In a few cases, respondents were asked to focus on more specific periods: before and after the Constitution of 1991 in the case of Colombia; before and after the end of the unified *Partido Revolucionario Institucional* (PRI) government in Mexico (1997); before and after the fall of the Stroessner regime (1989) in Paraguay; and before and after the introduction of popular elections for governors in Venezuela (1988). In this section, the values for each of these countries reflect the countries' performance in the latter ("after") period. Changes in these features of public policies within countries are discussed in Chapter 7.

[4] The methodology used to group countries in the different categories is explained in detail in the Data Appendix.

Box 6.1 State Capabilities

A State must have certain capabilities to perform certain essential functions. It must have the capacity to maintain macroeconomic stability and ensure economic growth; to make long-term promises credible, and implement and enforce policies over time; and to ensure that policies are not captured by special interests. A particularly good list of State capabilities has been drawn up by Kent Weaver and Bert Rockman.[1] They identify ten:

1. To *set and maintain priorities* among the many conflicting demands made upon them so that they are not overwhelmed and bankrupt
2. To *target resources* where they are most effective
3. To *innovate* when existing policies have failed
4. To *coordinate conflicting objectives* into a coherent whole
5. To *be able to impose losses on powerful groups*
6. To *represent diffuse, unorganized interests* in addition to those that are concentrated and well-organized
7. To *ensure effective implementation of government policies* once they have been decided upon
8. To *ensure policy stability* so that policies have time to work
9. To *make and maintain international commitments* in the realms of trade and national defense to ensure the State's long-term well-being
10. To *manage political cleavages* in order to ensure that the society does not degenerate into civil war.

These State capabilities tie in closely with the key features of public policies discussed in this chapter. The State Capabilities Survey used in this study added a few items to this list:

11. To *ensure policy adaptability* when changes in circumstances require it
12. To *ensure coherence* across policy domains, so that new policies fit well with existing ones
13. To *ensure effective policy coordination* among different actors operating in the same policy domain.

---

[1] Weaver and Rockman (1993).

---

to be incremental, building upon achievements of previous administrations, and tend to be achieved through consensus. In contrast, volatile policy environments are characterized by large swings and by lack of consultation with different groups in society. As discussed in Chapter 2, this study associates policy stability with the ability of political actors to strike and enforce inter-temporal agreements that allow certain fundamental policies (*Políticas de Estado*) to be preserved beyond the tenure of particular officeholders or coalitions. Thus, the notion of policy stability is closely linked to the notion of policy credibility discussed in Chapter 2.[5]

This study's measure of policy stability relies on both the GCR Executive Opinion Survey and the SC Survey. In addition, a variable on policy volatility based on the Fraser Index of Economic Freedom is used. This index, which has been published regularly since 1974 by the Fraser Institute, measures the degree to which policies and institutions of countries contribute to economic freedom (including dimensions such as the size of government, the protection of property rights, and freedom of international exchange). Given the focus on policy stability, this study is not interested in the level of economic freedom as measured by the index, but rather in the index's volatility. There are six components of the index of policy stability:

1. The standard deviation of the Fraser Index of Economic Freedom for the country[6]
2. The extent to which legal or political changes have undermined firms' planning capacity (from the GCR)
3. The extent to which new governments honor the contractual commitments and obligations of previous regimes (from the GCR)
4. The capacity of the State to set and maintain priorities among conflicting objectives (from the SC Survey)
5. The extent to which governments ensure policy stability (from the SC Survey)
6. The extent to which the State makes and maintains international commitments (from the SC Survey).

All the variables included in the index of policy stability were normalized to vary on the same scale (from 1 to 4, with 4 indicating greater stability), and each of them was given a similar weight. On the basis of the resulting index, cluster analysis techniques were applied in order to group countries into different categories for this dimension of public policy.[7] The country groupings for the stability dimension, as well as the other dimensions discussed in the following pages, are presented in Table 6.1.

Adaptability

It is desirable for countries to be able to adapt policies to changing economic conditions and to change policies when they are obviously failing. However, governments sometimes abuse the discretion to adapt policies by adopting opportunistic, one-sided

---

[5] This notion of policy stability is also closely related to the notion of resoluteness in Cox and McCubbins (2001), as discussed in Box 2.2.

[6] The series for each country was detrended before calculating the standard deviation, so that countries that moved steadily toward more (or less) free market policies throughout the period were not characterized as having volatile policies.

[7] Cluster analysis is a classification method that is used to arrange a set of cases into clusters. The aim is to establish a set of clusters such that cases within a cluster are more similar to each other than they are to cases in other clusters. For a more detailed discussion of the clustering methodology used, see the Data Appendix.

Table 6.1 Key Features of Public Policies since the 1980s

Country	Stability	Adaptability	Enforcement and implementation	Coordination and coherence	Public-regardedness	Efficiency	Policy index
Argentina	Low	Medium	Low	Low	Medium	Low	Low
Bolivia	Medium	High	Medium	Medium	Medium	Medium	Medium
Brazil	High	High	High	High	Medium	Medium	High
Chile	High	High	High	High	High	High	Very High
Colombia	High	High	High	Medium	Medium	Medium	High
Costa Rica	High	Medium	High	Medium	High	High	High
Dominican Republic	Medium	Medium	Medium	Medium	Low	Medium	Medium
Ecuador	Low	Medium	Low	Low	Low	Low	Low
El Salvador	High	High	High	Medium	Medium	High	High
Guatemala	Medium	Medium	Low	Medium	Low	Medium	Low
Honduras	High	Medium	Medium	Medium	Low	Medium	Medium
Mexico	High	Medium	High	Medium	Medium	High	High
Nicaragua	Medium	Medium	Medium	Low	Low	Medium	Low
Panama	Medium	Low	Medium	Low	Low	Low	Low
Paraguay	Medium	Low	Low	Low	Low	Low	Low
Peru	Medium	Medium	Medium	Medium	Medium	Medium	Medium
Uruguay	High	High	High	Medium	Medium	Medium	High
Venezuela	Low	Low	Medium	Low	Medium	Low	Low

Note: The key features of public policies are classified as "high," "medium," or "low" using cluster analysis (see Data Appendix). For the case of the policy index, because Chile outperforms all the other countries, it has been classified as "very high," and the remaining countries have been classified as previously noted.

These measures are intended to capture features of a country's public policies over the last couple of decades, or since the return to democracy, and do not necessarily reflect the characteristics of policies in the current administration.

Source: Stein and Tommasi (2005).

policies that are closer to their own preferences or those of their important constituents. This can result in policy volatility, as policies may shift back and forth as different groups alternate in power. In political environments that are not cooperative, political actors often agree to limit such opportunism by resorting to fixed policy rules that are difficult to change. This limits policy volatility, but at the cost of reducing adaptability. It is sometimes accomplished by embedding policies such as pension benefits or intergovernmental transfers into the constitution. In other cases, a political system regularly generates gridlock, making it difficult to achieve change. Whatever the reason, countries with low policy adaptability will be unable to respond to shocks adequately, or may get stuck in unsuitable policies for extended periods of time.

This study's index of policy adaptability (see Table 6.1 for country assessments) has two components, both from the State Capabilities Survey. The first asks about the extent to which there is innovation when countries' policies fail. The second asks about the extent to which governments ensure policy adaptability. Given the lack of questions on international surveys such as the GCR that are closely related to the concept of policy adaptability, this measure is not as reliable as that corresponding to policy stability, as well as some of the other indices of public policy discussed in this chapter.

Coordination and Coherence

Public policies are the outcome of actions taken by multiple actors in the policymaking process. Ideally, different agents acting in the same policy domain should coordinate their actions to produce coherent policies. However, this does not always occur. In some countries, policymaking on certain issues involves a large number of actors that do not communicate adequately with each other, leading to what Cox and McCubbins have called "balkanization" of public policies.[8] Lack of coordination often reflects the noncooperative nature of political interactions. It may occur among different agencies within the central government, between agencies in the central government and others at the regional or municipal level, or even among agents that operate in different stages of the policymaking process (such as when the complications that the bureaucracy might face during the implementation phase of a given policy are not taken into account during the design and approval stage of policymaking).

This study's measure of coordination and coherence (see Table 6.1 for country assessments)[9] has two components, both from the State Capabilities Survey. The first component measures the extent to which new policies are consistent with existing policies. The second component deals with whether different policymakers operating in the same policy domain (or related policy domains) coordinate their actions effectively.

---

[8] See Cox and McCubbins (2002). Balkanization refers to a process of fragmentation or division of a region into smaller regions that are often hostile or noncooperative with each other. In the case of public policies, the term refers to the fragmentation of policymaking, not necessarily along geographical lines.

[9] As in the case of adaptability, however, the measure is based on just two questions from the State Capabilities Survey, so the rankings for this category are probably not as reliable as some of the others, which are based on a wider range of variables.

Quality of Implementation and Enforcement

A policy could be very well designed, sail through the approval process unchanged, and yet be completely ineffective if it was not well implemented and enforced. In many countries in Latin America, the quality of policy implementation and enforcement is quite poor. This is associated in part with the lack of capable and independent bureaucracies, as well as the lack of strong judiciaries. To an important degree, the quality of policy implementation and enforcement in a given country will depend on the extent to which policymakers in that country have incentives and resources to invest in their policy capabilities.

This study's index of implementation and enforcement (see Table 6.1 for country assessments) was constructed from four components:

1. The extent of enforcement of the minimum wage (from the GCR)
2. The extent of control of tax evasion (from the GCR)
3. The consistency of environmental regulation (from the GCR)
4. The extent to which the State ensures effective implementation of public policies (from the State Capabilities Survey).

Public-Regardedness

Public-regardedness refers to the extent to which policies produced by a given system promote the general welfare and resemble public goods (that is, are public-regarding) or tend to funnel private benefits to certain individuals, factions, or regions in the form of projects with concentrated benefits, subsidies, or tax loopholes (that is, are private-regarding).[10] This dimension is closely tied to inequality, particularly since those favored by private-regarding policies tend to be the members of the elite, who have the economic and political clout to skew policy decisions in their favor.

This study's measure of public-regardedness (see Table 6.1 for country assessments) has four components:

1. The extent to which public officials tend to favor the well connected in their policy decisions (from the GCR)
2. The extent to which social transfers effectively reach the poor as opposed to the rich (from the GCR)
3. The ability of the State to impose losses on powerful actors (from the State Capabilities Survey)
4. The extent to which the government represents diffuse, unorganized interests, in addition to concentrated organized interests (from the State Capabilities Survey).

---

[10] See Cox and McCubbins (2001).

Efficiency

A key aspect of good policymaking is the ability of the State to allocate its scarce resources to those activities where they have the greatest returns. This feature of policies is somewhat related to public-regardedness since, to the extent that policymakers unduly favor specific sectors to the detriment of the public interest, they will be moving away from the most efficient allocation of resources. This study's index of efficiency (see Table 6.1 for country assessments) has two components:

1. Whether the composition of public spending is wasteful (from the GCR)
2. Whether resources are targeted where most effective (from the State Capabilities Survey).

The Overall Index of Quality of Public Policy

The preceding sections have identified a number of key features of public policies: stability, adaptability, coordination and coherence, quality of implementation and enforcement, public-regardedness, and efficiency. While there may be other relevant characteristics of public policies that have not been included in the analysis, in combination these features should provide a good picture of the quality of policymaking in Latin American countries.

The various indices we have constructed to measure these key features could be combined in different ways to come up with an overall index of the quality of public policies. This study gives the same weight to each of the key features discussed. That is, it uses the simple average of the different indices. However, the specific method used to aggregate the individual indices into the overall Index of Quality of Public Policy (or, for simplicity, the "policy index") is not driving the results,[11] or the grouping of countries into the categories shown in the last column of Table 6.1.[12]

How does Latin America compare with other regions with regard to these features of public policies? One important limitation in making an inter-regional comparison is the lack of comparable data for countries in other regions. In particular, data from the State Capabilities Survey conducted for this report are not available for other countries. However, the data from the Fraser Institute, and the data from the *Global Competitiveness Report*, are available for a much wider set of countries. It is not possible to compare Latin America directly with other regions using all the data. However, it is possible to do so using a modified version of the indices by including data only from the international data sets. Reassuringly, the correlation between the policy index for the countries in

---

[11] The correlation between the resulting overall index and an alternative in which the different qualities are weighted according to the number of subcomponents in each of them (six in the case of stability, two in the case of adaptability, and so on) is 0.99.

[12] As in the case of the individual indices, the countries were grouped using cluster analysis. In this case Chile, which had a significantly higher score than the rest of the countries on the policy index, was placed in a category of its own ("very high"); the rest of the countries were divided into the categories "high," "medium," and "low."

FIGURE 6.1 **Key Features of Public Policies Indices: An Inter-regional Comparison (using international data)**
(1–4 scale)

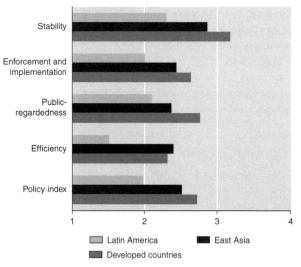

Sources: Stein and Tommasi (2005) and World Economic Forum (various years).

Latin America and the modified version using only the internationaly available data is 0.91, indicating that the comparison is meaningful.

Figure 6.1 presents the average index for four of the components,[13] as well as the international version of the policy index, for three different groups of countries: Latin America, East Asia, and developed countries. Two things are worth mentioning. First, Latin America lags behind East Asia and the developed world in each and every one of the different policy components. In the overall index, the average for Latin America is 1.98, on a scale of 1 to 4. Meanwhile, East Asian countries have an average index of 2.53, while the developed countries stand at 2.73. Second, the gap between Latin America and the other regions varies across features. Latin America lags behind the most in stability and efficiency, while it is closer to the rest, or at least to the East Asian countries, in terms of public-regardedness.

Features of Public Policies and Economic Development

The previous sections developed a series of indices to capture a number of key features of public policy. An important assumption behind the development of these indices was that the features of policies being measured, such as stability, adaptability, and the quality of implementation, should be important ingredients for economic development. This section provides some evidence in support of this hypothesis, by showing the association that exists between the different features discussed, as well as the policy index, and a number of measures of economic development.

---

[13] The indices for adaptability and coordination are not included in this comparison, since they were based exclusively on the State Capabilities Survey.

The measures of economic development used are the following:

- Per capita GDP growth, in U.S. dollars at purchasing power parity, between 1980 and 2002 (from the World Bank's *World Development Indicators*).
- The change in the value of the UNDP's Human Development Index (HDI) between 1980 and 2002. The HDI combines various measures of literacy and life expectancy with GDP per capita in order to measure a country's achievement in terms of human development.
- The reduction in poverty rates between 1980–90 and 1995–2000 (from the *World Development Indicators*).
- Two different measures of welfare, developed by the World Bank, that combine measures of income with different measures of income inequality, suggested by Amartya Sen and Anthony Atkinson, respectively.[14]

Table 6.2 presents the correlations between the different components and policy index and each of these five measures of welfare. The top portion presents these correlations for the case of Latin American countries, using the indices that combine international data with data from the State Capabilities Survey. The lower portion provides comparable information for a wider sample of developing countries, using international data only. For each political variable listed on the left, the top row of numbers presents simple correlations, while the bottom row of numbers presents partial correlations, controlling for the effects of initial (1980) per capita GDP, in order to account for potential convergence effects.[15]

As the correlations presented in the table show, the policy index is positively associated with each of the measures of development. In 14 out of 16 correlations, the association is statistically significant. In some cases, the correlations are very high. They tend to be higher for the Latin American sample, where the similarities among the countries are greater. The level of significance is higher for the developing country sample, however. This is not surprising, given the increase in the sample size. The individual indices also correlate well with most of the welfare measures used.

Relating Political Institutions and Policy Outcomes

The rest of this chapter pulls together information and findings on the features of policies in Latin America and some of the indicators of the workings of Latin American political systems developed in Part II. Correlations among the characteristics of public policies and a number of political and institutional variables appear in the following sections. This exploration is guided by the framework developed in Chapter 2, as well as some insights from the literature summarized in Part II.

---

[14] See Gasparini (2004) for a discussion of the welfare indices.

[15] In the case of partial correlations, the idea is to check whether countries whose policy index is higher than expected, given their initial per capita GDP, tend to have development indicators that are also higher than expected, given their initial income.

Table 6.2 Key Features of Public Policies and Economic Development: Simple and Partial Correlations

Latin American Countries

	Stability	Adaptability	Coordination and coherence	Implementation and enforcement	Public-regardedness	Efficiency	Policy index	No. obs.
GDP per capita growth	0.643***	0.543*	0.722***	0.653***	0.573**	0.674***	0.700***	18
	*0.453**	*0.445*	*0.505***	*0.545***	*0.287*	*0.512***	*0.509***	*18*
Human Development Index (change)	0.202	0.602***	0.186	0.519*	0.199	0.375	0.376	18
	*0.418**	*0.782****	*0.428**	*0.711****	*0.464**	*0.592****	*0.614****	*18*
Poverty reduction	0.467*	0.455*	0.427*	0.322	0.353	0.372	0.439*	17
	0.339	*0.377*	*0.268*	*0.235*	*0.177*	*0.226*	*0.300*	*17*
Welfare Index (Sen)	0.791***	0.685***	0.950***	0.688***	0.839***	0.856***	0.871***	16
	*0.649****	*0.610****	*0.800****	*0.590****	*0.639****	*0.739****	*0.730****	*16*
Welfare Index (Atkinson)	0.791***	0.630***	0.949***	0.635***	0.817***	0.826***	0.843***	16
	*0.647****	*0.548***	*0.796****	*0.528***	*0.605***	*0.704****	*0.695****	*16*

Developing Countries

	Stability	Adaptability	Coordination and coherence	Implementation and enforcement	Public-regardedness	Efficiency	Policy index	No. obs.
GDP per capita growth	0.489***	—	—	0.261*	0.193	0.467***	0.420***	52
	*0.491****			*0.331***	*0.236*	*0.476****	*0.445****	*47*
Human Development Index (change)	0.215	—	—	0.585***	0.485***	0.249*	0.400*	52
	0.199			*0.567****	*0.476****	*0.283**	*0.393**	*47*
Poverty reduction	0.511***	—	—	0.332**	0.222	0.448***	0.461***	42
	*0.514****			*0.327***	*0.202*	*0.445****	*0.450****	*37*

— Not available.
* Significant at 10 percent.   ** Significant at 5 percent.   *** Significant at 1 percent.

Note: For each political variable listed on the left, the first row presents simple correlations with each of the policy variables listed at the top of the columns, and the second row presents (in italics) partial correlations (controlling for 1980 GDP per capita).

Sources: World Bank (various years); Stein and Tommasi (2005); Gasparini (2004); and UNDP (various years).

The framework presented in Chapter 2 emphasized that good policymaking can be facilitated if political actors have relatively long horizons, and arenas for the discussion, negotiation, and enforcement of political and policy agreements are relatively encompassing and well-institutionalized. Some of the characteristics of key political actors and arenas that can enhance good policymaking are explored below.

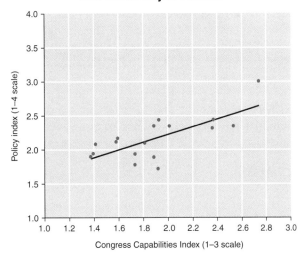

FIGURE 6.2 **Congressional Capabilities and the Quality of Policies**

Sources: Stein and Tommasi (2005) and authors' compilation.

The Policymaking Capabilities of Congress

Legislatures are critical to the functioning of democracy. Given its constitutional responsibility, the national legislature is the most natural arena for the discussion, negotiation, and enforcement of political agreements. Legislatures include broader representation than the executive branch, and as such they may serve as an arena for inter-temporal political agreements. A legislature made up of professional legislators, with technical capabilities for discussing and overseeing policies, and with adequate organizational structures, can facilitate the development of relatively consensual and consistent (stable) policies over time.

Chapter 3 presented an index, the Congress Capabilities Index, that attempts to capture the extent to which congress, as an institution, has the capabilities to serve such a policymaking function. The discussion focused on some aspects of congress as an organization, as well as on some characteristics of legislators. The index includes such variables as the strength and specialization of congressional committees, the confidence that the public has in congress as an institution, the level of education of legislators, their technical expertise, and the extent to which congress is a desirable career place for politicians.

Figure 6.2 presents a scatter plot relating the Congress Capabilities Index to the policy index.[16] The positive relation between both variables is quite clear. The correlation is 0.699, and it is significant at the 99 percent level of statistical confidence.

---

[16] Since the objective is to establish links between institutional variables and the quality of policies, and not to single out the countries with the best or the worst policies, the names of the countries are omitted from the scatter plots presented here.

While the figure shows a strong association between the Congressional Capabilities Index and the policy index, association does not necessarily mean causality. For example, both variables could be explained by a third one, such as the level of economic development. For this reason, we checked whether the link between these variables survives after controlling for the level of income per capita in 1980.[17] It does. Similar checks were conducted for the links between the policy index (and its components) and the other institutional variables used in this section. Table 6.3 presents information about the correlation of each of the policy characteristics identified earlier in the chapter and each of the political and institutional variables discussed. (For each institutional variable, the top number presents a simple correlation and the bottom number presents a partial correlation, controlling for GDP per capita.)

Characteristics of Political Party Systems

Parties are organizations whose function is to represent and aggregate diverse interests. As such, they are naturally encompassing organizations that should facilitate political bargains in the policymaking process.

As stated in Chapter 3, the structure and organization of political parties and party systems in a country can have an important influence on the policymaking process. Political parties can play a direct role in the policymaking process, but they also can play indirect roles through their interaction with various other institutions. For instance, in some countries parties are important actors in defining and articulating broad policy programs and are able to effectively engage in public policy debates, even when they are in the opposition. But characteristics of the party system in a particular country also affect the country's policymaking process somewhat more indirectly, such as by influencing the workability of executive-legislative relations, the possibilities for coordination in congress, and/or the incentives of elected officials to cater to narrower or broader sets of societal interests. This section focuses on some characteristics of parties and party systems that make parties more encompassing policy players, and explores the effects of these characteristics on the quality of public policies. One such characteristic is their degree of institutionalization. More institutionalized parties and party systems, particularly when parties are programmatic, are more likely to encourage long horizons and to prevent individual politicians from behaving opportunistically. They can also facilitate inter-temporal bargains, both within a party and among parties, since the commitments made by current party leaders are more likely to be respected in the future. Another characteristic that might facilitate encompassing parties is their relative focus on national issues, as indicated by measures of party system nationalization. How effectively parties play their roles in the PMP will also depend on the main incentives and orientations of key party actors.

---

[17] This check was conducted by using partial correlations instead of simple correlations. In the case of partial correlations, the idea is to check whether countries for which the Congress Capabilities Index value is higher than expected, given their income levels, tend to have values for the policy index that are also higher than expected, given their income levels.

Table 6.3 Correlations of Institutional and Political Variables with Key Features of Policies

	Stability	Adaptability	Coordination and coherence	Implementation and enforcement	Public-regardedness	Efficiency	Policy index	No. obs.
Congress Capabilities Index	0.740***	0.570**	0.754***	0.503**	0.624***	0.614***	0.699***	18
	*0.722***	*0.543***	*0.752***	*0.472**	*0.601***	*0.606***	*0.679***	*18*
Party system institutionalization	0.388	0.150	0.315	0.104	0.041	0.287	0.250	18
	*0.401**	*0.164*	*0.321*	*0.120*	*0.054*	*0.295*	*0.263*	*18*
Party system nationalization	0.505**	0.367	0.409	0.313	0.132	0.496*	0.420*	17
	*0.625***	*0.493***	*0.481**	*0.434**	*0.221*	*0.584***	*0.533***	*17*
Programmatic parties	0.431*	0.478**	0.478**	0.351	0.385	0.616***	0.499**	18
	*0.446**	*0.495***	*0.486***	*0.370*	*0.401**	*0.626***	*0.514***	*18*
Judicial independence	0.866***	0.705***	0.808***	0.722***	0.661***	0.751***	0.835***	18
	*0.850***	*0.678***	*0.809***	*0.693***	*0.637***	*0.745***	*0.816***	*18*
Cabinet stability	0.450	0.362	0.441	0.352	0.472	0.530	0.464	10
	0.442	*0.350*	*0.440*	*0.339*	*0.466*	*0.525*	*0.456*	*10*
Share of ministers in civil service	0.613*	0.312	0.340	0.420	0.200	0.317	0.411	8
	*0.669**	*0.343*	*0.463*	*0.400*	*0.263*	*0.383*	*0.467*	*8*
Civil service development	0.524**	0.562**	0.542**	0.536**	0.631***	0.452*	0.588***	18
	*0.526***	*0.548***	*0.611***	*0.503***	*0.646***	*0.482***	*0.599***	*18*
Proportionality of electoral system	−0.040	0.191	−0.210	0.036	−0.110	−0.208	−0.063	18
	−0.065	*0.163*	*−0.224*	*0.004*	*−0.139*	*−0.226*	*−0.089*	*18*
Effective number of legislative parties	−0.221	0.060	−0.168	0.019	−0.082	−0.261	−0.110	18
		−0.018	*−0.214*	*−0.070*	*−0.165*	*−0.325*	*−0.191*	*18*
Partisan powers of the president	−0.028	−0.168	0.040	−0.043	0.034	0.161	0.001	18
	0.029	*−0.108*	*0.070*	*0.031*	*0.100*	*0.207*	*0.062*	*18*

* Significant at 10 percent.
** Significant at 5 percent.
*** Significant at 1 percent.

Note: For each political variable listed on the left, the first row presents simple correlations with each of the policy variables listed at the top of the columns, and the second row presents (in italics) partial correlations (controlling for the 1980 GDP per capita)

Sources: Stein and Tommasi (2005); Jones (2005); Martínez-Gallardo (2005b); Zuvanic and Iacoviello (2005); World Economic Forum (2004); and authors' compilation.

Party System Institutionalization and Programmatic Orientation

In well-institutionalized party systems, parties are likely to have longer horizons and more encompassing interests than individual citizens or individual politicians. Parties are collective identities, with an interest in maintaining or enhancing their reputation over time. Well-functioning parties are likely to be able to control the free rider incentives of individual politicians to engage in activities that give them short-term benefits: whether material benefits in exchange for favors to narrow constituencies, or symbolic benefits of indulging in their personal ideological inclinations. Long-lasting, well-institutionalized parties are more likely to be consistent long-term policy players and contribute to generate inter-temporal cooperation.

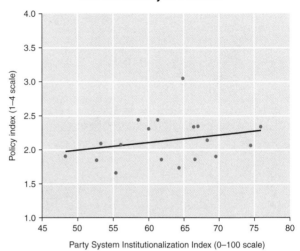

FIGURE 6.3 **Party System Institutionalization and the Quality of Policies**

Sources: Stein and Tommasi (2005) and Jones (2005).

A system with a relatively small number of parties that are expected to be around for a long time, alternating in government, is more likely to respect some basic rules of interaction, and to establish somewhat consensual sustained policy stances on crucial issues (known as *Políticas de Estado*).[18] Interactions among institutionalized parties with a focus on national policymaking can also add credibility and predictability to the policy-making system, complementing or even substituting for well-institutionalized legislative bargaining arenas.

Hence party system institutionalization is expected to have positive effects on key features of policies such as stability. The association between party institutionalization and the policy index presented in Figure 6.3, although positive, is not very tight. The reason is that the impact of this variable is not straightforward. In some countries, such as Colombia and to some extent Brazil, policies are relatively effective, despite the fact that the countries' party systems are not highly institutionalized. In these countries, the institutionalization of policymaking seems to take place in other arenas such as congress and the bureaucracy. In both countries, parties are more institutionalized in the con-

---

[18] At the same time, there are cases in which party systems are highly institutionalized and produce relatively effective policies, but at the cost of curbing political participation. Venezuela throughout the 1960s, 1970s, and 1980s is a case in point. For a more detailed discussion of Venezuela, see Monaldi and others (2005) and Chapter 11 of this report.

FIGURE 6.4 Party System Institutionalization, Programmatic Orientation, and the Quality of Policies

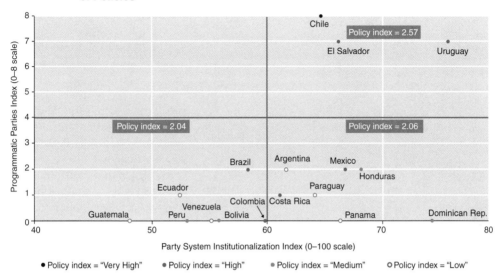

Note: The values in boxes show the average value of the policy index for the countries in that quadrant. Nicaragua has been omitted from this figure because its scores on the programmatic and institutionalization indices, when taken together, can be misleading (see note 14 in Chapter 3).

Sources: Stein and Tommasi (2005) and Jones (2005).

gressional arena (for instance, in their role in policy committees) than in the electoral arena—which is the one better captured in the index of party system institutionalization utilized in this study.

On the other hand, some parties are reasonably institutionalized, but are more focused on maintaining relatively narrowly based (often geographic) support networks than on the nature of public policies. Figure 6.4 shows the values of the policy index for different configurations of party system institutionalization and the extent to which parties are programmatic. The first thing to notice is that, as discussed in Chapter 3, there are no countries with programmatic parties that are not institutionalized (that is, the upper left quadrant of the figure is empty). The figure also suggests that institutionalization does not translate into better policies when parties are not programmatic. Policies are better only when party systems are institutionalized and programmatic.

Party System Nationalization

In a nationalized party system, parties tend to speak and act with a common national orientation, rather than being divided according to regional or subnational issues, and focused upon them. In highly nationalized party systems, national issues are likely to be central in legislators' careers. Under conditions of weak party nationalization, legislators' and politicians' concerns will tend to be less focused on national public policy questions.

FIGURE 6.5 **Party System Nationalization and the Quality of Policies**

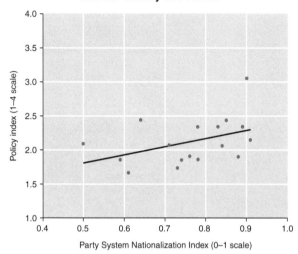

Party System Nationalization Index (0–1 scale)

Sources: Stein and Tommasi (2005) and Jones (2005).

More encompassing parties are likely to help generate better national policies. This study utilizes the Party System Nationalization Index score from Chapter 3 as a measure of nationalization of the party system. Figure 6.5 plots the policy index against the Party System Nationalization Index. The correlation between the two variables is 0.420, and it is significant at the 90 percent level. (The correlations are even stronger in the exercise controlling for GDP per capita.)

This result suggests that while having a more geographically decentralized political system may be beneficial in some respects ("getting government close to the people"), it may also have some harmful effects on the quality of national policymaking. The potential tension between increasing inclusiveness and representation, on the one hand, and complicating government effectiveness at the national level, on the other, is discussed further in Chapter 7, in the particular case of Colombia.[19]

Implementation and Enforcement

Policies with good properties are more likely to emerge in more cooperative policymaking environments. Adequate enforcement and implementation facilitate such cooperation and hence strengthen the quality of policies. The judiciary is the most obvious enforcer in the political system. The bureaucracy plays a predominant role in policy implementation, and thus some of its characteristics and capabilities are likely to have an effect on the quality of implementation. In addition, the quality of the bureaucracy can also affect the ability of other political actors to bargain and enforce inter-temporal policy agreements. In fact, delegation to a competent bureaucracy might in some cases be the way to enforce the inter-temporal implementation of political agreements. Ministers and, more broadly, cabinets also play a key role in the design, discussion, and implementation of public policies in Latin America.

The discussion that follows explores how some characteristics of the judiciary, the cabinet, and the bureaucracy affect the properties of public policies.

---

[19] See also the discussion in Chapter 11 regarding the impact of the introduction of elections for governors and mayors on the Venezuelan PMP.

The Judiciary

Of all the roles that the judiciary plays in the polity, one is especially important for the framework discussed in Chapter 2: the inter-temporal enforcement of prior political and policy decisions, as reflected in constitutions and laws. A judiciary that plays this role effectively will improve some characteristics of public policies, such as stability and quality of enforcement. The supreme court or equivalent institution is usually in charge of ensuring that the president does not encroach upon the powers of the congress, and that neither branch violates the constitution. The judiciary will be less able to perform this role if it is not independent of the executive in power.

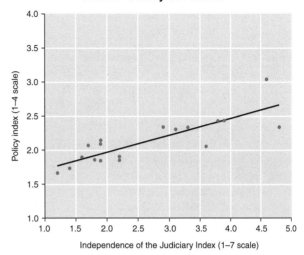

FIGURE 6.6 **Judicial Independence and the Quality of Policies**

Sources: Stein and Tommasi (2005) and World Economic Forum (2004).

Figure 6.6 plots the policy index against the World Economic Forum measure of independence of the judiciary discussed in Chapter 4. The correlation between those two measures is 0.835, and it is significant at the 99 percent confidence level. The presence of a reasonably independent referee thus turns out to be quite important in determining whether the political game generates high-quality policies. This seems to operate across the board on all policy features analyzed here.

The building of an independent judiciary is a complex business that usually takes a long time. This is suggested by Figure 6.7, which shows a strong correlation (0.771, significant at the 99 percent level) of judicial independence with the tenure of justices on the bench (see also Table 6.3). Clearly, a supreme court whose members change too often is unlikely to build up much independence. Since in most countries it is the president who nominates supreme court justices, in countries where the tenure of justices is short, most are likely to be nominated by sitting presidents. Individual justices who owe their position to the sitting president are less likely to show independence from the executive in their rulings.[20]

As explained in Chapter 4, the judiciary can play other roles, beyond the enforcement of existing political agreements. One such role is that of a potential veto player. The supreme court can be considered a potential veto player as long as its agreement is required to enact policy change.[21] Some observers have argued that policy change becomes more

---

[20] See, for instance, Iaryczower, Spiller, and Tommasi (2002).

[21] Sousa (2005).

difficult as the number of veto players increases.[22] The veto player theory would predict that stronger (more independent) courts would induce policy stability and policy immobility. That is, they would increase "decisiveness" but reduce "resoluteness," in the language of Cox and McCubbins.[23]

In order to test this hypothesis, this study looked at the correlation of the measure of judicial independence with the measures of policy stability (similar to resoluteness) and of policy adaptability (similar to decisiveness). It turns out that *both* policy characteristics correlate positively with judicial independence (0.866 and 0.705,

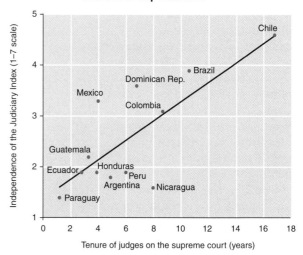

FIGURE 6.7 **Supreme Court Tenure and Judicial Independence**

Sources: World Economic Forum (2004) and Henisz (2000).

respectively, both significant at the 99 percent level). This finding argues against an emphasis on courts' role as veto player, which would suggest a negative relation to policy adaptability. It seems that independent courts in Latin America promote inter-temporal enforcement, which might even facilitate policy adjustment. On the other hand, weak judicial enforcement might induce political actors to attempt to implement their preferred policies in rigid manners to prevent future changes, limiting the adaptability of policies.

The Cabinet

Latin American cabinet ministers, either individually or collectively, play key roles in every stage of the policy process. Characteristics related to the formation, operation, stability, and structure of cabinets are likely to have important effects on the properties of public policies. For instance, a certain degree of cabinet stability is likely to be necessary to promote longer-term policies and to allow ministers to see programs and policy implementation through to completion. Frequent turnover of cabinet ministers is likely to promote a short-term orientation to policy and frequent policy switches. Longer tenures also allow the development of better relationships with permanent bureaucrats, which are essential for implementing policy efficiently. Frequent changes in the cabinet can leave leadership vacuums that may contribute to bureaucratic inertia and even

---

[22] See, for example, Tsebelis (2002).
[23] Cox and McCubbins (2001).

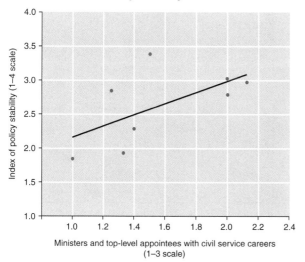

FIGURE 6.8 **Ministers and Top-Level Appointees with Civil Service Careers and Policy Stability**

Ministers and top-level appointees with civil service careers
(1–3 scale)

Source: Stein and Tommasi (2005), based in part on data from Rauch and Evans (2000).

corruption. Longer tenure allows ministers to accumulate valuable expertise specific to the policy area in which they work and to develop political and managerial skills that are likely to improve the quality of their performance in their different policymaking functions.

Of the many characteristics of cabinets that might have an impact on the features of policies, this study focused on two features that are particularly consistent with the emphasis on long horizons and on institutionalization: the stability/durability of ministers (the inverse of the number of ministers per portfolio in each administration discussed in Chapter 4), and the fraction of ministers that come from a civil service career (an indicator of institutionalization). Both variables have positive correlations with this study's policy features. More stable cabinets are positively correlated with policy features such as stability, adaptability, and coordination and coherence. The correlation with the overall policy index is 0.464. A high proportion of ministers and top-level political appointees with civil service backgrounds correlates quite highly with policy stability (0.613), as depicted in Figure 6.8.[24]

The Bureaucracy

A strong and capable bureaucracy is likely to improve the quality of implementation of public policies. It also has feedback effects on other stages of the policy process. Having a competent and independent bureaucracy to which some policy decision making and implementation may be delegated might facilitate inter-temporal agreements, par-

---

[24] See also Table 6.3. The measure of ministers and appointees with civil service careers used in Figure 6.8 is from Rauch and Evans (2000) and is based on responses to an expert survey that were coded on a scale from 1 to 3. For details, see Data Appendix. The correlation of the proportion of ministers and top-level appointees with civil service careers with the policy index is 0.411. While the correlations between both cabinet variables and the policy indices are not statistically significant, this is due to the very small size of the sample of countries (eight) for which cabinet data are available. Statistical significance is too demanding a criterion to impose on such a small sample.

ticularly in policy areas that are prone to politicization and political opportunism. In situations in which there is a choice between rules and discretion, and discretion may lead to political opportunism, delegation to a technically competent bureaucracy can facilitate adaptability while keeping political opportunism at bay. Conversely, when a competent bureaucracy is lacking, policies are more likely to deviate from the public interest. For instance, businesses affected by economic regulation (or by taxation) are likely to focus their efforts on evading regulation or taxation at the implementation stage.

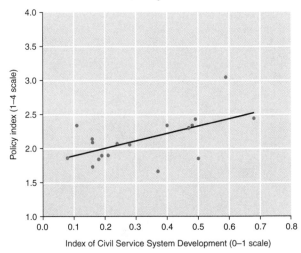

FIGURE 6.9 **Development of Civil Service System and the Quality of Policies**

Sources: Stein and Tommasi (2005) and Zuvanic and Iacoviello (2005).

Chapter 4 introduced an index of the development of civil service systems in each of the Latin American countries. This index has a strong correlation with most of the key features of policy. As predicted, a strong bureaucracy seems to prevent the excessive influence of special interests at the implementation stage, leading to public-regarding policies. The correlation with the policy index, depicted in Figure 6.9, is 0.588, significant at the 95 percent level.

Electoral Rules, Party System Fragmentation, and Partisan Powers of Presidents

Several characteristics of presidential democracies (other than the ones emphasized so far in this chapter) have received considerable attention because of their potential impact on governability (and hence policymaking). The results presented in Table 6.3 suggest that several of those predictions do not seem to hold for the measures and countries included in this study, at least at the level of simple and partial correlations. For brevity, only a brief example is discussed here.

The degree of proportionality of representation induced by electoral rules is a feature that has received considerable attention. More proportional electoral rules are expected to lead to better representation, but lower policy effectiveness.[25] Electoral rules that

---

[25] Payne and others (2002).

lead to a closer correspondece between share of votes and share of seats, as well as other features of the electoral system, are associated with more fragmented party systems and with presidents with lesser partisan powers (see Chapter 3 for a discussion of the various institutional sources of party system fragmentation and of partisan powers of presidents).

The last three rows of Table 6.3 present traditional measures of these concepts (proportionality of the electoral system, effective number of legislative parties, and presidential party's lower- or single-chamber contingent), and their correlation with policy characteristics. None of these measures appears to correlate significantly with this study's measures of policy effectiveness. This seems to suggest that it is difficult to generalize about direct effects of institutional rules and political configurations on the nature of policymaking and the characteristics of policies. As this study's framework suggests, more interactive and nuanced analysis seems to be necessary. That is a strong motivation for the type of country studies advocated by the framework. A first cut at such country studies is reflected in the Political Institutions, Policymaking Processes, and Policy Outcomes project, carried out by the Latin American Research Network of the Inter-American Development Bank. Some of that work is summarized in the next chapter.

Preliminary Conclusions

Table 6.4 summarizes the main correlations identified in this chapter. The countries (listed in the first column) are grouped in four categories with regard to the value of the policy index: "very high," "high," "medium," and "low." Countries are then presented alphabetically within each group. The other columns present values for some of the key variables identified in the foregoing analysis. Cases in which the country displays a relatively high value for the variable in question are shaded in dark blue. Cases of intermediate values are shaded in light blue. Cases of relatively low values are unshaded (white).

Countries with high values on the policy index tend to have high values for many of the institutional variables emphasized by this study. Note the country that has the highest value of the policy index: Chile. All the cells for Chile, with the exception of that corresponding to party institutionalization, are dark blue, indicating high values in the corresponding category. At the other end of the spectrum, countries with the lowest values of the policy index tend to have mostly white or light blue cells.

More generally, the table clearly shows that some of the main behavioral characteristics are inter-related. The high concentration of dark cells in the upper part of the table suggests that the variables are not independent. For instance, countries with stronger congresses tend to be countries with more independent judiciaries, and also with better policies.

This is not surprising, from the standpoint of this study's theoretical framework and the country studies conducted as background for this study. Several of the "institutional" variables, such as having a strong congress heavily involved in policymaking, or an independent supreme court, are the reflection of the equilibrium behavior of a number of relevant political actors. If a supreme court is able to maintain or develop its independence over time, it is because it is in the best interest of other relevant actors (such as

Table 6.4 Political Institutions and the Qualities of Policies

Country (by policy index level)	Congress Capabilities Index	Judicial independence	Party system institutionalization	Party system nationalization[a]	Programmatic parties	Development of civil service
Very High						
Chile	High	4.60	65	0.90	8.00	0.59
High						
Brazil	High	3.90	59	0.64	2.00	0.68
Colombia	High	3.10	60	—	0.00	0.47
Costa Rica	Medium	3.80	61	0.85	1.00	0.49
El Salvador	Medium	2.90	66	0.83	7.00	0.11
Mexico	Medium	3.30	67	0.78	2.00	0.40
Uruguay	High	4.80	76	0.89	7.00	0.48
Medium						
Bolivia	Medium	1.70	56	0.71	0.00	0.24
Dominican Rep.	Low	3.60	74	0.84	0.00	0.28
Honduras	Low	1.90	68	0.91	2.00	0.16
Peru	Low	1.90	53	0.50	0.00	0.16
Low						
Argentina	Low	1.80	62	0.59	2.00	0.50
Ecuador	Medium	1.90	53	0.74	1.00	0.18
Guatemala	Low	2.20	48	0.76	0.00	0.21
Nicaragua	Medium	1.60	70	0.88	8.00	0.19
Panama	Medium	2.20	67	0.78	0.00	0.08
Paraguay	Medium	1.40	64	0.73	1.00	0.16
Venezuela	Medium	1.20	55	0.61	0.00	0.37

—not available.

[a] Adequate data for party system nationalization are not available for Colombia for 2002. For the case of Ecuador, party system nationalization data correspond to 1998.

Note: Countries are classified first according to their policy index values ("very high," "high," "medium," and "low") and then alphabetically within those groupings. The values for each country on each variable are shaded such that dark blue represents "very high" or "high" values, light blue represents "medium" values, and white (no shading) represents "low" values.

Sources: Stein and Tommasi (2005); Jones (2005); Zuvanic and Iacoviello (2005); and World Economic Forum (2004).

the president) not to meddle with the supreme court in pursuit of short-term political benefits. Strong congresses and independent judiciaries are not built overnight, but are the outcome of processes of investing in the quality and credibility of such institutions. Such processes are inter-related.

These processes in some cases can lead to equilibria characterized by virtuous institutional dynamics. Executives will not attempt to change the composition of the supreme court, and this will help increase the court's independence and reputation. A strong and independent judiciary will tend to adequately enforce the domain and prerogatives of other institutional arenas such as congress, which will then enhance the incentives of legislators to invest in their individual and collective capabilities, and so forth.

But these processes can also result in vicious institutional dynamics, where the opposite will tend to happen. Executives will be inclined to meddle with the judiciary and encroach upon the powers of congress, lowering the incentives to invest in legislative careers and in the institutionalization and strengthening of congress.

This discussion suggests that the incentives of the president, the strength of congress, and the independence of the supreme court in a country are likely to be codetermined in equilibrium, and that all these factors together are likely to have an effect on the quality of policies in the country. This in turn suggests what economists might call the presence of multiplicity of equilibria. If for any reason a particular political system enters a virtuous circle, the political system is likely to build up its strength over time. The opposite will tend to happen when such virtuous circles do not have time to build or are broken.[26] This suggests that particular historical events or critical political junctures, as well as personalities and leadership qualities, will matter—inducing *path dependence*. The next chapter returns to the interdependencies among these factors in some Latin American countries. The related issue of governmental breakdowns in the form of constitutional interruptions is discussed in Box 6.2.

---

[26] Mailath, Morris, and Postlewaite (2001).

Box 6.2   Constitutional Interruptions

One of the central concerns in regard to political institutions and governability in Latin America is the history of interrupted governments. Until a few decades ago, coups d'état and military governments were frequent in Latin America. Most of the region's countries have steered clear of military governments in recent years, yet constitutional interruptions (when either presidents or congress do not complete the term for which they were elected) are still a recurrent occurrence. Since the early 1980s (or the return to democracy), there have been 14 constitutional interruptions in the 18 countries analyzed in this study. These interruptions (or more precisely, their absence) could be taken as an indication of the institutionalization of the political regime.

Not surprisingly, a high percentage of constitutional interruptions is associated with poor values on measures of several of the features of public policies, especially stability.[1] Also not surprisingly, constitutional interruptions are associated with low levels of some of the key variables describing the degree of institutionalization and quality of incentives in the policymaking process. Constitutional interruptions are associated with weak (and obstructive) congresses, dependent judiciaries, and weak party systems.

These findings reinforce the ideas developed in this report. Poorly functioning institutions are likely to breed the type of discontent that makes constitutional interruptions more likely. But such interruptions (and the expectation that they are likely to happen) in turn shorten the horizons of political actors, leading to more opportunistic short-term strategies and to the lack of investment in building policymaking capacities and better institutions.

Even though there are forces that make all these characteristics interdependent, there are institutional configurations that make constitutional interruptions more likely—a topic that has long preoccupied political scientists, particularly in the case of presidential democracies such as those in Latin America. Some scholars have argued that presidential systems, as opposed to parliamentary ones, pose special problems for democratic stability, given the weaker incentives inherent in presidential systems for forming and maintaining coalitions.[2] Others have argued that the stability of presidential democracies may be problematic mainly in the context of multi-party systems.[3] Recent work has suggested that presidential democracies in which the party in government does not control the legislature are a problem only to the extent that the president is unwilling or unable to form a majority (or near-majority) coalition.[4]

Following this lead, this study explored the links between constitutional interruptions and the type of government (majority or minority, single party or coalition) in a sample of 98 democratic governments in 18 Latin American countries between 1978 and 2005. The evidence, summarized in the table on the next page, is consistent with the findings of Chasquetti (1999) and Cheibub,

Box 6.2 — Continued

Przeworski, and Saiegh (2004). Democratic stability is more at risk in the case of minority governments. In fact, minority governments are five times more likely to suffer constitutional interruptions than governments that have a majority or near-majority in congress. However, whether majorities or near-majorities in congress are achieved through a single party, or through a coalition, does not seem to have an impact on the incidence of constitutional interruptions. Thus, particularly in the case of multi-party systems that tend to produce fragmented congresses, the ability of presidents to form and maintain majority coalitions is a very worthwhile area of inquiry. Chapter 7 further discusses these issues of policymaking in fragmented systems, focusing on the contrasting cases of Brazil and Ecuador.

Government Type and Constitutional Interruptions

	Near-majority			Minority		
	Number of governments	Number of constitutional interruptions	Share (%)	Number of governments	Number of constitutional interruptions	Share (%)
Single party	36	2	5.6	19	5	26.3
Coalition	28	2	7.1	15	5	33.3
Total	64	4	6.3	34	10	29.4

Sources: Payne and others (2002); Chasquetti (2004); and authors' compilation.

[1] The value for the correlation between constitutional interruptions and stability is −0.667, and is significant at the 99 percent level. Clearly, in these cases, causality is not unidirectional; the process is interactive. Constitutional interruptions are likely to induce shorter horizons, policy volatility, and poor coordination—but poor policies are likely to induce poor economic and social outcomes, which are a breeding ground for constitutional interruptions. For the purposes of this correlation, constitutional interruptions were measured as the share of presidential periods since 1978 or since the return to democracy that have been subject to interruptions, because either the president or the legislature did not complete their mandated terms.

[2] For example, Linz (1990).

[3] For example, Mainwaring (1993).

[4] Chasquetti (1999); Cheibub, Przeworski, and Saiegh (2004).

Chapter 7

Country Experiences in Policymaking

A general equilibrium approach is required to understand why similar political institutions may produce different policy outcomes in different countries.

Chapter 6 provides some perspective on the connections between the policy-making process (PMP) and policy outcomes. It shows how some key aspects of the policymaking process (such as whether congresses have policymaking capabilities, whether parties are institutionalized and programmatic, or whether judiciaries are independent) can have an important impact on the quality of public policies. While Chapter 6 emphasizes that these aspects are not independent of one another, it does not go all the way in terms of showing the full dynamic of policymaking processes as they function in general equilibrium, and the impact they have on public policies.

Rather than focusing on some particular aspects of the policymaking process, this chapter offers a glimpse of how the process works in a few countries. The chapter is largely based on the country studies from the Political Institutions, Policymaking Processes, and Policy Outcomes project of the IDB's Latin American Research Network. This project initially included ten countries in Latin America (Argentina, Brazil, Chile, Colombia, Ecuador, Mexico, Paraguay, Peru, Uruguay, and Venezuela) but was later extended to incorporate three more (Costa Rica, Guatemala, and Jamaica). In the interest of brevity, this chapter will discuss five of them.

The first is Chile. This choice is obvious, given that this country ranks at the top in each of the features of public policies discussed in Chapter 2. The other four countries were chosen to illustrate a number of important issues. One of them is the trade-off between representativeness (or inclusiveness) and policy effectiveness. A number of countries, including Colombia, Mexico, Paraguay, and Venezuela, have moved in the direction of more inclusiveness and participation. In some cases, however, this has come at the expense of some policy effectiveness. The second section in this chapter discusses this trade-off, using the changes in Colombia's PMP before and after the 1991 Constitution to illustrate the point.

The chapter's third section highlights the challenges involved in policymaking within the context of very fragmented political systems. The contrasting cases of Brazil and Ecuador are used to illustrate the issue. These countries have the most fragmented party systems in the region. They also share other important characteristics. In both, the president has strong legislative powers, designed in part to compensate for his weak partisan support. In both, legislators are elected using open lists, encouraging close connections between the legislators and the voters. Yet, while Brazil has a stable democracy and reasonably good public policies, in Ecuador the quality of policies is poor and presidents find themselves involved in difficult battles for political survival. While several factors help produce these contrasting results, especially important is the ability of the president in Brazil to build and maintain a stable coalition.

These sections are complemented with a box, based on the case of Costa Rica, which discusses an alternative (and, in this case, reasonably successful) way of making policies: one in which both presidents and legislatures are comparatively weak (in terms of their constitutional powers), and an important portion of policymaking is delegated to autonomous institutions.

Policymaking in an Institutionalized Setting: The Case of Chile[1]

Like any country, Chile must contend with many unfulfilled aspirations, and its social and economic outcomes, as well as the functioning of its policymaking system, have been subject to some criticism. Even though poverty fell by half from 1990 to 2003, dropping from almost 40 to 19 percent of the population, income inequality has not decreased. A large percentage of Chileans are dissatisfied with the "authoritarian enclaves" that were left over from the Pinochet government, and political participation, especially among the young, is low.[2]

Yet of all the countries included in this study, Chile is the one with the best policy characteristics. It has the highest value for the policy index and for most of the components of that index. These numerical measures are buttressed by the policy cases analyzed in the background study on Chile prepared for this report.[3]

Chile returned to democratic rule in March 1990, after almost 17 years of dictatorship. The workings of the recent Chilean polity and policymaking system present a mix of change and continuity with respect to the country's history of democracy before its period of dictatorship.

The constitution drafted in 1980 by the military authorities and reformed in 1989 and 1991 at the time of the transition to democracy established some important characteristics of Chilean political institutions, such as a very strong presidency, an

---

[1] This section is based largely on Aninat and others (2004). These authors are not, however, responsible for the interpretation in this chapter.

[2] See, for instance, the essays in Drake and Jaksic (1999). Most of these enclaves have been dismantled in recent years.

[3] Aninat and others (2004).

electoral system that favors the formation of two coalitions while overrepresenting the second-largest coalition, and the presence of an important number of "authoritarian enclaves."[4]

The Chilean president is very powerful (see Chapter 3, Table 3.5), with near-monopoly control over the legislative agenda, and with proposal and veto powers that make him the de facto agenda-setter.

While the president is very powerful, the Chilean policymaking system is studded with veto players, initially written into the constitution by the outgoing military government to impede policy changes by subsequent elected governments. These include a bicameral congress, a comptroller general, and an independent locus of judicial power, including regular courts, a constitutional tribunal, and an electoral tribunal. Less traditional (and more contested) checks on policy formation include the presence of unelected senators in the upper chamber of congress and the relative autonomy of the armed forces.

Yet some characteristics of the Chilean polity, with respect to its institutions and its policies, are surprising. While it has a strong executive in terms of constitutional prerogatives, Chile also has the strongest congress, as evidenced by its top ranking in the Congress Capabilities Index. While its system features numerous veto players, its policies in many areas are perceived as having the greatest capacity for adaptation among the countries examined in this study. The discussion that follows addresses these "puzzles" within the more general context of the workings of the Chilean policymaking process.

The Chilean Congress in the Latin American Context

Chilean legislators do not have access to technical input of the same quality as the executive does. And as noted, the legislative powers of the Chilean president are very strong.

Nonetheless, the Chilean Congress is the strongest congress in Latin America in terms of its role in the policymaking process. As shown in Table 3.6 in Chapter 3, Chile's Congress has one of the highest levels of technical specialization in the region (through its system of policy committees). Chilean legislators are fairly well educated, and they have long careers in congress. Consequently, their levels of technical expertise are high by Latin American standards. Even though public opinion of the congress is low in absolute terms in Chile (as it is in the whole region), it is the second highest in Latin America.[5] A seat in the lower chamber (and even more so, in the senate) is a high-profile and desirable position for Chilean politicians.

Despite the strength of the executive and the fact that some important negotiations within and among parties do not necessarily take place in congress, the Chilean Congress is an important political and policymaking arena. Crucial political and policy

---

[4] At the time of this writing, several of the main political parties had agreed on a constitutional reform that would purge many of these vestiges of the dictatorship from the constitution, and congress was debating the reform.

[5] According to a measure of the effectiveness of lawmaking bodies from the World Economic Forum (which can be read as "public" opinion from international business executives), Chile ranks first in Latin America.

matters are debated openly and later enforced in the national legislature.[6] The level of debate and transparency of the Chilean Congress is quite high.

The Making of Policy in Chile[7]

The Chilean president is constitutionally very powerful. Yet the three presidents who have served since democracy has been restored (Patricio Aylwin, Eduardo Frei, and Ricardo Lagos) have exercised that power in a relatively careful and consensual manner. The Chilean president is, undoubtedly, the agenda-setter in the policymaking process, and has enough tools at his disposal to be able, on occasion, to exert pressure to get his preferred policies through the PMP. Many important policies are developed primarily within the cabinet (with the assistance of technically capable and politically adroit ministers). There is a practice of negotiation and agreement that operates in several (usually sequential) stages.[8] Since Chile has relatively strong parties and party identities, the president initially tries to develop consensus for his policies inside his own party, and then within his own coalition, usually through negotiation with the leaders of the other parties in the coalition. Then interactions with the opposition take place, mostly through open forums such as congress.

Technical input enters the policymaking process at multiple nodes. The Chilean cabinet and bureaucracy are very solid by Latin American standards. Chile also has several well-established and reasonably well-staffed think tanks, with institutionalized links to different political parties and coalitions.

In a system with many veto players and a president with strong agenda-setting powers, policies are difficult to pass, but they are passed through negotiations, policy concessions, and, on occasion, distribution of a few particularistic benefits. Once policies are passed, any bargains struck during these negotiations are very stable, and policy is very credible (as seen in this study's indicators). This very policy stability makes policies a very strong currency in political exchanges. Moreover, the institutionalized nature of parties makes them important actors for the inter-temporal enforcement of these negotiations, minimizing transaction costs and associated distortions.

The Party System

Political parties in Chile are currently moderate, pragmatic yet programmatic, and strongly institutionalized. The tradition of three ideological blocs, left–center–right, has been maintained, but with a substantial degree of convergence. For instance, socialist parties still receive their historical share of electoral support, even though their Leftist ideological orientation has moderated considerably. Since 1990 there have been six par-

---

[6] Aninat and others (2004) present several illustrative cases.

[7] This description of policymaking in Chile is a stylized version of the PMP for many policy areas (including most economic and social policies). The process is distinct and more controversial in some policy areas, such as human rights.

[8] For simplicity, a "typical" sequence is described here, even though the specific negotiation sequence varies from issue to issue.

ties with congressional representation, organized into two national coalitions, the *Concertación* (Center-Left), and the *Alianza* (Right), which formed around the 1988 plebiscite called to decide whether Augusto Pinochet should remain as president.

The workings of the Chilean party system are influenced by a peculiar type of proportional-representation electoral system, with just two seats elected in each district ("binominal"). The lists (coalitions/parties) that receive the two highest shares of votes each win one of the two seats available in each district. Only if the first-place list wins by a ratio of more than two to one do both seats for the district go to the list that won the most votes.

This electoral system reduces the number of relevant actors by encouraging parties to coalesce. Together with the requirement that coalitions can be formed only at the national level (and thus are binding in every electoral district), it strengthens the national leadership of parties. There is a strong incentive to coalesce at the district level, since when the top vote-getter gets at least twice as many votes as its rival, it obtains all (100 percent) of the seats. If a list comes in second, even with only slightly more than half of the votes of the winning list, it gets half (50 percent) of the seats being contested. The provision that coalitions are binding at the national level leads parties to form encompassing national coalitions. Since it is difficult to form coalitions that secure more than two-thirds of the votes in each district, and it is relatively easy to secure one-third of the vote share, the most likely outcome is the formation of two national coalitions.

Any individual party would pay a high price for leaving a coalition. This has been important for keeping both coalitions in Chile united for many years, even though they include parties with different platforms on several issues and political leaders with strong personal rivalries. Despite publicized bickering within coalitions, both coalitions have remained united because of pressure exerted by the congressional members on their respective party leaderships. Congressional members know that their chances for reelection would be jeopardized should the coalitions break up.

Continuous party negotiations within coalitions to decide which candidates will be nominated to the coalition's list in each district strengthen the parties' national leadership (although nationally endorsed candidates must be appealing to their local districts). The legislative electoral system does not have term limits. This, together with the need for candidates with strong local support, encourages politicians to seek long legislative careers. In Chile, 75 percent of congressional members are renominated and about 60 percent are reelected. This reelection rate is one of the highest in Latin America.

The binominal system reduces the number of relevant actors to a few parties organized into two encompassing, stable coalitions. It strengthens the party leadership, but at the same time it encourages politicians to respond to their constituencies and have long legislative careers. Finally, given how difficult it would be for one coalition to obtain twice the vote share of the other in any given district, under the binominal system congressional representation for each coalition hovers at around 50 percent of the members of each chamber.[9]

---

[9] The binominal system also discriminates against third parties outside the two major coalitions. This "disproportionality" effect is one of the roots of the criticism of the system, which is considered by some to be another vestige of the dictatorship. This study suggests that when these trade-offs are evaluated, the general equilibrium effects of the system on the workings of the PMP should be considered.

Summary

The salient features of the Chilean PMP are a party system characterized by two long-lived coalitions, a powerful executive with de facto control over the agenda, a relatively independent judiciary, a bureaucracy that is relatively free from corruption (compared with OECD countries), and a series of veto points in the policymaking process that permit adversely affected actors to block policy change.[10] The small number of actors, which interact repeatedly, as well as the predictability of policy implementation and law enforcement, leads to a policymaking process in which transaction costs are low and inter-temporal political exchanges are credible.

Chile seems to be on a path of institutional and policy consolidation. The initial democratic governments have maintained the core of the economic reforms undertaken during the military dictatorship, while steadily (albeit slowly, according to some views) advancing on the social and democratic front. These steps have taken place according to a style of policymaking that is much more consensual and institutionalized than that of other Latin American countries.

The Trade-Off between Inclusiveness and Effectiveness: The Case of Colombia

After several decades in which most Latin American countries frequently switched between democratic and military governments, the countries of the region gradually returned to democratic rule in the 1980s. Democracies, however, come in different shapes and sizes. While some are fairly inclusive, others exclude certain parties or sectors of the population, either explicitly or because the electoral and constitutional rules prevent adequate representation of minorities. While some produce decisive governments that are able to adopt and implement their policies effectively, others tend to experience gridlock and suffer serious governability problems. It is quite obvious that both inclusiveness (or representativeness) and effectiveness are desirable traits. The problem is that sometimes there are trade-offs between these two characteristics.

Take, for example, the impact of electoral rules. A system of proportional representation with large district magnitudes will score high on representativeness, since the proportion of seats going to each party will be closely matched to the proportion of votes corresponding to each of them. In the limit of perfect proportionality, the number of parties would be large, and no sizable group of voters would be left unrepresented. Yet, unless the conditions are in place for the government to be able to form and sustain a majority coalition, multi-party systems are much more prone to gridlock, and even democratic interruptions. At the other end of the spectrum, plurality systems leave some groups without representation, but are much more likely to produce majority governments that can effectively implement their policy agendas.

---

[10] In the areas of human rights and military policy, the armed forces must be included among the set of veto players.

In recent decades, Latin American countries have tended to move toward greater inclusiveness. This is obvious in the cases of countries that have switched from dictatorships to democracy. But the movement is broader than that. In Peru, in addition to the return to democratic rule, the 1980s were characterized by a significant expansion of the franchise. Even countries that have been under democratic rule for many decades moved toward greater inclusiveness. In Mexico, the end of *Partido Revolucionario Institucional* (PRI) hegemony led to significant changes in terms of the representation of political minorities. Together with the adoption of elections for governors, this provided new opportunities for politicians to launch political careers outside of the control of the PRI party leaders. In Venezuela, discussed in more detail in Chapter 11, the introduction of elections for governors had a similar impact. It broke the strong control on political careers that had been firmly exercised by the national leaders of the two traditional parties, AD (*Acción Democrática*) and COPEI (*Comité de Organización Política Electoral Independiente*), and ended the collusive agreement between these parties that had been in place since the *Pacto de Punto Fijo*.[11] In Colombia, the adoption of the 1991 Constitution has also represented a movement in the direction of more inclusiveness, in a political system in which the Left had traditionally been excluded and had resorted to non-democratic means of expression (guerrilla movements).

Rather than covering each of the cases, this section focuses on just one of them—Colombia—to illustrate the delicate balance (or trade-off) between inclusiveness and policy effectiveness, as well as the quest to find a satisfying position on these two dimensions through institutional change.

The 1991 Constitution and Colombia's PMP

One key building block of the policymaking process in Colombia before the 1991 Constitution was the *Frente Nacional*, an agreement between the two traditional parties (*Liberal* and *Conservador*) to share power, with parties alternating in the presidency, and strict parity in key policymaking arenas such as congress, the cabinet, courts, governors, and mayors.[12] While the *Frente Nacional* was formally in effect between 1958 and 1974, several of the key features of the *Frente* extended well into the late 1980s.

During this extended period of the *Frente Nacional*, policymaking in Colombia was quite effective. Growth performance was strong, averaging 4.7 percent between 1950 and 1990. Fiscal deficits were low, and fiscal policy played a stabilizing role, aided by mechanisms such as the coffee stabilization fund. The perception in the region was that Colombia had avoided the populist tendencies that were prevalent in Latin America at the time.[13]

---

[11] The *Pacto de Punto Fijo* was signed by the main parties in 1958, and involved the sharing of power through the distribution of key cabinet positions and the implementation of common social and economic policies. See Chapter 11 for more details.

[12] For a more complete characterization of Colombia's PMP, see Cárdenas, Junguito, and Pachón (2005). This section is based on their work.

[13] This perception was strengthened by a well-known study by Urrutia (1991).

In the policymaking process that operated before 1991, the president was institutionally very powerful, as was the finance ministry, typically headed by a well-respected technocrat. The rules of the political game constrained the role of congress in economic policy and enhanced the decision making capacity of the government. The *Frente Nacional* coalition, sustained through cabinet and governorship appointments, ensured ample majorities in congress. While the structure of committees provided some incentives for legislators to specialize and gain policy expertise, electoral rules provided incentives for them to focus more on their constituents and less on national policymaking. Thus to some extent legislators focused on getting support for their local projects (in the form of *auxilios parlamentarios*) and for the most part delegated national policymaking—particularly macroeconomic policy—to the executive, which was able to rely on a bureaucracy that was relatively strong, at least by Latin American standards.[14] But even in cases in which the president could not count on the support of the legislature, he had ample powers to legislate by decree, through the use of economic emergencies or the declaration of the state of siege. As will be discussed in Chapter 8, these powers were instrumental in the passing of some important tax reforms during this period. The Supreme Court did exercise some control over the use of decrees, overturning about 25 percent of them, but was not as independent and active as today's Constitutional Court.

This policymaking process is reflected in the quality of public policies discussed in Chapter 6. Before 1991, Colombia ranked in the top five countries in the region in terms of stability, adaptability, coordination and coherence, and efficiency. If there was one weak spot in Colombia's PMP, it was linked to deficits in political participation. The *Frente* was an agreement of a collusive nature, which ensured cooperation among those included, but excluded important sectors of the population, notably the Left. Political participation at the subnational level was also lacking. Governors and mayors were appointed rather than elected, and on occasion had weak roots in the jurisdictions in which they held office. Additionally, this period was characterized by widespread use of clientelistic practices as a way to gather and maintain political support. The most obvious example was the discretionary and often arbitrary use by individual legislators of the resources they obtained through *auxilios parlamentarios*. Both factors—lack of participation and clientelistic practices—help explain the poor performance of the country in terms of public-regardedness, a dimension on which Colombia ranked near the bottom, in contrast to its relatively high rankings on most of the other dimensions.

Demands for further political participation at both the subnational and national levels were important factors in the transition to the new constitution. The process of decentralization, which had led to the election of mayors in 1988, coupled with the emergence of new sources of revenue associated with discoveries of oil, made it necessary to redefine the way the political and economic pie was going to be shared. The exclusion of the Left from regular channels of political participation had led to guerrilla activity and escalating violence, involving the drug cartels as well, which culminated with the assassination of three presidential candidates in the 1989 electoral campaign,

---

[14] The *auxilios parlamentarios*, which were discretionary funds that were assigned to each member of the legislature, were introduced in the 1968 constitutional reform and banned in the 1991 Constitution.

including the likely winner, Luis Carlos Galán. The idea of constitutional reform gained political support, at a time of political unrest when the incorporation of the insurgent groups into the political system was seen as a priority. This led to the adoption of a new constitution.

The 1991 Constitution introduced very important changes into the policymaking process. While the president is by no means weak compared to those in other systems in the region (see Chapter 3), the 1991 Constitution limited the power of the executive in a number of ways. It introduced the election of governors (which the president had previously appointed) and endowed them with significant fiscal resources. It reduced the discretion of the president (and congress) on a number of important policy issues: in some cases, such as pensions or intergovernmental transfers, because they were "hard-wired" into the constitution; in others, such as monetary and exchange rate policies, because they were left within the orbit of a newly independent central bank. The new constitution gave congress a more active role in policymaking by curtailing the ability of the executive to legislate by decree, and by making it easier for the legislature to overrule a presidential veto. It gave the judiciary a more active role, by creating a Constitutional Court endowed with *ex ante* constitutional review powers and appointment procedures that encouraged judicial independence.

The constitution also introduced reforms that weakened the partisan powers of the president. Rules for the election of presidents were modified from plurality to majority run-off elections, a system that encourages independents to run in the first round, and tends to reduce the president's legislative contingent. In addition, parties themselves became more fragmented. While electoral rules for congress had traditionally produced incentives for the fragmentation of political parties into a large number of very small and fairly independent factions, changes to campaign finance rules channeling public funding to factions rather than parties, as well as changes in the ballot structure, further weakened the ability of presidents and central party leaders to discipline their own legislative contingents (see Box 7.1).[15] In summary, not only did the constitution limit the legislative powers of the president, but his capacity to do the things that remained within his power was curtailed as well.

As a result of the changes introduced by the 1991 Constitution, the PMP in Colombia experienced significant alterations. Congress became increasingly involved in national policy discussions, introducing significant changes into legislation proposed by the executive. As the example of tax policies in Chapter 8 will make clear, passing legislation has become more costly. The executive must make more concessions, and more rewards need to be distributed in order to pass legislation, as the number of "sponsors" involved in each bill has substantially increased.[16] Even after legislation passes through congress, it can still be derailed by the Constitutional Court, which not only has made it more difficult for the executive to bypass congress (associated with its role as enforcer) but

---

[15] Changes to the ballot structure and campaign finance were not actually part of the constitutional reform, but were enacted by law shortly before the constitutional reform.

[16] Sponsors are legislators that participate directly in the discussion of bills. They typically have substantial impact on a bill's content, and they tend to obtain more "pork" than legislators who do not have this status.

| Box 7.1 | Extreme Party Fragmentation in Colombia: *Operaciones avispa* |

Until very recently, Colombia had an electoral system for the legislature that combined proportional representation with an allocation of seats by quotas and largest remainders. Multiple factions could present lists under the same party label. The largest-remainders formula was applied to factions, rather than parties, leading to party fragmentation and low party discipline.

The impact of the largest-remainders rule can be illustrated with an example. Consider a district with 1,000 voters and 10 seats (so the number of votes needed to gain a seat by quota is 100). Party A gets 650 votes, Party B gets 240, Party C gets 70, and Party D gets 40. Running as party lists, A would get 7 seats (6 by quota, 1 by remainder), B would get 2 (by quota), C would get 1 (by remainder), and D would get none. If Party B were to split into three equal factions of 80 votes each, the party would get 3 seats (all by remainder), taking one away from A. If Party A splits into eight equal factions, however, it would capture 8 seats (all by remainder), leaving only 2 seats (also by remainder) for the fragmented factions of Party B. It is easy to see that large parties, to maximize the number of seats, have incentives to fragment into small electoral vehicles (known in Colombia as *operaciones avispa*), most of which aim to elect a single individual to Congress.

These incentives for fragmentation were exacerbated just before the 1991 Constitution, when changes to the structure of the ballot were introduced, as well as the financing of parties. The party leadership, which had no control over the party label, after 1991 also lost control of the funds, which were directly allocated to the factions, further diminishing the influence of party leaders. As a result, the number of lists running for the lower house jumped from around 350 to more than 900 between 1990 and 2002. In 2002, 96 percent of the winning lists elected only one candidate to congress, the great majority of them by remainders. In this context, legislators have incentives to cater to their regional constituencies, rather than to follow the line of the party leaders, on whom they do not depend for reelection.

has also more generally become a more active—some observers say overly active—player in the policymaking game. Subnational governments have additionally become more important players in some aspects of policymaking, including social policies. This has sometimes had important implications for macroeconomic policies, as several departments and municipalities have incurred excessive debt and had to be bailed out by the national government.

In summary, the number of key players in the national policymaking game has increased, and cooperation among players has become more difficult to achieve. While these developments are positive in that they generate stronger checks and balances on the discretion of the executive, they can also have a negative impact on policy effectiveness. In fact, a few of the key features of public policies more directly linked with effectiveness (stability, efficiency, coordination, and coherence) declined after 1991 (see Figure 7.1).[17] On the other hand, the country achieved substantial improvements in terms of public-regardedness (which is still low, however). This improvement can be traced to at least four factors: the increase in checks and balances; increased participation, at both the national and subnational levels; more control on the clientelistic practices of politicians, particularly legislators, through the elimination of *auxilios parlamentarios*;[18] and more control over the discretion of the executive to distribute subsidies and credit to certain sectors of the population, as an independent central bank is subject to restrictions on lending to the private sector.

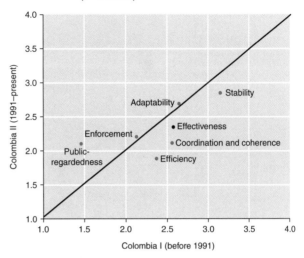

FIGURE 7.1   **Evolution of Key Features of Public Policies (Colombia)** (*1–4 scale*)

Note: The straight line is at a 45 degree angle, so that key features located in the upper triangle show improvement from period I to period II, and those that have deteriorated are located in the bottom triangle.

Sources: Stein and Tommasi (2005) and authors' calculations.

Colombia has not been the only country moving in the direction of more participation and inclusiveness. Other countries moving in that direction include Mexico and Paraguay.[19] In all these cases, the improvement in terms of inclusiveness has occurred alongside some declines in policy effectiveness (see Figure 7.2). However, the rate at which countries have sacrificed effectiveness in the quest for more inclusiveness differs greatly across countries. The challenge is to try to increase inclusiveness and participation without losing effectiveness in the process.

---

[17] While this study's imperfect measure of adaptability based on just a couple of survey questions shows slight improvement, the "hard-wiring" of a number of aspects of policy, as well as the discussion of tax reforms in Colombia before and after the reform of the constitution (see Chapter 8), suggests that, at least in a number of areas, adaptability has also decreased in recent times.

[18] The impact of the elimination of the *auxilios*, however, has been the subject of some debate. Some authors argue that, although formally eliminated, the *auxilios* have continued in practice in a more informal and opaque way. Furthermore, they argue that the funds involved in these practices have increased with these changes, rather than decreased. See, for example, Vargas (1999) and Echeverry, Fergusson, and Querubín (2004).

[19] The case of Venezuela, which also conforms to this pattern, is discussed in detail in Chapter 11.

FIGURE 7.2 **Evolution of Key Features of Public Policies** (*1–4 scale*)

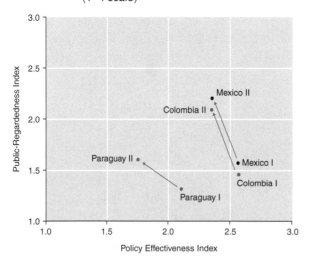

Note: For Colombia, Mexico and Paraguay, policy indices were calculated for two sets of data, corresponding to different periods in time. The periods are as follows: Colombia I = before 1991, Colombia II = 1991–present; Mexico I = 1950–mid 1990s, Mexico II = 1990s–2003; and Paraguay I = 1954–1989, Paraguay II = 1989–2003.

Sources: Stein and Tommasi (2005) and authors' calculations.

In Colombia, recent reforms have passed through congress that seek to improve effectiveness, hopefully without compromising inclusiveness and participation to any significant extent. One change involves the reelection of the president, a trend that has been present in many Latin American countries. Probably the most important one, from the perspective of this study, relates to changes in the electoral rules for the legislature. Political parties can now present only a single party list in each electoral district. In addition, a threshold was introduced (equivalent to 2 percent of the national electorate) that precludes small local movements from participating in elections. These changes should help reduce fragmentation and increase party discipline. Thus they should enhance the role of parties as encompassing institutions interested in policymaking at the national level, where inter-temporal bargains can be reached. They should also help facilitate the passage of some legislation through congress.

Policymaking in Fragmented Political Systems: The Contrasting Cases of Brazil and Ecuador[20]

One of the main concerns about the workings of presidential democracies is the potential for governability problems. In contrast to his counterpart in parliamentary democracies, the president in a presidential democracy is not guaranteed a winning coalition that will allow him to pass his agenda through the legislature. Lack of support for the president in the legislature has been associated with difficulties in obtaining approval of welfare-enhancing reforms and in adapting to shocks, and even with an increased likelihood of constitutional interruptions. These concerns are particularly relevant in the case of fragmented political systems, in which the party of the president typically does not hold a majority of the seats in the legislature. In these cases, policy adaptability and,

---

[20] This section draws heavily on Araujo and others (2004), Alston and others (2005a), and Mueller and Pereira (2005).

more generally, democratic governability will depend on the ability of the government (and of the president in particular) to form and maintain a winning coalition.

This section looks at policymaking in Brazil and Ecuador. These two countries have the most fragmented party systems in Latin America. As a result, in both cases the presidential party's contingent in the legislature is among the lowest in the region (see Figure 7.3).[21]

Yet Brazil and Ecuador differ considerably with regard to the quality of their public policies. According to the policy index developed in Chapter 6, Brazil appears in the group with relatively good policies, while Ecuador appears in the group in which the quality of policies is low. In fact, Brazil ranks above Ecuador in each of the features of public policy presented in Table 6.1 (see also Figure 7.4). Furthermore, democracy in Brazil is stronger and more stable than in Ecuador, where none of the last three popularly elected presidents (Abdalá Bucaram, Jamil Mahuad, and Lucio Gutiérrez) has been able to complete his term.

In addition to their political fragmentation, political institutions in Brazil and Ecuador share other important features. In both countries, the president has been endowed with unusually strong constitutional powers. Legislators in both countries are elected using similar electoral rules: open-list proportional representation systems, which provide them with incentives to cater to their geographical constituencies. Given their important common elements, how can the contrasting political and economic policy outcomes of Brazil and Ecuador be explained? The answer does not lie in any single factor.

To some extent, differences in policy outcomes may be associated with substantial differences in the quality of the institutions that Chapter 6 identified as essential for good policymaking. While Brazil has a congress with relatively

FIGURE 7.3 **Effective Number of Legislative Parties and President's Chamber Contingent**

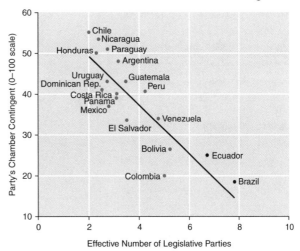

Sources: Jones (2005) and Saiegh (2005).

Differences in policy outcomes in the two countries may be associated with substantial differences in the quality of the institutions that are basic building blocks for good policymaking.

---

[21] In the case of Brazil, the figure refers to fragmentation and the presidential contingent in the lower chamber.

good policymaking capabilities, a strong bureaucracy, and
an independent judiciary, Ecuador lacks all of these things.
While in Brazil the president's
main focus (at least in recent
times) has been on maintaining macroeconomic stability,
the president of Ecuador on occasion becomes engaged in an
uphill battle for political survival, which prevents him from
focusing on the long run.

In addition, there is another
important difference between
the policymaking process in
Brazil and Ecuador. While the
president in Brazil seems to have
the tools he needs to engage in
political exchanges with legislators and sustain a coalition in
congress, in Ecuador coalitions
are very fickle and tend to collapse as the presidential term

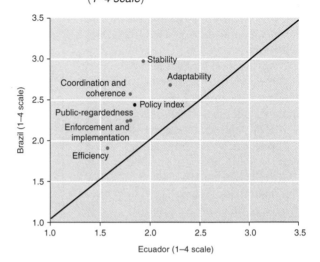

FIGURE 7.4 **Key Features of Public Policies
(Brazil and Ecuador)**
(*1–4 scale*)

Note: The straight line is at a 45 degree angle; points above the line
represent features on which Brazil scores higher than Ecuador.
Source: Stein and Tommasi (2005).

progresses and elections draw near. The rest of this section explores each of these factors
in more detail.[22]

Policymaking Capabilities and the Role of Congress

Brazil and Ecuador differ substantially with regard to the policymaking capabilities of
their legislatures and the role they play in the PMP, in spite of important similarities in
the electoral rules for the legislature.

Brazil

Legislators in Brazil are elected for a period of four years under an open-list, proportional
representation system. Having an open list means that voters can vote for an individual
candidate within the party list and help shape which candidates get elected. This electoral system typically provides incentives for legislators to respond according to the

---

[22] As discussed in Chapter 6, several of these factors are determined jointly. In addition, these factors
are endogenous to other important factors such as income, degree of ethnic fractionalization, and the
economic structure of the country, dimensions on which Brazil and Ecuador differ significantly. In line
with the focus of this report, the discussion that follows will abstract from these issues, and consider
instead the role of political institutions and policymaking processes in explaining these differences in
economic and political outcomes.

preferences and demands of their districts, rather than respond to the wishes of party leaders. Not surprisingly, their reelection chances depend crucially on their ability to deliver on those demands.

However, in Brazil these decentralizing electoral forces are compensated for by other features that lead to greater party discipline. Party leaders have the power to appoint and substitute members of the legislative committees, which play a relatively important role in policymaking. Perhaps more importantly, interactions between the executive and legislators are not handled individually, but through the mediation of party leaders, who act as brokers in the exchange. Thus, by controlling the access of individual legislators to the benefits that may affect their chances for reelection, party leaders can get individual legislators to vote according the party's preferences, resulting in a relatively high degree of party discipline. This is why, in spite of "decentralizing" electoral rules, political parties in Brazil tend to be strong and cohesive within the legislative arena, increasing the scope for cooperative inter-temporal exchanges.[23]

A number of other factors contribute to the policymaking capability of congress in Brazil. Reelection rates for legislators are relatively high, at least in regional perspective. Nearly 70 percent of legislators in the lower chamber seek reelection, and about 70 percent of those who run are reelected. Thus close to 50 percent of legislators have prior legislative experience, which contributes to an accumulation of policy expertise, as well as a longer-term focus.

The technical capacity of the legislature for policymaking purposes is further aided by a large technical staff that provides legislative support (see the discussion of knowledge actors in Chapter 5). More than 500 staff members in the two chambers provide technical support. Most of them are specialists in different areas of policy. They are highly educated and well paid, and they obtain their positions through a highly competitive selection process. These legislative support offices, developed mostly during the 1990s, have helped improve the technical level of legislative deliberations, as well as the quality of the policies that are discussed in congress. In this dimension, Brazil is at the top of the ranking of the countries in Latin America.

As a result of these factors, Brazil ranks high within the region on the index of policymaking capabilities of congress, lagging behind only Chile. These capabilities allow the Brazilian Congress to play a constructive role in policymaking, a role characterized by a workable relationship with the executive, despite the high level of political fragmentation. The mechanisms through which the executive can keep the coalition together and advance its agenda are discussed in more detail below.

---

[23] Much of the political science literature dealing with Brazil in the early 1990s focused on how incentives derived from the electoral and party system, including the open-list and proportional electoral system, would be expected to lead to difficulties for the executive in gaining approval for its agenda (Ames 1995, 2001; Mainwaring 1997). By contrast, a subsequent wave of scholarship focused on how the rules and structures that organize the legislative process and the power of the executive shape the behavior of the legislature and result in a more centralized decision making process (Figueiredo and Limongi 2000; Pereira and Mueller 2004).

Ecuador

In Ecuador, electoral rules for the legislature have been subject to a number of changes. Until 1997, Ecuador had a mixed electoral system in place for its unicameral congress. While "national" deputies were elected from a single district for a period of four years, "provincial" deputies (comprising more than 80 percent of the total) were elected from provincial districts under proportional representation, for a period of just two years. Immediate reelection was banned by the constitution until 1994. As a result, the legislative experience of the Ecuadorian legislators was by far the lowest in the region. These short tenures led to legislators with short horizons, without policymaking capabilities, and without incentives to develop them.

The midterm elections for provincial deputies had another important drawback. They typically reduced the size of the president's legislative contingent even further, making it more difficult for the president to build a winning coalition that would allow him to pass his agenda. As an example, during the Rodrigo Borja administration (1988–92) the share of seats controlled by the ruling party, the *Izquierda Democrática*, dropped from 42.3 percent in the first half of the term to 19.4 percent after midterm elections. During the Sixto Durán-Ballén administration, the share corresponding to the *Partido Unión Republicana* fell from 15.6 percent to just 3.9 percent. More generally, the size of the coalition supporting the president in congress declined substantially throughout the presidential term, with the midterm elections accounting for an important share of the decline.

In recent years, electoral rules for the legislature have been subject to a number of changes. The ban on immediate reelection was lifted in time for the 1996 election. The electoral system was switched to one with open lists in 1997. Midterm elections were eliminated, and the tenure of provincial deputies was extended to four years in the constitutional reform of 1998. For the 2002 elections, deputies were elected only out of provincial districts. In addition, the rules for electing the president were also changed in 1998, in an attempt to provide the executive with a larger legislative contingent. The recent episodes of democratic interruptions suggest that the impact of these changes has been insufficient. The legislative contingent of Ecuadorian presidents continues to be very small; only a small portion of legislators (about 27 percent) are reelected, which means that they still tend to be focused on the short run and have weak policymaking capabilities.

As a result of scant legislative support, particularly toward the end of the presidential terms, executives have often resorted to using their considerable constitutional powers to carry out their agendas. These attempts to bypass congress have led to a highly adversarial relationship between the executive and the legislature, with the president often trying to legislate by decree, and congress threatening to impeach cabinet members.

The contrasting roles of the legislatures in Brazil and Ecuador are reflected in the rate of success of the executive in passing legislation, presented in Chapter 3. While Brazilian presidents have been able to pass 72 percent of their initiatives through congress, Ecuadorian executives have been successful only 42 percent of the time.[24]

---

[24] While both presidents have very significant powers, the nature of these powers is different. Brazil's president has very strong decree powers but weak veto powers. The opposite is true in Ecuador. These differences may also contribute to explaining the different success rates.

Judiciaries and Bureaucracies

Brazil and Ecuador also differ substantially with regard to the strength and independence of the judiciary and the bureaucracy. As discussed in Chapter 6, both are important building blocks that contribute to good policymaking.

Brazil

In Brazil, supreme court justices are nominated by the president and confirmed by the senate for lifetime terms, but must retire at age 70. Tenures of supreme court justices have averaged over ten years, making Brazil second only to Chile within Latin America (see Figure 4.6 in Chapter 4). As a result, each president typically appoints a small number of the 11 supreme court justices. For example, during the eight years of the Cardoso administration, only three justices were appointed to the supreme court. The independence of the courts has been enhanced by the 1988 Constitution, which established that the judiciary would determine its own budget, and the courts themselves would appoint lower-court judges. All this translates into a reasonably high degree of judicial independence that, according to the World Economic Forum, places Brazil in third place in Latin America, with a score of 3.9 out of 7 (see Table 4.3 in Chapter 4).[25]

The judiciary in Brazil has played the important role of enforcer of the constitution, ensuring that the other branches of government do not overstep their boundaries. There have been a number of high-profile cases in which the supreme court ruled against the executive on issues that were of vital importance to the executive. One of these was the attempt by the Cardoso administration to tax retired workers, a measure that was seen as an important component of a fiscal restraint program. The measure, which was passed through congress after considerable effort, was highly controversial because it involved acquired rights and entitlements. In the end, the supreme court declared the measure unconstitutional. Alston and others discuss this and other cases that support the notion that the judiciary in Brazil has a reasonable degree of independence.[26]

The bureaucracy in Brazil also contributes to the high quality of public policies. In fact, according to most measures of bureaucratic quality, Brazil has the strongest bureaucracy in Latin America. This is reflected in the indices presented in Chapter 4, in which Brazil appears at the top of the rankings. Most appointments are handled through a well-institutionalized system of competitive entrance examinations. Employment conditions (tenure and competitiveness of salaries) are attractive, and there are ample resources available for training of personnel.[27] While there are a significant number of positions that are reserved as political appointments (called "DAS positions"), the number is

---

[25] For comparison, Uruguay, the highest-ranked country in the region, has an index of 4.8. Brazil appears in sixth place within the region in Feld and Voigt's (2003) de facto judicial independence index.

[26] Perhaps the greatest concern regarding the judiciary in Brazil is the system's slowness. Delays have on occasion been used strategically by governments, particularly with regard to tax legislation, since a reversal by the courts may end up imposing constraints only on future governments. See Alston and others (2005a).

[27] This includes public administration schools such as the *Escola Nacional de Administração Pública* (ENAP), and the *Escola de Administração Fazendária* (ESAF).

limited by law, and in making these appointments technical criteria are still taken into consideration.[28] Brazil's bureaucracy, which combines a high degree of autonomy with strong technical capabilities, is an important institutional actor that can constrain the executive, and at the same time contribute to policy stability and the public orientation of policies.

Ecuador

In Ecuador, the judiciary has traditionally been highly politicized. On occasion, the ability of the executive to influence the courts has even been used as a token of exchange in order to build political support for the government coalition. Before 1998, the tenure of supreme court justices was formally six years, and their terms could be renewed beyond that. In practice, however, the average tenure of supreme court justices until the mid-1990s was 2.8 years, among the shortest in Latin America. The constitutional reforms of 1997 and 1998 introduced important changes, aimed at providing the judiciary with independence from political pressures. Tenure for supreme court justices was extended from six years to lifetime terms, and the appointment of members (31, including the court's president) was assigned to an administrative branch of the judiciary, the *Consejo Nacional de la Judicatura*. The constitutional reform also introduced the nine-member Constitutional Tribunal as the supreme entity for constitutional oversight.

In spite of these efforts, the judiciary in Ecuador continues to be politicized. The best example of this was the removal of 27 of the 31 supreme court justices in December 2004. That the justices would be removed was decided by pro-government deputies, with the support of the *Roldosista* Party, the party of ex-president Bucaram, whose trial on charges of corruption was immediately voided. Public demonstrations against Bucaram's impunity became the trigger that eventually contributed to President Gutiérrez's dismissal, in April 2005. This episode is yet another example demonstrating that changes to the letter of the law do not necessarily change institutions in the long run.

The bureaucracy in Ecuador presents a stark contrast to that in Brazil. Both appointments and dismissals tend to be politically motivated, and a substantial number of people enter and exit the bureaucracy with every new administration. Ecuadorian legislation as far back as the 1980s has introduced merit criteria for the appointment of civil servants, but there is a large gap between the letter of the law and established practice. The frequent constitutional interruptions experienced by Ecuador in the recent past have contributed to the lack of stability of the civil service. In terms of the indices presented in Chapter 4, Ecuador ranks 13th out of 18 countries in the combined index of civil service development presented in Figure 4.4.

---

[28] DAS stands for *Direção e Assessoramento Superior*. Currently, the number of DAS positions is around 17,000, or 3.5 percent of the civil service. These positions do not carry tenure, and most of them are filled from within the civil service, as a reward for good performance. See Shepherd and Rinne (2005).

Forming and Maintaining Coalitions

Box 6.2, on constitutional interruptions, clearly showed that minority governments have a substantially higher risk of democratic instability. It also showed that a fragmented party system does not need to be a problem, provided that the president is able to form and sustain a majority or near-majority coalition that can provide political support in congress. In Brazil, coalitions tend to be stable and have for the most part allowed the president to pass a significant part of his agenda during the entire presidential period. In contrast, in Ecuador coalitions are typically weak and short lived, tend to provide ad hoc support for selected initiatives, and typically break down as new elections approach. Thus, it is important to examine the mechanisms through which coalitions are built and maintained in each case.

Brazil

The president in Brazil has many instruments for building and maintaining the support of the coalition. Perhaps most important is his strong budgetary powers.[29] The budget approved each year in congress typically includes a number of amendments introduced by legislators, involving small projects such as roads or sanitation infrastructure in their districts. Even after these amendments are approved, the president has discretionary power during the budget execution stage to decide which amendments get funded and which do not. This constitutes a powerful bargaining chip, which the president can use to build political support for his agenda. Legislators' electoral success depends on getting their projects implemented in their districts, so they are often willing to make policy concessions in exchange for these investment projects.

A second tool used by the president is his power to distribute positions in the federal government. Within certain limits described above, the president can use appointments to DAS positions to reward coalition partners or their supporters, in order to help cement the coalition.

A third mechanism used to build support in congress is the power to appoint cabinet ministers. All major parties in the coalition are granted ministries, typically in proportion to their share of votes in congress, although the extent to which this resource is utilized varies from administration to administration. While the president has to "concede" certain ministries to coalition partners in exchange for their support, he still is able to dictate the major policy guidelines and holds the authority to reclaim any position at any moment.

In Brazil, these exchanges are credible because they are part of a repeated game among actors that tend to be long-term players. Presidents can be reelected, and party leaders, who act as brokers in these transactions, are long-term players, as are many individual legislators, who stand a good chance of reelection. If the government were to frequently renege on implicit promises made in the course of these exchanges, it would debase the bargaining chips it holds, and coalitions would break down.

---

[29] See Alston and others (2005a) and Pereira and Mueller (2004). For a more detailed discussion of the role of budgetary discretion in Brazil, see Chapter 11.

Recently, some allegations regarding illegitimate political exchanges in Brazil have attracted considerable attention. In this context, it is important to point out that the particular transactions discussed in the last few paragraphs are legitimate ways for Brazil's president to gather political support and pass his agenda, in the context of a very fragmented party system. While some observers may find these political transactions objectionable as a matter of principle, the transactions play a vital role in helping cement stable coalitions, and they contribute to governability. Eliminating these opportunities for political exchange would either put governability at risk, or increase the likelihood that other less legitimate and less transparent forms of exchange might take place. The case of Ecuador is a vivid example of what can happen in fragmented party systems in the absence of stable coalitions.

Ecuador

If the president in Brazil can overcome the weaknesses associated with party fragmentation by forming a stable coalition that allows him to pass his agenda, the question is, why can the president in Ecuador not do the same? The contrasting results are puzzling given that, like his Brazilian counterpart, the Ecuadorian president is also endowed with a number of resources—pork-barrel projects, cabinet positions, positions in the bureaucracy, policy concessions, contracts—that he can offer in exchange for support for his agenda. As usual, there are no single-factor explanations to account for the inability of presidents in Ecuador to maintain a stable coalition.

It is worthwhile to begin by examining the three types of mechanisms identified for the case of Brazil and attempting to understand why they do not seem to contribute to the building of stable coalitions in the case of Ecuador. The first of these was the exchange of projects for political support. In Brazil, the president can deliver these projects, because of his discretionary power over the budget, and legislators value this, since it contributes to their reelection. In Ecuador, as in Brazil, legislators are elected from open lists and can be reelected, so they should have similar incentives to deliver projects to their districts. However, presidents in Ecuador do not have discretionary power over the budget. They previously had the power to make discretionary use of off-budget allocations, but lost this power in 1995.[30] Even before that date, these types of exchanges would not have been very useful, since at the time legislators could not be reelected and were elected from closed lists. Thus, they had a weaker electoral connection with their voters, and they did not have the kind of incentives to deliver investment projects to their communities that Brazilian legislators have.[31]

The second bargaining chip discussed in the case of Brazil was public employment. While the DAS positions discussed in Brazil are very prestigious and well paid, this is not the case for civil service positions in Ecuador. In addition, while these positions in Brazil may last up to eight years in case of reelection of the president, in Ecuador both entry to and exit from the civil service tends to be highly political, and there is a great deal of turnover (particularly in the case of political appointees) every time there is a change

---

[30] See Araujo and others (2004).

[31] They could have been interested in delivering transfers to particular social or ethnic groups, however.

in administration. The absence of immediate presidential reelection further shortens the expected length of these appointments. In the case of Ecuador, the result is less prestigious and shorter-term positions, which are likely to be less attractive. Naturally, as the end of the presidential term draws near, this loses most of its value as a token of exchange.

The third bargaining chip discussed in the case of Brazil was cabinet ministries. As can be seen in Figure 4.1, Ecuador is the country with the greatest degree of cabinet instability among the 12 Latin American countries for which data are available.[32] The study of the PMP in Ecuador presents evidence showing that, out of 292 ministers that occupied cabinet positions between 1979 and 2002, 61 percent did not finish the presidential term, and 90 percent of these either resigned or were dismissed by the executive.[33] In other words, tenure of ministers is short and uncertain, and the president, who awards these positions, can also take them away when he needs to build a coalition along a different policy dimension. This reduces the credibility of the reward, and thus the attractiveness of cabinet positions for coalition partners, as well as the value the president can expect to receive in exchange for a cabinet position. Interestingly, the background study of Ecuador's PMP conducted for this report also states that Ecuador has one of the lowest shares of partisan ministers in Latin America. It is likely that short tenure and the lack of credibility surrounding the reward may be contributing to this result.

But there is another important component to the explanation of why coalition partners do not find cabinet positions attractive, and more importantly, why coalitions in Ecuador are unstable. There is an embedded perception in the Ecuadorian political culture, reinforced by the electoral calendar, that collaborating with a government (or being a "*gobiernista*") can be a politically costly move, especially if this involves the support of unpopular adjustment policies. This anti-government attitude—and the liability of being associated with the government—increases when the president's job approval ratings decrease over time. With decreasing levels of presidential popularity, potential coalition partners often prefer to engage in what have been called "ghost coalitions": secret agreements whereby party leaders agree to collaborate with the government on a narrow set of ad hoc policy issues, but avoid—and sometimes publicly deny—any long-term commitment that may affect their own electoral chances.[34] These exchanges are made possible by the absence of roll calls in the legislature. In this way, parties can obtain the benefits of coalition membership, without having to pay the political costs of being associated with the government.

The cost of being a part of the government coalition increases as the term of the presidency advances, new elections draw near, and party leaders need to position themselves for the elections. At the same time, the benefits of being in the coalition decline as the presidential term approaches its end, since positions in the bureaucracy, and

---

[32] Brazil is second in this dimension, so there is actually not much difference between the two countries in this regard.

[33] Interestingly, while impeachments in Ecuador have been a subject of great debate, only 7 percent of the 292 ministers in the sample have been removed by congress using this procedure.

[34] Mejía Acosta (2004).

FIGURE 7.5   **Evolution of the President's Coalition in Congress over the Period 1984–2002** (*monthly averages*)

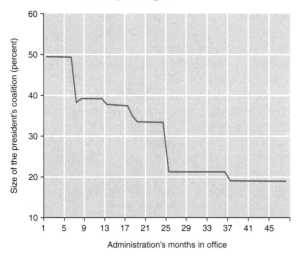

Source: Mejía Acosta (2004).

even ministries, become shorter in expected tenure and thus less valuable. It is therefore not surprising that the size of the coalition declines substantially over the presidential term (see Figure 7.5).

As should be clear from the above discussion, none of the political mechanisms that seem to work in Brazil as a way of cementing stable coalitions appear to be working in the case of Ecuador. These mechanisms are further hindered by the relatively short tenure of the political actors that participate in them. All these factors contribute to explaining the relative instability of democratic governance in Ecuador.

The contrasting cases of Brazil and Ecuador also illustrate the need for a general equilibrium view of political institutions and policymaking processes. Focusing on just a few institutional dimensions, such as the extent of presidential powers, the electoral rules for the legislature, and the degree of party fragmentation, may lead to the wrong conclusions, however important these dimensions may be. Policymaking processes are very complex, and understanding them requires attention to details such as presidential budgetary discretion and roll calls in the legislature, which may affect in an important way the nature of the political transactions among the relevant political actors. This point is further illustrated by the discussion of the case of Costa Rica, in which a key element of the policymaking process is the delegation of important policymaking responsibilities to autonomous institutions (Box 7.2).

| Box 7.2 | Policymaking through Delegation: The Case of Costa Rica* |

Costa Rica has had a competitive political system for more than 100 years, and has been a full democracy for almost the last 50. Significant advances were made in 1949 with the adoption of a constitution that laid the foundation not only for the institutionalization of a stable democratic system, but also for the more general characteristics of Costa Rica's policymaking process. This policymaking framework permitted a fourfold increase in GDP per capita between 1950 and 2000, whereas in the Latin American region as a whole GDP per capita barely doubled. The country also has one of the lowest rates of income inequality in the region and compares favorably with upper-middle-income countries in respect to basic education and health outcomes. Underlying these positive development results are broadly effective public policies. Costa Rica ranks among the top five countries in the region in respect to all but one of the key features of public policies discussed in Chapter 6, including stability, coordination/coherence, implementation and enforcement, and public-regardedness. Only in respect to the characteristic of adaptability does Costa Rica rank more toward the middle tier of countries.

Effective policies have been possible in Costa Rica in part because highly competitive and fair elections centered on two main political parties/coalitions provide incentives for politicians to orient their policy decisions toward satisfying the interests of the median voter, and, therefore, to design institutions to meet ambitious social welfare objectives. The 1949 Constitution also establishes a distinctive institutional design which limits the scope of conflict between the elected branches of government and devolves important policy responsibilities to autonomous bureaucratic institutes. Neither the president nor legislators—all of whom are elected on separate ballots for concurrent, four-year terms—can stand for immediate reelection. In addition, the constitution limits the ability of the president to shape the legislative agenda and creates "fast-track" procedures for enacting the annual budget. The legislative assembly must modify or approve the executive's budget within 90 days, and the president can subsequently veto it. These procedures have succeeded in preventing the budget from getting bogged down in inter-branch conflict.

As a result of steady expansion since 1949, the decentralized State sectors now consist of more than 100 autonomous institutions. In these sectors, including health care, old-age pensions, election management, housing, higher education, and monetary policy, the autonomous institutions are the key players. Although in total they spend as much as the central government, autonomous institutions do not have to submit their budgets to either the president or the legislature. They have programmatic, budgetary, and administrative autonomy and often rely on specific or protected revenue sources. The comptroller general of the republic,

Box 7.2   Continued

an auxiliary institution of the legislature, exercises oversight of the decentralized State sectors.

As a consequence of these long-term inter-temporal agreements by key partisan actors to delegate policy authority to autonomous agencies, important areas of policy have been safeguarded against the instability and incoherence that might otherwise have resulted from government turnover and partisan conflict. An independent supreme court has enforced these agreements by repeatedly upholding the autonomy of the institutions in its rulings, especially during the 1960s. The desire of politicians to regain some control over this large portion of the State apparatus led to a constitutional reform in 1968 and other statutory reforms in the 1970s, which affirmed the executive and legislative branches' authority to set general policy in the sectors and permitted more partisan-based appointments in their directorates. Nonetheless, the institutions largely retained their budgetary and administrative autonomy.

Policymaking in areas pertaining to the central State was fairly centralized from the 1950s until around 1990. The unicameral legislature and the relatively cohesive party system (2.5 effective parties) limited the number of distinct actors in the policymaking process, which permitted some degree of policy adaptation despite the weakness of the president in respect to constitutional powers. Adaptability was facilitated by the relatively large share of seats (48 percent) typically controlled by the governing party and the president's influence in determining who is nominated and elected to the congress from his party. But the president's partisan powers and ability to enact laws weaken during the course of the four-year presidential term. Term limits make presidents "lame ducks" by the third year as legislators, even from the governing party, distance themselves from the incumbent. Legislators focus instead on aligning themselves with a future president, hoping perhaps for a cabinet or senior bureaucratic post in the new administration, or for an advantage in the world of local government.

Since the early 1990s policymaking in Costa Rica has become more fragmented. Growing disenchantment with the two-party system contributed to an increasing vote for parties and candidates not affiliated with the National Liberation Party (PLN) and the Social Christian Unity Party (PUSC) and a reduction in the share of legislative seats controlled by the governing party. In addition, the establishment of the Constitutional Chamber in 1989 entailed the introduction of a new veto player that has the power to prevent bills from becoming law even while they work themselves through the legislative process. Thus, the flexibility of policymaking in respect to the areas under the control of the central State has diminished as a consequence of electoral and institutional changes.

---

* Based on Lehoucq (2005).

Part IV

The Policymaking Process in Action

However beautiful the strategy, you should occasionally look at the results.

Winston Churchill

Much of this report looks into the general characteristics of policymaking in different countries, with the implicit assumption that such general characteristics will tend to permeate policymaking in all areas of public policy. Yet policymaking processes may differ across sectors, as a result of the different actors and institutions that may be relevant, as well as differences in the nature of the transactions required for policy implementation.

The chapters in Part IV look into the making of policy in a number of different sectors. They provide cross-country comparisons of policymaking in these sectors and show how policy outcomes in each of them can be linked to the characteristics of their policymaking process. Chapters 8, 9, and 10 focus on tax policy, public services, and education, respectively. Chapter 11 is somewhat different in nature. Rather than looking at the impact of the policymaking process on policy outcomes, it focuses on feedback effects from policy reform to the policymaking process and illustrates these effects with examples from the areas of decentralization and budget processes.

The chapters in Part IV constitute an important step toward one of the main purposes of this report: to provide guidance in and orientation toward understanding the policymaking processes surrounding specific reform initiatives in particular areas in particular countries at particular points of time.

Chapter 8

The Art of Tax Policies

*The art of taxation consists in so plucking
the goose to obtain the largest amount of feathers,
with the least possible amount of hissing.*

—Jean-Baptiste Colbert, Treasurer to Louis XIV[1]

Tax policies are a good starting point for seeing the policymaking process in action. First and foremost, a good number of public policy decisions are related to taxation, and taxation touches almost every aspect of the economy and society. The size of the State, the amount of redistribution from the rich to the poor, and decisions to consume and invest are all related to this fundamental area of policy. Given its potentially large effects on efficiency and equity, tax policy is perhaps the area of public policy where the most interests are at stake.

Thus the policymaking process (PMP) for taxes tends to be a good reflection of the broader ("global") PMP: that is to say, the process through which a host of interests, both public and private, work their way through the wheels of political negotiation in the making of public policies. As a general rule, actors that play key roles in the broader ("global") PMP are also active players in the process of discussing, enacting, and implementing tax policies. This applies not only to actors that are central in the PMP in every country—notably the executive (whose powers and constraints strongly influence the quality of tax policies) and the legislature—but also to other actors whose influence is more specific to certain countries, such as regional authorities in Argentina and Brazil, the judiciary in Colombia after the 1991 Constitution, or business groups in Guatemala.

Despite the far-reaching economic impact of taxes, economic considerations do not go very far in explaining the features of tax policies. Countries with similar levels of income, income distribution, or sectoral composition of output have very different tax structures. There is clearly no economic model that explains tax policy outcomes.

Moreover, the tax structures and policies that countries put in place are often far from ideal. Some countries have tax revenues that are too low or too high, even when

---

[1] As cited in *The Economist,* May 29, 1997.

most of the main actors and observers acknowledge that this is a problem (for example, Guatemala and Brazil). There are countries that rely heavily on inefficient or distortionary tax revenues (Colombia) or have tax systems that are full of exemptions (Costa Rica and Paraguay), although simpler and more efficient systems would be technically preferable. Then there are those countries that approve reform after reform because each gets watered down in the approval process (Colombia). These outcomes cannot be justified by economic considerations alone.

Furthermore, each and every country in Latin America has faced the same external shock to its economy in the past 15 years: the trend toward globalization. This has increased the international mobility of goods, investments, and financial capital around the world, thus limiting the possibilities of taxing them. Globalization trends have forced countries to slash import tariff rates and trim tax rates on business. In response to this common shock, countries throughout the region have come up with a wide range of tax structures and tax policies. This variation across countries exemplifies how, even in response to a common shock, different political institutions and political actors can result in different policy outcomes.

This chapter examines four very different country cases—Brazil, Colombia, Guatemala, and Paraguay—and discusses the general features of the tax policymaking process. The analysis reveals that to a large extent, differences in taxation reflect differences in political institutions and structure, which interact with some important features of tax policies.

Profound Changes in Tax Regimes

At first glance, the landscape of tax policies in Latin America is hardly encouraging. Tax revenues of the typical central government in Latin America reached 13.2 percent of GDP on average in the first years of the current decade, a decrease from the average of 14 percent in the late 1980s, and less than half the current average of 30 percent in developed countries. Only a handful of countries in the region, including Brazil, Bolivia, and the Dominican Republic, succeeded in raising tax collections by more than 3 percentage points of GDP over that period. But such a superficial evaluation turns out to be mistaken. Behind this apparent stagnation in taxes are hidden very profound changes in tax regimes that countries have had to make to respond to globalization.

Specific features of tax policies go a long way toward explaining the peculiarities of the tax systems ultimately put in place in each country.

In the face of the challenges of globalization, taxation policy has been a very active area of reform. Every Latin American country has undertaken important reforms in this area since 1990—an average in the region of 4.2 such reforms—and 11 Latin American countries have overhauled their tax systems since that time. Taxes on the incomes of businesses and individuals have risen from 2.7 percent of GDP in the 1980s to 3.9 percent at present, although they remain very low in comparison to averages worldwide or in developed countries (12 percent of GDP). The loss of revenues from the reduction of import tariffs has been largely compensated for by the revenues produced by the value-added tax (VAT), which was introduced in most countries between the mid-1980s and the mid-1990s and now generates more than a third (37 percent) of all tax revenues of the region's central governments: equivalent to 5.5 percent of GDP, on average.

Why, given this surge of activity, have the policies adopted often been less than ideal? While tax policymaking proceeds against the backdrop of each country's broader ("global") PMP, specific features of tax policies constrain the possibilities for policy reform. These constraints go a long way toward explaining the peculiarities of the tax policies discussed, enacted, and ultimately implemented and enforced.

Among the main features of tax policies that must be kept in mind, four are especially important. First, taxes have wide-reaching effects throughout the economy. This means that many players will be active in the policymaking process. If they perceive that their interests are directly or immediately affected, they are likely to be more intensely involved. The policymaking game in taxation is therefore more likely to have a large number of players.

Second, taxation is subject to severe common-pool problems. That is, taxation may be viewed as a game in which each individual player wins or loses depending on his ability to extract more than he contributes to a common pool of resources. Each individual has incentives to minimize contributions to the pool: for instance, by being exempted from paying taxes or by taking advantage of a loophole to pay less than others. Each individual also has incentives to extract as much as possible from the common pool by earmarking some taxes or assigning some share of the tax pool for specific uses or regions he favors, as is the case in Argentina, Brazil, or Colombia.

Third, the effective implementation of tax policies relies heavily on the capabilities of the tax administration office. The experience, resources, and administrative capabilities, and even the preferences and biases of the tax administrators, determine what is put into practice. Thus, as is often said, "In developing countries, tax administration *is* tax policy."

Fourth, once tax systems are structured in a given way, they are very hard to change. In the parlance of social scientists, they are strongly path-dependent. What makes tax systems so remarkably hard to improve? In principle, any common-pool problem can be solved by a cooperative agreement among the participants—provided the costs and uncertainty of the negotiation are low compared with the expected benefits, and enforceable mechanisms can be put in place to avoid opportunistic behavior and ensure compliance.

Unfortunately, these conditions rarely exist in taxation issues, for several reasons. Most fundamentally, since economic power is usually very concentrated and powerful elites are able to influence the political system through a variety of channels, they tend to be protected from the vagaries of the political system: richer taxpayers are often able to prevent reforms that would affect them negatively. This argument can be labeled the elite resistance hypothesis.[2]

Further complicating matters, the revenue and distributional effects of structural changes to the tax system cannot be easily predicted. Given that many Latin American

---

[2] For a short review of the literature on this hypothesis, see Melo (2004).

countries face a precarious fiscal situation, fiscal authorities are often deterred from pursuing deep reforms in the face of uncertainty about revenues in the short and the medium run, even when there might be confidence in the long-term benefits of reform. Tax administrators are intrinsically very conservative, as implied in the adage "Good taxes are old taxes." This explanation can be called the uncertainty hypothesis.

Moreover, if a country is beset by political instability or polarization, a government or a political party in power may prefer not to pursue a reform that makes the tax system more efficient and productive for fear that, while the political costs of the reform will fall upon the government or party itself, the benefits will be showered upon the next government. This is the strategic argument.[3]

Finally, there is the enforcement argument, which states that welfare-enhancing reforms can be implemented only if an "enforcement technology" can be put in place to ensure compliance and punish defectors. The superiority of self-compliance over punishment has been well documented in the literature on tax compliance. But a culture of self-compliance is hard to build and easy to destroy, because it rests on trust in public institutions, the legitimacy of those in power, and a feeling of fairness, transparency, and reciprocity in the collection and use of public revenues. In the absence of such a culture, some external enforcement mechanism is necessary to facilitate effective reform. The IMF has played this role in some countries: the probability of tax reform is higher during a fiscal adjustment program undertaken in the context of an IMF loan agreement.[4] The exact channel is not clear, but it may have something to do with greater consistency of tax policies or control over expenditures, or it may simply be that the IMF shifts the political costs away from the government. An effective and transparent tax administration can also be seen as an additional enforcement mechanism, as will be discussed below.

The Immediacy, Pervasiveness, and Complexity of Taxation Effects

The effects of taxation vary in their immediacy, pervasiveness, and complexity, complicating both policymaking and the analysis of tax policymaking. Some taxes work many of their effects through the economic system in a short period of time. Others have long-term consequences that are far more important (think of taxes that affect saving and investment decisions). Another challenge is disentangling the direct or partial equilibrium effects of taxation, as opposed to the indirect or general equilibrium effects. For example, some taxes displace productive activities in important ways, therefore reducing the base for collection (an increasingly relevant factor in a globalized economy). General equilibrium considerations are of particular importance in relation to the burden of many taxes, which may be transferred from those that initially face the obligation to other firms or individuals. In general, the

Since meddling with the many features of tax systems is essentially a political game, it is not surprising that tax systems are not only complex but also subject to continuous change.

---

[3] Cukierman, Edwards, and Tabellini (1989).

[4] Mahon (2004).

burden of direct taxes, such as income and property taxes, is less easily transferable than that of indirect taxes, such as sales or value-added taxes, which tend to be shifted to the final consumers. Thus the visibility of the burden varies from tax to tax, and in many cases depends heavily on technical details usually beyond the grasp of those ultimately affected. Finally, the effects of taxation are in many cases highly uncertain, introducing another complexity into the PMP.

There are two important implications of the immediacy, pervasiveness, and complexity of taxation effects. First, as noted, since taxes have such far-reaching economic and policy impacts, the PMP for tax policy tends to mirror a nation's broader ("global") PMP. Second, tax systems should be expected to have multiple bases, varied rate structures, and a myriad of special provisions as a result of the policymaking process.[5] Since it is reasonable to assume that support for any political party depends on how that party affects the interests of its current and potential supporters, every party will try to tailor the tax mix in order to best suit those interests. As a result, a variety of tax bases, rate structures, and special provisions should be expected. Even a one-party system will be interested in introducing some complexity into the tax system because, by doing so, it may cater to a variety of its supporters.

However, in any political system, the forces that push toward making the tax system more complex are constrained by at least two factors. First, each party's supporters may also benefit from the expenditures that are financed by the common pool of taxes. Thus for some specific aspects, the players may find it more beneficial to shift the policymaking game toward the budget process. Second, tax collection costs will increase as the tax system becomes more complex. This will divert resources from other uses that may produce higher political benefits and will reduce total tax revenues. Thus there is pressure to reduce costs and keep the system simpler if this would lead to higher tax revenues, which can potentially improve the outcomes for some or all players. Tax systems can be seen as the result of these conflicting forces.

Since meddling with the many features of tax systems is essentially a political game, it is not surprising that tax systems are not only complex but also subject to continuous change. However, most changes are gradual, rather than radical. Countries with tax revenues that are too low remain in that situation for long periods; tax systems that are clearly inefficient are improved only slightly year after year; and so on.

The last feature of tax policies that needs to be stressed is the central role that the tax administration office plays in the implementation of tax decisions.[6] In the tax policy process, there is a clear separation between the stages of policy enactment and policy implementation. Although the tax administration office usually contributes to drafting tax reform proposals, it plays an entirely passive role during the process of discussion in congress. Often, congress introduces changes into the draft that may look inconvenient or impracticable to the tax administrators, without consulting them. However, once the reform is approved, the tax administration office has wide latitude in deciding how, when, and where the new tax code will be implemented.

---

[5] For a summary of the theoretical and empirical support for this argument, see Winer and Hettich (2003).

[6] See Shome (1999).

Tax administrators are usually under pressure from the minister of finance to increase effectiveness in the collection of tax revenues. Faced with this pressure, tax administrators prefer to concentrate collection efforts on the largest contributors through large-taxpayer units. Over the last two decades, to facilitate compliance among small firms and to reduce the costs of monitoring and collecting revenues, tax administration offices have introduced simplified taxation schemes for small firms (whereby a single combined payment is made for income taxes, VATs, and excise taxes). Although usually effective in reducing collection costs, these systems may introduce important horizontal inequities and displace the burden of some taxes in ways that lawmakers did not intend.

A Look at Four Countries

Colombia: Changes in the Balance of Power

Colombia has been a very active reformer since the early 1990s, but the reforms have come out of congress substantially diluted and altered. The changes in the PMP introduced by the 1991 Constitution, discussed in detail in Chapter 7, are largely responsible for these difficulties, as they weakened the executive vis-à-vis the legislature and the judiciary.

Since 1991, the size of the State and its mandate has grown considerably. Until 1991, the public sector was relatively small by regional standards. Between 1990 and 2003, aggregate public expenditures jumped from 21.2 to 33.7 percent of GDP, reflecting a deliberate intention in both the constitution and the political system to increase the size of the State and use fiscal expenditures for redistribution. The fact that total revenues grew from 20.6 to 29.7 percent of GDP in the same period suggests that the decision to raise government expenditures was accompanied by an important effort on the revenue side—although an insufficient one. The central government's deficit has been close to 6 percent of GDP since the late 1990s.

The Colombian experience highlights how changes in the balance of power between the executive and other branches influence the enactment of tax reforms.

The executive's major objective in the tax reform process has been to increase tax revenues as a means of re-establishing fiscal balances. However, the draft tax reform projects submitted to congress have also given importance to the structure of the tax system, an area in which successive administrations have been only partially successful. Reliance on the VAT has been increasing, and the VAT rate has increased from 10 to 16 percent through the various reforms since 1990. However, the most recent attempts to widen the VAT base or raise the rate have had very limited success, in part because the legislature assigns greater priority to the progressivity of the tax system than to its efficiency—regardless of the progressivity of the expenditure structure. This has severely limited attempts by the executive to reduce the dispersion of VAT rates and the number of exemptions.

Colombia is characterized by very high income tax rates, and is one of the few countries (along with Argentina and Bolivia) that has increased corporate and personal income tax rates since 1990. Currently, the corporate tax rate is 38.5 percent, the highest in Latin America, and the personal income tax rate is 35 percent. The effectiveness of these rates, however, is severely undermined by a host of exemptions and loopholes. Consequently, very few pay direct taxes, but those who do pay bear an excessive share of the burden. Similarly, although the average VAT rate has increased substantially, the tendency has been to increase the number of rates, with the declared intention of making the system more progressive (by assigning lower VAT rates to basic goods and higher rates for luxury goods), thus distorting it considerably. As a result of the high tax rates and their low effectiveness, the tax system as a whole is considered one of the least neutral in Latin America.

As a consequence of congress's reluctance to widen the income and value-added tax bases, the executive has introduced new—and highly distortionary—tax sources. In 1998, a temporary 0.2 percent financial transactions tax was adopted through an emergency decree. This was raised to 0.3 percent and made permanent in the 2000 tax reform, and raised to 0.4 percent in the 2003 reform. In the same vein, through an extraordinary "internal commotion" decree, the Uribe government adopted a temporary net wealth tax earmarked for the strengthening of democratic security in Colombia: the proceeds go to financing the military and social operations necessary for ending the guerrilla and terrorist insurgency. This tax was extended for three additional years in 2003. Thus revenue pressures have led to decisions that disregard the basic principles of an equitable and efficient tax structure. For example, as a concession to the business community for enacting this tax, a temporary tax holiday was enacted simultaneously, consisting of a 30 percent deduction for reinvested earnings in capital, which according to the ministry of finance ended up costing the Treasury more than what the net wealth tax yielded in 2004.

The inability of the political system to deliver more efficient tax reforms is explained in part by the changes introduced into the PMP in the Constitution of 1991. While the constitution preserved the prerogatives that make the Colombian president the main agenda-setter in most policy areas, it reduced presidential powers in a number of dimensions. It deliberately curbed the legislative powers of the president by limiting to 90 days the declaration of either a state of internal commotion or a state of economic emergency, and by establishing that the decrees issued remain in force after the emergency only if congress enacts them in regular sessions. In this way, the constitution severely curtailed a method that had been used several times to enact major tax reforms. For example, the government used special legislative powers to enact the 1974 tax reform—which incorporated many of the recommendations of international experts. In 1997, the Samper administration attempted to use economic emergency powers to tax capital inflows, but the Constitutional Court declared this unconstitutional because it did not consider conditions pressing enough to justify an emergency. Nonetheless, against the backdrop of two economic emergencies (during the 1998–2002 Pastrana administration) and one internal commotion (during the 2002–06 Uribe administration), various administrations have been able to introduce new temporary taxes, which were extended by regular legislation with the approval of the Constitutional Court. Accustomed to these practices, Colombians say that "nothing is more permanent than a temporary tax."

Since 1991, the Constitutional Court has been a key player in the policymaking process. (It is more active and independent than its predecessor, the Supreme Court.) The main reason is that many policy issues, particularly tax reform issues, were elevated to constitutional status by the Constitution of 1991. Around 10 percent of the total legal claims on economic matters handled by the Constitutional Court since 1991 have been tax issues. In 1999, a ruling on the financial transactions tax limited the executive's scope in the use of resources. More recently, the Constitutional Court denied the approval of the generalization of the VAT and the taxation of specific activities.

Another trend that has been reinforced by the constitution—the increase in the number of political parties and the factionalization of existing parties—has made the normal passage of legislation through congress more difficult for the executive. Electoral rules traditionally used in Colombia (the "Hare" quota system, whereby the majority of seats end up being allocated to the largest remainder of candidates) generate incentives for parties to fragment into factions, presenting multiple lists of candidates for congressional elections in each district.[7] The result is that parties have increased the number of lists over time, maximizing their share of seats, while enhancing decentralization and factionalization. While the constitution did not change the electoral rules, the trend toward party fragmentation was reinforced around the time of the constitutional reform with the introduction of a system of direct public funding for congressional and presidential campaigns, where the political movement rather than the party is the recipient of the funds. These reforms lowered the costs of challenging party hierarchies and created room for small party factions to influence the legislative process. To some extent these centrifugal forces are contained in congress, where the main committees, such as the budget and tax committees, are controlled by recognized party leaders with deep knowledge of fiscal affairs, who lead the debate and who are influential in the legislative outcome. However, to ensure the support of the larger number of parties, the executive resorts to nominating a larger number of sponsors for each bill—which implies that it must deliver a larger amount of "pork" to get the bills passed. In addition to increasing the cost of passing tax bills, the legislative process also reduces the benefits by watering down government proposals. This cost-benefit analysis led the Uribe government to withdraw its latest tax proposal in December 2004. The government proposed a VAT reform, but legislators wanted to raise wealth taxation instead. The government opted for keeping the status quo.

In sum, the Colombian experience highlights how changes in the balance of power between the executive and other branches influence the enactment of tax reforms. In earlier decades, congress largely rubber-stamped the tax reforms the executive submitted, oftentimes through emergency legislation. Since the early 1990s, however, legislative involvement in the design of tax packages has been increasing. Congress has passed eight tax reforms since 1990, but it tends to water down the proposals during debate, not only in terms of revenues, but also, more importantly, in terms of the quality of the reforms. Likewise, in earlier decades, the judiciary played no significant role in the process of approval of reforms. However, the greater independence and extended powers it received from the revised constitution to oversee the enactment of laws has severely limited the room for maneuver of both the executive and the legislature in tax issues.

---

[7] For a discussion of the impact of the Hare system on party fragmentation, see Chapter 7, Box 7.1.

Brazil: Inaction in the Face of Uncertainty

Brazil is a puzzling case. It has a cumbersome and inefficient tax system that has resisted a badly needed overhaul. Yet over the last two decades, total revenues have increased and the productivity of the major taxes compares very well with that in other Latin American countries. Brazil now has the highest tax burden in Latin America and one of the highest in the developing world. As a federal country, Brazil is one of the most fiscally decentralized countries in Latin America—so much so that its main source of fiscal revenue, the VAT, is collected mainly at the state level, a feature seldom observed in the developing world. As in other decentralized countries, vertical imbalances across states are partly compensated for by transfers of national tax revenues to the states. The possibility that the states can resort to VAT revenues

A powerful executive and a capable and well-respected tax administration may not be enough to introduce deep reforms into the tax system.

reduces the probability of states running large deficits that can sometimes be associated with large vertical imbalances, at the cost of creating inefficiencies and problems of coordination and competition among states. How has Brazil managed to weather the coordination and enforcement problems of its complex tax system? As will be argued, much of the answer lies in the combination of a powerful executive and a strong tax administration office.

Gross federal government tax revenues increased from an average of 16.5 percent of GDP in 1985–89 to 24.4 percent in 2000–02. The total national tax burden reached 34 percent of GDP in 2000–02, up from 24 percent in 1985–89, as state and provincial taxes also have increased. It is predicted to rise to 38 percent of GDP by 2005: a rate roughly similar to that of Great Britain in the 1990s.

The centerpiece of the tax system is Brazil's version of the VAT, the ICMS, which is collected by the states and represents about a third of all tax revenues (excluding social security). As a result of changes in the Constitution of 1988, which gave governors a central role as part of the transition to democracy, states were allowed to set different rates for the ICMS. The constitution also deepened the process of fiscal decentralization by increasing the mandated transfers to municipalities and states of the main federal tax revenues, namely, the income and industrial products (IP) taxes. These transfers currently represent 3 percent of GDP, or about half the federal revenues of those taxes.

The case of Brazil illustrates the great difficulty in moving to a new equilibrium, especially when the system has become more complex.

The constitution imposed other rigidities in the use of fiscal resources, reducing the flexibility of the executive. This has led the federal government to resort to taxes that are not shared with the municipalities and states, contributing to an increasingly inefficient tax system. The two major sources of additional revenues are the financial transactions tax (CPMF), which was introduced at the end of 1993 and has been abolished and reintroduced several times since then; and the Social Security Financing Contribution (COFINS), which was associated with increases in tax rates and a series of court rulings favoring the federal government. Since the mid-1990s, temporary (so-called "extraordinary") revenues have become commonplace and widely used. Extraordinary revenues peaked at over 3 percent of GDP in 1999 and contributed 2.5 percent of GDP in 2000–02, on average, suggesting that temporary taxes were a success in terms of revenues. However, as a result, the structure of the tax system has deteriorated.

As in Colombia, the new constitution introduced fiscal rigidities that weakened the central government and reduced the discretion of the executive in tax issues. However, unlike in Colombia, the executive was able to regain its capacity to impose its fiscal preferences. While governors were central during the democratic transition, their power lessened with the passage of time (as noted in Chapter 4), partly because of the executive's significant powers to shape the legislative agenda and to build support for the enactment of legislation. In fiscal issues, the governors derived their power from their substantial tax powers, and the prerogative of the states to own banks and public enterprises. However, after the monetary stabilization of the *Plan Real* (1994), the fiscal situation of the states deteriorated. As a condition for extending federal bailouts, the federal government was able to impose privatizations of banks and public enterprises, as well as other conditions. This culminated with the enactment of the Fiscal Responsibility Law of 2000, which acts as an enforcement mechanism that improves the effectiveness of the subnational tax system and mitigates the common-pool problem of the federal tax system (Box 8.1).

An effective tax administration has also been instrumental in maintaining the productivity of the tax system, despite all its complexities. Since its inception in 1969, the Brazilian Internal Revenue Service (*Secretaria da Receita Federal, SRF*) has received the support of the government and society at large, partly due to a long tradition of strong public administration that goes back to the process of formation of key bureaucracies during the period of the monarchy in the 19th century. Brazil was one of the first countries in the world to introduce a comprehensive VAT, generating revenues equal to 26 percent of GDP by 1971. The more than 13,000 tax auditors at the federal level were among the best-paid career civil servants in Brazil throughout the 1980s and 1990s. Meritocratic recruitment and low turnover have been permanent features of the SRF, except under the Collor administration (1990–92), which politicized the agency and curtailed its administrative and functional autonomy.[8] Since then, modernization has continued unabated and the SRF's enforcement capabilities have been strengthened. Information on tax collections, tax legislation, and taxpayer services is provided on the Internet. About 90 percent of personal income tax returns are filed through the Internet, and all corporate income taxes are filed electronically. A 2001 law allows bank secrecy to be broken for tax enforcement purposes. Paradoxically, the effectiveness of the tax administration office may have eased the pressure to overhaul the cumbersome tax system.

As noted, the power of the executive has been instrumental in introducing discipline in the tax relations between the national and the subnational governments and also in strengthening the tax enforcement capabilities of the tax administration office. However, the federal government has not been able to implement comprehensive tax

---

[8] Melo (2004).

| Box 8.1 | An Intergovernmental Enforcement Mechanism: Brazil's Fiscal Responsibility Law |

The Fiscal Responsibility Law (FRL), approved in May 2000, imposes order and accountability on spending by the states through a general framework for budgetary planning, execution, and reporting, applicable to all levels of government. On revenues, the law mandates the withholding of discretionary federal transfers to states and municipalities that do not collect their own taxes effectively. This reinforces a constitutional amendment of 1993 that allows the federal government to withhold transfers to a state if it defaults on its obligations to the federal government. The FRL mandates the publication at every level of government of an analysis of the impact of tax exemptions in the year they take effect, as well as the next two years. The FRL also requires that governments match any permanent spending decision with a corresponding increase in permanent revenues (or a reduction in other permanent spending items).

The FRL has some noticeable consequences for the broader ("global") policymaking process. In particular, it further weakens the power of governors to influence national policies, since it makes the states more responsible for their own fiscal problems, thus reducing their ability to hold the federal government hostage on fiscal grounds.

reform. This failure illustrates the great difficulty in moving to a new equilibrium, especially when the system has become more complex. In late 1997, and not for the first time, the idea of a deep tax reform began to circulate. The government considered some proposals that were quite radical. The main proposal was to discard turnover and cascading taxes,[9] as well as state VATs, and replace them with three new taxes: a consistent broadbased nationally managed VAT; a new federal excise tax on a small number of goods and services; and a local retail sales tax. After the Asian and Russian crises and election to a second term, President Cardoso decided to raise the issue in public in 1999. Over the next 18 months, tax reform dominated the political debate. Eventually, it was impossible to coordinate such a move; only opposition and stalemate resulted. While it may have superficially looked like a situation where the executive did not push hard enough on reform, once one considers the complexity of the change expected, it is not surprising. There was uncertainty about the revenues that the new tax system would raise, uncertainty as to whether the intergovernmental compensation rules would continue, and uncertainty about whether the distribution across states would be preserved.[10]

---

[9] Cascading taxes are those "in which an item is taxed more than once as it makes its way from production to final retail sale" (Wikipedia 2005). For example, some sales taxes (in particular, those in which an item is taxed at more than one stage of production) are cascading taxes.

[10] Werneck (2000).

Thus, although everyone agrees that the indirect tax system in Brazil needs to be reformed to remove cascading taxes, no agreement has been reached on how to get there. While the president is typically able to pass his own agenda, the overhaul of the tax system has been prevented mainly by the uncertain fiscal effects of such reform, not only on aggregate tax revenues, but also on each state's tax revenues and composition. For instance, São Paulo would have lost revenues from the introduction of a general consumption VAT, but would have benefited from the elimination of the VAT on exports; the opposite would have happened to Paraná. The difficulty in measuring whether the gains would offset the losses, combined with an aversion to losing revenues, meant that it was hard to build a winning coalition that would support the passage of the reforms.

In 2003 President Lula's government once again made a concerted effort to arrive at a consensus on tax reform. Originally the main pillars of the reform were unifying the VAT, putting the 27 state codes under a single national value-added tax, and converting the main cascading taxes into a non-cumulative tax. Although the reform was planned to be revenue-neutral at every level of government, congress did not support it. The government decided to concentrate on measures that had the best chance of being approved, and postponed or shelved the most controversial aspects of the reform. The unification of the VAT was thus postponed to 2005, and the number of tax rates allowed was reduced to five (as opposed to one). The proposed reform of the cascading taxes was watered down. Moreover, tax relief for exports and capital goods was granted. The federal government enjoyed partial success with the replacement of the payroll tax with a turnover tax and the extension of two temporary taxes. But the price was a transition to lower-quality taxes. Despite all the progress in the negotiation process, politics took over. With so many interests and players in such a complex issue, the reform process was temporarily shelved in 2004. The biggest problem, once again, was uncertainty created by the multidimensional nature of the reform.

While overhauling the tax system has been impossible, the government has been able to pass piecemeal tax reforms through ordinary legislation several times in the last few decades. Some important reforms have resulted, including the restructuring of the corporate taxation system, the introduction of norms to curb transfer pricing, and the creation of an entirely new simplified system for taxing small business.

In sum, the Brazilian case clearly shows that although a powerful executive and a capable and well-respected tax administration are instrumental in enforcing the tax code and inducing cooperative behavior, both from the subnational levels of government and the taxpayers at large, they may not be enough to introduce deep reforms into the tax system. Path-dependence is difficult to break when there is a high number of players and multidimensional reforms are needed to overhaul the tax system, thus creating uncertainty about the revenue effects for each individual player.

Guatemala: Exploring the Political Underpinnings of Low Taxation

There is broad social and political consensus in favor of increasing taxation in Guatemala, yet attempts to raise the tax burden substantially have failed repeatedly. A key reason why has been the lack of an effective political counterweight to the strength of the business sector.

Tax revenues in Guatemala have traditionally been among the lowest in Latin America. The tax burden was 7.9 percent of GDP, on average, in the second half of the 1980s, and it declined further, to just 7.4 percent of GDP, in the first half of the 1990s. Following the stabilization of the economy and a series of tax reforms, tax revenues increased significantly, to 8.9 percent of GDP in the second half of the 1990s, and to 10.2 percent of GDP in 2000–2002.

Instrumental to these improvements were the Peace Accords signed in 1996. To finance the social and infrastructure expenditures identified as priorities to cement peace, a 12 percent tax burden was widely agreed upon as a target that should be met (originally in 2000). Most of the increase in tax revenue was produced not by taxes on business profits or income taxes, but by the VAT, which jumped from 2.5 to 4.4 percent of GDP between the early 1990s and 2000–2002. Income taxes increased, but only from 1.6 to 2.4 percent of GDP, through the introduction of a new tax on the income of agricultural and business firms (known as IEMA, for its Spanish acronym).[11] However, even this incomplete achievement proved to be short lived. In 2004 the new tax was overturned by the Constitutional Court in response to legal action by some organizations in the private sector, and tax revenue remained at 10.3 percent of GDP in 2004, the same figure as in 2003. New attempts by the administration of Óscar Berger to reach the 12 percent target have faced opposition not only from some business groups but, surprisingly, also from some popular organizations.[12]

The effectiveness of the business sector in preventing tax increases in Guatemala is due to the relative weakness of State institutions.

The history of Guatemala is replete with instances of failed attempts to increase taxation. During the administration of Julio César Méndez Montenegro (1966–70), the minister of finance, Alberto Fuentes Mohr, was removed from office after pushing for a tax reform that was opposed by certain business interests. In 1982, under the de facto administration of Efraín Ríos Montt, the entire economic cabinet was dismissed after attempting to introduce a package of ambitious tax reforms to curtail the fiscal deficit. In 1984, the new military government of Óscar Humberto Mejía Víctores decreed several new export and consumption taxes and raised others, prompting opposition from some business organizations. These organizations retaliated by leaving the goods affected by the taxes in customs and successfully pressed for repeal of the measures.[13]

The influence of business interests in tax matters left its mark on the Constitution of 1985, which limits the power of the State to levy tax revenues through "constitutional locks" that prevent any type of "double taxation." This legal provision has been invoked on several occasions, apart from the recent repeal of the IEMA. For instance, in 1987–88, during the administration of Vinicio Cerezo, the Program for National Reorganization lost its economic base when taxes that had been previously agreed upon with the business sectors were later challenged on the basis of provisions in the new constitution.

---

[11] Agricultural and Business Firms Tax (IEMA).

[12] ASIES (2005).

[13] ASIES (2005).

As this brief history of taxation reveals, the ability of some private interests to block or reverse tax measures is deeply entrenched in Guatemala. Business and business organizations around the world pursue their interests in a variety of ways, depending on the perceived opportunities for influence offered by the political system. As discussed in Chapter 5, business is most likely to mobilize against the adoption of a certain policy when its costs are immediate and certain. This is the case with several taxes, such as direct taxes on business profits. It is not surprising, then, that some business organizations in Guatemala oppose attempts to raise taxation. What needs to be explained is why they are so effective in achieving their objectives. Part of the explanation is that the business sector has traditionally been under the control of a small number of families and concentrated in a few sectors of economic activity, especially agriculture and commerce. These two features, according to the discussion of the role of business in Chapter 5, would mitigate problems of collective action, and lead to more intense and effective participation by the business community. But this is hardly the whole explanation. The effectiveness of the business sector in influencing policies essentially rests on the relative institutional weakness of the Guatemalan State.

As the Association of Research and Social Studies of Guatemala, a prominent policy research group, explains, "a government that starts almost from scratch every four years, political parties that do not know if they will survive legally after governing, and a diffuse social movement, without significant representation and with little capacity to formulate and advance policy proposals, do not create an adequate context for the emergence of an organized business participation with a focus on the long-term. It is rather an appropriate context for the development of narrow and short-term business interests that prevail in the exercise of their disproportionate influence."[14]

A vivid example of the effectiveness of the business sector in the face of weak institutions is the recent history of the Fiscal Pact. When it became clear that it would be impossible to meet the target of a 12 percent tax burden in 2000, as agreed in the Peace Accords, the Peace Accord Accompaniment Commission, at government request, agreed in 1998 to reprogram the target for 2002. Along with the postponement, a series of additional actions were taken: extension of a temporary tax (IEMA), the elimination of the deductions related to the VAT and income tax; changes to the Free Zone Law; resumption of the IUSI property tax; the contracting of activity verifiers for foreign trade; and, most importantly, the promotion of a consultation process on a Fiscal Pact, under the auspices of the ministry of public finance and the Accompaniment Commission itself.

A committee of prominent professionals prepared a draft Fiscal Pact in consultation with various economic and political groups. After the public presentation of the source document, the issues were widely publicized and discussed in a rich and very participatory process including representatives from universities, study centers, labor unions, *campesino* organizations, women's organizations, chambers of commerce, departmental consultation groups, mixed and non-mixed committees, peace institutions, nongovernmental organizations (NGOs), and cooperative federations. Political parties participated only to a limited extent, although party participation increased appreciably at the time of the signing of the pact. The process ended successfully with the signing

---

[14] ASIES (2005).

of the Fiscal Pact by the heads of the three branches of government, together with the Accompaniment Commission and representatives of the participating social, political, and economic groups.

In the political climate at the moment, which was not particularly auspicious to the business sector, leading private representatives participated in and supported this process, adopting an attitude of dialogue and cooperation, even on issues that directly touched their interests, such as tax breaks and exemptions (although not in relation to the "constitutional locks").[15] However, a short time later, the balance of power moved back in favor of the business sector—and the Fiscal Pact was never fully implemented. Although the highest authorities of the State had formally backed the process and various political parties had endorsed the document at the last moment, the executive and legislative branches ultimately did not support or respect the pact for various political reasons.

The new tax reform proposed in 2004 by President Óscar Berger also failed to obtain political backing. Paradoxically, on this occasion, the strongest opposition came not from the business sector but from a group of popular organizations and NGOs. Despite the attempt to incorporate progressivity and control of evasion into the bill, they decided to reject the changes, viewing the changes as originating with a government which they perceived as being too closely allied with the business sector.

The result was the reinstatement of the status quo: one in which lack of confidence in the capacity of the State, in the context of a system in which parties are weakly disciplined and relatively unprogrammatic, confers great de facto power on groups that tend to oppose attempts at reform.

Paraguay: Laying the Groundwork for Major Change

In sharp contrast with Brazil, Paraguay does not have a tradition of strong public administration that commands the respect of the public and facilitates the enforcement of the tax code. However, unlike the tax system of Brazil, that of Paraguay is free from many of the complexities of decentralization and the diversity of interests and fears that have prevented Brazil from overhauling its tax system. A recent tax reform became possible when a progressive party sided with the executive to respond to public demands for transparency and effectiveness.

The tax burden in Paraguay is one of the lowest in Latin America. The tax revenues of the central government barely increased from 8.5 percent to 9.7 percent of GDP between the late 1980s and 2000–2002. There is no personal income tax, other tax rates are low, exemptions are plentiful, and evasion is pervasive,[16] the latter reflecting a very weak and poorly financed tax administration and a very high level of informality in the economy.

---

[15] Several reasons contributed to explain this about-face on the part of the business community. Business interests had generally opposed newly elected President Alfonso Portillo, resulting in a decline in their influence during this juncture. In this context, the effective mobilization of the rest of society around the Peace Accords and the pressure of the international community encouraged business leaders to behave cooperatively, rather than risk becoming isolated.

[16] The IMF (2005) estimates that evasion is between 45 and 55 percent for the VAT.

Since 1990, when Paraguay moved toward democracy and witnessed the reduction of tariff barriers of its large neighbors, Argentina and Brazil, a 50-year-old paradigm of smuggling across borders has begun to break down. Among the early reforms to address the high level of informality was tax reform legislation, Law 125/91. The original law was biased against the industrial sector, while the agricultural sector was barely taxed. There was no personal income tax, and it was not particularly hard for small businesses to be exempt from the VAT. Initially the law had two features: it afforded considerable flexibility to the executive, which could decide which articles to apply, and it even allowed some latitude for the executive to decide the rate and base of various taxes. Various aspects of the law and its regulations were ambiguous and subject to interpretation, thus opening up the measure to a series of changes. Taking advantage of its authority to initiate bills on tax issues and bills targeted to the private sector, congress passed some 42 reform laws over the following decade,[17] adding several exemptions, particularly for the industrial sector. The largest was a five-year holiday on all taxes for firms that presented reasonable investment projects, even if they were never carried out. This clearly allowed any firm to be eligible for the tax holiday, and to continue reapplying.

Even in tax systems that are underperforming, major change is possible when political circumstances shift to enable the executive and public-minded politicians to introduce sweeping changes.

Although the tax rate on profits was kept at 30 percent, firms on average effectively paid a tenth of that as a result of exemptions and quasi-legal alternatives. Moreover, politically and economically powerful agricultural interests, well represented in the government and congress, prevented the updating of land values for tax purposes. Partly as a consequence, the tax base value of agricultural land in Paraguay averages only 5.6 percent of its market price.[18]

The agricultural sector accounts for more than 20 percent of GDP, but directly contributes less than 2 percent of total tax revenue, as extremely low land taxation makes it very cheap to preserve idle land in Paraguay. A personal income tax was established only recently and is not expected to be fully operational for years to come. The VAT rate of 10 percent (the lowest in South America) also had numerous exemptions, many introduced through amendments in the 1990s. (Most of these exemptions were eliminated by a law passed in 2004.) Another important indirect tax is the excise tax on diesel fuel (used by 85 percent of the vehicles in Paraguay). The price of diesel is regulated, and so the tax rate has suffered various modifications, the result of negotiations between the state oil company, Petropar, the central government, and the agricultural sector.

Paraguay has historically had a two-party system. The Colorados retained power the longest, even through non-democratic means, until the early 1990s. Attempts at overhauling the tax system began in 2001, but repeated efforts never acquired enough steam to get through congress, particularly in the face of a progressively weaker government with low credibility, a highly factionalized Colorado Party, and determined opposition

---

[17] World Bank (2003).

[18] Molinas, Pérez-Liñán, and Saiegh (2005).

spearheaded by the Liberal Party in congress. A new reformist party, *Patria Querida*, gained considerable popularity during the presidential election race in 2003, as it ran on a platform of change and opposing corruption, an endemic problem in Paraguay. The party was led by a group of progressive technocrats from various sectors of society, particularly from the business sector. As a result, the two-party hegemony broke down. Although the Colorado Party candidate, Nicanor Duarte Frutos, won the election, his party did not win a majority in congress. The seats were more or less equally divided among the three parties: Colorado, Liberal, and *Patria Querida*. Moreover, Duarte came from the reformist faction of the Colorado Party, and while the rhetoric was populist and appealed to the rural less-well-off constituents, in practice the policies were pragmatic and reformist and thus met with some resistance from the traditional faction of his own Colorado Party.

Duarte was elected on a promise to attack corruption at the highest levels. Immediately after taking office, he replaced the top levels of government with individuals who were renowned for their integrity and professionalism and were independent of the traditional Colorado Party apparatus. This included replacing the heads of the tax and customs administrations (which were perceived as the most corrupt institutions in Paraguay) and providing full support to a technocratic group of policymakers. The government then proposed its own strong reform agenda. One of the most important aspects was tax reform. The draft tax law in its purest version essentially eliminated tax exemptions and equalized the rates of both direct and indirect taxes at 10 percent, strengthened tax administration by adding independence and accountability, and increased financing by earmarking a percentage of tax revenues for the tax administration authority. The government made very strong efforts to include as broad a set of groups as possible in the dialogue on tax reform, including civil society, business groups, and trade union groups. To create additional external pressure, the administration secured a commitment for funding from multilateral and bilateral development organizations, conditional on an IMF program. In the end, the ruling Colorado Party supported the law, the Liberal Party opposed it, and *Patria Querida* was left in a very strong bargaining position to support the law on the condition that certain features opposed by its special interests were removed. It thus became the main veto player. In the end, the law was watered down. The share of taxes to be paid by the agricultural sector increased, but remained relatively small. Nonetheless, through a significant broadening of the tax base and the elimination of some egregious exemptions, the law was estimated to increase the tax revenue yield by 1.3 percent of GDP in the long run.[19]

Although the new law (*Ley de Reordenamiento Administrativo y de Adecuación Fiscal*) clearly moved in a desirable direction, in practice the traditional pressure groups continue to lobby for the postponement of some aspects of the law. (The executive has the power to decide the timing of implementation of the articles of the law.) Remarkably, even before the law went into effect, the new government was able to increase tax revenues by 40 percent between August 2002 and 2003, in part through some efficiency measures, but mostly as a result of better compliance and a reduction of internal corruption in the tax administration.

---

[19] IMF (2005).

The experience of Paraguay suggests that major change is possible in tax systems that are seriously underperforming when the political circumstances shift to enable the executive and public-minded politicians to introduce sweeping changes. Of course, this story has yet to unfold fully. Two main challenges persist. First, the tax and customs administrations are not sufficiently financed or independent to perform their mandates adequately. The recent successes in tax collection may not be sustainable unless the resources and powers of the tax administration are increased and maintained. Second, the trend toward eroding the law through amendments may repeat itself. Congress can initiate reforms that benefit particular interests that are very strong and have influence in the political parties and with individual politicians. As the other case studies have highlighted, the executive must exert its power to prevent those trends from eroding a very promising tax reform.

Conclusion

Why do some countries have higher tax revenues relative to their GDPs than others? Why do some countries opt for indirect taxes, while others prefer direct ones? Why do some countries have simple tax regimes, while others prefer complex structures with large numbers of exemptions? Why is taxation so hard to change?

To answer these questions, this chapter has explored some political and institutional aspects of the tax policymaking process. Drawing closely from the experiences of Brazil, Colombia, Guatemala, and Paraguay, the analysis has found that, to a large extent, differences in taxation reflect differences in political institutions and structures, which interact with some important features of tax policies. The wide-reaching effects of taxation throughout the economy make cooperative solutions difficult when the number of players is large. The common-pool nature of taxation revenues creates incentives to renege on cooperative agreements. It also necessitates enforcement mechanisms to implement tax policies effectively. These problems may be acute in fiscally decentralized countries, especially if subnational authorities have strong powers vis-à-vis the executive and, in general, in countries where political power is fragmented. Taxation systems are very highly path-dependent because of the resistance of elites; uncertainty about the revenue consequences of the reforms; the strategic interests of weak governments or parties in polarized political systems; and the difficulty of putting enforcement mechanisms in place. Path-dependence is more likely to be overcome in more centralized systems, especially when the balance of power favors the executive and leadership is strong.

Chapter 9

Politicization of Public Services[1]

Because regulation...is sometimes used to promote redistributional or ideological purposes...it can be highly politicized.

—Oliver Williamson, *Public and Private Bureaus*

The policymaking process (PMP) strongly influences the quality of the regulation of public services (telecommunications, electricity, gas, water and sanitation, and the like). As in other policy areas, the stability, adaptability, credibility, and transparency of policies depend on how they are proposed, discussed, and put into action. The regulation of public services does not emerge solely from technical criteria aimed at designing the economically ideal system of incentives. In practice, regulatory mechanisms and institutions are the result of complex processes of political negotiation, which in turn are affected by the inherent characteristics of the regulated sectors and of underlying political institutions. In each country, these institutions are shaped by history, values, and other factors unique to the country. All these factors set the limits within which the actors involved in these processes can act.

Unlike the case of tax policy, analyzed in Chapter 8, in which the tax policymaking process mirrors the country's general policymaking process, the policymaking process for the public services sectors is molded not only by how policies are formulated in general in each country, but also by the characteristics and institutions specific to these sectors. Reform policies often alter the domestic institutional arrangement in these sectors; thus reforms can also affect how policy is made in the future. So, while the general political ground rules tend to persist over time, the relevant elements of the political game in the area of public services tend to change considerably during the actual process of reforming these sectors. This is because new key agents appear (such as new companies), new forms of interaction emerge (based on explicit contracts or new legal conditions, for example), and new political alignments develop for strategic or ideological reasons (for or against certain forms of ownership).

---

[1] This chapter is based on Bergara and Pereyra (2005).

Why are regulatory policies so susceptible to politicization? The explanation lies with three features that characterize the sectors. First, public services require large specific and permanent fixed investments (which economists call "sunk costs" because they cannot be recovered for alternative uses). Second, they have large economies of scale and scope. For example, electricity may be generated more cheaply in generators exceeding a certain size, and the same can be said of water treatment plants. Although electricity and water may be delivered by different suppliers, it makes no sense for each generator to have its own distribution network. Third, public services are consumed by very extensive groups within the population.

Although none of these features is decisive, the combination of all three works in favor of the politicization of regulation of the sectors. As Spiller and Tommasi note:

> First, the fact that a large component of infrastructure investments is sunk implies that once the investment is undertaken the operator will be willing to continue operating as long as operating revenues exceed operating costs. Since operating costs do not include a return on sunk investments (but only on the alternative value of these assets), the operating company will be willing to operate even if prices are below total average costs. Second, economies of scale imply that in most utility services, there will be few suppliers in each locality. Thus the whiff of monopoly will always surround utility operations.
>
> Finally, the fact that utility services tend to be massively consumed, and thus that the set of consumers closely approximates the set of voters, implies that politicians and interest groups will care about the level of utility pricing. Thus massive consumption, economies of scale, and sunk investments provide governments (either national or local) with the opportunity to behave opportunistically vis-à-vis the investing company. For example, after the investment is sunk, the government may try to restrict the operating company's pricing flexibility, may require the company to undertake special investments, purchasing, or employment patterns, or may try to restrict the movement of capital. All these are attempts to expropriate the company's sunk costs by administrative measures. Thus expropriation may be indirect and undertaken by subtle means.[2]

While the risk of expropriation of public utility companies is serious, it is only one of the political risks that can hamper the functioning of the public services sectors. Another risk is capture of regulatory agencies by the regulated companies. These companies have much at stake in the process of regulation. They are typically endowed with abundant resources and often engage in different activities to influence policy outcomes in their favor (such as lobbying, and sometimes even outright corruption) to try to capture the executive bodies or the regulatory agencies that set the parameters within which these companies operate (see Figure 9.1).

Because of the possibilities of politicization, the institutional environment plays a crucial role. Well-functioning institutions can provide credibility and stability to policies in these markets. They can also limit the possibility that the regulated firms will capture the executive bodies or regulating agencies in charge of defining and enforcing the rules of the game.

---

[2] Spiller and Tommasi (2005, p. 519).

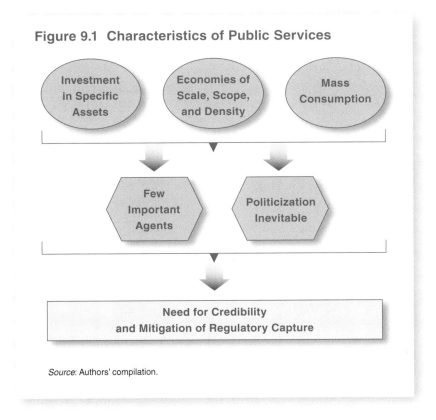

Figure 9.1 Characteristics of Public Services

Source: Authors' compilation.

The incentives for expropriation tend to be stronger under certain conditions:

1. When formal and informal procedures for decision making are not well established.
2. When regulatory decision making is centralized in agencies that are subordinated to the executive and are susceptible to political pressure.
3. When the judicial system does not have the tradition or the power to review all administrative decisions.
4. When the government's time horizon is relatively short.

To reduce the risks to investors of expropriation, and to prevent investors from influencing the design of the policies in their favor, the design of the relevant institutions must lend credibility to the policymaking process. In this respect, the promise that investors' rights will be respected and that their obligations will be enforced must be credible.

Although all the public services sectors share the three characteristics mentioned above as making them particularly susceptible to politicization, they differ with respect to whether competition is technically possible and, if so, how rapidly competition can translate into visible results. For example, it is easier to generate competition in the telecommunications sector than in the electricity sector. Moreover, competition in international long-distance telephony and cellular telephony produces improvements in efficiency, yields price reductions, introduces new services, and increases market volume more efficiently than the introduction of competition into the energy sectors. Obviously, these aspects are crucial for the success and long-term sustainability of reforms.

Various attempts have been made to reform public services markets in Latin America. The most notable have been those related to the areas of telecommunications, energy, and water and sanitation. In the 1990s, governments, with the help of international organizations, made great efforts to find mechanisms to privatize companies that had traditionally provided these basic services.

FIGURE 9.2 **Total Private Investment in the Infrastructure Sectors in Latin America, 1990–2003[a]** (*as percentage of GDP*)

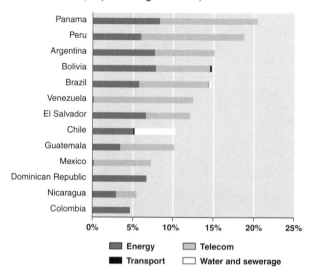

[a] Includes investment in acquiring government assets and investment in facilities.
Note: Cumulative values of the investments as a percentage of the annual gross domestic product.
Source: Authors' calculations based on World Bank (2005) and World Bank (various years).

The outcomes were very mixed because the intensity of the privatization process differed greatly from one country to another (see Figure 9.2) and because the processes were not always introduced and carried through as part of a clearly defined strategy to restructure the affected sectors. Rather the reforms were often a response to the fiscal needs of governments, to political circumstances that favored potential buyers, and even to purely personal factors. The common element in the processes was politicization—the result of the three characteristics of the services sectors described above. Such politicization has often acquired ideological trappings, in a struggle between the virtues and vices of "market" versus "State."

The attempts at privatization in the 1990s yielded mixed results, particularly in countries such as Argentina and Peru, where the quality and coverage of public services were very low at the outset. In these cases, State provision of the services had proven to be basically deficient. This experience, added to the government's fiscal needs and a political environment more open to supporting privatization, initially facilitated the sale of assets and the participation of private agents in the provision of services. Since the crux of the discussion was the relative virtues of different forms of ownership, the central aspect of the process was privatization rather than the introduction of a competitive framework, especially in the case of telecommunications, where in several countries the State monopoly was simply replaced by a private monopoly.

The incomplete implementation and limited results led many to question the approach of the reform adopted. For reasons of substantial technological progress, as in the case of telecommunications, the approach to the reforms gradually changed, giving primacy to competition and leaving the nature of the ownership of the companies that provide the public services as a secondary consideration. In electricity, for reasons of organizational learning, the ground rules themselves acquired more importance, apart from whether they applied to public or private companies, and whether competition could be introduced.

It has become critically important to set up regulatory agencies that are independent from economic agents.

In this process of promoting competition and regulating the noncompetitive segments of the market (for instance, electricity or water distribution), it has become critically important to set up regulatory agencies that are independent from economic agents, particularly existing companies. The creation and strengthening of these agencies is part of a process of redesign of the role of the State that aims to define who is responsible for policy design, who is responsible for the regulation of the market, and who is responsible for providing the service, in cases where State companies still exist. As part of this process, the creation and design of regulatory agencies has been the subject of considerable debate and institutional dispute.

Debate has also centered on the institutional location of the regulatory agencies, as well as their relation to the authorities responsible for overseeing competition. In all these aspects of regulation, the difficult balance between technical and political criteria has been affected by institutional constraints. The case studies below illustrate these points.

Case Studies

Institutional Weakness and Volatile Results: The Case of Argentina

Since the early efforts at reform in the sector, public services policy in Argentina has been characterized by volatility, considerable influence by special interests, and insufficient attention to the institutional capacity of the regulatory agencies.

The opening of telecommunications to the private sector in the early 1990s was Argentina's first experience with privatization. At that time, telecommunications services were provided by *Empresa Nacional de Telecomunicaciones* (ENTEL), a public company with a legal monopoly, which suffered from major financial and administrative problems that impacted the quality of service and the network's rate of expansion. After ENTEL was privatized, the provision of telecommunications services was in the hands of two companies (*Telefónica* and *Telecom*), which operated in the southern and northern parts of Argentina,

In a political and institutional context largely unfavorable to inter-temporal agreements, the result has been substantial volatility in public services policies.

respectively, and shared the Buenos Aires market equally. These companies acquired exclusive operating licenses for basic services (voice transmission except mobile telephony) for seven years. This exclusivity was intended to trigger an accelerated investment process, in order to boost development of Argentina's telecommunications capacity (and increase the proceeds of the sale). For this, the companies made specific investment commitments to expand the network and improve the quality of the service. At the same time, a regulatory agency, the National Telecommunications Commission (CNT), was established, but it operated independently for only one year. In 1991, the executive intervened and placed the CNT under the control of the ministry of public works.

In March 1998, a telecommunications liberalization plan was approved. It implemented the decision to move the sector gradually toward competition. New licenses were granted for basic services, which favored existing operators, whether providers of fixed or mobile telephony, or other services. The exclusive licenses for the telephony providers were extended for two more years (until 1999), even though they had not fully complied with their investment commitments.

The absence of adequate institutions to manage the regulation process has helped make policies in the telecommunications sector even more volatile than in other infrastructure sectors in Argentina, where regulators have maintained greater independence. It is therefore not surprising that the most serious conflict over regulation of public services in Argentina during the 1990s took place in the telecommunications sector. At issue were the criteria for tariff-setting, following the introduction of exchange rate convertibility in 1991. A special feature of telecommunications privatization (compared with the processes for other public services that came later) was that the preexisting tariff structure was transferred to the new operators. This structure entailed a series of cross-subsidies that were even higher than those that had historically existed in the country. When peso-dollar parity was adopted, firms were prevented from adjusting tariffs in line with the consumer price index (CPI), undermining the arrangement of price cap regulation with indexation to the CPI that had been established in the privatization agreement.

In 1996, the ministry of economics took control of negotiations with the firms, assuming the place of the regulator. Tariffs and adjustments to them were dollarized: in line not with prices in Argentina, but with prices in the United States—without changing the productivity factor. The firms saw this as an expropriation and began legal actions to recover the difference with respect to the old formula. These actions ultimately failed.

The privatization agreement led to other disagreements. The firms faced lost revenues because developments in technology were presenting users with the possibility of finding alternative providers for the services for which the firms were charging the highest tariffs. Thus firms demanded tariff rebalancing. A series of public hearings was held to discuss the rebalancing, with the participation of different actors (the ombudsman, consumer groups, legislators) that opposed the measure. Aside from the fact that the rebalancing had sound economic justification and that it was clearly needed even before privatization, the important aspect was the contentious way in which the political and social agents interacted. After the rebalancing was approved, claims of illegality were filed in court. In some cases, the courts upheld, on procedural grounds, the claims of those who opposed rebalancing.

Following these legal decisions, the companies either stopped invoicing (in an attempt to delay billing until the legal claims had been resolved) or ignored the decisions and sent out invoices under the new tariff scheme. Both procedures were poorly received by the public, which also perceived the regulatory agency as having been captured by the companies.[3] Negative public opinion, aggravated by the regulator's inability to explain the reasons for the tariff rebalancing and regain credibility, influenced the position that other key agents adopted later in the conflict. The resolution to adjust tariffs issued by the ministry of economics in 1996 was never enforced because of political opposition. The issue was ultimately resolved by the president, and in 1997 the tariff rebalancing was approved by presidential decree.

These difficulties arose because the private companies had inherited an inadequate tariff structure from ENTEL. This resulted from the government's eagerness to initiate the reform process in public services as quickly as possible, to pave the way for reform in the other services sectors. The government was trying to capitalize on the period when it held a majority to introduce legal change. This was a reasonable stance, in view of Argentina's PMP, which offers few possibilities for inter-temporal cooperation between governmental and other political actors.[4] The regulatory scheme adopted—which is characterized by the regulator's lack of independence and various technical and institutional deficiencies—should be understood as the result of the interaction between the special characteristics of the telecommunications sector and the institutions and practices of the national political game, in which short-term agendas often take priority over any inter-temporal agreement, leaving little room for long-term institutional development.

When Argentina ended exchange rate parity in 2002, deepening the economic recession, the contracts governing privatization of the companies would have allowed them to keep the tariffs unchanged in (indexed) dollar terms, which implied nearly three times their present value in pesos. Congress passed a law that repealed the contracts' dollar adjustment provision and prohibited any indexation based on the indices of other countries (or any other indexation mechanism), and set the tariffs in pesos, based on the old exchange rate of one peso per dollar. The law also authorized the executive to renegotiate contracts for provision of public services, setting up the Renegotiation Commission for Public Works and Services Contracts. As a result of these measures, the telecommunications sector fell into a deep crisis, various companies defaulted on their debt payments, and others shut down their operations.[5]

Public services policy in Argentina has been highly volatile. A policy of private sector participation in public service provision has been in effect for about 20 years without the development of regulatory institutions that are significantly independent of the political system. This has led, in some cases, to a degree of capture by the regulated companies. When the institutional design produced a more independent regulator (as in electricity and gas in the 1990s), capture did not occur. However, some decisions were made and actions taken that imposed financial losses on the private providers and thus amounted to some degree of expropriation. This was aggravated by the difficulty of settling complex cases through the judicial system. The political system was not willing to lose its discretionary capacity in regard to the sectors. Thus the regulatory institutions that were created in the privatization process were rapidly incorporated into the political sphere. This, in

---

[3] Vispo (1999), cited in Celani (2000).

[4] Spiller and Tommasi (2003).

[5] See AHCIET (2003).

turn, resulted in limitations on their areas of responsibility, technical capacity, and financial resources. In this context, it is debatable whether the special agendas and political interests of the actors involved in the regulatory process had more influence on the decisions made (in rebalancing telecommunications tariffs, extending exclusivity periods, and delaying the introduction of competition, for example) than the broader public interest. The successive changes of government at the turn of the century produced a substantial policy shift. The situation moved from one of relative capture by the regulated companies to one of open conflict with the private providers (linked to the "pesification" of the contracts), making this a paradigmatic example of policy volatility.

The reforms of the 1990s profoundly changed Argentina's PMP at the sectoral level. The key actors were now the privatized companies: mainly multinational firms with large amounts of capital in the sector at the international level. The regulatory agencies appeared as potentially important but institutionally weak actors with inadequate funding. Public opinion was initially favorable to the reform because of deficiencies in the existing provision of services. However, as the regulatory process developed, there was a widespread perception that the regulatory agencies had been captured, and that the regulatory process was providing important benefits to companies at the expense of consumers. This led to the appearance of actors such as the ombudsman, consumers' associations, and even groups of legislators that opposed the way in which tariff problems were dealt with. The economic shock of 2002 was clearly unfavorable to investors, and it occurred at a time when the privatized companies were poorly perceived by the public. Against this backdrop, the response to the shock yielded important political benefits. Thus, in a political and institutional context largely unfavorable to inter-temporal agreements, the result has been public services policies characterized by substantial volatility.

Institutional Consistency and Stable Results: The Case of Chile

Chile has been a world pioneer in the introduction of various forms of privatization and the adoption of policies to promote competition in public services sectors. These policies have been based on an institutional framework that includes regulators with a high degree of technical capacity—although without a high degree of political independence—and an independent competition protection agency with a high level of involvement in sectoral policies. The policies have generally been stable, benefiting from the economic stability of the country. However, they have exhibited some deficiencies in their ability to respond to shocks. The policies for each sector have been guided by technical objectives specific to that sector, as opposed to political considerations, and are consistent with fiscal policy. The institutional design and operation of regulatory institutions has effectively protected privatized companies from the risk of indirect expropriation, although at some cost in terms of efficiency, and in some cases giving rise to extraordinary profits.

Policymakers have come to recognize the limitations of direct regulation and the disciplinary power of market competition. This has led to a real transformation of policymaking in the area of public services.

Perhaps the best illustration of these characteristics is the reform of the telecommunications sector. In the mid-

1970s, telecommunications services in Chile were in the hands of two public companies. *Compañía de Telecomunicaciones de Chile* (CTC) provided local telephony to almost the entire country, while *Empresa Nacional de Telecomunicaciones* (ENTEL) offered domestic and international long-distance services. In the early 1980s, the market structure was changed radically. Both firms passed into private hands, and the first steps were taken to introduce competition into the sector. The regulation of telecommunications became the responsibility of the sub-secretariat of telecommunications (SUBTEL), attached to the ministry of transport and telecommunications. Its powers include design and regulation of sectoral policy, as well as the application of tariff-setting procedures. The Telecommunications Law of 1982 set guidelines for the development of the sector, establishing transparent processes for granting concessions, with exceptions made only on technical grounds (shortage of spectrum in mobile telephony). The law allows providers to set prices—except in cases in which the Antitrust Commission (established in the early 1970s) decides that there is insufficient competition. In these cases, prices are regulated.

In 1994, during the opening of the international telephony market to competition, there was a debate on whether the fixed-telephony operating companies should be allowed to operate in the international market. SUBTEL asked the Antitrust Commission for its opinion. The commission authorized the fixed-telephony firms' operation in that market, provided that before their entry, the government established a multi-carrier system, and the firms established separate independent companies to participate in the international market. In turn, SUBTEL established additional conditions for approving the application of the fixed-telephony firms to operate long-distance services. The pressures exerted by the firms on regulators to authorize vertical mergers, with a view to exploiting economies of scale, were dealt with by the Antitrust Commission. This prevented capture and favored solutions in which the integration of companies did not impede competition in the competitive segments of the market.

In the electricity sector, the privatization process began with the separation of regulatory activity from the public utility before 1980, at the same time as regulatory changes were introduced to allow private participation. Chile's three integrated public electricity companies were separated into multiple generating and distribution companies and then privatized, with the privatization taking place through the sale of shares in the new firms. Unlike in the telecommunications sector, the reforms did not impose vertical disaggregation on the companies, as the largest generator (*Endesa*) kept the property of the central electricity grid. Furthermore, generation and distribution companies were sold separately, but nothing prevented a generation company from buying a distribution company. This approach was criticized because it allowed the same business conglomerate to maintain a dominant market position by controlling large portions of all segments of the industry. The electricity sector privatization legislation left almost no room for the regulator to introduce more efficient solutions to problems that later arose that the legislation could not foresee or to resolve ambiguities in interpretation (on such issues as indices for tariff adjustment and setting of transmission tolls).

The technological characteristics of the electricity sector and the rigidity and ambiguities of the privatization legislation led to many conflicts related to the possibilities of vertical integration in the production stages and the (anti)competitive conduct of the integrated companies. However, these conflicts made it clear that independent judicial intervention was able to prevent (indirect) expropriation of the privatized companies and that competition, as a principle embodied in the legislation, was deeply rooted in the working of the Antitrust Commission and the regulatory agency.

But even in Chile, there have been episodes in which politicization has played an important role. Regulatory action failed most clearly in response to the energy crisis of 1988–89. In those years, Chile was hit by a record drought, which led to the reduction of hydroelectric potential. In addition to its error in estimating the extent of the drought, the government did not impose restrictions on the use of water reserves until the last minute, having hesitated for fear of the political costs that such an unpopular measure would entail. The government's stance subjected the regulator, which was directly dependent on the government, to politicization—on an issue that was clearly technical in nature and had an obvious technical solution.

The regulatory decisions at the time of the crisis (to keep the cost assigned to unprovided energy low in spite of scarcity, to reduce the wholesale price of energy, and to refrain from establishing voluntary rationing quotas for unregulated large consumers) provided inadequate incentives for both producers and consumers. The legislature later passed a law establishing how energy rationing should be implemented. The law did not adhere to the principles of technical efficiency in managing the crisis, and instead introduced incentives that were harmful to the long-term development of the sector.[6] The way in which the crisis was handled reflected the regulator's abandonment of technical solutions in favor of political considerations, with inefficient results. Strong politicization was clearly evident in this episode.

At the onset of privatization, Chile adopted a system of regulation by price caps. It includes a regular review of prices, based on a model that leaves very little room for discretion by the regulator. The price cap system involves setting prices based on a markup of profit over costs and capital in an efficient "ideal" model company with the capacity to meet the demand. Tariffs are set every five years and are indexed in the periods between adjustments. The utilities themselves carry out the tariff-setting studies and propose tariff adjustments, and the regulator comments on their proposals. The differences are submitted for arbitration to an expert committee. The regulator usually accepts the committee's decision, because the courts are generally disinclined to overrule the experts.[7]

Changes in the electricity distribution tariffs in 1992 and 1996, and those for the telephone companies in 1994, reveal that the processes for setting tariffs are extremely conflictive: the companies expended massive amounts of resources to influence decisions and used minor legal arguments to delay the tariff-setting process and negotiate an unjustifiably high tariff in response to their demands. They were able to attain returns of 20 to 40 percent, which are excessive considering the level of risk assumed. However, the gradual strengthening of regulatory institutions seems to be having a beneficial impact

---

[6] Basañes, Saavedra, and Soto (1999).

[7] Fischer and Serra (2002).

in relation to tariff-setting, as the margins have gradually declined to normal levels following the excesses that characterized the early years.

In the water and sanitation sector, the tariff-setting process followed the general
scheme described above. In 2000, the first tariff review of the privatized companies led
to a 20 percent increase in real terms. The tariff-setting system was clearly resistant to
political pressures because, even in an election year, a significant increase was approved.
However, the increase had a negative impact on public opinion in regard to privatization. It also influenced the policy adopted in subsequent privatizations of companies in
this sector, in which, in contrast to the previous privatizations, a concession scheme was
adopted instead of a sale of assets, given that the regulatory system in this sector was still
too weak to regulate privatized companies adequately.[8]

In general, public services policy in Chile has been characterized by stability. The
structural reforms in the direction of the privatization of public companies and the introduction of competition, which began during the dictatorship, have proceeded without major shifts. Developing competition has been a priority, and the privatizations of
the 1990s avoided granting protected markets to the privatized firms. Consistent with
these principles, the importance of the Antitrust Commission in the regulation of public
services has grown over time, in line with its gradual institutional strengthening.

Regulatory agencies in Chile have considerably more human and economic resources
than comparable agencies in the rest of the region, which has given them a higher level
of technical competence. However, in terms of institutional setup and operation, they
are no more independent of political influence than other agencies of their kind. So how
can the stability of policy be explained? At least part of the answer is that the political-
institutional system in Chile offers better possibilities for inter-temporal cooperation,
particularly in a context in which preferences and ideological positions on privatization
and the role of the market are less polarized than in other countries.

The results of the regulatory process have been varied. When protection of competition has been at stake, decisions have been consistent and stable. However, this has not
been the case when the subject of the decision has been technically complex. For example, in the design of the operation of the electricity market, the regulator was subject to
some capture by the regulated companies. In the case of the 1988–89 drought, its actions
were influenced by fear of the political costs of a decision to ration use of limited water
reserves. However, in cases in which regulatory intervention has been related to aspects
of tariff-setting for monopolistic services, the dispute settlement mechanisms and judicial action have operated as effective institutional guarantees for the firms against the
risks of expropriation by the regulator.

The reforms initiated in the early 1980s radically changed Chile's sectoral PMP.
Public companies were replaced by private companies, regulatory agencies appeared on
the scene, and the Antitrust Commission began to play a central role. The relationship
between the new companies and public institutions has been dynamic, partly as a result
of a gradual learning process in public institutions. The most important lesson learned
in the regulatory field has been policymakers' recognition of the limitations of direct
regulation and the disciplinary power of market competition. This has led to a real

---

[8] Gómez-Lobo and Vargas (2002).

transformation of policymaking in the area of public services. The case illustrates how an environment characterized by strong and well-defined institutions and acceptance of competition can reduce room for discretionary policy decisions and limit the influence of special interests in such decisions.

Direct Democracy and Resistance to Privatization: The Case of Uruguay

Policies aimed at opening and modernizing the public services sectors have been unstable in Uruguay. In the last decade, the legislature has passed a series of reform-minded laws, which were then threatened by referendum or plebiscite, or repealed. The impasse that this has created has not prevented progress in improving the functioning of public companies. Policies in this area have produced important fiscal benefits and have been very stable—mainly because the preferences of the public and the political system have aligned on keeping these companies public but improving their provision of services and are favorable to the companies.

Reforms have been limited because the potential losers have found mechanisms to block change.

Although the regulatory institutions created in the reform process lack adequate technical and economic resources, the bureaucracy of the public companies has been greatly strengthened, allowing them to operate more efficiently and effectively than is typical of this kind of company in developing countries. Moreover, their monopolistic power has been curbed in recent years by a series of legal decisions—despite the rigidity imposed by direct democracy mechanisms and popular resistance to measures that could weaken public companies.

Direct democracy is promoted in the current constitution, which offers a number of mechanisms that can be activated by citizens or lawmakers. Since the return of democracy in 1985, two mechanisms have been used. The first is referendum by popular initiative, which can block a law from being implemented if so approved by an absolute majority of the voters registered for that purpose (at least 25 percent of all registered voters). With only one exception—a referendum on amnesty for military personnel accused of violating human rights during the dictatorship—the procedure has been used exclusively to attempt to block laws related to public services (though not always successfully). A second procedure has been plebiscite by popular initiative. This mechanism can be initiated on the approval of as little as 10 percent of registered voters. Votes occur at the time of the national elections, and the mechanism can even be applied to amendments to the constitution. This procedure has been used for changes in the water and sanitation sector and in social security.

Direct democracy mechanisms for public services have all been promoted by the labor unions of the public companies affected. Political groups on the Left have also lent organized support and provided significant capacity for mobilizing voters (although in some cases with discordant opinions on the introduction of competition without privatization).

An important factor driving the reforms has been the desire to strengthen public companies as a source of public revenue. Unlike tax increases, adjustments to tariff rates for public companies do not require legislative approval—an advantage for the government, especially in times of severe fiscal constraints. This apparent advantage, however, works against the objectives of reforming public services sectors.

Recent legislation has begun to break the monopolistic powers of State companies, with varying degrees of success. In 1997, the monopoly of *Administración Nacional de Usinas y Trasmisiones Eléctricas* (UTE) on electricity generation was eliminated. (Its monopoly on transmission and distribution was maintained.) In 2001, the monopoly held by *Administración Nacional de Telecomunicaciones* (ANTEL) on telecommunications activities was eliminated, with the exception of local and national long-distance telephony. This opened the way for the entry of competitors into international telephony markets, in addition to data transmission and mobile telephony. In 2002, congress repealed the 2001 legislation—in light of its imminent repeal by referendum. This prevented new competitors from entering international telephony markets. However, the companies that entered these markets while the legislation was in force continue to operate. In 2003, a law was passed to end the public monopoly on the refining and marketing of fossil fuels by 2006, and to open the way for the association of the State oil company, *Administración Nacional de Combustibles, Alcohol y Portland* (ANCAP), with the private sector. However, the law was repealed by referendum in late 2003.

The process of reforming public services in Uruguay has been relatively volatile. Many reforms passed by congress have been repealed by referendum. The ones that have escaped this fate (such as that involving the electricity sector) have suffered years of delay in their implementation, influenced by the political factors inherent in the public services sectors. Since the preferences of the population clearly incline toward public provision of services and the protection of public companies, opposition to reform attempts produces substantial political benefits. This makes it easier for unions to successfully promote direct democracy mechanisms. The preference for public ownership of utilities is widespread (although the need for competition in the public services markets is accepted). This preference can be traced to historical reasons (the strong presence of the State in the country's "golden era" in the mid-20th century), as well as the fact that the coverage and quality of services is not deficient, as it was in some other countries at the start of their privatization processes. Another factor working against the opening of services sectors to private investment has been the government's need for fiscal revenue from public companies. This factor has even led to delays in the implementation of legislation, introducing an additional element of volatility and uncertainty into those sectors.

Since reforms have not been very deep, the way public services policies are discussed and implemented in Uruguay has changed little. Public companies continue to be the key actors, with the broad support of the population. Reforms have been limited because the potential losers have found mechanisms to block change. The setting up of regulatory agencies has been the most important institutional advance toward establishing some level of market competition in the public services sectors, but little has been invested in strengthening these agencies technically, administratively, or financially. The agencies have some institutional independence, but face a fundamental limitation in that they do not regulate the tariff-setting of the monopolistic sectors (a power that remains with the executive). They also have limited ability to prevent anticompetitive conduct in a context in which public companies are vertically integrated and competition protection agencies are limited. In addition, public companies have large and competent bureaucracies, with more capacity to affect political decisions than the regulator itself, and strong possibilities of delaying the implementation of decisions. The role played by the regulatory agencies in maintaining the main advances in liberalization should be emphasized, because there are no other key actors pushing in that direction.

Institutional Weakness and Attempts to Build Credibility: The Case of Peru

Because investors suffered direct and indirect expropriations in the 1980s, the main challenge facing public services policymaking in Peru in the last 15 years has been to generate credibility in a very weak institutional context. The outcome has been relatively successful, but at the cost of creating serious rigidities in sectoral policy. Although the policies promoted by successive administrations have consistently aimed to stabilize the policies for the sectors, in practice policy implementation has been volatile in view of the resistance by the legislature to most of the initiatives promoted by the current government.

The case of Peru illustrates the difficulties confronting regulatory policy when there is a deficit of credibility in relation to investors.

With the arrival of the Fujimori administration in 1990, Peru introduced a sweeping reform program in the infrastructure sectors, based on the privatization of public companies in the telecommunications and energy sectors. This program was part of a strategy to remove the State from all business activities and stabilize the economy. The reform program was the response of the government to a legacy of earlier nationalizations that had occurred without compensation (especially in the banking sector) and a variety of episodes of indirect expropriation, which had soured investors on investing in Peru.

To carry forward a privatization process in this adverse institutional environment, the government attempted to create credibility through a series of framework laws that offered greater legal certainty in regard to private investment, especially foreign investment. The laws introduced the possibility of signing legal stability agreements with foreign investors. These agreements, with the status of law, preclude the government from changing tax conditions, imposing labor obligations, or setting limits on companies' ability to transfer profits or capital out of the country. Thus, the government was willing to sacrifice its own powers to achieve credibility. It signed international investment protection agreements that allowed recourse to international arbitration bodies to settle disputes, as well as a series of bilateral investment protection agreements. If the domestic institutions for protection of investors were not sufficient, the government was willing to import such institutions when necessary.

To encourage private investment in public services, the Commission to Promote Private Concessions was set up, with responsibility for the partial or total sale of equity in public companies to the private sector. Regulatory agencies were also created for each sector (energy, telecommunications, water and sanitation, and transport), all of which were directly dependent on the executive branch.

The main characteristics of the reform process for public services are illustrated by the case of the electricity sector. Before privatization, electricity generation and distribution service in Peru was provided mainly by a single public utility, *Electroperú*. Distribution was provided by various public utilities, subsidiaries of *Electroperú*, including *Electrolima* (which also provided generation for the city of Lima). At the start of the reform, less than half of households had access to electricity, one of the lowest electrification rates in Latin America. Public companies produced 70 percent of the country's energy; industry self-generated the remaining 30 percent. Electricity tariffs were set at very low levels for political reasons, covering less than 40 percent of the operating costs of the sector. This was an enormous obstacle to the investment process. In 1992, the Electricity Concessions Law was passed, which separated the functions of generation and distribution, established a new tariff system, and authorized privatizations. Between 1993 and 1997, five generating utilities and five distribution utilities were privatized, with explicit commitments to increase generating capacity. With Peru's integrated electricity companies having been disaggregated by these privatizations, integration was prohibited as a procompetition measure, reinforced by the passage of the Electricity Sector Anti-Monopoly and Anti-Oligopoly Law.

Since the end of the final Fujimori administration in 2000, part of Peru's electricity sector has remained in the hands of public companies: the hydroelectric generating utility of the Mantaro basin and the distributors in the south of the country. State-owned *Electroperú* operates one-third of the country's generating capacity, while transmission is almost totally in private hands. The State is still an important operator in distribution, although the main distributors have been privatized. In the years following the privatizations in the electricity sector, installed generating capacity grew 25 percent, electrification coverage expanded 20 percent (30 percent, in privatized areas), and operating losses fell by 40 percent. In return, residential tariffs rose over 80 percent.[9] Simultaneously with the privatizations, two institutions were created for sectoral regulation: the Organization for Supervision of Private Investment in Energy (OSINERG), and the Energy Tariffs Commission (CTE). These were later merged.

The country's main distributor, *Electrolima*, representing more than half of power distribution in the country, was split in two in 1993 and awarded as an indefinite-term concession, in the first major privatization of the Fujimori period. The concession agreements established the main aspects of the relationship between the privatized firms and the regulator, including tariff-setting and dispute settlement mechanisms.

Several points of contention left their mark on the regulatory system after the initiation of the privatization process in the electricity sector. One of them, between the regulator and the distribution firms in Lima, arose during the initial definition of tariffs in relation to the method for determining the replacement value of the firms' assets. The regulatory scheme adopted for the electricity sector used a cost-based tariff for the segments of the industry that were considered natural monopolies. An important part of the costs was associated with the fixed assets, which were valued at replacement cost for the purpose of the calculation. In 1997, the regulator published its estimates for the

---

[9] Torero and Pascó-Font (2001).

new replacement value, which the companies strongly challenged in administrative and judicial bodies, and through a strong advertising and information campaign. The regulator maintained its position, with public support from the country's main political authorities, including President Fujimori, and the companies finally abandoned the litigation.[10]

Although the Electricity Sector Anti-Monopoly and Anti-Oligopoly Law prohibited concentration in different market segments and greatly limited integration of the industry, both horizontal and vertical concentration occurred in practice, as a result of mergers of business groups that controlled different firms in the electricity sector.[11] This obvious inconsistency between reality and rules was resolved by changing the rules—thus abandoning one of the central pillars of the regulatory system in favor of the special interests of investors. Affected sectors, such as business organizations, were notoriously absent from this process. And the political parties showed no interest, as if it were merely a technical discussion without economic and political implications.

The Toledo administration attempted to revive the reform process, which had lost momentum in the final years of the Fujimori administration. It promoted the privatization of two distribution utilities in Arequipa in the south of the country. Their sale was the subject of a constitutional appeal (*amparo*) filed by the mayor of the city of Arequipa, which claimed that the region, not the national government, was the owner of the distribution companies. A series of regional social groups organized around opposition to the privatization of the distribution companies. Popular demonstrations grew so large that they led to an indefinite general strike in the region, spilling over to neighboring areas, and the declaration of a state of emergency by the government. Finally, the government abandoned its intention to privatize the utilities and two ministers resigned. The demonstrations were led by local groups composed in some cases of *campesinos* and urban workers, but also including local chambers of commerce and even mayors.[12] The Mantaro generating complex, *Electroperú*'s main asset, was also selected for privatization—until congress passed a law to abandon the plan, influenced by strong opposition to it.

The case of Peru shows the difficulties confronting regulation policy when there is a lack of credibility in relation to investors, and a shifting balance of power between the executive and legislative branches. To encourage private investment, it was crucial to offer broad guarantees. All relevant interests were aligned in support of this objective, and the legislature responded without objection, given its subordination to the executive during the first Fujimori administration.

Peru's experience with privatization altered the policymaking process in the public services sectors. Powerful private companies interested in exploiting potential monopolistic profits entered the market. Regulatory agencies also appeared on the scene, with a certain degree of operating independence and technical capacity, but under the control of the executive. Simultaneously, the balance of power of the executive vis-à-vis the

---

[10] Campodónico (2000).

[11] Aguilar (2003).

[12] The area is among the places where President Toledo had the highest electoral support, and opposition to the privatizations was part of his election platform.

legislature changed. This was due in part to a fragmentation of the party system, which reduced the executive's chances of obtaining majority support in congress. The presumption of corruption surrounding the Fujimori privatization process further strengthened opposition to privatization and hindered efforts to continue the privatization process under the Toledo administration.

As circumstances changed, it also became clear that a regulatory agency dependent on the executive could not be isolated from politicization. Thus attempts to strengthen the credibility and stability of regulatory policy were frustrated because ultimately they were based on a circumstantial alignment of interests and on the temporary supremacy of the executive, rather than on a process of consensus-building and longer-term inter-temporal agreements among enduring political agents.

Conclusion

Policies in regard to and regulation of public services sectors are susceptible to politicization because of very high sunk costs, large economies of scale and scope, and mass consumption. These characteristics offer governments and politicians the possibility of behaving opportunistically to expropriate the provider companies—directly or indirectly—and take over their quasi-rents to benefit the Treasury or consumers. These characteristics also encourage firms to adopt monopolistic behavior, so they must be regulated to promote efficiency and protect the welfare of consumers. The risk of capture of the regulators by the regulated introduces further complexities into the public services sectors.

All regulatory agencies confront conflicting interests in the short term: not only between providers and consumers, but also between existing companies and potential new entrants, and among companies in the various segments of a sector (for example, between electricity generators and distributors). This makes the policymaking process for public services especially complex. It is influenced not only by the general policymaking process in the country, but also by complex institutional, political, and technical factors inherent in the sectors. As the process moves ahead and the economic and institutional structure of the market changes, public services reforms tend to alter policymaking in the affected sectors by introducing new agents into the process, by changing the balance of power among them, and by altering the possibilities for the relevant actors of reaching sustainable inter-temporal agreements.

The case of Argentina suggests that it is not possible to isolate public services policy from the more general policy context. In the absence of strong institutions that facilitate consensus-building and the forging of inter-temporal agreements, the regulation of public services is prone to volatility: sometimes favoring investors, and sometimes favoring the interests of politicians or consumers in the short term.

Chile has achieved stability in public services policy, thanks to the possibilities of cooperation offered by the political-institutional system. Such cooperation is further encouraged by low levels of polarization in preferences and ideological positions on privatization. This environment supports a system of public services that encourages not only the participation of private capital, but also competition in the provision of services.

In Uruguay, a certain convergence of preferences in favor of public companies, coupled with mechanisms of direct democracy that allow the electorate to express these preferences readily, has also lent stability to public services policies—although with a cost in efficiency. In spite of the difficulties of advancing reforms, legal decisions in some sectors have reduced the monopoly power of State companies in Uruguay.

The case of Peru is a convincing demonstration that the credibility required for good performance by public services sectors cannot be achieved overnight or imported. It must be built upon the foundation of a stable balance of power among the branches of government and backed by the technical competence and political and operational independence of the regulator, in tune with the perceptions and preferences of the majority of the population.

Chapter 10

Two Kinds of Education Politics

There is not one but rather two kinds of education politics:
the politics of expansion and growing enrollments,
and the politics of quality and efficiency improvements.

Education is an area that has undergone intensive reform in Latin America in the last decade and a half. Every country in the region has undertaken significant changes in its educational system. Paradoxically, all this activity has occurred alongside a generalized perception that educational change is very difficult to achieve in practice and that some fundamental things have hardly changed at all. Why?

In-depth analysis reveals that there is not one but rather two kinds of education politics. The first involves a group of core policies, dealing with quality and efficiency improvements, that is very rigid and resists fundamental change. The other involves a group of peripheral policies, dealing with expansion and growing enrollments, that is highly adaptable and even volatile: subject to regular—perhaps too frequent—modification.

Understanding why change is difficult involves understanding the main actors, their preferences and time frames, their alignments of interests—and thus the potential for conflict or cooperation—and the arenas where policymaking takes place. It also requires understanding what is distinctive about the policymaking process (PMP) in the education sector, and how that sectoral PMP interacts with the general PMP in a particular country.

The discussion that follows examines six examples of the education policymaking process in four countries: Argentina, Brazil, Chile, and Mexico. One type of policy examined is a core policy, touching the very essence of the political economy of education: the introduction of teacher incentives and evaluation. The other is also fairly widespread across the region but more peripheral, dealing with decentralization.

The discussion helps explain why it is that not every change in the area of education is politically feasible, while showing that some worthwhile changes can take place. They require, as much as in any other sector, if not more, the help of a sound general policymaking process.

Distinctive Features of Education Policymaking: A General Model

In the education sector around the world, providers (teachers) typically are well organized and highly aware of policy decisions that could affect their welfare. By contrast, beneficiaries—consumers of education or, more accurately, their families—are highly dispersed, are usually not organized, and receive little information about what is going on in schools. These asymmetries in organization and information are the starting point of most of the distinctive features of education policymaking. When it comes to government action—even the most routine budget allocations or the enforcement of rules, much less policy reforms—interest groups representing teachers find few if any checks on their views and designs.

Education policymaking in Latin America is biased toward policies focusing on expansion and access rather than on quality and efficiency. This bias means that most policymaking will be about expansion, most of the time.

The political economy of education has several other important features:

- There is no overall organizing principle. Education lacks a basic definition that, once made, lends coherence across the system. This sets it apart from other policy areas, such as social security, with its pay-as-you-go principle. It is possible to partially modify particular characteristics of education provision without realigning education policy as a whole. Waves of policy change and reform typically accumulate one on top of another.

- Contracting problems are severe and pervasive. That is, teachers' actions are extremely hard to observe, even by their direct superiors, the school principals or supervisors. School performance is difficult to monitor for both education authorities and parents. The very large size of public school systems—thousands of schools, hundreds of thousands if not millions of teachers, and millions of students—creates severe difficulties in coordination. Thus low-powered incentives are the rule, since there is almost no possibility of distinguishing individual effort and its contribution to the final product. The products of the education process also are not easily measured. Only in the medium and long term, as students grow up and enter the labor force, do the products become truly visible and measurable.[1]

- Policy implementation is complex. Implementation usually requires the participation of numerous actors—teachers, principals, students, supervisors, central and subnational bureaucracies, parents—or at least the absence of active opposition on their part. Time-specific and place-specific information is very important for making the system work. Notably, tracking down whether centralized decisions are being carried out in practice is a daunting task.

---

[1] Navarro (2002).

The combination of these distinctive features has an important political implication. Education systems operate under a constant risk of capture by providers, with regard to teaching and administrative posts and control over key decisions and processes within education organizations, including appointments, disciplinary actions, distribution of perquisites or incentives, training, management, and personnel management systems.

Education systems can avoid or curtail this propensity toward being captured through the operation of a series of countervailing forces. Two such forces are key. The first is a strong State: one that can count on a well-functioning public services regime and that incorporates strong accountability mechanisms. The second is a firmly rooted professional culture that socializes teachers and other important actors into values of proper conduct, high standards of competency, and public-regardedness.

In Latin America, both of these countervailing forces tend to be weak. Typically, the union will have considerable staying power, while the government tends to have a very short time horizon. Moreover, there is not a sizable corps of public servants with the ability to steer or to preserve long-term policies. A teachers' union is often the largest labor organization in a country, and it has and does exercise the right to strike, with consequences that ripple all the way to the nation's political stability. A history of conflicts has weakened the government's ability to commit to inter-temporal deals with the union, in some cases because current administrations lack the ability to tie the hands of future administrations, in others because previous labor agreements have not been honored.[2]

Such inability on the part of the State to enter into inter-temporal deals tends to produce education systems with an extreme reliance on rigid rules and institutional definitions that become untouchable and non-negotiable, no matter how much the economic environment of the education system changes. Outstanding among these are what this study calls core policies of an education system in Latin America, namely:

- The public/private market share
- Free public education at all levels
- Absolute job stability and almost unchangeable rules regarding teacher hiring, promotion, and retirement
- Preservation of the nationwide scope—and hence the full bargaining power—of the teachers' union(s).

Not a single case of significant alteration in any of these core policies has occurred anywhere in the region over the past decade and a half.[3] Extreme swings in economic circumstances have come and gone without producing modifications in these core policies, most notably unchanging—or even expanding—teacher payrolls during periods of economic adjustment when public employment was contracting and other public sector

---

[2] Indeed, pervasive conflict often is at least as much the product of the unchecked power of the unions as it is the direct result of the State not paying salaries or honoring related commitments in due time. The unions strike and win concessions because they can. The State commits itself to things it cannot deliver; when it fails, conflict flares yet again.

[3] The exception that proves the rule is Chile, analyzed later in this chapter. It should also be pointed out that the framework presented here assumes business as usual in the PMP. Radical regime changes or extreme undemocratic circumstances may alter some of the core policies.

salaries were reaching an all-time low. As described below, decentralization processes have taken place without nationally organized unions losing their strong unified bargaining position, except for short periods of time.

In contrast with this rigidity of core policies, the relative weakness of the State translates into acute volatility regarding non-core policies, as administrations—or even leaderships within the same administration—change. This applies to such areas as teacher training; design, production, and distribution of textbooks and teaching materials; curricula; integration of technology into the learning process; and an array of education innovations. Here the lack of an organizing principle comes into play by making it relatively easy for any new administration to undertake new programs that overturn former policy guidelines or modify them in some areas without this becoming an ostensible or unsustainable lack of coherence.

Additionally, there is little of a deeply rooted and widely shared professional culture among teachers. Some teachers have been poorly educated in pedagogic institutes of questionable quality and have entered the profession through practices in which all sorts of non-professional criteria have prevailed (whether political patronage or corruption, through the purchase of teaching positions from union officials or other authorities). On the other hand, these teachers are managed by a bureaucracy that tends to be unqualified to manage the education system.

Teachers' unions are the one actor with unquestionable veto power in the education PMP in the region.

Accordingly, if no other significant organized groups stand in the way, as is typical, the unions will have the upper hand in education in Latin America, to the point that they can be described as the one actor with unquestionable veto power in the education PMP in the region.

Before moving ahead, it is time to ask whether there is room for cooperation at all. The picture so far may seem too dark. Here the recent literature on education reforms comes to the rescue, allowing for a more nuanced view. Various studies have pointed out that even though reforms in the 1990s largely aimed at improving quality and efficiency, much of what has been going on has to do with adding capacity—building schools, providing them with furniture and equipment, training more teachers, and so on.[4] From this generalization, it follows that there is not one but rather two kinds of education politics: the politics of expansion and growing enrollments, and the politics of quality and efficiency improvements.

When an expansion in enrollments is at stake, all parties involved nearly always agree. Parents and children want more education. Teachers and their unions see enrollment expansion as more jobs, and authorities in both the executive and the legislature tend to like the kind of policy that allows them to show their constituencies very concrete results: more children attending school, new school buildings, and the like. International lending organizations also support this type of reform, since expanding capacity involves large investments with relatively tangible products and uncomplicated implementation processes. This type of educational policy and change was typical of the 1960s, 1970s, and 1980s in most countries. It remains widespread and significant in

---

[4] Kaufman and Nelson (2004); Grindle (2004a).

all of them. There is even considerable enthusiasm for a novel variety of expansionary policy based not on supply but on the subsidization of demand, such as rapidly spreading cash transfer programs like PROGRESA/*Oportunidades* (Mexico) and *Bolsa Escola* (Brazil), which provide benefits to families conditional on the children attending school.

Yet expansionary steps have proven insufficient in terms of improving the quality of education or encouraging a more efficient use of resources. In the 1990s, this fact generated impatience among modernizing elites concerned about the development prospects of Latin American countries. Embarking on a sweeping wave of economic and institutional reforms, and feeling the pressure of Asian competition in an increasingly global economy, many governments felt the need to act forcefully, not only to expand access, but also to produce reforms that would improve the quality of education systems.

As it turns out, cooperation does not emerge as easily in this type of education policy. Influencing the quality and effectiveness of an education system often means initiating actions that imply a substantial reorganization of teachers' work, through the introduction of incentives, supervision systems, and greater accountability through decentralization or intense parental involvement. Even fixing inequities that remain after across-the-board enrollment expansions, such as attending to excluded populations (the extremely poor or indigenous populations), can cause conflict since this requires redistributional decisions. This can also be the case with reforms in financing that aim to distribute educational spending more fairly, typically taking resources away from previously privileged groups or jurisdictions.

When an expansion in enrollments is at stake, all parties involved—parents, children, teachers, teachers' unions, and the authorities—nearly always agree.

Simplifying a bit, it could be argued that the main policy game played in Latin America over the past 15 years has had two main actors: the unions and the executive. The unions are in a dominant position and have often felt threatened by the reforms typical of this period, not only insofar as the interests of their membership have been affected, but also regarding their own viability and power as organizations. This study identifies the other main player as the executive for a combination of reasons. First, a modernizing and sometimes technocratic team at key ministries, often the ministry of education or the ministry of planning, has always initiated the reforms, which have often moved forward with the backing or even the proactive leadership of the president himself. Second, no other branch of government has exercised leadership. Legislatures have tended to play minor roles, and the judiciary has been almost invisible—in contrast to the prominent role the courts have played in the United States, for instance.

The emergence of proactive executives as forceful actors suggests that the depiction of the education policymaking game as one between a strong union and a weak State may need to be redefined to allow for the case in which education authorities declare education policy a priority for a host of reasons related to growth or equity, and become far more energized players than usual through presidential and technocratic support.

The only other actors of significance that approach the relevance of unions and the executives are subnational power players (see Table 10.1). These regional actors gained considerable influence as education decentralization was being attempted. This influence extended to many areas of education policy—the structure of the formal education system, the curriculum, and the introduction of innovations and region-specific reforms that later were disseminated nationally—but it reached veto power in the area of whether particular transfers of responsibility for education were actually being made to subnational levels. Other actors—business, the media, and families—have played a supporting role, at best, in some cases.

Summing up, education policymaking in Latin America will be disproportionately biased toward policies focusing on expansion and access rather than on quality and efficiency.

Table 10.1 Actors with Veto Power in the Education PMP, Selected Countries

Country	Unions	Executive	Subnational
Argentina	x	x	x
Bolivia	x	x	n.a.
Brazil	x	x	x
Chile	x	x	n.a.
Colombia	x	x	x
Ecuador	x	x	n.a.
Mexico	x	x	x
Nicaragua	x	x	n.a.
Uruguay	x	x	n.a.
Venezuela	x	x	x

n.a.: Not applicable.

Source: Authors' meta-analysis of the literature on the political economy of education in Latin America during the 1990s.

This bias means that most policymaking will be about expansion, most of the time. It also means that a fair share of education policymaking will develop along cooperative lines, since the preferences of the main actors are aligned.

This bias tends to create pressure to address quality and efficiency issues, as it becomes clear for some political, economic, and intellectual elites that expansion alone will not produce quality education, improve the use of resources, or reach those marginalized after massive expansion. Typically, steps to redress quality and efficiency are championed by an executive, elected with a mandate to undertake education reforms. There is no alignment of interests on this type of reform (see Box 10.1). Conflict will ensue, primarily between union(s) and the executive, and regional power players will become involved wherever issues of decentralization are at stake. Moreover:

• Inter-temporal deals are very difficult to reach (mostly given the inability of the executive to commit).
• Lack of effective enforcement mechanisms makes it difficult to monitor any agreement (since other actors such as the judiciary, the legislative, and public opinion tend to be very weak).
• The main actors tend to have starkly opposed ideologies.

Given these dynamics, the main outer features of education policy will be:

• Rigidity in the face of economic shocks, particularly extreme in the case of core policies

Box 10.1	The Preferences of the Main Actors in the Education PMP

The three actors with veto power in education policymaking have complex preferences. These preferences are presented below in order of their approximate intensity (meaning, for instance, that if a union has to choose between more jobs and job security for those teachers already employed, it will tend to prefer the latter).

Executive: Improvement of education as part of larger modernization and development agendas, maintaining overall political stability, use of the education payroll as a channel of patronage, votes, keeping budgets under control. Short-term horizon. Modernization, efficiency-oriented ideologies play a role.

Unions: Job security, more teaching positions, control over appointments and functioning of the education system (capture), preservation of nationwide bargaining power, better salaries. Long-term horizon. Labor and Leftist ideologies are often present.

Subnational players: Creation and/or expansion of opportunities for patronage, votes, avoidance of unfunded mandates and constraints on discretionary spending, improvement of local economy in a context of interjurisdictional competition.

- Lack of stability in policies in light of short-term political changes (electoral shake-ups, cabinet shuffles), particularly in non-core policies
- A tendency to leave a great deal to be determined at the implementation stage, given the involvement of so many bureaucrats, schools, teachers, and families.

Given the nature of the players and the game, absence of cooperation, or open conflict, tends to occur in a limited set of arenas. The most common arena is direct and private negotiations between the executive and the union(s), which this study refers to as occurring "behind closed doors." It is characterized by a low level of public accountability and the exclusion of any other stakeholder. In decentralized settings, subnational power players are allowed behind the closed doors. More accurately, coordination among levels of government can become a primary arena for conflict.

Not surprisingly, this kind of arena often is unable to keep conflict confined. Conflict spills over to "the street" in various degrees of intensity, ranging from simple strikes to events that disrupt the civil and political order. Finally, given the importance of implementation in education policy, the "street-level bureaucracy" becomes the fourth key arena where conflicts are played out. This refers to the legion of teachers, school principals, and supervisors who in the end exercise a great deal of control over what happens in schools and within classrooms, which constitute the end delivery point of education services.

Education Politics and the General PMP: Some Examples

Having characterized the education PMP, it is time to turn to specific episodes of policymaking that illustrate and provide nuance to the model. Argentina and Mexico went through an ambitious decentralization of their education systems in the 1990s, and also attempted to introduce teacher incentives. Brazil had decentralized its education system by the early 1990s, but the system was widely recognized to be deficient and unable to tackle extremely serious deficits in educational outcomes. Thus in the mid-1990s Brazil undertook a radical overhaul of the status quo in matters of decentralized financing and the distribution of responsibilities among levels of government—although it made no nationwide attempt to introduce incentives for teachers. This type of incentive is the focus of the last case in the chapter, which looks at Chile.

Mexico: Decentralization

In 1992, negotiations between the executive (the president and minister of education) and the teachers' union produced the National Agreement for Modernization of Basic and Normal Education (known as ANMEB, for its Spanish-language initials). This agreement dictated that the education system in Mexico would become decentralized, and state governments would begin to assume direct responsibility for providing public education to 13 million primary and secondary education students.

ANMEB was advanced as a remedy for excessive centralization of the Mexican education system, regarded as the main source of its deficient coverage and poor quality. Yet another important objective of the initiative was to curb the power of the teachers' union, the SNTE.[5] The SNTE is in a league of its own when it comes to general political influence and control over the education system, even by the standards of Latin America. By the early 1990s, it had successfully defeated several other decentralization initiatives and had co-opted a deconcentration policy. The SNTE had considerable control over appointments to teaching positions and a significant share of administrative positions in the education system. Its financial position was secure, thanks to mandatory membership fees, and its monopoly was enshrined in a law barring competing unions. Its close association with the long-term governing party, the *Partido Revolucionario Institucional* (PRI), translated into political positions in the administration for union members and a non-negligible share of seats in Congress. A public-regarding, modernizing presidency would likely see such power as part of the problem rather than a solution.

Core policies were threatened by the initial proposal—but in the end left untouched.

The ANMEB was presented to the SNTE as an all-or-nothing package.[6] That the union took the deal says something about the capacity of a strong, competent, and committed executive to move forward even in the face of opposition from such a powerful

---

[5] See Hanson (1997); Grindle (2004b).
[6] Grindle (2004b).

actor. That this did not happen before the proposal was modified to allow the SNTE to emerge as a winner in many significant respects shows that, in terms of the framework, the union exercised its veto power.

Why did the executive succeed this time, where previous administrations had failed? By 1992, and in contrast with 10 or 15 years before, some governorships were in the hands of opposition parties.[7] With the federal executive's proposed transfer of responsibilities at stake, subnational governments were allowed behind the closed doors, where they expressed their support for decentralization. While this was not enough to tailor the entire initiative to their preferences, it was good enough to tilt the balance in favor of the view that the time had come to correct the excesses of centralization and open the door to better accountability and more diversity in the education system.

The semi-corporatist structure of the Mexican political system played a direct role in preventing discussions about the policy initiative from spilling over to the streets. SNTE was also a section of the PRI, the party in power. The president and the minister of education were prominent party figures, and the party had an overall interest in political stability and in not letting the conflict emerge from behind the closed doors. Once the governors were let in and the agreement was reached, the necessary legislative reforms passed congress in a matter of days, even modifying an article of the constitution.

As for the SNTE, core policies were threatened by the initial proposal—but in the end left untouched. Most notably, the union's nationwide bargaining power was preserved. To this day, salary negotiations occur through meetings between representatives of the SNTE in Mexico City and representatives of the secretary of public education. In addition, the monitoring and enforcement mechanisms of the decentralization process were left weak, leaving critical details to be worked out in regard to decentralized financial arrangements and coordinating education policy between the states and the federal government.

Mexico: Teacher Incentives and Evaluation

The initiative that led to the ANMEB was bundled with an innovative program aimed at linking teachers' remuneration and promotions to performance. This was a radical move, given that no such provision had ever existed, and it affected a core policy. Although the program, *Carrera Magisterial*, also sought to intensify teacher training,[8] its merit pay component presented the strongest potential for conflict.

Teachers' unions have opposed pay for performance incentives all around the world. Mexico in the 1990s was no exception. Generally, teachers' unions strongly prefer across-the-board salary raises that benefit all their constituencies. Salary improvements that

---

[7] Lehoucq and others (2005).

[8] Teacher training, particularly in-service training, probably has been the only policy directly aimed at improving teaching with respect to which the preferences of unions and the executive are fully aligned. It is hardly surprising that for a long time, and beyond its intrinsic benefits, it has been one of the most common components of education plans that have remained silent regarding other fundamental issues, such as pre-service training, incentives, licensing, or mechanisms regulating recruitment and entry into the profession.

benefit only a subgroup of members cannot plausibly be claimed as the product of the union's own lobbying and negotiation, opening the way for teachers to conclude that their remuneration is not mainly a function of the union, but rather of their individual or team effort.

The union's approach was not to oppose the performance evaluation reform head on, but rather to make sure that it would stay under its control and acquire features that would prevent any substantive impact on core policies.

This noted, it is important to recognize that the design of an efficient teacher incentive program is plagued with serious agency problems. It is not easy to separate the contribution of different teachers to the learning process of a student. Moreover, teaching is an important input to learning, but not the only one, and the product is difficult to measure, particularly in the short term. In this sense, union opposition rests on plausible economic and educational arguments that have strengthened opposition to merit pay.[9] Moreover, in Latin America, the widespread use of the teacher payroll for political patronage adds to the mistrust of any system that enlarges administrators' discretionary power regarding teacher salaries.

The SNTE approach was not to oppose the performance evaluation component of *Carrera Magisterial* head on, but rather to make sure that, once adopted, it would stay under its control and would acquire features that would prevent any substantive impact on core policies. Once again negotiations occurred behind closed doors. Open conflict was not in the interest of any of the veto players, given that the union was affiliated with the PRI, and it was a PRI government that was trying to introduce reforms. In its initial period in 1993, the *Carrera Magisterial* program mandated the use of performance as only one of several criteria to assess salary increases for individual teachers—35 points out of 100 on a scale in which seniority and formal education still retained the most important weight. Even though the relative weight of performance has since increased, to this day the program works under a joint committee in which the SEP and the SNTE have parity representation.

Over the years, *Carrera Magisterial* has benefited more than 700,000 teachers. Given that it is massive, and that it produces permanent salary increases rather than one-time bonuses, it has come to resemble an entitlement rather than an incentive proper. Until 2001, the federal government allocated an amount to each state and the state government was responsible for deciding who would get the award. In practice, the state government allocated as many awards as funds would allow, starting with teachers at the top of the scale. This meant that the cutoff point was not a standard of performance but was dictated by the availability of funds in a particular state for a particular year. SNTE's considerable degree of capture of state education administrations made sure that the implementation of the instrument remained in union hands for all practical purposes.

Generalizing from these episodes, the extreme political leverage of the teachers' union has led the education policy process to dictate some important features of the larger policymaking process in Mexico. The SNTE has become a major power player in

---

[9] Navarro (2002).

congress and in most large-scale political negotiations, beyond education issues. Conversely, this episode also illustrates how larger features of the Mexican policymaking process have influenced the way education conflict has played out. This is particularly clear in the way the corporatist structure of the political system has affected the "choice" of arenas for conflict. The fact that the union did not go to the street despite the radical nature of the proposals advanced by the executive is closely related to the fact that conflict was taking place between a PRI administration and a PRI union, which had conflicting preferences on education policy but a joint interest in party unity and overall political stability. The newly elected opposition governors may also have tipped the SNTE strategy toward accommodation and co-optation as opposed to outright rejection of reforms.

Argentina: Decentralization

In August 1989, the Menem administration announced that decentralization would be the centerpiece of its education policy. A first decentralization bill was introduced in 1990 but remained dormant in the congress. This changed drastically with a change in the minister of finance in early 1991.

The executive viewed decentralization as a way to unburden the federal government of responsibility for education spending. A 1991 law stipulated the transfer of responsibility for secondary education to the provincial governments; primary education had been transferred in 1977. It dictated that there would be no specific additional transfer of fiscal resources from the federal to the provincial level, so the functioning of the education systems would have to be financed out of each province's own resources.

Provincial unions delayed, co-opted, or impeded the execution of the most basic mandates of the new legislation.

The governors and the unions immediately opposed the proposal. Governors rejected the proposition of proceeding with the transfer of responsibility without any accompanying transfer of resources. The national federation of unions, CTERA, clearly saw the threat decentralization could pose to its national bargaining power—not nearly comparable to the power of the SNTE in Mexico. Yet it was unable to mobilize a coherent opposition in the face of an administration at the height of its popularity, given the fresh success of the convertibility plan. In the end, the only significant modification to the original decentralization proposal was a guarantee of a minimum level of federal contributions to provincial education spending.

The process of decentralization was completed by a 1993 law. Again the executive took the initiative, and this time the bill sent to congress threatened several core policies. CTERA, now stronger, succeeded in eliminating those threats. Although the new law was approved, it was stripped of any mention of school autonomy or tuition fees, or any emphasis on private education. Governors joined the coalition against the proposal.

The arena in which the conflict was played out was clearly affected by the characteristics of the larger PMP in Argentina.[10] The close ties between governors and senators,

---

[10] Spiller, Stein, and Tommasi (2003).

given the electoral rules, led senators to initiate a counter-proposal that was the polar opposite of the executive's proposal. From then on—unusually for the education policy-making process—congress became the main arena for negotiations until the compromise bill, stripped of threats to core policies, was approved. The provinces were also satisfied with investment guarantees, as well as with a strong mandate in the law to activate the Federal Council of Education, whereby the federal minister of education and his provincial counterparts would jointly consider the main decisions of the education system.

After 1993, Argentinean schools were in the hands of the provinces, which administered and paid for day-to-day operations and were responsible for paying teachers' salaries. The federal ministry remained in charge of assessment, curriculum design, and large infrastructure investment. Provinces' incomes, however, originated largely in direct transfers from federal tax receipts, creating substantial fiscal imbalances.[11] The structure of the school systems and curricula were considerably modified. The structural reforms and the adoption of new content became a responsibility of the provincial ministries of education.

The shift to the provincial level also led to a shift to provincial union activity. As the implementation phase began, the most active arena of education policymaking in Argentina for over half a decade became the street. CTERA's strong opposition to decentralization on many grounds, including ideological ones, translated into vigorous opposition by provincial teachers' unions to the implementation of the 1991 and 1993 laws. Provincial unions delayed, co-opted, or impeded the execution of the most basic mandates of the new legislation. The result, by the end of the decade, was a mosaic of structures across provinces, in degrees that ranged from full implementation to none at all.[12]

Argentina: Teacher Incentives in Name Only

As the end of the decade approached, labor unrest among teachers was on the rise. While fueled by opposition to decentralization, the main determinant of such unrest lay in the fiscal crisis of the provinces. The economic downturns of 1995 and 1999 hurt the provinces' ability to keep pace with the expansion in enrollments, leading to all sorts of measures aimed at salary reductions—or even nonpayment.[13] Strikes flared and many days of school were lost.

The national executive argued that salaries were a provincial responsibility, and that the federal government was fulfilling its commitment to invest heavily in infrastructure and special programs that provided strong support for the provinces. Although formally correct, the executive's position was unable to prevent the conflict over teacher salaries from spilling out to the street and the national stage. In April 1997, groups of teachers, with the support of CTERA, started a public demonstration across the street from the building of the national congress, setting up a White Tent in which teachers took turns in a vigil, declaring their unwillingness to leave until their salary grievances were

---

[11] Tommasi (2002).

[12] Rivas (2004).

[13] Kweitel and others (2003).

resolved. The White Tent proved effective in creating and sustaining political pressure on the executive and it won widespread public support. The ministry of education broke with the official position of the finance ministry, declaring openly by the end of 1997 that teachers were not well paid.[14]

Then came a policy proposal, the *Fondo Nacional de Incentivo Docente* (FONID). In previous years, the ministry had been exploring the idea of creating some pay-for-performance mechanism in the form of a special fund that the federal government would transfer to the provinces.

The consequence of the whole episode was the creation of an ongoing source of contention between the executive and the unions.

After the White Tent campaign started, the unions and the provinces stepped up their pressure on the federal government to do something about teacher salaries. The ministry of education proposed a supplement to salaries paid by regional governments. After rapid debate in the Federal Council of Education—including the participation of CTERA and other prominent teacher unions—a law was passed by the end of 1998 creating the FONID. By then the idea of pay for performance was nowhere to be seen. The provinces were granted large transfers, to be distributed equally to teachers as an entitlement, to supplement their regular salaries. The substantial amounts involved made it difficult to win support from the ministry of finance. In the end, it was won over by stipulating that the FONID would be financed through the proceeds of a newly created tax, to be paid by motor vehicle owners, an episode revealing the strength of the actors involved in the education PMP.

This strength proved to be limited, however, when the executive, facing imminent public protests by the transportation sector, eliminated the tax. In 1999 the new De la Rúa administration came to power and managed to convince the CTERA that the White Tent should be taken down—after 1,003 days—in exchange for the executive's commitment to finance the incentive out of the general budget for at least two years.

The consequence of the whole episode was not to eliminate or reduce the FONID, but rather a commitment by the federal government to pay for a new entitlement for teachers. To this day, the need to pay for FONID has had two major effects: an endemic threat to the overall fiscal situation of the central government and considerable distortion in education spending, since the federal government has had to cut investments in such areas as infrastructure and teacher training to amass resources to finance FONID. The federal government, in the act of creating FONID, accepted the principle that teacher salaries were a shared responsibility of the provinces and the national government, thus reversing one of the main themes of the decentralization process at the start of the decade.

The financial arrangements worked out after 1991 proved unable to withstand economic downturns. As soon as the federal government faltered in its fiscal transfers to the provinces, the budget situation of the provinces, by now spending around 25 percent of their resources on education, worsened—in some cases to the point of collapse.[15]

---

[14] Corrales (2004).

[15] Tommasi (2002).

From a political economy point of view, the most important outcome of the combination of a fiscally distorted decentralization process and a short-sighted response to labor unrest was the creation of an ongoing source of conflict between the executive and the unions whenever payments have not been made on time. Disputes involving FONID—calculating it, distributing it, reauthorizing it, financing it—have become a major focus of policymaking in Argentina. This constitutes a prime example of the functioning of the education PMP spilling out to create conflict and distortions in the larger PMP at the national level.

Brazil: Fixing Decentralization

The Brazilian education system had been considerably decentralized for decades when the Cardoso administration was inaugurated in 1995. At the time, Brazil's poor educational performance was becoming a major focus for modernizing elites pushing for economic and public sector reform. Extreme regional inequalities and widespread political patronage characterized the education system and constituted major obstacles for any serious program aimed at improving its equity and quality.

FUNDEF, which set a nationwide minimum expenditure per student, was one of the most consequential education reforms introduced in Latin America in the 1990s.

The Cardoso administration assembled a technocratic team, headed by the minister of education, that set out to transfer specific programs to states and municipalities, as well as to build capacity at the level of the federal ministry to design and manage effectively what would become an ambitious reform program. The cornerstone of the reform was the creation of a fund, FUNDEF, that redefined the organization and financing of decentralized education in Brazil, together with two major education measures approved by congress in late 1996.

FUNDEF had less to do with the amount of resources dedicated to education and more to do with the distribution of existing funds. Indeed, the reform of financing was seen as a precondition for more ambitious reform. The constitution required states and municipalities to spend 25 percent of revenues on education, yet there was very wide variation among them in terms of per student expenditures. Teacher salaries and training were unregulated, leading to great variation across regions and levels of government. Little correspondence existed between the sharing of tax revenues among states and municipalities and the sharing of responsibilities for education.

FUNDEF set out to address these issues by setting a nationwide minimum expenditure per student (primary level only), regardless of schools' governance structure (state or municipal). If a state could not meet this minimum, the federal government was required to make up the difference. By equalizing and stabilizing primary school spending across Brazil, and by creating incentives for subnational governments to include rather than exclude children, FUNDEF was arguably one of the most consequential education reforms introduced in Latin America in the 1990s.

Between 1998 and 2000, annual per student spending increased significantly nationwide and enrollments shot up.[16] More students found their way into the secondary level, which in turn led to a considerable expansion of secondary education down the road.

FUNDEF also had an important redistributive effect. It effectively redistributed resources away from relatively wealthy state-level schools toward poorer municipal schools. As federal resources compensated states falling below minimum standards of expenditure, inequities among states were reduced. Teachers' salaries improved as well.

How could such a consequential reform have been adopted and implemented, especially since creating FUNDEF required reforming the constitution? First, the Cardoso reform did not directly touch any core policy. Job stability, hiring and firing rules, unionization, and private/public market shares were not affected by either FUNDEF or the new education legislation. The only provisions affecting the interests of teachers were fully aligned with state union preferences: more training and higher salaries.

Second, Brazil, alone among Latin American countries, lacks a nationally organized teachers' union of political significance. Teacher unionism is alive and well at the state level, but the federal government does not face anything in the same league as SNTE, CTERA, or FECODE in Colombia.

Yet much of the reason why FUNDEF passed congress in less than two weeks can be found in some general characteristics of the Brazilian PMP. Particularly relevant is the power of the presidency in Brazil with regard to the legislature.[17] Unlike in Argentina, Chile, or Mexico, political parties in Brazil are relatively fragmented and their composition and loyalties in congress are fluid. Beyond this, the line-item veto puts the president in a position to win the support of members of congress far beyond his own party. With the veto, he can secure (or deny) investments in public projects in particular electoral districts that critically affect members' chances for reelection. In Brazil, in contrast with Argentina, this power tends to supersede the control that governors and other regional power players have in securing nominations for congressional seats. It has led to the curious extreme of relatively easy constitutional reforms, a distinctive feature of the Brazilian PMP.

The government proposal of FUNDEF conflicted with some preferences of governors, notably taking away considerable discretionality from state governments. The most economically developed states stood to be forced to reduce funds for their spending priority, secondary education, while the poorer jurisdictions would be forced to provide primary education at levels they had not been willing or able to do before.[18]

Yet not only was there no noticeable opposition from unions, there was also no open conflict with governors before the measure was adopted—less than one month after its introduction in congress. The executive secured early support for the measure from two important education regional power players, the CONSED (National Council of State

---

[16] Draibe (2004).

[17] Alston and others (2005a).

[18] Draibe (2004).

Secretariats of Education) and the UNDIME (National Association of Municipal Education Directors), which played a role in neutralizing opposition from governors.

The FUNDEF was stipulated to begin operations in early 1998. In 1997, opposition spilled out to the street through union opposition in some states such as São Paulo and vocal complaints from state legislatures and governors about the fund's implications. Significantly, they did not amount to much, and did not turn into grassroots resistance from the street-level bureaucracy. Thus implementation, once started, was not undermined.

Currently, there is widespread consensus in Brazil about the benefits of FUNDEF. It has, in combination with the subsequent education law, considerably improved coordination of education policy among levels of government. The episode that led to its adoption seems to present a counter-example of easy education politics, as well as an example of public-regarding, welfare-enhancing educational policies. As previously explained, however, only the combination of some particular characteristics of the general Brazilian PMP, notably the fact that it allows for "easy" constitutional reforms, and a particular characteristic of the education PMP, that it lacks a strong nationally organized teachers' union, explain much of the outcome.

Moreover, even in this "easy" case of reform, the strategy of the executive was to create an important source of rigidity in the system: the imposition of a fixed rule across the immensely varied fiscal and educational landscape of Brazilian states. On top of this, the fact that the reform was the first of its kind, well prepared both technically and politically and rushed through congress, meant that potential opposition was "surprised" and had little time to react. By contrast, plans by the Lula administration to enact a new FUNDEF for secondary and/or pre-school education have faced stronger resistance precisely because state governments are now aware of the possible consequences of such measures for their spending discretionality.

Chile: Exception to the Rule? The Introduction of Teacher Incentives

In 1996 the Chilean government successfully put in place a nationwide incentive pay system for teachers, known as SNED (*Sistema Nacional de Evaluación del Desempeño Docente*). The teachers' union initially resisted this development, yet ultimately proved unable to block it. This achievement stands out as the only significant exception to the rule that education systems in Latin America do not change some core policies closely aligned with the interests of teachers' unions.

The executive undertook a sustained series of steps that led to the building of trust and predictability in the relationship with the teachers' union.

Chile certainly has a nationwide teachers' union (the *Colegio de Profesores de Chile*). This organization is a major player in education policy, as is typical in the region. Much of the policymaking process revolves around negotiations in which the only parties involved are the executive and union leaders. Generally speaking, the union has opposed the highly activist and reformist education policy developed by the executive during the past decade and a half, most of which has focused on improving the quality and efficiency of education in the country.

The original and long-lasting source of antagonism between the union and the executive, once a democratic order was reestablished in 1990, was the decision made early on by the leaders of the ruling coalition (the *Concertación Democrática*) to preserve two key features of education reforms introduced by the former dictatorship: the transfer of public schools to municipal administration, and the voucher system that allowed for a drastic expansion in the market share of private schools in the 1980s.

At the same time, the new democratic administration made the equally key decision to re-create a teacher statute, the special labor regime that had been abolished by the authoritarian government. This measure was highly favored by the union and its constituency. It granted them the tenure, status, and benefits that had disappeared when their labor contracts were placed under the jurisdiction of mainstream labor legislation under the Pinochet regime. Crucially, this statute reestablished their nationwide bargaining power in salary negotiations with the executive.[19]

This decision was also controversial. From the standpoint of many in the opposition and even within the coalition government's political parties, it undermined a key feature of the model that aimed to produce stronger incentives for teacher performance. Even more importantly, it threatened to disrupt the ability of municipalities to maintain their fiscal balance by forcing them to incur payroll commitments that were not backed by their own financial resources.[20]

From the perspective of the policymaking process, however, it marked the beginning of a sustained series of steps on the part of the executive that led to the building of trust and predictability in the relationship with the union. Given that it is just this kind of lack of mutual trust that characterizes education policymaking across the region, the importance of this development cannot be underestimated. It was paramount to ensuring the political feasibility of the nationwide incentive pay system (SNED) several years down the road.

The trust-building process was a foundation for the avoidance of open conflict, a distinctive feature that has characterized education policymaking in Chile since 1990. The building of trust had other important components far beyond the original reenactment of the teacher statute:

- A particularly important part of the story also concerns the sustained increases in teacher salaries that started immediately after democracy was restored and have continued to this day—far beyond the date of the adoption of SNED. Such an unbroken long-term upward trend in teacher pay has no parallel in any other

---

[19] The first minister of education of the post-dictatorship period, Ricardo Lagos, openly recognized this step as an important component of a political compromise between unions and the executive: "I gave priority to the teachers, since they were concerned about a teacher statute. The Statute for the Professionals of Teaching, as much as other examples of the education policy of the *Concertación Democrática*, represented an appropriate equilibrium between continuity and change" (Espínola and de Moura Castro, 1999, p. 46).

[20] The adoption of the statute led to the anticipated fiscal shortfall in many municipalities, eventually forcing the national government to supplement teacher salaries, further undermining the voucher system. Some corrective measures were eventually adopted, starting in 1995. For details of the politics of this phase of education policymaking in Chile, see Angell, Lowden, and Thorp (2001).

country in the region. Earnings for Chilean teachers doubled, on average, between 1990 and 1997, quadrupling the average increase in salaries for workers in the private sector and outstripping those for other public sector employees.[21]

- More generally, many of the education programs initiated by the executive starting in 1990 aimed to enhance the skills and working conditions of teachers, as well as the social prestige associated with the profession.
- In addition, no matter how much education policy in Chile focused on quality, considerable expansion was taking place as well. Secondary education enrollments were growing rapidly. As a byproduct of several new programs that were more "teacher intensive," more teachers per students were needed, leading to a 10 percent increase in the teaching workforce in the early 1990s. As noted, better salaries and more teaching positions are areas where the preferences of the union and the executive align.[22]

Despite the general betterment in the condition of teachers, union opposition to many quality-enhancing reforms continued. Yet teacher strikes led to the loss of only 26 days of classes between March 1990 and March 2001; recourse to the street as an arena for conflict was exceptional.[23] Union opposition took the form of public statements made by union leaders and intense horse-trading at the bargaining table at the time of major contract negotiations with the executive—but it always came with a sizable dose of cooperation.

This mix of opposition and cooperation was evident in the process surrounding the establishment of the nationwide incentive pay system (SNED). The proposal was introduced in 1996, in the aftermath of the endorsement, by all political parties, of the "Framework Agreement for the Modernization of Chilean Education," a groundbreaking report produced by the National Commission on the Modernization of Education appointed one year earlier by President Eduardo Frei, Jr. The report formalized a widespread political consensus regarding the top priority that educational development should have in both public and private efforts in Chilean society. As one of a very short list of priorities, the report specified the need to strengthen the teaching profession. The commission issued the report after extensive consultation across the political spectrum. Significantly, the teachers' union was reluctant to get involved in the consultation phase, yet in the end endorsed the report. The strong pressure the leadership of the union felt not to be left isolated from the rest of the political forces in play led to this endorsement.[24]

Against this backdrop of solid presidential and multi-party support, the ministry started negotiations with the union. At stake, to begin with, was the salary increase that

---

[21] Mizala and others (2002).

[22] Underlying this expansionary policy is the fact that public expenditure on education also was growing in Chile in the 1990s. So was private funding for education, a non-negligible issue, given that the share of private schools in primary and secondary education in Chile is exceptionally high: nearly 40 percent of enrollment. The prosperity of the Chilean economy during this period represents the best possible economic prerequisite for such an expansion to occur and be sustained.

[23] Cox (2003).

[24] Núñez (2003).

had become routine at every round of contractual negotiations. But the executive actually offered far more than routine salary raises. In exchange, it demanded substantial concessions on the union side. Both turned out to be impossible for the union to refuse. First, the executive insisted on some flexibility regarding certain aspects of the teacher statute approved in 1991. This was intended to give municipalities breathing room to better plan and manage their education budgets. Notably, this implied slightly backtracking from the 100 percent tenure protection granted by the 1991 statute. Second was the introduction of merit pay.

Remarkably, SNED was then created, with the reluctant acceptance of the *Colegio*. It has continued to be implemented. Public opinion research clearly indicates that teachers, once they have experienced the system, become more receptive to the idea that some kind of performance review is legitimate. The trust built into the education system by a long succession of policies over the previous six years, as well as the generalized political consensus created around significant policy reforms, had paid off. In this process, the union was relegated to the exercise of a vocal opposition—which risked isolating it politically. Moreover, as teachers continued to enjoy visible improvements in their living and working conditions, continuing opposition by union leaders would have risked alienating the leadership from its membership base.[25]

Several other factors were also important. From a technical standpoint, the merit pay proposal put forward by the administration in Chile reflected an elevated degree of awareness of the serious incentive and contracting problems that had been impeding effective performance incentives for teachers.[26] From the beginning, the plan was designed and later implemented as a "team incentive," payable to all teachers in a particular school, rather than as an individual payment to a particular teacher. It established a complex yet workable series of criteria according to which performance would be established, including groupings of schools. For instance, each school was to be compared to others in similar initial conditions, and estimates of value added, rather than absolute progress in student learning, were used. The approach taken reflected the best research available on incentive regimes for teachers. And it effectively turned the system into something teachers could relate to, since it accommodated many of their concerns regarding evaluation of their performance.[27]

The second factor has to do with the overall characteristics of the public policymaking process in Chile after democracy was restored. The Chilean PMP is a system with exceptionally strong presidential agenda-setting powers and many veto players, in which policies must pass through prolonged negotiations and concessions to be enacted.[28]

---

[25] Opinion polls taken at the time consistently show a significant degree of support for education reforms among the teachers (Núñez 2003). This seems to support the observation made by several ministers of education from the period regarding their ability to establish a direct dialogue between the ministry and the base of the union, rather than only with its leadership, as one of the keys of the success in adopting reforms (Espínola and de Moura Castro 1999).

[26] Delannoy (2000); Navarro (2002).

[27] For a detailed description of the technical aspects of SNED, see Mizala and others (2002).

[28] Aninat and others (2004).

Once those policies are enacted, however, the Chilean PMP tends to produce very stable and credible arrangements.

This stability in turn becomes a key tool in the negotiation of long-term deals. The enforcement of such deals is aided by the institutionalization of political parties. In a context such as this, education policymaking stands out as an area in which sector-specific investments have been made in order to rebuild a political environment in which complicated inter-temporal deals affecting core policies could be struck between the executive and the union. Yet it also must be seen as part and parcel of a larger PMP that has provided the right environment for trust-based politics to grow. Serious differences of opinion between the union and the executive existed in Chile during the extraordinary period of reforms. The PMP of the sector mirrored the larger PMP of the country in allowing for a constructive resolution of those differences in the form of stable and public-regarding policies.

Conclusion: The Joint Dynamics of the Education and National PMPs

Amidst a highly varied landscape of situations and institutions in different countries and a variety of policymaking episodes, some underlying threads of coherence in education policymaking can be found:

- The key veto players are teachers' unions, the executive (in particular, the modernizing or "impatient" executive), and regional power players. Other players are relatively minor.
- Each of these players has a particular structure of preferences that goes from almost full alignment when it comes to the expansion of coverage to acute conflict in education policies oriented toward improving quality or efficiency.
- Agency problems are pervasive. Moreover, it is generally difficult to strike inter-temporal deals. Thus, even when transcendent policy changes are accomplished, they institute new rigidities, rather than increase adaptability.
- A clear distinction exists between core and non-core policies. Core policies are only rarely challenged and never actually reformed. Non-core policies are susceptible to change, to the point of volatility. The differing fortunes of policy reform in the case of these two types of policies result from an underlying difficulty in reaching long-term deals between veto players in the education PMP. The only exception found, the introduction of teacher incentives in Chile, is closely related to an exceptional PMP in which such difficulty has been counteracted by a series of investments in trust and enforcement mechanisms.

Finally, this discussion has shown how the outcome in each episode reviewed must be seen as the combination of the specifics of the education policymaking process in action with the influence of the general policymaking process of each country at hand. The relative strength of the executive with respect to congress, the degree of articulation between unions and political parties, the importance of regional elites, and other fundamental pieces of the general PMP differ from one country to the next because of a host of institutional and historical factors. These features clearly interact with the peculiar politics of the education sector to produce certain outcomes.

The evidence reviewed indicates that the general PMP affects three key aspects of the education PMP. The first is the selection of the arena(s) in which conflict will play out. The second is the likelihood that reforms or policy changes will actually be adopted. The third is the likelihood that—and the avenues through which—education politics will transcend and affect the country's general PMP by escalating conflicts, creating large fiscal imbalances, or generating political actors that move beyond the boundaries of the education sector and become contenders on the national scene.

Chapter 11

Decentralization, Budget Processes, and Feedback Effects

While policymaking processes have a strong impact on policy outcomes, policy outcomes and policy reforms can have a significant impact on the PMP. Thus there are important feedback effects between the PMP and policy outcomes.

Chapters 8, 9, and 10 looked at the impact of the policymaking process (PMP) on policy outcomes in three different sectors: tax policy, public utilities, and education. Each of these sectors has its own specific actors and its own specific sectoral policymaking games. Moreover, each sector has its own challenges, associated with its specific political economy. In each, political and technical considerations interact during the processes of policy design, approval, and implementation. In each, policy outcomes are not independent of the nature of political institutions and policymaking processes.

But the link between policymaking processes and policy outcomes goes both ways. While policymaking processes have a strong impact on policy outcomes, policy outcomes and, in particular, policy reforms can have a significant impact on the PMP. Thus the link between the PMP and policy outcomes is characterized by important feedback effects. This chapter focuses on these feedback effects, illustrating them with a few examples taken from two different policy areas in which these effects can be particularly intense: decentralization and budget processes.

Feedback effects from policy reforms to policymaking processes may vary along a number of dimensions. They can vary in terms of their intensity or their scope. In some policy areas, the feedback effects of reforms tend to be restricted to the policymaking game in the specific policy area subject to reform. In others, feedback effects are broader and can affect the general policymaking process by introducing new actors that play across the board, or by changing the nature of the exchanges that are available to participants.

In addition, feedback effects can be intentional or unintentional. Where they are intentional, the impact of the reform on the PMP is precisely one of the considerations that leads to its adoption. But some reforms can have unwanted or unanticipated effects. A good understanding of the workings of the policymaking process in the countries in question may help limit such unwanted effects.

Chapter 9, on public services, provided a good illustration of feedback effects that are intense but narrow in scope. The process of privatization and regulation generates new actors, such as privatized firms and regulatory agencies, that subsequently change the dynamics of how the policymaking game is played in the public services sector. Yet these new actors are unlikely to have an important impact on the broader policymaking game.

In contrast, in some sectors, policy reforms have the potential to affect the entire PMP. The areas of decentralization and budget processes fall into this category, as well as the area of civil service reform. Not only are the effects of reforms in these areas likely to be broad, but they are also potentially intense.

Political decentralization—such as the introduction of elections for mayors or governors in countries where they were previously appointed—can affect the policymaking process through different channels. It introduces new actors that can play an important role in the national policymaking game, at least in some countries. It may alter the political landscape by encouraging the creation of new parties (often with a regional base of support) and by providing alternative opportunities for politicians to launch and build their political careers, away from the control of the national party leadership.

Fiscal decentralization—in the form of decentralization of revenue, debt, and expenditure responsibilities—may also significantly alter a country's PMP by shifting the balance of power in favor of regional actors, at the expense of others that have a national base of support. Apart from increasing their role in the design and implementation of policies such as health and education, fiscal decentralization provides governors and mayors with a variety of resources (financial resources, government positions, and the like) that can be used to influence the behavior of other actors, such as legislators, who play a key role in the national policymaking process.

Budget reform can also have a significant impact on the broader policymaking game. After all, the budget process is the arena in which the allocation of society's scarce resources is determined. As such, it constitutes a fundamental element of the PMP. Many public policies are decided in this arena. Even those that are agreed upon elsewhere must go through the budget to ensure that the resources will be available to implement them effectively. The budget process is also the arena where many of the exchanges occur that allow certain policies to be implemented.

As is the case with the PMP more generally, the budget process involves a multiplicity of actors with different powers and incentives—the president, the finance minister, legislators, bureaucrats—that interact in the process of fiscal decision making according to certain rules of engagement. Changes in those rules—whether numerical rules that set limits on spending or debt; rules that alter the balance of power among the different actors involved in the budgetary process; or rules that affect the transparency and visibility of the budget—can affect the nature of the exchanges that are feasible, and thus have a substantial impact on the PMP.

The reform of the civil service also can have profound effects on the general PMP. In particular, in countries in which civil service positions are regularly used as a political resource, a reform that seeks to professionalize the civil service can affect the type of exchanges that political actors engage in to build and maintain political support. It is precisely because political actors are aware of these feedback effects that the reform of the civil service has been such a difficult undertaking.

The rest of the chapter will focus on a few cases that illustrate the feedback effects that reforms can have in the overall policymaking process. The first case, associated with the area of decentralization, focuses on the introduction of elections for governors in Venezuela. This reform, which took place in 1988, activated the federal aspects of the Venezuelan Constitution, which had been latent until then. While the reform had an impact through a variety of channels, probably the most important was its effect on the configuration of the party system. By opening new channels of participation and new opportunities for parties and politicians to enter the political arena, the introduction of elections for governors had a profound (and unintended) impact on the party system. It significantly diminished the power of the national party leaders of the two traditional parties, which had been major players in the policymaking game.

The second case focuses on one particular dimension of budget processes: the discretionality of the president and the executive in allocating budget resources. It compares the cases of Brazil and the Dominican Republic. Rather than focusing on reforms that have actually taken place, the discussion looks at this particular feature of budget processes and the role it plays in the PMP of the two countries. Interestingly, while in Brazil budgetary discretion allows the president to engage in political transactions that are instrumental to his ability to approve and implement his agenda, in the Dominican Republic presidential discretion over the budget seems to be an impediment to cooperation. Thus the same institutional feature has very different consequences, depending on the institutional context in which it plays out. In this way, the comparative cases of Brazil and the Dominican Republic clearly illustrate the need for a general equilibrium view of policymaking processes.

The Introduction of Elections for Governors and Mayors in Venezuela[1]

The introduction of elections for governors and mayors in Venezuela is a good example of the impact of political decentralization on the PMP. Prior to decentralization, the policymaking process was characterized by relatively few and stable key players, and was highly cooperative (even collusive) in nature. At the heart of the Venezuelan PMP during the period prior to decentralization (late 1950s to late 1980s) was the *Pacto de Punto Fijo*, signed by

Some reforms can have unwanted or unanticipated feedback effects. A good understanding of the workings of the policymaking process in the countries in question may help limit such unwanted effects.

---

[1] This case is based on Monaldi and others (2005) and Monaldi (2005).

the two traditional parties, *Acción Democrática* (AD) and *Comité de Organización Política Electoral Independiente* (COPEI), in 1958.[2] The *Pacto*, which was signed in reaction to the political instability generated by the hegemonic style of rule during the 1950s, involved power sharing and the implementation of common social and economic policies regardless of the results of electoral competition. Oil revenues, which played a key role, were also distributed through key political actors from both parties, regardless of electoral results.

Within this context, political parties, and in particular party leaders, played a very important role. The party system that emerged from the *Pacto*, as well as from the electoral rules in place,[3] was characterized by low party fragmentation, high party centralization, and high party discipline. The party leadership controlled the nominations (who gets on the list) and the order of election (who gets elected first). The lack of elections at the regional and local levels did not provide alternative career opportunities for politicians and regional leaders outside the party, making it very costly to defect. The role of parties and party leaders in political and public life was so great that it led one analyst to call Venezuela a "partyarchy."[4]

The process in the AD for nominating candidates for the legislature is illustrative of the power of central national party leaders. Regional party authorities would propose a list of candidates with three times more names than the number of legislative seats corresponding to the district. The National Executive Council (CEN) reserved the right to pick one-third of the candidates from outside the list and had free rein in establishing the order of the list. In practice, this meant that the CEN decided who could be elected. Other parties had slightly more democratic nomination procedures, but in all parties, the national party leadership had the most prominent role, providing an important incentive for legislators to follow the wishes of party leaders.[5]

The power of the parties and their leaders led to an arrangement where the legislature had a relatively marginal role. Most important decisions were made outside the realm of congress, which to a large extent would rubber-stamp the decisions agreed upon by the president and the party leaders (most of whom were longstanding members of the legislature)—sometimes with the participation of corporatist actors such as the workers' union, CTV, and the peak business association, FEDECAMARAS.

Poor economic performance during the 1980s, partly due to a fall in oil prices but also due to fiscal mismanagement of the oil booms of the 1970s, led to demands to expand the channels of political participation. To a large extent, these demands were a reaction to the dominance of the traditional political parties, which were perceived as being responsible for poor economic and social outcomes. In response to these demands, President Lusinchi created the Commission for the Reform of the State, which proposed significant political reform, including elections of mayors and governors, reform of

---

[2] A third party that signed the *Pacto de Punto Fijo*, the *Unión Republicana Democrática* (URD), left the coalition in 1960.

[3] In particular, the closed and blocked candidate lists for the legislature, and the concurrency of legislative and presidential elections.

[4] Coppedge (1994).

[5] See Crisp (2001).

electoral rules, and democratization of party structures. While the traditional parties resisted these measures, these reforms took center stage during the presidential campaign in 1988, and some of them, including the election (and reelection) of governors and mayors, were approved. The first elections for subnational executive positions took place in 1989.

Subnational elections significantly changed political and party dynamics in Venezuela. The greater number of arenas open to political competition made it more difficult for the national party leaders to keep control of nominations. Because they had to present candidates in more than 20 states and 300 municipalities, they had to rely on local politicians with local or regional appeal in order to select candidates with a greater chance of success. The increase in the number of contests also provided small parties—which had previously had no chance of survival in national elections—with the chance to compete at the regional and local level, initially through the formation of alliances with the national parties. Eventually, several of these parties, such as *Causa R* and *Proyecto Carabobo*, used these regional niches as foundations for building national structures and thus entering national politics.

A number of additional factors also helped enhance the independence of regional political actors. The decentralization of expenditure responsibilities that came with political decentralization and the close relationship with the constituents, together with the fact that regional elections were held separately from the presidential elections, created the means and the incentives for governors and mayors to become more independent from the national parties, and to develop their own political machinery. The introduction of a mixed electoral system in 1993, in which some of the legislators were chosen in districts with only one party nominee, further weakened the control of the party leadership over legislators, and strengthened the bonds between legislators and regional leaders.

All these changes caused an increase in party fragmentation (measured by the effective number of parties) and party volatility, in both presidential and legislative elections (see Table 11.1). The reforms also changed the nature of the policymaking process. Before 1989, bargaining took place among a small number of actors that acted cooperatively in more opaque arenas. In the 1990s, policymaking involved a larger number of actors in more open arenas, and policymaking became more contentious. National party leaders could no longer decide on policies outside the legislature. Not only did they have to deal with more parties, but once they lost control over nominations, they also lost control over their own legislative delegations. Congress became a more important arena, and legislators became more involved in policymaking, as illustrated by the increase in the share of laws initiated by the legislature (as opposed to the executive). Regional actors became more influential, and local/regional policies became a more important token of exchange.

The introduction of elections for governors and mayors in Venezuela very clearly illustrates the feedback effects from policy and institutional reform on the nature of the PMP. The weakening of the national parties and their leaders was an unintended consequence of the reform. These parties, after all, were the ones that had approved the reforms, even if they did so under the pressure of popular demand. The change in the policymaking process also brought about changes in the features of public policies, similar to those dis-

Table 11.1 Party Fragmentation, Party Volatility, and the Role of Congress in Venezuela before and after Decentralization

	Pre-decentralization	Post-decentralization
Effective number of parties in congress	2.65[a]	4.6[b]
Party volatility in congress (percent)[c]	18.9[d]	38.1[e]
Volatility in the presidential vote (percent)[f]	13.9	52.0
Share of ordinary laws initiated by the legislature (percent)	34.0	64.0

[a] Average between 1973 and 1988. See Data Appendix for an explanation of the method for computing the effective number of parties.
[b] Average between 1989 and 2003.
[c] See Data Appendix.
[d] Average between 1958 and 1988.
[e] Average between 1989 and 2000.
[f] See Data Appendix.

Source: Monaldi and others (2005).

cussed in the case of Colombia (see Chapter 7). In line with the increased level of political participation, policies became more public-regarding. But the breakdown of cooperation meant that, at the same time, policies became less stable and less adaptable.

Presidential Budgetary Discretion in Brazil and the Dominican Republic

Like decentralization, the reform of budget procedures may also have profound effects on the PMP. These effects are particularly important, given the role that the budget plays as an arena where policies are funded, where losers can be compensated, and, more generally, where important political transactions can take place. Different dimensions of budget procedures may be subject to reform, and each of them may impact the PMP in a different way.[6] Since the objective of this chapter is to illustrate the importance of feedback effects with some examples, this section will focus on a particular dimension of budget procedures: the discretion of the executive to modify the allocation of funds during the budget execution stage.

---

[6] See Filc and Scartascini (2005).

The discussion will center on a comparison between two countries in which presidents enjoy a substantial amount of budgetary discretion: Brazil and the Dominican Republic. Interestingly, while in Brazil budgetary discretion seems to foster inter-temporal agreements and cooperation, in the Dominican Republic, executive discretion in budgetary matters can make it more difficult to reach agreements. The different role played by budgetary discretion in these two countries can be attributed to differences in the precise nature of the budgetary discretion in each country and, more importantly, to substantial differences in the broader political and institutional context in which this particular feature of budget processes is embedded.

The same institutional feature can have very different consequences, depending on the institutional context in which it plays out. This result clearly illustrates the need for a general equilibrium view of policymaking processes.

Brazil[7]

According to the Brazilian budget process, the executive branch is quite powerful in relation to the legislature. This difference in relative power is evident in different stages of the budget process. During budget approval, for example, the executive has the ability to veto any amendment proposed by the legislature that it does not favor. Despite this high level of executive control, congress nevertheless systematically proposes and approves a large number of amendments (collective and individual) to the annual budget. Even though the resources involved are small relative to the whole budget, it may seem surprising that the executive would allow its proposal to be moved from its preferred position in such a manner, given the instruments at its disposal.

The reason why the executive allows this to happen is that it still retains a considerable amount of discretion during budget execution. More specifically, the president can impound the funds associated with any of the amendments proposed by the legislators, provided actual revenues fall short of budgeted revenues (which tends to be the case rather frequently). Thus the approval of these amendments provides the opportunity for the president to use his powers of budgetary appropriation to obtain political support for his agenda from the members of the legislature and thus keep the coalition together, even in the context of a highly fragmented party system.

For these political transactions to occur, two things must come together. First, there must be gains to both participants in the transaction. Second, the executive must be credible in its promise to execute the amendments in exchange for the support it receives in congress. Both conditions seem to be present in Brazil.

One of the most important dimensions on which the president is judged is his ability to deliver macroeconomic stability. Macro stability has become an important electoral issue and can greatly affect a president's chances for reelection. To deliver stability, the president needs support for certain reforms, such as pension reform. Legislators also

---

[7] This section is based on Alston and others (2005a, 2005b).

seek reelection. As discussed in Chapter 7, the electoral rules in place (open-list proportional representation) provide incentives for legislators to deliver local investment projects to their jurisdictions. Except when legislators have strong preferences opposing the administration's reform agenda, this combination of factors creates opportunities for gains from trade. Legislators support the executive on crucial votes in the legislature in exchange for the disbursement of funds for local investments (a bridge, a hospital, a school) in their jurisdictions.

It is important to stress that the type of political exchange described here is perfectly legitimate. The president is seeking to further the national public good, and the legislators are acting in line with the preferences of their constituents. Moreover, such an exchange may allow the president to pass his agenda, even if he controls a small share of legislative seats.

These exchanges also require an important element of credibility. Empirical research suggests that the executive delivers on its promise: the execution of budget amendments proposed by individual legislators is highly correlated with the share of votes in which the legislator voted in favor of the administration's position.[8] Moreover, the research shows that the execution of legislators' amendments significantly increases their probability of electoral success and political survival.

Dominican Republic

As in Brazil, the president of the Dominican Republic also has a high degree of budgetary discretion, although the extent of this discretion has declined in recent years. Yet while this element contributes to facilitating political transactions in Brazil, the impact is quite the opposite in the Dominican Republic. The contrast between these cases clearly shows that the consequences of discretionary power depend on how budgetary rules operate in conjunction with the remaining features of the PMP.

Historically, the executive has had discretion over a large portion of the budget because of the combination of various rules that have limited the prerogatives of the legislature. Congress cannot propose budget increases, modify any expenses, or move allocations between budgetary items in different budget chapters without having a two-thirds majority of the total membership in each chamber.[9] When congress is not in session, the president can freely move resources between budget chapters by decree. Most importantly, until fairly recently the president controlled the "1401 Account" and had discretionary control over its distribution. The funds in this account had two origins: 75 percent of any revenues above and beyond budget estimations, and 100 percent of any "unutilized" funds by any executing unit. It was not unusual for the executive to underestimate revenues and control expenditures through cash management in order to have more control over the distribution of budget expenditures.[10] Primarily through the

---

[8] Alston and others (2005a).

[9] In effect, it is more demanding to introduce or modify expenses in the national budget than to reform the constitution.

[10] It is important to point out that the rules regarding the use of the 1401 Account changed in 2002. As a result, the discretion of the president in distributing resources has been significantly reduced.

use of this account, the Office of the President executed more than half (50 percent) of the budget every year between 1986 and 1996.[11]

In the context of the Dominican PMP, the executive's discretionary powers over budget matters seem to increase the cost of passing reforms and approving legislation. The difference can be traced to the two elements that are necessary for efficient transactions to occur: gains from trade and credibility. In Brazil, the gains from trade are clear. In the Dominican Republic, the opportunities for trade are less clear, in the context of a clientelistic party system. The reason is that both presidents and legislators tend to be judged according to their ability to deliver public goods and transfers to specific groups of voters. In this regard, they are competing for the distribution of the same pool of resources.

Credibility has also been lacking in the Dominican Republic, for a simple reason: credibility suffers when the bargaining chip one holds is costly to sacrifice. Unlike in Brazil, where the executive can decide whether or not to execute an amendment (without the power to change the destination of the funds), until recently the budget process in the Dominican Republic allowed the president to gain control of the funds by limiting budget execution on any item. In effect, a president seeking political support to pass legislation through congress would be subject to what the literature refers to as a *time-consistency* problem. He could promise to deliver budget resources in order to build a coalition to pass key legislation—but he would not be able to credibly commit to deliver.

In the presence of time-consistency problems, the "market" for political exchanges breaks down. In this case, the result was difficulty for the president in passing key legislation or economic reform, and a contentious relationship between the executive and congress. Given the relative lack of party discipline in the Dominican political system, this difficulty persisted even during periods in which the government's party controlled a majority of the legislative seats. Examples of legislation that was severely delayed or blocked in congress include the monetary and financial code, which took almost a decade to clear congress,[12] and various attempts to increase tax revenues, which were repeatedly blocked.[13]

The contrasting cases of Brazil and the Dominican Republic illustrate how particular features of the PMP may have different effects when they are embedded in different institutional contexts. Examination of such contrasting cases highlights the need for a nuanced view of policymaking processes that takes into account a multiplicity of institutional dimensions and their interactions.

---

[11] Central Bank of the Dominican Republic (2005).

[12] Some observers believe its earlier approval could have prevented the financial crisis that took place in the country in 2003.

[13] Interestingly, attempts to lower taxes are typically approved without much complication.

Part V

Conclusion

> *We need to raise
> other people's children.
> Good policy initiatives started
> by others must be cared for at
> least as much as our own.*
>
> Antanas Mockus, former mayor of Bogotá

Chapter 12

A New Lens for the Future

Development depends not so much on choosing the right policies from a technical standpoint as on negotiating, approving, and implementing them in a way conducive to their political survival and their effective application.

The approach used in this report has profound implications for the theory and practice of development. In general, development has been viewed as a technical problem amenable to solution by technically correct policies. This is the conception that has prevailed until recently, guiding the work of countries and of bilateral and multilateral development institutions. Over the years, these technically correct policies have undergone major transformations, with the focus shifting from capital investment to import substitution or, more recently, to the necessity of eliminating distortions in the efficient functioning of markets—the dominant theory of the so-called Washington Consensus. From these perspectives, it was important for countries to adopt the correct policies. Institutions were seen as a mere residual factor in the process of policy implementation.

In recent years, the wisdom of an approach based exclusively on a single model of technically correct policies has begun to be questioned. For instance, it is debatable whether across-the-board privatization, low and flat tax rates, or unrestricted international trade decisively contribute to stable and consistent growth and development paths. Moreover, the more successful countries in the region, such as Brazil, Chile, and Mexico, have combined some proposals of the orthodox model with others that are clearly different from it. At the same time, other countries, such as Argentina and Bolivia, that have led the way in structural reforms have displayed lower than expected performance on certain indices and have suffered grave political and economic crises. All this indicates that economic and social development is possible as long as policies are adopted that fall within a reasonable range but that are able to adapt to each country's challenges and circumstances—without conforming to any one specific model. The problem then consists of asking what makes countries adopt policies that are technically reasonable and well adapted to their context.

This document, while not claiming to have discovered the touchstone of development, explores an area increasingly emphasized by the specialized literature in recent years: the importance not only of policies, but also of the institutional framework producing the incentives that shape policies in practice. The focus is on the processes of policy formulation and implementation, and on the actors that interact to make and execute decisions. This point of view recognizes that policies are important, not only for their technical content, but also because they may possess certain features, such as stability, adaptability, coherence, the ability to be implemented effectively, an orientation toward the public interest (public-regardedness), and efficiency. The extent to which policies attain these features depends on the way in which actors in the policy process interact. The cycles of the policy process are vicious or virtuous according to the institutional incentives influencing the behavior of various actors in the process and according to the dynamic effect that interactions among these actors produce in the final result.

Institutions and processes are not neutral or merely instrumental; they are the crucible in which policies are forged and shaped and acquire their true form and meaning.

Policies are filtered through processes, and what initially seems to be a design that is correct and in line with the best international practices can turn out to have disappointing results. Institutions and processes are not neutral or merely instrumental; they are the crucible in which policies are forged and shaped and acquire their true form and meaning. This explains the dangers of replicating policy solutions from one country in another. For example, the extension of certain schemes of privatization adopted in more advanced countries to other countries that lack their institutional foundations has led to more problems than solutions.

The strengthening of democracy throughout the region has brought to light the critical importance of processes in the design and implementation of policies. Democracy divides and redistributes power—from the executive to the legislature, from the center to the periphery, from traditionally powerful classes to less powerful classes and to long-excluded groups and communities. The political process becomes increasingly dense, but also increasingly transparent, open, and exposed to influence by new formal and informal actors, such as the media and social movements. The viability of policy proposals often has more to do with their legitimacy than their technical correctness. The experience with privatization policies in the region provides an illustration of this point. Although their results have been technically evaluated as beneficial, the majority of the population is opposed to them and actively mobilizes against any effort in this area. Acceptability to the population, in addition to technical correctness, is therefore a requisite for the effectiveness of policies.

These considerations relate to some of the main messages presented in the introduction to this report. Political processes in a democracy must incorporate the dual requirement of representativeness and effectiveness. This makes it indispensable to develop certain institutions and processes that generate the qualities of stability, adaptability, coherence, public-regardedness, and effectiveness in policies. This study underscores the importance of certain basic institutions to the processes of approving and implementing public policies: a professional and stable bureaucracy, an independent judiciary, an institutionalized party system, and a legislature with the ability to contribute actively to the discussion of public policies.

All of the foregoing has many implications for the work of the Inter-American Development Bank and other development institutions in the countries of the region, and for the countries themselves in the process of formulating and implementing policies. Affirming that development depends not only on the adoption of certain technically correct policies, but also on the development of appropriate political processes, presents a formidable challenge. To orient the work of the Bank and the development community, a series of strategic recommendations is presented in the following section.

Strategic Recommendations

The first group of recommendations has to do with the necessity of fitting policies to the institutional contexts in which they are implemented.

1. The tendency to think of policies first and institutions later may be the source of many problems and errors. Politics and institutions are inseparable, and should be considered jointly in the analysis and design of strategies and operations. It is necessary to test designs in the institutional framework in which they are going to operate and leave room for adaptation to that framework—even though this may lead to questioning of some aspects of the initial design. Referring (as is habitually done) to failed reforms as good ideas that could not be put into practice is illogical, as their infeasibility makes them bad ideas to begin with. Overcoming the reasoning behind statements of this type is an enormous challenge for governments and bilateral and multilateral development institutions.

2. A vision of development from the perspective of processes and not only from policies expands and complicates the work of analysis. It is necessary to analyze the processes of policy formulation and implementation in detail in specific countries and sectors. This calls for the systematic institutional analysis of countries. Detailed analyses of this type can help to identify the possibilities for adopting policy reforms—and the constraints. They also can help open discussion about the evolutionary possibilities of institutions, identifying factors that might lead to possible imbalances or crises, and zeroing in on actors that might serve as agents of reform, as well as possible coalitions that might support them.

3. A key component of institutional diagnosis is deepening the empirical indicators of governability, which make the analysis as objective as possible. This report makes extensive use of these instruments. Nonetheless, there is still a long way to go in this regard. It is necessary to advance from indicators based on perceptions, which are relevant but somewhat superficial, to indicators that more directly and specifically measure and analyze the capacities of particular institutions and their relationship to the broader configuration of State institutions. This in turn requires the development of models that associate the desirable attributes

of institutions with the intrinsic characteristics of institutions, which presents a conceptual and analytical challenge of enormous proportions.

The second group of recommendations relates to initiatives that alter the framework of incentives in which actors operate. Reforms along the lines of these initiatives have proven difficult, and little is known about the way in which institutions change, or how to have a positive influence on their transformation. Nonetheless, some lessons can be extracted on the basis of years of experience.

4. It is difficult to produce institutional change by addressing an institution in isolation. To intervene effectively, it is important to understand the complex interdependencies that exist among institutions. For example, trying to professionalize the bureaucracy when it traditionally has been used as a political resource requires reforming the political institutional framework and, in particular, the incentives of the political parties themselves. Similarly, trying to strengthen the legislature to improve its technical contribution to the design and implementation of policies requires changing the incentives for legislators to invest in such capacities, which in turn may require changing the electoral system or the party system.

5. Institutions represent political and cultural expressions and should be understood as such. Institutional reform is more than a technical change whereby some rules are replaced by others. It is necessary to act through processes that are incremental and, with few exceptions, slow, in which old conceptions, ideas, and interests gradually lose their strength and are replaced by new ones. Change of this type requires developing these processes through diverse initiatives over time. Efforts that ignore this deep logic of institutions and employ mechanical means such as laws and other formal instruments may be insufficient to change deep-seated political practices and attitudes. An example of this in many countries is the existence of two parallel budgets, one formally approved and the other informal, carried out through cash transfers that determine the allocation of resources.

6. In the process of institutional change, demand factors, such as internal crisis and political will, outweigh supply factors, such as the availability of resources and knowledge from outside. Accordingly, countries must assume ownership of their reforms and generate the political will necessary to carry them out. Political will should not be conceived of as a blank check; it must be built over time, and the amount of it can be increased or diminished according to the results obtained. Conceiving of reforms as a matter not of achieving an ideal model, but of improving the existing model on the basis of available resources and existing restrictions, is a very important orientation toward the development of political will. The countries of the region that have most successfully reformed their institutions, such as Chile and Brazil, have been characterized by prudence and gradualism in their processes, supported by broad consensus.

7. Importing institutional models without taking into account the underlying conditions that make them possible can produce serious problems. Experience

demonstrates the dangers of conceiving institutional change on the basis of ideal schemes or best practices without considering the broader institutional requisites for their success. Such has been the case with the creation of schemes of participation or private investment in public services, in the absence of capacity for regulation and control; the creation of government bodies in the judiciary that exacerbate politicization rather than prevent it; and the decentralization of the provision of services, without ensuring incentives for fiscal discipline. Inspiration from successful models is a great stimulus, but only to the extent that those models can be assimilated by the recipient countries. Although it may sometimes be a justifiable option to bypass stages of institutional development, most of the time it is advisable to avoid universal models that may in some cases represent the state of the art but may not be applicable to all institutional settings.

8. Financial resources—which are often the fundamental tool utilized by international financial institutions—are a double-edged sword in relation to institutional change. It is important to understand that contributing financial resources does not change institutions per se. It is necessary to ensure that financing is directed toward removing the obstacle that is blocking change, because often what is required to remedy a lack of technical capacity generates significant resistance from opposing interests. If the problem is the compensation of potential losers, it is useless to apply resources to the development of capacity, and vice versa. Additionally, the amount of resources applied can hardly be proportional to the problems addressed or to the costs of solving them, which are difficult to assess. It is not unusual for an abundance of resources to become a perverse incentive, once political problems are disguised as technical problems and projects become capital-intensive with the focus on buying equipment and developing systems. None of this confronts the real problems of institutional transitions.

The viability of policy proposals can be determined more often by their legitimacy than by their technical correctness.

9. Financial resources can be an important catalyst for the process of change if their application is proportionate and strategic. Institutional innovations can be achieved when three elements coincide that permit the system of incentives to be realigned:

   - A window of opportunity opens, as a result of a crisis or political change, that demonstrates the costs associated with not changing.
   - The ideas and the technical knowledge that legitimize change and make it possible are transferred to actors that may benefit from change.
   - A coalition of actors emerges that adopts these ideas, perceives them as consistent with their interests, and assumes a leadership role in the process of change.

Resources can have value as catalysts for the second and third elements, by supporting various activities of technical assistance, training, and dissemination—to the extent that their application is opportune in the political climate of reform.

10. Finally, institutional development is impossible without the development of political, economic, and social leaders who can take advantage of crises that produce changes in the incentives of the main actors. In such times, systems are open to being restructured, incorporating new actors, and modifying the relative power and roles they play. Leadership permits the opening of institutional opportunities that can generate further cycles of policy formulation and implementation and institutional renewal. The way in which windows of opportunity and leadership create virtuous cycles of reform is little understood and difficult to explain. Institutional change can thus be understood as a process of trial and error in which there are no recipes ready and waiting to be applied. The willingness to make mistakes and learn from experience is a prerequisite for contributing to institutional change.

In the last decade, evidence of a connection between the quality of institutions and development has become increasingly strong. Latin America is a particularly relevant case for testing this connection. This study seeks to deepen the analysis of this connection, opening new paths to analyzing the relationship between institutions, political processes, and the quality of public policy. The emphasis is on making it clear that the quality of policy is not merely dependent on the interaction among individual desires and preferences. Rather, it can be explained on the basis of the dominant institutional arrangements in each country. Although what we do not know is far more than what we do, this study attempts to present a compilation of knowledge and stimulate new horizons that may allow us to continue learning in order to advance the region's economic and social progress.

Data Appendix: Description of Variables and Technical Concepts

Variables are grouped by subject matter in order of appearance in text. Except where indicated, all variables are cross-section measures by country for the latest available year.

Variable	Description	Source	Chapter(s)
Public Policies			
Overall Index of Quality of Public Policy	Average of six indicators describing the quality of public policies: (1) stability, (2) adaptability, (3) coordination and coherence, (4) enforcement and implementation, (5) public-regardedness, and (6) efficiency. The index and all components and subcomponents are normalized on a scale of 1–4, with higher levels indicating better quality of public policies.	Stein and Tommasi (2005)	2, 6
1. Stability	Average of six components: (1) the standard deviation of the detrended Fraser Index of Economic Freedom, (2) the extent to which legal or political changes have undermined firms' planning capacity (GCR), (3) the extent to which new governments honor the contractual commitments and obligations of previous regimes (GCR), (4) the capacity of the State to set and maintain priorities among conflicting objectives (SC Survey), (5) the extent to which governments ensure policy stability (SC Survey), and (6) the extent to which the State makes and maintains international commitments (SC Survey). Index on a scale of 1–4, with higher levels indicating greater policy stability.	Stein and Tommasi (2005), based on Fraser Institute (various years), World Economic Forum's *Global Competitiveness Report* (GCR) (various years) and State Capabilities (SC) Survey (a survey of more than 150 experts in 18 countries in Latin America conducted for this report; see Box 6.1)	2, 6
2. Adaptability	Average of two components: (1) the extent to which there is innovation when policies fail (SC Survey) and (2) the extent to which governments ensure policy adaptability (SC Survey). Index on a scale of 1–4, with higher levels indicating higher policy adaptability.	Stein and Tommasi (2005), based on State Capabilities (SC) Survey	2, 6
3. Coordination and coherence	Average of two components: (1) the extent to which new policies are consistent with existing policies (SC Survey) and (2) whether different policymakers operating in the same policy domain (or related policy domains) coordinate their actions effectively (SC Survey). Index on a scale of 1–4, with higher levels indicating more coordination and coherence of public policies.	Stein and Tommasi (2005), based on State Capabilities (SC) Survey	2, 6

Variable	Description	Source	Chapter(s)
4. Implementation and enforcement	Average of four components: (1) the extent of enforcement of the minimum wage (GCR), (2) the extent of control of tax evasion (GCR), (3) the consistency of environmental regulation (GCR), and (4) the extent to which the State ensures effective implementation of public policies (SC Survey). Index on a scale of 1–4, with higher levels indicating better enforcement and implementation of public policies.	Stein and Tommasi (2005), based on World Economic Forum's *Global Competitiveness Report* (GCR) (various years) and State Capabilities (SC) Survey	2, 6
5. Public-regardedness	Average of four components of policy stability: (1) the extent to which public officials tend to favor the well connected in their policy decisions (GCR), (2) the extent to which social transfers effectively reach the poor as opposed to the rich (GCR), (3) the ability of the State to impose losses on powerful actors (SC Survey), and (4) the extent to which the government represents diffuse, unorganized interests, in addition to concentrated, organized interests (SC Survey). Index on a scale of 1–4, with higher levels indicating that public policies are more public-regarding.	Stein and Tommasi (2005), based on World Economic Forum's *Global Competitiveness Report* (GCR) (various years) and State Capabilities (SC) Survey	2, 6
6. Efficiency	Average of two components: (1) whether the composition of public spending is wasteful (GCR) and (2) whether resources are targeted where most effective (SC Survey). Index on a scale of 1–4, with higher levels indicating higher policy efficiency.	Stein and Tommasi (2005), based on World Economic Forum's *Global Competitiveness Report* (GCR) (various years) and State Capabilities (SC) Survey	2, 6
Political Parties			
Party System Institutionalization Index	Following Mainwaring and Scully (1995), this is an aggregate index which is an average of four component measures: (1) the stability of inter-party competition, (2) the extensiveness of parties' roots in society, (3) the legitimacy of parties and elections, and (4) the strength of party organizations. Index on a scale of 0–100, with higher levels indicating more institutionalized party systems.	Jones (2005)	3

Variable	Description	Source	Chapter(s)
1. Stability of inter-party competition	Average of two indicators: (1) the volatility of votes (percentage of valid votes) and (2) the volatility of seats (percentage of seats), for the two most recent lower house (or national assembly) elections. Volatility is measured following Pedersen (1983), with higher levels indicating higher levels of volatility.	Jones (2005)	3
2. Extensiveness of parties' roots in society	Average of two indicators: (1) the percentage of the population reporting some form of identification with a political party (LB) and (2) 100 minus the percentage of legislators who believe that political parties are distant from society (PELA).	Jones (2005), based on data from Latinobarometer (LB) (2003) and Proyecto de Elites Latinoamericanas (PELA) survey (2005)	3
3. Legitimacy of parties and elections	Average of two indicators: (1) the legitimacy of parties, measured as the combination of the percentage of citizens who stated that political parties were indispensable (LB 2003) and the percentage of the population that had "a great deal of" or "some" confidence in political parties (LB 2004) and (2) the legitimacy of elections, measured as the combination of how respondents rated the elections in their country on a scale from 1 *(clean)* to 5 *(not clean)* (LB 2000) and to what extent respondents agreed with the statement that election offers voters a real choice between parties and candidates on a scale from 1 *(strongly agree)* to 4 *(strongly disagree)*.	Jones (2005), based on data from Latinobarometer (LB) (2000, 2003, 2004)	3
4. Strength of party organizations	Average of two components: (1) party age and (2) party continuity. Party age is the average of the percentage of parties holding at least 10 percent of the seats in the lower house (or national assembly) that as of 2004 had been in existence for at least 10 years and (2) the percentage of such parties that as of 2004 had been in existence for at least 25 years. Party continuity is based on a question from a survey (PELA 2005) that asked legislators whether they considered their party organization to be continuous or merely an electoral vehicle.	Jones (2005), based on Mainwaring (1998, 1999) and Proyecto de Elites Latinoamericanas (PELA) (2005)	3

Variable	Description	Source	Chapter(s)
Programmatic Parties Index	This index measures the extent to which parties are programmatic. This in turn is derived from three components: (1) the level of programmatic politics among party supporters (electorate), (2) the level of programmatic politics among the party elite (legislators), and (3) the extent of electoral volatility in the country (see *Party volatility in congress*). The following equation is used to calculate the index from the components: *Prog. Parties = (Prog. Electorate + Prog. Elite) – Electoral Volatility* The index is constructed on a scale of 0–8, with higher levels indicating more programmatic parties.	Jones (2005), based on data from the Latinobarometer (2002, 2003, 2004) and the Proyecto de Elites Latinoamericanas (PELA)	3
Ideological self-placement of parties	Legislators from different parties are asked to place their parties on an ideological scale from 1 *(Left)* to 10 *(Right)*.	Jones (2005), Saiegh (2005), based on data from the Proyecto de Elites Latinoamericanas (PELA) survey (2002)	3
Effective number of legislative parties	Following Laakso and Taagepera (1979), this is a measure of legislative fragmentation in the lower house (or national assembly), following the two most recent legislative elections. It is calculated by taking the inverse of the sum of the squares of all parties' seat shares. If, for example, there were three parties competing that received close to an equal share of the vote, then the value of the index would be close to 3. But if two of the three parties received about 45 percent of the seats each, and the third party received only 10 percent, then the value would be about 2.4. The index attempts to capture the fact that despite both having three parties, the functioning of the latter system is closer to that of a two-party system, whereas the former functions more purely like a three-party system.	Jones (2005)	3, 11
Presidential party's chamber contingent	Average percentage of seats held by the president's party in the lower house (or national assembly) in the two most recent legislative elections.	Saiegh (2005), Jones (2005)	3

Variable	Description	Source	Chapter(s)
Proportionality of the design of the electoral system	This index measures the extent to which the electoral system, given its design, would be expected to allocate seats in a proportionate manner; that is, the extent to which the parties' share of legislative seats corresponds to the parties' share of the vote. The index is constructed on a scale of 1–5, where 1 = *majority system* (average district magnitude [ADM] = 1), 2 = *low proportionality* (ADM = 2–4), 3 = *moderate proportionality* (ADM = 4–10), 4 = *high proportionality* (ADM = 10–20), 5 = *very high proportionality* (ADM = 20–national district).	Authors' calculations based on Payne and others (2002)	3
Type of government	Governments are classified by looking at two dimensions: (1) whether they have majority or minority in congress and (2) whether they belong to a single party or a coalition. Using this criterion, 98 democratic governments in 18 Latin American countries between 1978 and 2005 were coded from 1 to 6, where 1 = *single-party majority in all legislatures*, 2 = *near single-party majority in all legislatures (45 percent and above)*, 3 = *stable coalition majority*, 4 = *coalition or single-party majority for a significant part of the presidential term (50 percent or more) or near coalition majority for most of the term*, 5 = *coalition or single-party majority for less than half the term*, and 6 = *minority governments (only ad hoc or very short-lived coalitions, if any)*.	Authors' compilation	3, 6
Party Central-ization Index	This is an aggregate index calculated as the simple sum of its six individual components: (1) candidate nomination, (2) electoral system, (3) presidential elections, (4) autonomous governors, (5) intra-party democracy, and (6) presidential primaries. The index is constructed on a scale of 6–18, with higher levels indicating more highly centralized party systems.	Jones (2005)	3
1. Candidate nomination	Assessment of the party's control over the nomination of legislative candidates. Index on a scale of 1–3, according to who principally makes the nomination decision: 1 = *individual candidates*, 2 = *regional party leaders*, and 3 = *national party leaders*.	Jones (2005), based on Alcántara Sáez and Freidenberg (2001)	3

Variable	Description	Source	Chapter(s)
2. Electoral system	Assessment of the electoral system for legislative elections, based on the type of electoral districts (national, regional, single-member, or some mixture thereof) and the presence or absence of preference voting (closed list vs. open list). Added to the resulting number is 0.5 in those cases in which a fused vote is utilized for the election of the president and the legislature as well as those cases in which there exists a national threshold that a party must cross in order to obtain some legislative seats. The index is constructed on a scale of 1–3, with higher levels indicating a more centralized arrangement of the electoral system.	Jones (2005)	3
3. Presidential elections	Assessment of the timing of presidential and legislative elections. Index on a scale of 1–3, according to the extent to which presidential and legislative elections are held concurrently: 1 = *in fewer than one-third of the cases*, 2 = *in one-half of the cases*, and 3 = *always*.	Jones (2005)	3
4. Autonomous governors	Assessment of the autonomy possessed by regional officials. Index on a scale of 1–3, where 1 = *governors possess an important degree of political and administrative autonomy*, 2 = *governors possess limited political and administrative autonomy*, and 3 = *there are no directly elected governors*.	Jones (2005)	3
5. Intra-party democracy	Measurement of the extent of members' participation in parties' decision making processes. Based on a survey question (PELA 2005) that asked legislators to evaluate the extent of internal democracy in their parties. From these responses an index was constructed on a scale of 1–3, with higher levels indicating systems that are less democratic in the decision making process.	Jones (2005), based on Proyecto de Elites Latinoamericanas (PELA) (2005)	3
6. Presidential primaries	Assessment of the extent to which direct primary elections have been used to choose the major parties' candidates in recent presidential elections. The index is constructed on a scale of 1–3, with higher values indicating that a smaller number of major parties held democratic primaries.	Jones (2005), based on Alcántara Sáez (2002), Carey and Polga-Hecimovich (2004), and Freidenberg and Sánchez López (2002).	3

Variable	Description	Source	Chapter(s)
Party System Nationalization Index	This index shows the party system nationalization scores (PSNS) for Latin American countries based on the votes in the lower house elections held closest to 2002. Following Jones and Mainwaring (2003), the PSNS is calculated as the sum over all parties of 1 minus the Gini coefficient for the distribution of each party's vote (its party nationalization score [PNS]), multiplied by its share of the national valid vote.	Jones (2005), based on Jones and Mainwaring (2003)	3

Legislatures

Variable	Description	Source	Chapter(s)
Legislative success rate	Measures the percentage of executive legislative initiatives that are approved by the legislature.	Saiegh (2005)	3
Reelection rates	Average percentage of legislators in the lower house (national assembly) that are reelected in the following legislature.	Saiegh (2005) and authors' compilation	3
Congress Capabilities Index	This is an aggregate index calculated as the simple average of the following eight components: (1) confidence in congress, (2) effectiveness of lawmaking bodies, (3) average experience of legislators, (4) percentage of legislators with university education, (5) number of committee memberships per legislator, (6) committee strength, (7) whether congress is a good place to build a career, and (8) technical expertise of legislators. All components are rescaled to a scale of 1–3, such that the aggregate index is on a scale of 1–3, with higher levels indicating better congressional capabilities of legislators.	Authors' compilation based on Latinobarometer (1996–2004), World Economic Forum (2005), Proyecto de Elites Latinoamericanas (PELA) (various years), and Saiegh (2005)	3, 6
1. Confidence in congress	Average percentage of respondents who stated they had "a lot of" or "some" confidence in congress.	Latinobarometer (1996–2004)	3, 6
2. Effectiveness of lawmaking bodies	Average score given by business executives to the question "How effective is your national parliament/congress as a lawmaking and oversight institution?" Index on a scale of 1 *(very ineffective)* to 7 *(very effective)*.	World Economic Forum (2005)	3

Variable	Description	Source	Chapter(s)
3. Average experience of legislators	Assessment of the average years of experience of legislators (E), calculated on the basis of the reelection rate of legislators (r) and the average length of the legislative term (D). The equation is as follows: $$E = \frac{D}{2} + \sum_{i=1}^{10} r^i D$$ For the cases of Dominican Republic, Nicaragua, and Venezuela, because there were no available data for the reelection rate, reelection rate values were estimated on the basis of a regression of the reelection rate of legislators (for the available countries) on the percentage of new legislators (PELA 2002).	Saiegh (2005), authors' compilation, and Proyecto de Elites Latinoamericanas (PELA) (2002)	3
4. Legislators with university education	Percentage of legislators with a university education.	Proyecto de Elites Latinoamericanas (PELA) (2002)	3
5. Committee specialization	Average number of committee memberships per legislator.	Saiegh (2005)	3
6. Committee strength	Qualitative assessment of the strength of the committees by Saiegh (2005), based on the number of committees, their jurisdictions, and the overlap with other ministries from the executive. Other sources included the country studies from the Political Institutions, Policymaking Processes, and Policy Outcomes project of the IDB's Latin American Research Network. Index on a scale of 1–3, where 1 = *low*, 2 = *medium*, and 3= *high*.	Saiegh (2005) and authors' compilation	3
7. Place to build career	Qualitative assessment on whether congress is a good place to build a career by Saiegh (2005), based on results from the PELA survey and the country studies from the Political Institutions, Policymaking Processes, and Policy Outcomes project of the IDB's Latin American Research Network. Index on a scale of 1–3, where 1 = *low*, 2 = *medium*, and 3 = *high*.	Saiegh (2005), Proyecto de Elites Latinoamericanas (PELA) (2005), and authors' compilation	3

Variable	Description	Source	Chapter(s)
8. Technical expertise	Qualitative assessment on the technical expertise of legislators by Saiegh (2005), based on results from the PELA survey and the country studies from the Political Institutions, Policymaking Processes, and Policy Outcomes project of the IDB's Latin American Research Network. Index on a scale of 1–3, where 1 = *low*, 2 = *medium*, and 3 = *high*.	Saiegh (2005), Proyecto de Elites Latinoamericanas (PELA) (2005), and authors' compilation	3
Party volatility in congress	This is the Pedersen index of electoral volatility, derived by adding the absolute net change in percentage of seats, in the lower house (or national assembly), for each party from one election to the next, then dividing by two.	Monaldi and others (2005), based on Payne and others (2002)	11
Share of ordinary laws initiated by the legislature	This represents the percentage of all the ordinary laws approved in a year that were initiated into the legislative process by members of the legislature (as opposed to the executive or in a very few cases the supreme court). Ordinary laws are the regular laws that can be initiated by legislators (as opposed to other legislative decisions, like the appointment of ambassadors, that have to be initiated by the executive or the supreme court).	Monaldi and others (2005)	11

Presidents

Variable	Description	Source	Chapter(s)
Constitutional powers of the president	This index is the average of three variables: (1) proactive powers, (2) reactive powers, and (3) plebiscite powers. Index on a scale of 0–1, with higher numbers representing greater power.	United Nations Development Programme (UNDP) (2005)	3
1. Proactive powers	These are powers that contribute to the president's ability to unilaterally change the status quo. They have two components: (1) decree and agenda-setting powers (whether the president has the power to directly make laws by issuing decrees) and (2) budgetary powers (whether the president has the power to prepare the budget with few interventions from the congress). Aggregate index on a scale of 0–1, with higher numbers representing greater powers of the president.	United Nations Development Programme (UNDP) (2005)	3

Variable	Description	Source	Chapter(s)
2. Reactive powers	These are powers that allow the president to oppose efforts by the legislature to change the status quo. They have three components: (1) package veto (power of the president to block the enactment of a law approved by the congress to which he objects), (2) partial veto (power of the president to veto particular provisions of an approved bill to which he objects), and (3) exclusive initiative (relates to cases in which the constitution gives the president the exclusive right to introduce legislation in specific policy areas). Aggregate index on a scale of 0–1, with higher numbers representing greater powers of the president.	United Nations Development Programme (UNDP) (2005)	3
3. Plebiscite powers	These are powers by which the president can convoke a plebiscite or referendum. Index on a scale of 0–1, with higher numbers representing greater power to convoke a plebiscite without restrictions.	Payne and others (2002), based on data from United Nations Development Programme (UNDP) (2005)	3
Legislative powers of the presidents	See *Constitutional powers of the president.*		
Partisan powers of the presidents	See *Presidential party's chamber contingent.*		
Constitutional interruptions	Cases in which either presidents or members of congress do not complete the term for which they were elected.	Chasquetti (1999) and authors' compilation	6
Size of president's coalition	Percentage of seats controlled by the parties in the president's coalition in congress over the period 1984–2002 (monthly averages).	Mejía Acosta (2004)	11
Volatility in the presidential vote	This is the Pedersen index of presidential electoral volatility, derived by adding the absolute net change in percentage of presidential votes for each party from one election to the next, then dividing by two.	Monaldi and others (2005), based on Payne and others (2002)	7

Variable	Description	Source	Chapter(s)
Cabinets			
Cabinet stability	Inverse of cabinet instability, which is measured as the average number of different individuals that served in a given ministry from 1988 to 2000.	Martínez-Gallardo (2005b)	4, 6
Fraction of ministers and top-level political appointees in civil service	Average of an index constructed on the basis of responses to the question "Of political appointees to higher official positions (roughly the top 500 positions in the core economic agencies), what proportion are likely to already be members of the higher civil service?" Index on a scale of 1–3, where 1 = *less than 30 percent*, 2 = *30–70 percent*, and 3 = *more than 70 percent.*	Rauch and Evans (2000)	6
Bureaucracy			
Index of Civil Service System Development	Average of three indicators of the bureaucracy: (1) the Bureaucratic Merit Index, (2) the Bureaucratic Functional Capacity Index, and (3) the Bureaucratic Efficiency Index. Index on a scale of 0–100, with higher levels indicating more developed civil service systems.	Authors' compilation based on IDB's Network on Public Policy Management and Transparency (www.iadb.org/int/DRP/Ing/Red5/transpmain.htm)	4
1. Bureaucratic Merit Index	Measures the degree to which effective guarantees of professionalism in the civil service are in place and the degree to which civil servants are effectively protected from arbitrariness, politicization, and rent-seeking. Index on a scale of 0–100, with higher levels indicating more autonomous bureaucratic systems.	Authors' compilation based on IDB's Network on Public Policy Management and Transparency	4
2. Bureaucratic Functional Capacity Index	Measures the degree to which the bureaucracy has salary compensation systems and systems for evaluating the performance of public officials. Index on a scale of 0–100, with higher levels indicating systems with higher technical capacities and more incentives for performance.	Authors' compilation based on IDB's Network on Public Policy Management and Transparency	4

Variable	Description	Source	Chapter(s)
3. Bureaucratic Efficiency Index	Measures the degree to which the bureaucracy is efficient in assigning human capital, given a fiscal policy constraint. Index on a scale of 0–100, with higher levels indicating more efficient bureaucratic systems.	Authors' compilation based on IDB's Network on Public Policy Management and Transparency	4
Bureaucracy size	Percentage of total population employed in the public sector.	Authors' compilation based on IDB's Network on Public Policy Management and Transparency	4
Judiciary			
Tenure of supreme court judges	Average tenure (years) of supreme court judges for the period 1960–1995.	Henisz (2000)	4
Independence of the Judiciary Index (WEF)	Measures the degree to which the judiciary is independent of the political influence of members of government, citizens, or firms. Index on a scale of 1 *(heavily influenced)* to 7 *(entirely independent)*.	World Economic Forum (2004)	4
De facto judicial independence (Feld and Voigt)	Simple average of eight components, each of which is coded between 0 and 1 or normalized to vary between 0 and 1: (1) Effective average term length of the members of the highest court; (2) Deviations between actual term length and that which would be expected given legal setting; (3) Have members of the highest court been removed before the end of their terms? (4) Number of times the number of judges has been changed since 1960; (5) Have incomes of judges at least remained constant since 1960? (6) Has the budget of the highest court at least remained constant in real terms since 1960? (7) How often have the relevant articles of the constitution (or the law on which the highest court is based) been changed since 1960? and (8) In how many cases has one of the other government branches remained inactive when its action was necessary for a decision of the highest court to become effective?	Feld and Voigt (2003)	4, 7

Variable	Description	Source	Chapter(s)
Unions			
Union coverage	Workers affiliated with unions as a percentage of the economically active population.	McGuire (1997)	5
Macro-economic Variables			
GDP per capita growth	Average per capita GDP growth (in U.S. dollars at purchasing power parity) between 1980 and 2002.	World Bank (various years)	6
Human Development Index	Combines measures of life expectancy at birth and adult literacy, the combined gross enrollment ratio for primary, secondary, and tertiary schools, and a measure of income GDP per capita (in U.S. dollars at purchasing power parity), in order to measure a country's achievement in terms of human development. In this study we used the change in the value of the index between 1980 and 2002.	United Nations Development Programme (UNDP) (various years)	6
Poverty Reduction Index	The inverse of the change in the poverty rate between 1980–90 and 1995–2000. The poverty rate is measured as the percentage of the population that has an income of less than 1 U.S. dollar at purchasing power parity a day.	World Bank (various years)	6
Aggregate Welfare Index (Sen)	This is an aggregate measure of welfare that combines GDP per capita at purchasing power parity with Sen's inequality index (equal to the mean times [1 minus the Gini coefficient]). See Lambert (1993) for technical details. For this study, we used the average of the index for the period 1990–2002.	Gasparini (2004)	6
Aggregate Welfare Index (Atkinson's)	This is an aggregate measure of welfare that combines GDP per capita at purchasing power parity with Atkinson's inequality index (which takes a constant elasticity of substitution [CES] function with a given parameter of inequality aversion). See Lambert (1993) for technical details. For this study, we used the average of the index for the period 1990–2002.	Gasparini (2004)	6

Variable	Description	Chapter(s)
Technical and Statistical Concepts		
Cluster analysis	Cluster analysis is a technique used to identify homogenous groups of observations. Using this technique it is possible to classify observations with similar characteristics into different subgroups.	3, 6
	This document follows Anderberg (1973) and uses K-means cluster analysis (KMC). KMC is based on *nearest centroid sorting*, which consists of assigning to a given cluster the observations that are the least distant from the center of the cluster *(centroid)*. As the number of clusters is defined *ex ante* and clusters are assigned iteratively, the groupings are identified solely based on the distances between observations, and not by selection on the part of the researcher.	
	For this particular study, cluster analysis was used to classify countries according to different variables (key features of public policies, political variables, etc.). For the case of the Overall Index of Quality of Public Policy, the clustering was performed excluding Chile, whose score was significantly higher than those of the rest of the countries in the sample. Because of its high score, Chile was placed in a separate category, *very high*. The rest of the countries were then classified, using three clusters, into the *high*, *medium*, and *low* categories.	
Correlation	Correlation analysis is a statistical technique that can show whether and how strongly pairs of variables are related. The correlation coefficient can range between –1 and 1 and is a measure of the degree of linear relationship between two variables. A correlation coefficient of 1 indicates that two variables always move together in the same direction, in which case they are said to be perfectly correlated. A correlation coefficient of –1 indicates that two variables always move together, but in the opposite direction, in which case they are said to be perfectly negatively correlated. A correlation coefficient of 0 indicates that a pair of variables move independently of one another, with no association between the movement of one and the movement of the other. The correlation coefficient r between two variables x and y can be calculated as follows:	6

$$r = \frac{n\sum xy - \sum x \sum y}{\sqrt{n\left(\sum x^2\right) - \left(\sum x\right)^2}\sqrt{n\left(\sum y^2\right) - \left(\sum y\right)^2}}$$

where n is the number of observations.

Variable	Description	Chapter(s)

It is possible to test whether a correlation coefficient is significantly different from zero by computing the t-statistic of the coefficient and then comparing the computed value with the t-statistic tabulations that are available in most books of statistical analysis. To use a t-statistics table, it is necessary to know the degrees of freedom (in this case $n - 2$) and choose a confidence level (usually 5 percent, but 10 percent and 1 percent are also commonly used). If the computed value is higher than the tabulated value, then it is possible to say that the correlation coefficient is significantly different from zero with the chosen level of confidence.

The t-statistic is computed as follows:

$$t = \frac{r\sqrt{n-2}}{\sqrt{1-r^2}}$$

where r is the correlation coefficient and n is the sample size.

| Partial correlation | Partial correlation is a statistical technique that can show whether and how strongly pairs of variables are related, while controlling for the effect of other variables. In order to compute the partial correlation between x and y, while controlling for a third variable z, it is necessary to perform a regression of x on z and then recover the residuals of this regression (i.e., the component of x that cannot be explained by z). Next it is necessary to perform a regression of y on z and then recover the residuals of this second regression (i.e., the component of y that cannot be explained by z). The correlation between these two sets of residuals will yield the partial correlation (controlling for z) between x and y. | 6 |

In this study, partial correlations were performed to isolate the correlation between two variables from a country's level of economic development. Economic development was defined as GDP per capita in 1980, measured in U.S. dollars evaluated at purchasing power parity.

References

Acemoglu, Daron, Simon Johnson, and James A. Robinson. 2001. The Colonial Origins of Comparative Development: An Empirical Investigation. *American Economic Review* 91(5):1369–1401.

———. 2002. Reversal of Fortune: Geography and Institutions in the Making of the Modern World Income Distribution. *Quarterly Journal of Economics* 117(4):1231–94.

Aguilar, Giovanna. 2003. *El sistema tarifario del servicio público de electricidad, una evaluación desde el punto de vista de los usuarios.* Working Paper no. 224. Pontificia Universidad Católica del Perú, Lima.

Alcántara Sáez, Manuel. 2002. *Experimentos de democracia interna: las primarias de partidos en América Latina.* Working Paper no. 293. Kellogg Institute for International Studies, University of Notre Dame, Notre Dame, IN.

Alcántara Sáez, Manuel, and Flavia Freidenberg, eds. 2001. *Partidos políticos de América Latina.* 3 vols. Salamanca, Spain: Ediciones Universidad de Salamanca.

Alston, Lee, Marcus Melo, Bernardo Mueller, and Carlos Pereira. 2005a. *Political Institutions, Policymaking Processes and Policy Outcomes in Brazil.* Latin American Research Network Working Paper no. R-509. Washington, DC: Research Department, Inter-American Development Bank.

———. 2005b. Who Decides on Public Expenditures? A Political Economy Analysis of the Budget Process: The Case of Brazil. Inter-American Development Bank, Washington, DC. Unpublished.

Altheide, David L. 1996. *Qualitative Media Analysis.* Thousand Oaks, CA: Sage.

Ames, Barry. 1995. Electoral Rules, Constituency Pressures, and Pork Barrel: Bases of Voting in the Brazilian Congress. *Journal of Politics* 57(2):324–43.

———. 2001. *The Deadlock of Democracy in Brazil.* Ann Arbor: University of Michigan Press.

Anderberg, Michael R. 1973. *Cluster Analysis for Applications.* New York: Academic Press.

Angell, Alan, Pamela Lowden, and Rosemary Thorp. 2001. *Decentralizing Development: The Political Economy of Institutional Change in Colombia and Chile.* Oxford: Oxford University Press.

Aninat, Cristóbal, John Londregan, Patricio Navia, and Joaquín Vial. 2004. Political Institutions, Policymaking Processes and Policy Outcomes in Chile. Latin American Research Network, Research Department, Inter-American Development Bank, Washington, DC. Unpublished.

Araujo, María Caridad, Andrés Mejía Acosta, Aníbal Pérez-Liñán, Sebastián M. Saiegh, and Simón Pachano. 2004. Political Institutions, Policymaking Processes, and Policy Outcomes in Ecuador. Latin American Research Network, Research Department, Inter-American Development Bank, Washington, DC. Unpublished.

Asociación Hispanoamericana de Centros de Investigación y Empresas de Telecomunicaciones (AHCIET). 2003. *La regulación de las telecomunicaciones en Iberoamérica: situación actual.* Madrid: AHCIET.

Asociación de Investigación y Estudios Sociales (ASIES). 2005. Instituciones políticas, proceso de formulación de políticas y resultados de las políticas en Guatemala. Guatemala City. Unpublished.

Barro, Robert J., and David B. Gordon. 1983. A Positive Theory of Monetary Policy in a Natural-Rate Model. *Journal of Political Economy* 91(4):589–610.

Basañes, C. Federico, Eduardo Saavedra, and Raimundo Soto. 1999. *Post-privatization Renegotiation and Disputes in Chile.* Working Paper no. IFM-116. Inter-American Development Bank, Washington, DC.

Bennett, Lance. 2003. *News: The Politics of Illusion.* 5th ed. New York: Addison-Wesley Longman.

Bergara, Mario, and Andrés Pereyra. 2005. El proceso de diseño e implementación de políticas y las reformas en los servicios públicos. Paper prepared for Inter-American Development Bank Workshop on State Reform, Public Policies and Policymaking Processes, February 28–March 2, Washington, DC.

Bresser-Pereira, L. C. 2003. The 1995 Public Management Reform in Brazil: Reflections of a Reformer. In B. R. Schneider and B. Heredia, eds., *Reinventing Leviathan: The Politics of Administrative Reform in Developing Countries.* Coral Gables, FL: North-South Center Press/University of Miami.

Brewer-Carías, Allan R. 1997. La jurisdicción constitucional en América Latina. In Domingo García Belaúnde and Francisco Fernández Segado, eds., *La jurisdicción constitucional en Iberoamérica.* Madrid: Editorial Dykinson.

Calvo, Guillermo A. 1996. *Money, Exchange Rates, and Output.* Cambridge, MA: MIT Press.

Calvo, Guillermo A., and Allan Drazen. 1998. Uncertain Duration of Reform: Dynamic Implications. *Macroeconomic Dynamics* 2(4):443–55.

Campodónico, Humberto. 2000. Privatización y conflictos regulatorios: el caso de los mercados de electricidad y combustibles en el Perú. *Serie recursos naturales e infraestructura* 8 (March):1–84.

Cárdenas, Mauricio, Roberto Junguito, and Mónica Pachón. 2005. *Political Institutions and Policy Outcomes in Colombia: The Effects of the 1991 Constitution.* Latin American Research Network Working Paper no. R-508. Washington, DC: Research Department, Inter-American Development Bank.

Carey, John M., and John Polga-Hecimovich. 2004. Primary Elections and Candidate Strength in Latin America. Dartmouth College, Hanover, NH. Unpublished.

Carey, John M., and Matthew Soberg Shugart. 1995. Incentives to Cultivate a Personal Vote: A Rank Ordering of Electoral Formulas. *Electoral Studies* 14(4):417–39.

Carlson, Ingrid, and J. Mark Payne. 2003. Estudio comparativo de estadísticas de empleo público en 26 países de América Latina y el Caribe. In Koldo Echebarría, ed., *Red de gestión y transparencia de la política pública. Servicio civil: temas para un diálogo.* Washington, DC: Regional Policy Dialogue, Inter-American Development Bank.

Celani, Marcelo. 2000. *Reformas en la industria de las telecomunicaciones en Argentina.* Working Paper no. 18. Centro de Estudios Económicos de la Regulación (CEER), Universidad Argentina de la Empresa, Buenos Aires.

Central Bank of the Dominican Republic. 2005. Estadísticas económicas: sector fiscal. Available at http://www.bancentral.gov.do/estadisticas.asp?a=Sector_Fiscal.

Chasquetti, Daniel J. 1999. Compartiendo el gobierno: multipartidismo y coaliciones en el Uruguay (1971–1997). *Revista Uruguaya de Ciencia Política* 10:25–46.

———. 2004. Democracia, multipartidismo y coaliciones en América Latina: evaluando la difícil combinación. In Jorge Lanzaro, ed., *Tipos de presidencialismo y coaliciones políticas en América Latina.* Buenos Aires: Consejo Latinoamericano de Ciencias Sociales (CLACSO).

Cheibub, José Antonio, Adam Przeworski, and Sebastián M. Saiegh. 2004. Government Coalitions and Legislative Success under Presidentialism and Parliamentarism. *British Journal of Political Science* 34(4):565–87.

Collier, Ruth Berins, and David Collier. 1991. *Shaping the Political Arena: Critical Junctures, the Labor Movement, and Regime Dynamics in Latin America.* Princeton: Princeton University Press.

Coppedge, Michael. 1994. *Strong Parties and Lame Ducks: Presidential Partyarchy and Factionalism in Venezuela.* Stanford: Stanford University Press.

Corrales, Javier. 2004. Multiple Preferences, Variable Strengths: The Politics of Education Reforms in Argentina. In Robert R. Kaufman and Joan M. Nelson, eds., *Crucial Needs, Weak Incentives: Social Sector Reform, Democratization, and Globalization in Latin America.* Washington, DC: Woodrow Wilson Center Press.

Cox, Cristián. 2003. Las políticas educacionales de Chile en las últimas dos décadas del siglo XX. In Cristián Cox, ed., *Políticas educacionales en el cambio de siglo: la reforma del sistema escolar en Chile.* Santiago, Chile: Editorial Universitaria.

Cox, Gary W., and Mathew D. McCubbins. 2001. The Institutional Determinants of Economic Policy Outcomes. In Stephan Haggard and Mathew D. McCubbins, eds., *Presidents, Parliaments, and Policy.* New York: Cambridge University Press.

———. 2002. Agenda Power in the U.S. House of Representatives, 1877 to 1986. In David W. Brady and Mathew D. McCubbins, eds., *Party, Process, and Political Change in Congress: New Perspectives on the History of Congress.* Stanford: Stanford University Press.

Cox, Gary W., and Scott Morgenstern. 2002. Epilogue: Latin America's Reactive Assemblies and Proactive Presidents. In Scott Morgenstern and Benito Nacif, eds., *Legislative Politics in Latin America.* Cambridge: Cambridge University Press.

Crisp, Brian F. 2001. The Impact of Candidate Selection Processes on Legislator Behavior in Venezuela. Paper prepared for the 23rd International Congress of the Latin American Studies Association, September 6–8, Washington, DC.

Cukierman, Alex, Sebastian Edwards, and Guido Tabellini. 1989. *Seigniorage and Political Instability.* Working Paper no. 3199. National Bureau of Economic Research, Cambridge, MA.

Dakolias, Maria. 1996. *The Judicial Sector in Latin America and the Caribbean: Elements of Reform.* Technical Paper no. 319. World Bank, Washington, DC.

Delannoy, Françoise. 2000. *Education Reforms in Chile, 1980–98: A Lesson in Pragmatism.* Education Reform and Management Publication Series, vol. 1, no. 1 (June), World Bank, Washington, DC.

Di Palma, Giuseppe. 1990. *To Craft Democracies: An Essay on Democratic Transitions.* Berkeley and Los Angeles: University of California Press.

Dixit, Avinash K. 1996. *The Making of Economic Policy: A Transaction-Cost Politics Perspective.* Cambridge, MA: MIT Press.

Draibe, Sônia M. 2004. Federal Leverage in a Decentralized System: Education Reforms in Brazil. In Robert R. Kaufman and Joan M. Nelson, eds., *Crucial Needs, Weak Incentives: Social Sector Reform, Democratization, and Globalization in Latin America.* Washington, DC.: Woodrow Wilson Center Press.

Drake, Paul, and Iván Jaksic. 1999. *El modelo chileno: democracia y desarrollo en los noventa.* Santiago, Chile: LOM Ediciones.

Drazen, Allan. 2000. *Political Economy in Macroeconomics.* Princeton: Princeton University Press.

Echeverry, Juan Carlos, Leopoldo Fergusson, and Pablo Querubín. 2004. *La batalla política por el presupuesto de la nación: inflexibilidades o supervivencia fiscal.* Working Paper no. 740. Centro de Estudios sobre Desarrollo Económico (CEDE), Universidad de los Andes, Bogotá.

Espínola, Viola, and Claudio de Moura Castro, eds. 1999. *Economía política de la reforma educacional en Chile: la reforma vista por sus protagonistas.* Washington, DC: Inter-American Development Bank.

Etchemendy, Sebastián, and Vicente Palermo. 1998. Conflicto y concertación: gobierno, congreso y organizaciones de interés en la reforma laboral del primer gobierno de Menem (1989–1995). *Desarrollo Económico—Revista de Ciencias Sociales* 37(148):559–90.

Feld, Lars, and Stefan Voigt. 2003. Economic Growth and Judicial Independence: Cross-Country Evidence Using a New Set of Indicators. *European Journal of Political Economy* 19(3):497–527.

Figueiredo, Argelina C., and Fernando Limongi. 2000. Presidential Power, Legislative Organization, and Party Behavior in Brazil. *Comparative Politics* 32(2):151–70.

Filc, Gabriel, and Carlos Scartascini. 2005. Instituciones fiscales. In Eduardo Lora, ed., *El estado de la reforma del Estado.* Washington, DC: Inter-American Development Bank. Forthcoming.

Fischer, Ronald, and Pablo Serra. 2002. Evaluación de la regulación de las telecomunicaciones en Chile. *Perspectivas* 6(1):45–78.

Foweraker, Joe. 1998. Institutional Design, Party Systems, and Governability—Differentiating the Presidential Regimes of Latin America. *British Journal of Political Science* 28(4):651–76.

Fraser Institute. Various years. *Economic Freedom of the World.* Available at www.freetheworld.com.

Freedom House. 2004. *Freedom in the World 2004: The Annual Survey of Political Rights and Civil Liberties.* Lanham, MD: Rowman and Littlefield.

Freidenberg, Flavia, and Francisco Sánchez López. 2002. ¿Cómo se elige un candidato a presidente? reglas y prácticas en los partidos políticos de América Latina. *Revista de Estudios Políticos* 118:321–61.

Gasparini, Leonardo. 2004. Different Lives: Inequality in Latin America and the Caribbean. In David de Ferranti, Guillermo E. Perry, Francisco H. G. Ferreira, and Michael Walton, eds., *Inequality in Latin America: Breaking with History?* Washington, DC: World Bank.

Gómez-Lobo, Andrés, and Miguel Vargas. 2002. La regulación de las empresas sanitarias en Chile: una revisión crítica. *Perspectivas* 6(1):79–110.

Grindle, Merilee S. 2004a. *Despite the Odds: The Contentious Politics of Education Reform*. Princeton, NJ: Princeton University Press.

———. 2004b. Interests, Institutions, and Reformers: The Politics of Education Decentralization in Mexico. In Robert R. Kaufman and Joan M. Nelson, eds., *Crucial Needs, Weak Incentives: Social Sector Reform, Democratization, and Globalization in Latin America*. Washington, DC: Woodrow Wilson Center Press.

Hanson, E. Mark. 1997. *Educational Decentralization: Issues and Challenges*. Occasional Paper no. 9. Partnership for Educational Revitalization in the Americas (PREAL), Inter-American Dialogue, Washington, DC.

Henisz, Witold. 2000. The Institutional Environment for Economic Growth. *Economics and Politics* 12(1):1–31.

Hirschman, Albert O. 1967. *Development Projects Observed*. Washington, DC: Brookings Institution Press.

Hughes, Sallie. 2005. The Role of the Latin American News Media in the Policymaking Process: A First Look. Paper prepared for the convention of the Association for Education in Journalism and Mass Communication, August 10–13, San Antonio, TX.

Iaryczower, Matías, Pablo T. Spiller, and Mariano Tommasi. 2002. Judicial Independence in Unstable Environments: The Argentine Supreme Court, 1936–1998. *American Journal of Political Science* 46(4):699–716.

International Labour Organization (ILO). 1999. *Panorama Laboral 1999: América Latina y el Caribe*. Available at www.oit.org.pe/spanish/260ameri/publ/panorama/1999/texto.pdf.

International Monetary Fund (IMF). 2005. *Paraguay: 2004 Article IV Consultation and Second Review under the Stand-By Arrangement and Requests for Waiver and Modifications of Performance Criteria*. Country Report no. 05/59. Washington, DC: IMF.

Israel, Arturo. 1987. *Institutional Development: Incentives to Performance*. Baltimore: Johns Hopkins University Press.

Jones, Mark P. 2005. The Role of Parties and Party Systems in the Policymaking Process. Paper prepared for Inter-American Development Bank Workshop on State Reform, Public Policies and Policymaking Processes, February 28–March 2, Washington, DC.

Jones, Mark P., and Scott Mainwaring. 2003. The Nationalization of Parties and Party Systems: An Empirical Measure and an Application to the Americas. *Party Politics* 9(2):139–66.

Jones, Mark P., Sebastián M. Saiegh, Pablo T. Spiller, and Mariano Tommasi. 2002. Amateur Legislators—Professional Politicians: The Consequences of Party-Centered Electoral Rules in a Federal System. *American Journal of Political Science* 46(3):656–69.

Kaufman, Robert R., and Joan M. Nelson, eds. 2004. *Crucial Needs, Weak Incentives: Social Sector Reform, Democratization, and Globalization in Latin America*. Washington, DC: Woodrow Wilson Center Press.

Kweitel, Mercedes, Ariana Koffsmon, Federico Marongiu, Florencia Mezzadra, Axel Rivas, and Pablo Rodríguez del Pozo. 2003. *Análisis fiscal de los servicios descentralizados de educación y de salud en Argentina*. Working Paper no. 2. Center for the Implementation of Public Policies Promoting Equity and Growth (CIPPEC), Buenos Aires.

Laakso, Markku, and Rein Taagepera. 1979. "Effective" Number of Parties: A Measure with Application to West Europe. *Comparative Political Studies* 12(1):3–27.

Lambert, Peter J. 1993. *The Distribution and Redistribution of Income.* 2nd ed. Manchester, UK: Manchester University Press.

Latinobarometer. Various years. Latinobarometer: Latin American Public Opinion. Available at www.latinobarometro.org.

Lehoucq, Fabrice. 2005. Policymaking, Parties, and Institutions in Democratic Costa Rica. Paper prepared for Inter-American Development Bank Workshop on State Reform, Public Policies and Policymaking Processes, February 28–March 2, Washington, DC.

Lehoucq, Fabrice, Francisco Aparicio, Allyson Benton, Benito Nacif, and Gabriel Negretto. 2005. *Political Institutions, Policymaking Processes, and Policy Outcomes in Mexico.* Latin American Research Network Working Paper no. R-512. Washington, DC: Research Department, Inter-American Development Bank.

Levy, Brian, and Pablo T. Spiller. 1994. The Institutional Foundations of Regulatory Commitment: A Comparative Analysis of Telecommunications Regulation. *Journal of Law, Economics and Organization* 10(2):201–46.

Linz, Juan J. 1990. The Perils of Presidentialism. *Journal of Democracy* 1(1):51–69.

Linz, Juan J., and Alfred Stepan, eds. 1978. *The Breakdown of Democratic Regimes.* Baltimore: Johns Hopkins University Press.

Lipset, Seymour M., and Stein Rokkan. 1967. Cleavage Structures, Party Systems, and Voter Alignments: An Introduction. In Seymour M. Lipset and Stein Rokkan, eds., *Party Systems and Voter Alignments: Cross-National Perspectives.* New York: Free Press.

Longo, Francisco. 2005. Diagnóstico institucional comparado de sistemas de servicio civil: informe final de síntesis. Paper prepared for the Fifth Meeting of the Public Policy Management and Transparency Dialogue: Civil Service Reform, March 17–18, Inter-American Development Bank, Washington, DC.

Mahon, James E. 2004. Expanded Discussion of Data Analysis from "Causes of Tax Reform in Latin America," *Latin American Research Review,* Spring 2004. Available at http://64.233.161.104/search?q=cache:dyVemrv_hw8J:www.williams.edu/PoliSci/mahon/TaxReformDataAnalysis.htm+&hl=en.

Mailath, George J., Stephen Morris, and Andrew Postlewaite. 2001. Laws and Authority. Yale University, New Haven, CT. Unpublished.

Mainwaring, Scott. 1993. Presidentialism, Multipartism, and Democracy: The Difficult Combination. *Comparative Political Studies* 26(2):198–228.

———. 1997. Multipartism, Robust Federalism, and Presidentialism in Brazil. In Matthew Soberg Shugart and Scott Mainwaring, eds., *Presidentialism and Democracy in Latin America.* New York: Cambridge University Press.

———. 1998. *Rethinking Party Systems Theory in the Third Wave of Democratization: The Importance of Party System Institutionalization.* Working Paper no. 260. Kellogg Institute for International Studies, University of Notre Dame, Notre Dame, IN.

———. 1999. *Rethinking Party Systems in the Third Wave of Democratization: The Case of Brazil.* Stanford: Stanford University Press.

Mainwaring, Scott, and Timothy R. Scully. 1995. Introduction: Party Systems in Latin America. In Scott Mainwaring and Timothy R. Scully, eds., *Building Democratic Institutions: Party Systems in Latin America*. Stanford: Stanford University Press.

Mainwaring, Scott, and Matthew Soberg Shugart. 1997. Presidentialism and Democracy in Latin America: Rethinking the Terms of the Debate. In Matthew Soberg Shugart and Scott Mainwaring, eds., *Presidentialism and Democracy in Latin America*. New York: Cambridge University Press.

Martínez-Gallardo, Cecilia. 2005a. Designing Cabinets: Presidents, Politics and Policymaking in Latin America. Ph.D. dissertation, Department of Political Science, Columbia University, New York.

———. 2005b. The Role of Latin American Cabinets in the Policymaking Process. Inter-American Development Bank, Washington, DC. Unpublished.

McGuire, James W. 1997. *Peronism without Perón: Unions, Parties, and Democracy in Argentina*. Stanford: Stanford University Press.

Mejía Acosta, Andrés. 2004. Ghost Coalitions: Economic Reforms, Fragmented Legislatures and Informal Institutions in Ecuador. Ph.D. Dissertation, Department of Political Science, University of Notre Dame, Notre Dame, IN.

———. 2005. The Policymaking Process in Jamaica: Fiscal Adjustment and Crime Fighting Policies. Paper prepared for Inter-American Development Bank Workshop on State Reform, Public Policies and Policymaking Processes, February 28–March 2, Washington, DC.

Melo, Marcus André. 2004. Explaining Tax Reforms and the Capacity to Tax: The Divergent Paths of Argentina and Brazil. Paper prepared for the Workshop on Taxation and Development: Essays on the New Politics of Taxation and Accountability, Danish Institute for International Studies/Institute of Development Studies (DIIS), June 14–15, Copenhagen.

Mizala, Alejandra, Pablo González, Pilar Romaguera, and Andrea Guzmán. 2002. Chile: la recuperación de la profesión docente es posible. In Juan Carlos Navarro, ed., *¿Quiénes son los maestros? Carreras e incentivos docentes en América Latina*. Washington, DC: Latin American Research Network, Inter-American Development Bank.

Molinas, José R., and Aníbal Pérez-Liñán. 2005. Who Decides on Public Expenditures? A Political Economy Analysis of the Budget Process in Paraguay. Inter-American Development Bank, Washington, DC. Unpublished.

Molinas, José, Aníbal Pérez-Liñán, and Sebastián M. Saiegh. 2005. *Political Institutions, Policymaking Processes, and Policy Outcomes in Paraguay: 1954–2003*. Latin American Research Network Working Paper no. R-502. Washington, DC: Research Department, Inter-American Development Bank.

Monaldi, Francisco. 2005. The Role of Sub-national Political Authorities in the National Policymaking Process: A Comparative Perspective of Latin American Cases. Paper prepared for Inter-American Development Bank Workshop on State Reform, Public Policies and Policymaking Processes, February 28–March 2, Washington, DC.

Monaldi, Francisco, Rosa Amelia González, Richard Obuchi, and Michael Penfold. 2005. *Political Institutions, Policymaking Processes, and Policy Outcomes in Venezuela*. Latin American Research Network Working Paper no. R-507. Washington, DC: Research Department, Inter-American Development Bank.

Morgenstern, Scott. 2002. Towards a Model of Latin American Legislatures. In Scott Morgenstern and Benito Nacif, eds., *Legislative Politics in Latin America*. Cambridge: Cambridge University Press.

Mueller, Bernardo, and Carlos Pereira. 2005. The Cost of State Reform in Latin America. Paper prepared for Inter-American Development Bank Workshop on State Reform, Public Policies and Policymaking Processes, February 28–March 2, Washington, DC.

Murillo, María Victoria. 1999. Recovering Political Dynamics: Teachers' Unions and the Decentralization of Education in Argentina and Mexico. *Journal of Inter-American Studies and World Affairs* 41(1):31–57.

———. 2005a. Partisanship amidst Convergence: Labor Market Reforms in Latin America. *Comparative Politics* 37(4):441–58.

———. 2005b. The Role of Labor Unions in the PMP. Inter-American Development Bank, Washington, DC. Unpublished.

Murillo, María Victoria, and Andrew Schrank. 2005. With a Little Help from My Friends: External and Domestic Allies and Labor Rights in Latin America. *Comparative Political Studies* 38(8):971–99.

Navarro, Juan Carlos, ed. 2002. *¿Quiénes son los maestros? Carreras e incentivos docentes en América Latina*. Washington, DC: Latin American Research Network, Inter-American Development Bank.

Navia, Patricio, and Julio Ríos-Figueroa. 2005. The Constitutional Adjudication Mosaic of Latin America. *Comparative Political Studies* 38(2):189–217.

North, Douglass C. 1990. *Institutions, Institutional Change and Economic Performance: Political Economy of Institutions and Decisions*. Cambridge: Cambridge University Press.

Núñez, Iván. 2003. El profesorado, su gremio, y la reforma de los años noventa: presiones de cambio y evolución de la cultura docente. In Cristián Cox, ed., *Políticas educacionales en el cambio de siglo: la reforma del sistema escolar en Chile*. Santiago, Chile: Editorial Universitaria.

Oszlak, Oscar. 2003. Profesionalización de la función pública en el marco de la nueva gestión pública. In David Arellano, Rodrigo Egaña, Oscar Oszlak, and Regina Pacheco, eds., *Retos de la profesionalización de la función pública*. Caracas: Centro Latinoamericano de Administración para el Desarrollo (CLAD); Agencia Española de Cooperación Internacional (AECI); Ministerio de Administraciones Públicas (MAP); Fundación Internacional y para Iberoamérica de Administración y Políticas Públicas (FIIAPP).

Payne, J. Mark, Daniel Zovatto G., Fernando Carrillo Flórez, and Andrés Allamand Zavala. 2002. *Democracies in Development: Politics and Reform in Latin America*. Washington, DC: Inter-American Development Bank.

Pedersen, Mogens N. 1983. Changing Patterns of Electoral Volatility in European Party Systems, 1948–1977: Explorations in Explanation. In Hans Daalder and Peter Mair, eds., *Western European Party Systems: Continuity and Change*. London: Sage.

Pereira, Carlos, and Bernardo Mueller. 2004. The Cost of Governing: Strategic Behavior of the President and Legislators in Brazil's Budgetary Process. *Comparative Political Studies* 37(7):781–815.

Persson, Torsten, and Guido Tabellini. 2000. *Political Economics: Explaining Economic Policy*. Cambridge, MA: MIT Press.

———. 2003. *The Economic Effects of Constitutions*. Cambridge, MA: MIT Press.

Pritchard, David. 1992. The News Media and Public Policy Agendas. In J. D. Kennamer, ed., *Public Opinion, the Press, and Public Policy: An Introduction*. Westport, CT: Praeger.

Proyecto de Elites Latinoamericanas (PELA). Various years. Proyecto de Elites Latinoamericanas, 1994–2005. Manuel Alcántara, Director. Salamanca, Spain: Universidad de Salamanca.

Rauch, James E., and Peter B. Evans. 2000. Bureaucratic Structure and Bureaucratic Performance in Less-Developed Countries. *Journal of Public Economics* 75:49–71.

Rivas, Axel. 2004. *Gobernar la educación: estudio comparado sobre el poder y la educación en las provincias argentinas*. Buenos Aires: GRANICA–Universidad de San Andrés.

Roberts, Kenneth. 2002. Social Inequalities without Class Cleavages in Latin America's Neoliberal Era. *Studies in Comparative International Development* 36(4):3–33.

Rodríguez, Victoria E. 1997. *Decentralization in Mexico: From Reforma Municipal to Solidaridad to Nuevo Federalismo*. Boulder, CO: Westview.

Rodrik, Dani. 1989. Credibility of Trade Reform: A Policy Maker's Guide. *World Economy* 12(1):1–16.

———. 1995. Political Economy of Trade Policy. In Gene M. Grossman and Kenneth Rogoff, eds., *Handbook of International Economics*. Vol. 3. Amsterdam: Elsevier.

Saiegh, Sebastián M. 2005. The Role of Legislatures in the Policymaking Process. Paper prepared for Inter-American Development Bank Workshop on State Reform, Public Policies and Policymaking Processes, February 28–March 2, Washington, DC.

Santiso, Javier, and Laurence Whitehead. 2005. Ulysses and the Sirens: Political and Technical Rationality in Latin America. Paper prepared for the Workshop on State Reform, Public Policies and Policymaking Processes, February 28–March 2, Washington, DC.

Sartori, Giovanni. 1976. *Parties and Party Systems: A Framework for Analysis*. New York: Cambridge University Press.

Schneider, Ben Ross. 2004. *Business Politics and the State in Twentieth-Century Latin America*. New York: Cambridge University Press.

———. 2005. Business Politics and Policy Making in Contemporary Latin America. Paper prepared for Inter-American Development Bank Workshop on State Reform, Public Policies, and Policymaking Processes, February 28–March 2, Washington, DC.

Shapiro, Martin, and Alec Stone Sweet. 2002. *On Law, Politics, and Judicialization*. Oxford: Oxford University Press.

Shepherd, Geoffrey, and Jeff Rinne. 2005. Brazil. In Building on Strengths: Lessons from Comparative Public Administration Reforms. Prepared for the Government of the Russian Federation by Nick Manning and Neil Parison, with Kathy Lalazarian, Jana Orac, and Jeff Rinne. World Bank, Washington, DC. Unpublished.

Shetreet, Shimon. 1985. Judicial Independence: New Conceptual Dimensions and Contemporary Challenges. In Shimon Shetreet and Jules Deschênes, eds., *Judicial Independence: The Contemporary Debate*. Dordrecht: Nijhoff.

Shirley, Mary M. 2005. Institutions and Development. In Claude Ménard and Mary M. Shirley, eds., *Handbook of New Institutional Economics*. New York: Springer.

Shome, Parthasarathi. 1999. La tributación en América Latina: tendencias estructurales e impacto de la administración. Paper prepared for the 11th Regional Seminar on Fiscal Policy of the Economic Commission for Latin America and the Caribbean (ECLAC), January 25–28, Brasilia.

Shugart, Matthew Soberg, and Stephan Haggard. 2001. Institutions and Public Policy in Presidential Systems. In Stephan Haggard and Mathew D. McCubbins, eds., *Presidents, Parliaments, and Policy*. New York: Cambridge University Press.

Sousa, Mariana. 2005. Judicial Reforms, the PMP, and Public Policy. Inter-American Development Bank, Washington, DC. Unpublished.

Spiller, Pablo T., Ernesto Stein, and Mariano Tommasi. 2003. Political Institutions, Policymaking Processes, and Policy Outcomes: An Intertemporal Transactions Framework. Inter-American Development Bank, Washington, DC. Unpublished.

Spiller, Pablo T., and Mariano Tommasi. 2003. The Institutional Foundations of Public Policy: A Transactions Approach with Application to Argentina. *Journal of Law, Economics and Organization* 19(2):281–306.

———. 2005. The Institutions of Regulation: An Application to Public Utilities. In Claude Ménard and Mary M. Shirley, eds., *Handbook of New Institutional Economics*. New York: Springer.

Stein, Ernesto, and Mariano Tommasi. 2005. Democratic Institutions, Policymaking Processes, and the Quality of Policies in Latin America. Inter-American Development Bank, Washington, DC. Unpublished.

Swanson, David L. 2004. Transnational Trends in Political Communication: Conventional Views and New Realities. In Frank Esser and Barbara Pfetsch, eds., *Comparing Political Communication: Theories, Cases, and Challenges*. New York: Cambridge University Press.

Tate, C. Neal. 1992. Comparative Judicial Review and Public Policy: Concepts and Overview. In Donald W. Jackson and C. Neal Tate, eds., *Comparative Judicial Review and Public Policy*. Westport, CT: Greenwood.

Tommasi, Mariano. 2002. *Federalism in Argentina and the Reforms of the 1990s*. Working Paper no. 147. Center for Research on Economic Development and Policy Reform, Stanford University, Stanford, CA.

Torero, Máximo, and Alberto Pascó-Font. 2001. *El impacto social de la privatización y de la regulación de los servicios públicos en el Perú*. Working Paper no. 35. Grupo de Análisis para el Desarrollo (GRADE), Lima.

Tsebelis, George. 2002. *Veto Players: How Political Institutions Work*. Princeton: Princeton University Press.

United Nations Development Programme (UNDP). 2005. *Democracy in Latin America: Towards a Citizens' Democracy*. Buenos Aires: Aguilar; Altea; Taurus; Alfaguara, S.A.

———. Various years. *Human Development Report*. New York: Oxford University Press.

Urrutia, Miguel. 1991. On the Absence of Economic Populism in Colombia. In Rudiger Dornbusch and Sebastian Edwards, eds., *The Macroeconomics of Populism in Latin America*. Chicago: University of Chicago Press.

Vargas, Jorge Enrique. 1999. Las relaciones entre el Ejecutivo y el Legislativo. In Miguel Gandour and Luis Bernardo Mejía, eds., *Hacia el rediseño del Estado: análisis institucional, reformas y resultados económicos*. Bogotá: Departamento Nacional de Planeación and Tercer Mundo Editores.

Vispo, Adolfo. 1999. *Los entes de regulación: problemas de diseño y contexto. Aportes para un urgente debate en la Argentina*. Buenos Aires: Grupo Editorial Norma.

Weaver, R. Kent, and Bert A. Rockman, eds. 1993. *Do Institutions Matter? Government Capabilities in the United States and Abroad*. Washington, DC: Brookings Institution Press.

Werneck, Rogério L. F. 2000. *Tax Reform in Brazil: Small Achievements and Great Challenges*. Working Paper no. 83. Center for Research on Economic Development and Policy Reform, Stanford University, Stanford, CA.

Wikipedia. 2005. Sales tax. Available at http://en.wikipedia.org/wiki/Sales_tax.

Winer, Stanley L., and Walter Hettich. 2003. The Political Economy of Taxation: Positive and Normative Analysis When Collective Choice Matters. In Charles K. Rowley and Friedrich Schneider, eds., *The Encyclopedia of Public Choice*. Vol. 1. Dordrecht: Kluwer Academic.

World Bank. 2003. *Country Assistance Strategy for the Republic of Paraguay 2004/2007*. Report no. 27341-PA. Washington, DC: World Bank.

———. 2005. Private Participation in Infrastructure (PPI) project database. Available at http://ppi.worldbank.org/.

———. Various years. *World Development Indicators*. Washington, DC: World Bank.

World Economic Forum. 2004. *The Global Competitiveness Report 2003–2004*. New York: Oxford University Press.

———. 2005. *The Global Competitiveness Report 2004–2005*. New York: Oxford University Press.

———. Various years. *The Global Competitiveness Report*—Executive Opinion Survey. Available at www.weforum.org.

Zuvanic, Laura, and Mercedes Iacoviello. 2005. El rol de la burocracia en el PMP en América Latina. Inter-American Development Bank, Washington, DC. Unpublished.

List of Acronyms

AD Acción Democrática (Venezuela)

ADM Average district magnitude

ANCAP Administración Nacional de Combustibles, Alcohol y Portland (Uruguay)

ANEF Agrupación Nacional de Empleados Fiscales (Chile)

ANMEB Acuerdo Nacional para la Modernización de la Educación Básica (Mexico)

ANTEL Administración Nacional de Telecomunicaciones (Uruguay)

APRA Partido Aprista Peruano (Peru)

ASIES Asociación de Investigación y Estudios Sociales (Guatemala)

CAF Corporación Andina de Fomento

CARICOM Caribbean Community

CEN Comité Ejecutivo Nacional (Mexico)

CERES Centro de Estudios de la Realidad Económica y Social (Uruguay)

CGT Confederación General del Trabajo (Argentina)

CIEN Centro de Investigaciones Económicas Nacionales (Guatemala)

CIEPLAN Corporación de Estudios para Latinoamérica (Chile)

CINVE Centro de Investigaciones Económicas (Uruguay)

CNT Comisión Nacional de Comunicaciones (Argentina)

COFINS Contribuição para o Financiamento da Seguridade Social (Brazil)

CONSED Conselho Nacional de Secretários de Educação (Brazil)

COPEI Comité de Organización Política Electoral Independiente (Venezuela)

CPI Consumer price index

CPMF Contribuição Provisória sobre Movimentação Financeira (Brazil)

CTC Compañía de Telecomunicaciones de Chile S.A.

CTE Comisión de Tarifas Eléctricas (Peru)

CTM Confederación de Trabajadores de México (Mexico)

CTV Confederación de Trabajadores de Venezuela (Venezuela)

DAS Direção e Assessoramento Superior (Brazil)

ECLAC Economic Commission for Latin America and the Caribbean

ENAP Escola Nacional de Administração Pública (Brazil)

ENTEL Empresa Nacional de Telecomunicaciones S.A.

ESAF Escola de Administração Fazendária (Brazil)

FEDESARROLLO Fundación para la Educación Superior y el Desarrollo (Colombia)

FIEL Fundación de Investigaciones Económicas Latinoamericanas (Argentina)

FONID Fondo Nacional de Incentivo Docente (Argentina)

FRG Frente Republicano Guatemalteco (Guatemala)

FRL Fiscal Responsibility Law

FSE Fundo Social de Emergência (Brazil)

FUSADES Fundación Salvadoreña para el Desarrollo Económico y Social (El Salvador)

GCR *Global Competitiveness Report*

HDI Human Development Index

ICE Instituto Costarricense de Electricidad (Costa Rica)

IDB Inter-American Development Bank

IEMA Impuesto a las Empresas Mercantiles y Agropecuarias

ILO International Labour Organization

IMF International Monetary Fund

INCAE Instituto Centroamericano de Administración de Empresas (Costa Rica)

JLP Jamaica Labour Party

MST Movimento dos Trabalhadores Rurais Sem Terra (Brazil)

NGO Nongovernmental organization

OSINERG Organismo Supervisor de la Inversión en Energía (Peru)

PAN Partido Acción Nacional (Mexico)

PELA Proyecto de Elites Latinoamericanas

PJ Partido Justicialista (Argentina)

PLN Partido Liberación Nacional (Costa Rica)

PMP Policymaking process

PNP People's National Party (Jamaica)

PRD Partido de la Revolución Democrática (Mexico)

PRI Partido Revolucionario Institucional (Mexico)

PT Partido dos Trabalhadores (Brazil)

PTB Partido Trabalhista Brasileiro (Brazil)

PUSC Partido Unidad Social Cristiana (Costa Rica)

SNCF Sistema Nacional de Coordinación Fiscal (Mexico)

SNED Sistema Nacional de Evaluación del Desempeño Docente (Chile)

SRF Secretaria da Receita Federal (Brazil)

SUBTEL Subsecretaría de Telecomunicaciones (Chile)

UNDIME União Nacional dos Dirigentes Municipais de Educação (Brazil)

UNDP United Nations Development Programme

URD Unión Republicana Democrática (Venezuela)

UTE Administración Nacional de Usinas y Trasmisiones Eléctricas

VAT Value-added tax